12 $\frac{50}{\_\_}$

4/86

D1175824

THE ARCHITECT
IN HISTORY

DA CAPO PRESS SERIES IN
ARCHITECTURE AND DECORATIVE ART

General Editor: ADOLF K. PLACZEK
Avery Librarian, Columbia University

THE ARCHITECT
IN HISTORY

By Martin S. Briggs

DA CAPO PRESS · NEW YORK · 1974

Library of Congress Cataloging in Publication Data

Briggs, Martin Shaw, 1882-
    The architect in history.

    (Da Capo Press series in architecture and decorative art)
    Reprint of the 1927 ed. published by Clarendon Press, Oxford.
    Includes bibliographies.
    1. Architects. 2. Architecture—History.
I. Title.
NA203.B7   1974   720'.9   69-15613
ISBN 0-306-70584-2

This Da Capo Press edition of *The Architect in History* is an
unabridged republication of the 1927 edition published in Oxford.
This reprint has been authorized by the Clarendon Press, Oxford.

Published by Da Capo Press, Inc.
A Subsidiary of Plenum Publishing Corporation
227 West 17th Street, New York, N. Y. 10011

THE ARCHITECT
IN HISTORY

FIG. I. INIGO JONES

From the reputed self-portrait in the Burlington-Devonshire Collection
(R. I. B. A. Library)

THE ARCHITECT
IN HISTORY

BY

MARTIN S. BRIGGS
F.R.I.B.A.

OXFORD
AT THE CLARENDON PRESS
1927

Printed in England at the OXFORD UNIVERSITY PRESS
by John Johnson Printer to the University

TO THE ROYAL INSTITUTE
OF BRITISH ARCHITECTS

PREFACE

THERE is no mystery about the purpose of this book. It is an honest attempt to claim for the architect the position in history that is his due, and to expose prevailing fallacies about his work where substantial evidence or reasonable inference permits. My frequent quotations will show that most recent architect-writers on the various periods support my main conclusions ; but it is pleasant to welcome the timely aid of a layman, Professor Hamilton Thompson, whose interesting and learned researches into the ways of medieval architects confirm the views advanced in my fourth chapter, which was written before the publication of his book, *The Cathedral Churches of England*, and has only needed slight revision as a result. During the last stages of preparing my work for the press, my attention has been drawn to some articles on ' The Architect in History ' by A. L. Frothingham, in *The Architectural Record* (New York, 1908–9) covering the same ground as my second, third, and part of my fourth chapters. These articles, too, agree in the main with my own views, as expressed in the following pages. Another work, that does not appear in my bibliographies but contains references to architects in Dalmatia, is Sir Thomas Jackson's *Dalmatia, the Quarnero, and Istria* (Oxford 1887). Among the latest contributions to our knowledge of the architect are Mr. A. H. Smith's paper at the R.I.B.A. on *Building Inscriptions of the Acropolis* and Mr. S. J. Wearing's *Georgian Norwich* : *its Builders*, which I have noticed in post-scripts to Chapters II and VIII respectively. Since I wrote the description of the Smithson drawings (pp. 243–9), that fine collection has been acquired by the Royal Institute of British Architects on the advice of a small committee of which I had the honour to be a member.

Up to the end of the Middle Ages I have dealt with the evolution of the architect in Europe generally ; for the Renaissance period I have followed his progress in Italy, France, and England ; and for the nineteenth century I have confined my attention to England. Only by some such limitation can the subject be brought within one volume. The Index at the end of this book includes references to Competitions, Drawing, Town-planning, Assistants, Use of Models, Education, Remu-neration of Architects, &c., enabling a reader to follow the various aspects of architectural practice through successive periods of history. The sources of my illus-trations are acknowledged in the List on pp. x–xii. I also have to thank the Editor of the R.I.B.A. Journal for the use of sixteen blocks.

M. S. B

April 1927.

CONTENTS

LIST OF ILLUSTRATIONS

I

THE FIRST ARCHITECTS

THE modern architect is often taunted with living too much in the past. It may therefore be felt that a study of his position in history is superfluous, and, indeed, that it affords only another instance of his habit of help-less retrospection. Again and again he is adjured to throw away his copybooks and his precedents, to forget the past that has shackled him so long, and to study modern problems of building without leaning so heavily on his forefathers. With much of this criticism every sensible modern architect will agree. There is no doubt that, as a profession, we have tended to be too conservative, and that the long succession of revivals that have swept over this and other countries during the last hundred years has sometimes weakened our capacity for imaginative design on modern lines.

Nevertheless we cannot and must not forget that we who are architects are practitioners of 'The Mistress Art', and members of one of the oldest and noblest professions in the world. The dignity that is conferred on the architect by his long history is a thing to be proud of, and dignity in architecture is an essential part of its value to the com-munity. It inspires and sustains even those of us whose work is mainly humdrum and utilitarian, it restrains us from undue eccentricity, and it forms a beacon to light the student on his arduous path.

Recent movements within the profession have succeeded in establishing the architect's status among the general public, and an increasing interest is being displayed in his aims and methods of work. At the same time the

whole system of training architectural students has under-
gone sweeping changes, and the present moment seems
particularly opportune for considering the stages of the
architect's evolution through history.

But, when we look back to the past, we cannot fail to
be astonished by the meagreness of the available material.
While innumerable books have been written on the history
of architecture, little has been said about the lives and
personalities of the men whose brains created our greatest
buildings, especially up to the close of the Middle Ages.
Certainly the architect has not received due recognition
in history.

Too often his name has been concealed or his office
misrepresented, as when we are asked to believe that our
Gothic minsters were the work of simple-minded and
unlettered masons, sustained only by the faith that was
in them. We, at any rate, must know that the design
and erection of every large and complicated building in
the past involved the control of some master-brain, that
no group or committee could have taken its place, and
that neither Salisbury Cathedral nor the Parthenon could
have leapt from the ground at the behest of a handful of
rustic craftsmen.

In considering the personality of these great ancestors
of ours, there is no need to dispel the glamour that has
hitherto enhanced their work just because it has popularly
been regarded as anonymous. In many of the best periods
of the past there has been a close-knit comradeship of
craftsmen that we should emulate rather than regret,
a single-minded selflessness of purpose that is altogether
admirable. Nevertheless, we may claim honour where it
is due, and, if the glory of our greatest buildings has
sometimes effaced the identity of their designers, there is

no sacrilege in drawing aside the curtain to reveal the human interest that lies behind.

What manner of men were the architects of the past ? How were they trained, and how did they work ? What were their difficulties ? In attempting to answer such questions, it is not necessary to dig up dry bones or to dispel romance.

But, before commencing our survey, we must pause to consider the term ' Architect ', its origin, and its significance. It is a Greek word of high antiquity (ἀρχιτέκτων) originally meaning, according to Liddell and Scott's *Lexicon*, ' a chief artificer, master-builder, &c., director of works, architect, engineer, opposed to χειροτέχνης ' (an artisan or manual worker). It then appears in its Latin form, *architectus*, and as such is used not only in Roman days and during the Dark Ages, but occasionally in medieval times in Latin documents. It found its way with slight modification into the French, Italian, and Spanish tongues, and seems to have been first printed in its modern English spelling on the title-page of a book by John Shute in 1563. On this occasion it was applied to a professional English architect without qualification. From that date onwards it has been used in English in its modern sense, and therefore presents no difficulties. But it has also had a figurative application, as when Shakespeare wrote in 1588—' Chiefe Architect and plotter of these woes '—or in speaking of—' The Great Architect of the Universe '—thus denoting a controlling and directing mind, or the creator of something. So also in medieval Latin the rare word *architectus* does not always mean an architect, but sometimes merely a man who has created or contrived something (see pp. 58–60).

But even in comparatively modern English, after the

date of John Shute's book, we find other forms of the word, such as ' Architectist ' (in 1650), ' Architector ' (in 1637, 1702, &c.), ' Architectur ' and ' Architecter ' (in John Shute), and even ' Architecture ' (apparently a corruption of the French *architecteur*, or from medieval Latin or Italian forms). Other derivatives from the same root are ' Architectress ' (but apparently this generally meant a woman who had invented or created something), and ' Architecturalist ', a Victorian word which, as describing ' a professed student of, or connoisseur in, architecture ', labels that large class of amateur critics who write more freely and floridly about our art than practising architects, hampered by hard facts, are able or willing to do. The ' Architecturalist ' is chiefly to blame for the scanty recognition that has been accorded to the architect in history. Another variant occurs in Ben Jonson's *Tale of a Tub* (Act IV, Scene i), where he writes of Inigo Jones

> . . . But I am truly,
> *Architectonicus Professor*, rather
> That is (as one would say) an architect.

But besides all the forms of the word ' Architect ', many Latin and other words were used during the Middle Ages to describe those men who occupied that position, such as the *cementarius*, the *ingeniator*, and the ' master-mason '. Their status is fully discussed on pp. 60–5 in this book ; and here we need only remark that the ' Architecturalists ' who will not admit the existence of the medieval architect are ready enough to swallow his counterpart if suitably disguised under any other name.

Returning to the modern word ' Architect ', we find it defined in the *New English Dictionary* as ' a master builder ', or, more precisely, ' a skilled professor of the art of building, whose business it is to prepare the plans of edifices, and exercise a general superintendence over the course of their erection '. Thus no distinction is drawn between ' architecture ' and mere ' building ', for under the former head we find ' the art or science of building or constructing edifices of any kind for human use ', though later we read, ' Architecture is sometimes regarded solely as a fine art.' It is beyond the scope of this book to venture on so thorny a topic as the difference between architecture and building.

To most of us, Ruskin's definition that, ' Architecture is the art which so disposes and adorns the edifices raised by man . . . that the sight of them contributes to his mental health, power, and pleasure ' is far preferable to Sir Gilbert Scott's dictum that—' Architecture, as distinguished from mere building, is the decoration of construction '. The latter view, constantly fomented by Ruskin himself, did infinite harm to English architecture in Victorian days, and is still too common among the general public, but especially among engineers, who persist in regarding an architect primarily as one who applies ornament to structures. Another ridiculous statement was made by Ruskin to the effect that : ' No person who is not a great sculptor or painter *can* be an *architect*. If he is not a sculptor or painter, he can only be a *builder*.' [1] The broadcasting of rubbish such as this all over Victorian England has often caused people to forget that the architect is simply one who designs buildings and superintends their erection : they may or may not be ' ornamental ', but to constitute works of architecture they must be both well proportioned and well constructed. All intelligent readers of this book are probably aware already of the

[1] *Lectures on Architecture*, Add. 113.

nature of an architect's duties ; in the following pages they will be able to trace the story of his relationship to the builder, the engineer, and other personages connected with the conduct of building work.

. . . . . .

It is perhaps idle to surmise as to the identity of the first architect. We may rummage among Biblical and pagan myths and legends without much success and with no certainty. Sir Reginald Blomfield has written [1] that : ' Among the cavemen there were admirable draughtsmen, but they had to make their drawings on the sides of caves.' In the building of cromlechs and dolmens some degree of skill may be involved, but one can hardly be expected to unravel from the darkness that surrounds their origin any evidence as to their designers, and it is even a question whether they should be regarded as architecture. On the other hand, the erection of such primitive structures as huts of wattle and daub obviously called for little dexterity of hand and brain, and they may be ruled out.

We may, therefore, look to Egypt to provide the commencement of our story. Much has been discovered during the past century that illuminates the conditions under which the great tombs and temples were built. The tragic tale of the Captivity has been confirmed, and, though some famous authorities [2] are inclined to discount the hardships of the *corvée*, it appears fairly certain that the chief buildings in the Nile valley were raised only by means of a prodigal waste of human life and labour. But the personality of the architect in ancient Egypt is by no means clear.

[1] Sir R. Blomfield, *Greek Art and Architecture*, p. 55. (Oxford, 1922.)

[2] e. g. Sir W. Flinders Petrie, *Social Life in Egypt*, pp. 24, 26–7. (London, 1923.)

He has left us long inscriptions, which are found on many tombs at Thebes where the chief royal architects are buried. But these epitaphs consist simply of pompous boasts as to the greatness of the departed. A few examples will soon cloy the reader's palate.[1] Thus Ineni, who erected an obelisk at Thebes, after assuring us that he was ' a really first-class engineer and immensely popular ', continues :

. . . ' I became great beyond words; I will tell you about it, ye people; listen and do the good that I did—just like me. I continued powerful and met with no misfortune; my years were spent with gladness. I was neither traitor nor sneak, ,and I did no wrong whatever. I was foreman of the foremen and did not fail.'

His official titles were ' Pasha, Count, Chief of all the works in Karnak, Controller of the Double-houses of Silver and Gold, Sealer of all contracts in the House of Amūn, and Excellency in Charge of the Double Granary '.

Sennemūt, another architect of obelisks, went to Punt (Somaliland) in Queen Hatshepsōwet's expedition, was her chief architect, and, incidentally, supervised her daughter's education. He describes himself as—

' Pasha, Count, Royal Seal-bearer, Sole Companion, Chief of the Prophets of Monthu in Armant, Controller of the Fields Gardens and Cattle of Amūn,' &c. . . . ' I was the greatest of the great in the whole land ; one who had audience alone in the Privy Council. I was a real favourite of the King ; foreman of foremen ; superior of the great ; one to whom the affairs of Egypt were reported ; ' . . . ' I was a noble who was obeyed ; I had access to the writings of the prophets ; there was nothing which I did not know concerning what had happened since the beginning.'

Dhutij is described, *inter alia*, as ' Director of Works ',

[1] All taken from R. Engelbach, *The Problem of the Obelisks,* pp. 92–112. (London, 1924.)

and Beknekhonsu as ' Pasha, Count, High Priest of Amūn, and Chief Overseer of Works '. He also gives us a useful outline of his professional career :

' I passed four years as an infant.

I passed twelve years as a youth, being chief of the training-stable of King Menmirē [Seti I].

I acted as priest of Amūn for four years.

I acted as Divine Father for twelve years.

I acted as third prophet of Amūn for fifteen years.

I acted as second prophet of Amūn for twelve years.'

From these wearisome epitaphs we can make certain deductions. It is clear that the Egyptian architect was closely connected both with the temple and the court. If one practitioner began his career as a stud-groom, many more approached their profession by way of mathematics learned in the temple, for we know that education was entirely in the hands of the priesthood,[1] and that Egyptian architecture, from the Pyramids onwards, is based on a profound knowledge of geometry. The control of the ' Works Department ', as we should call it, was vested in a high officer of Church or State, and he may or may not have taken an active part in the design of buildings. Perhaps he relied for this on technical architects whose names have not been preserved. Yet Ineni himself is said to have been at one time a foreman on one of the gates at Karnak, then on a temple, and not until later did he obtain the ' superintendence of the King's building projects '. He also says that he ' made fields of clay for plastering the tombs of the Necropolis '. Dhutij made shrines, thrones, and small furniture for the temple at Karnak, besides doing his ordinary architectural work.[2]

[1] Petrie, *Religious Life in Egypt*, p. 41. (London, 1924.)

[2] Engelbach, *op. cit.*, pp. 95, 106.

The scantiness of the records thus makes it impossible to generalize further as to the architect's training and functions ; his status was evidently satisfactory.

Sir Flinders Petrie has recently informed me that the names of many Egyptian state architects have been preserved. The usually well-informed Cairo correspondent of *The Times* (16 Jan. 1926), in describing recent discoveries at Sakkara, mentions that the colonnade of the temple there ' is the work of Imhotep, the first known architect, who was afterwards canonized and worshipped as the patron saint of wise men, scribes, &c.'.

In a very interesting study of the conventions employed by Egyptian draughtsmen, Professor Capart has described their methods of drawing plans.[1] He mentions one plan of a royal tomb, drawn on papyrus, and now preserved in the Turin Museum. He does not state whether these were merely records, or whether they were drawn before the building was erected ; but, seeing that they were capable of drawing such plans, it is reasonable to suppose that architects would use them as they do nowadays.

In the great buildings of Babylonia and Chaldea, as in the work of the later empires that flourished in the Mesopotamian plain, some considerable degree of skill must have been required. Some official must have planned and supervised their erection and even laid them out to form an ordered city. But the name of no architect has been preserved. Where any record exists of these vast projects, it is only the king or the queen who is commemorated.

Milizia [2] and other writers have seen in the craftsmen

---

[1] J. Capart, *Egyptian Art*, pp. 145–8. (London, 1923.)

[2] F. Milizia, *Lives of Celebrated Architects*, trans. Mrs. Cresy, i. 6. (London, 1826.)

employed by Moses to build the Tabernacle the counterpart of the modern architect :

' The Lord hath called by name Bezalel . . . and he hath filled him with the spirit of God, in wisdom, in understanding, and in knowledge, and in all manner of workmanship ; and to devise cunning works, to work in gold, and in silver, and in brass, and in cutting of stones for setting, and in carving of wood, to work in all manner of cunning workmanship. And he hath put in his heart, that he may teach, both he, and Oholiab ' . . . ' Them hath he filled with wisdom of heart, to work all manner of workmanship, of the engraver, and of the cunning workman, and of the embroiderer, in blue, and in purple, in scarlet, and in fine linen, and of the weaver, even of them that do any workmanship, and of those that devise cunning works.' [1]

It cannot be pretended, however, that this passage enlightens us very much in our quest, especially as the Tabernacle is generally believed to have been little more than a large tent or marquee.[2] Nor is there anything bearing very definitely on the status or functions of the architect in the legendary history of Crete.

This brings us to the early days of Greece.

GENERAL BIBLIOGRAPHY

(for special bibliographies see end of each chapter)

Architectural Publication Society's *Dictionary*, s.vv. ' Architect ', and ' Drawing '. (London, 1853–92.)

Berty, A. *Les grands Architects français*. (Paris, 1860.)

Blomfield, R. T. *Architectural Drawing and Draughtsmen*. (London, 1912.)

Egger, H. *Architektonische Zeichnungen Alter Meister*. (Vienna, N. D., recent.)

[1] Exodus xxxv. 30–5 (R.V.).
[2] See Dr. Schick's restoration at Jerusalem.

Félibien, J. F. *La Vie et les Ouvrages des plus célèbres Architectes.*
(Paris, 1690.)
Lance, A. E. *Dictionnaire des Architectes français.* (Paris, 1872.)
Milizia, F. *Le Vite dei più celebri architetti.* (Rome, 1768.)
Monaldini, G. A. *Le Vite de' più celebri architetti d'ogni nazione e
d'ogni tempo.* (Rome, 1768.)
Sturgis, R. *Dictionary of Architecture and Building*, s.v. ' Architect '.
(New York, 1901.)
Velasco, P. *An Account of the Lives and Works of the Most Eminent
Spanish Painters, Sculptors, and Architects.* (London, 1739.)
Wasmuth, E. (publisher). *Architektur-zeichnungen.* (Berlin, 1922.)

II

GREECE

IN early Greek writings there are indications of the architect's existence. Six times at least in the *Iliad*, and twice in the *Odyssey*, Homer mentions the τέκτονες (craftsmen) from whom the architect or master-craftsman derived his name in later years (ἀρχός = chief ; τέκτων = craftsman). In other passages we find references to Daedalus, who is credited with invention of the saw and other tools ; to Trophonius and Agamedes, like Daedalus, of royal birth ; and to Euryalus, said to have introduced the making of bricks and the construction of dwelling-houses into Greece for the first time. All of these were claimed as architects by later Greek writers. It appears that the τέκτονες were not masons, but rather workers in wood or metal (i. e., carpenters and smiths) on buildings and on ships, and that the architect was a master-carpenter or a master-smith rather than a master-mason.[1] On the other hand, the word Ἀρχιτέκτων is also used in contradistinction to χειροτέχνης (manual worker).[2]

Trophonius and Agamedes, mentioned above, are commonly cited as early architects, but the references to them are so vague and so confused with legendary lore that we cannot take them very seriously. Thus, when they built a temple to Apollo, Homer gives us to understand that the god not only chose his site but actually got to work with architects and masons and apparently finished the building before he discovered that the site was haunted.[3]

---

[1] C. Lucas, s.v. ' Architectus ', in Daremberg et Saglio, *Dictionnaire des Antiquités grecques et romaines*. (Paris, 1877, &c.)

[2] Liddell and Scott, s.v. αρχιτέκτων.

[3] Homer, *Hymn to Apollo*, 356.

Finally, they are said to have asked the god for a reward for their labours. Apollo promised them the best of all gifts, and consequently within three days they were both found dead.[1]

Milizia [2] records the names of a score or so of Greek architects who flourished during the centuries subsequent to legendary times and prior to the age of Pericles. He bases his statements largely on the writings of Vitruvius (who lived in Rome hundreds of years later), Strabo, Pausanias, and other Greek historians, but fails to create any definite picture of the architect as a human personality. Yet he tells us [3] that the ingenious Hermogenes, getting into trouble with the triglyphs of the Doric order when a certain temple was well under way, changed his mind and adopted the Ionic, though the stone was already cut and waiting on the site. This seems to indicate that Hermogenes was a privileged person, of recognized professional status, or, alternatively, of noble birth. Then there was Callimachus, who became famous for his legendary modelling of the Corinthian capital from a basketful of growing acanthus. He is also credited with the invention of a lamp that burned for a year without replenishment, a testimonial to his ability to hoodwink the public.[4] There were Ctesiphon and Metagenes, his son, who designed and built the Temple of Diana at Ephesus, using many mechanical contrivances to surmount difficulties encountered in the construction ; [5] and four architects who worked together on the Temple of Jupiter at Athens.[6] Archimedes has been described by some writers as one of the seven chief Greek architects,

---

[1] Cicero, *Tusc. Disp*. i. 47. [2] Milizia, *op. cit*. i. 16–41.
[3] Vitruvius, iv. 3. [4] *Ibid*. iv. 1 ; Pausanias, i. 26.
[5] Vitruvius, x. 6. [6] *Ibid*. vii, preface.

though he specialized in mechanics and mathematics. There were architects who wrote books on their art, such as Tarchesius, Argelius,[1] and Hermogenes already mentioned. There were some whose reputation rested on one building, such as Andronicus, who designed the Tower of the Winds at Athens ; [2] and Libon of Messena or Elis, to whom is ascribed the Temple of Jupiter at Olympia.[3] Others seem to have enjoyed a large provincial temple-practice, among them Chirisophus the Cretan, at Tegea,[4] and Pheaces, at Agrigentum.[5] Meticus laid out a square in Athens, and eventually it was named after him.[6] Chirisophus had a statue erected in his honour in one of the temples he built.[7]

Bupalos practised the arts of sculpture and architecture at Ephesus, and also found time to caricature his neighbour, the poet Hipponax, who retaliated in verse.[8] Another sculptor-architect was probably Pytheos, to whom Dr. Percy Gardner is inclined to attribute the great chariot-horses on the Mausoleum at Halicarnassus, which are ' heavy and rough '. Pytheos is said to have planned not only this famous mausoleum but also the Temple of Athena at Priene.[9] Yet from all these miscellaneous and doubtful statements there emerges but a shadowy figure of the architect in primitive Greece. We are told nothing of his training, nothing of his remuneration, and little of his methods of work. In some cases he seems to have been a person of consequence ; and even in those early days he had contracted the habit of writing about architecture, sometimes in the familiar form of rules for the

[1] Vitruvius, iv. 3.
[2] *Ibid.* i. 6.
[3] Pausanias, v. 10.
[4] *Ibid.* viii. 53.
[5] Diodorus Siculus, xi. 2 ; and xiii. 12.
[6] Jul. Pollux, viii. 10.
[7] Pausanias, viii. 53.
[8] *Journal of Hellenic Studies*, x. 9.
[9] *Ibid.* xiii. 193–4.

Orders, more often describing and perhaps advertising his own buildings.

Perhaps the most definite picture of a building enterprise at this period is to be found in the records of the fifth temple at Delphi, erected in the latter half of the sixth century B. C. to replace the fourth temple which was destroyed in 548 B.C. It was decided to open a fund for rebuilding it, the cost to be contributed as to 75 talents by the people of Delphi, and the remaining 300 talents collected by Delphians from the rest of the civilized world. The architect selected by the Amphiktyons was a Corinthian named Spintharus—an otherwise unknown name.[1] A contract was drawn up between the Amphiktyonic Council and the wealthy family of Alcmaeonidae, builders, and the temple was to be of local limestone, but with great liberality the contractors made the columns of the front of white Parian marble.[2] The building was probably ready for use by the end of the century, but the external sculpture was not completed.

As we pass out of these misty centuries into the brilliant light of the Periclean age, we naturally expect to find adequate records of those architects who did so much for the beautification of Athens. Yet even here history is singularly silent, and all the wealth of learning that for a century has been lavished on the Athenian Acropolis has failed to reveal anything tangible about Ictinus, Callicrates, and the rest.[3] This may be due partly to the prominent part played by Pericles and Pheidias in the rebuilding and embellishment of Athens in their day. Pheidias was a sculptor, but, though architects were employed on the

[1] Pausanias, x. v.   [2] Herodotus, v. 62
[3] See G. Graindor, 'L'architecte Kallikrates et le mur est de l'Acropole', in *Rév. Arch.*, 1924, i. 174.

various temples, &c., it was to him that the superintendence of the great building projects was entrusted.[1]
Pericles, who for many years had been a generous patron
and connoisseur of the arts, may even have entered the
field of architecture himself : ' By conversing with the
most able architects, and from the instruction of his great
friend Anaxagoras, a philosopher of the first rank, and
president of architecture, he acquired that science.' [2]

If Milizia is correct in his rendering, we may hail in
Pericles the first of those ' gifted amateurs ' who, at
intervals through history, have developed from connoisseurs into practitioners of our art. He is said to have
' superintended ' the Odeon at Athens.[3]

On the other hand, the professional status of the architect (now definitely labelled as ἀρχιτέκτων) seems to
have become generally recognized, although he was not
always accorded full credit for his work. Pausanias,
writing many centuries later, states that in most Greek
towns the authorship was ascribed to the gods, to mythical
heroes, or to local worthies. Valerius Maximus writes
that Athens was rightly proud of its Arsenal, an admirable
work, and that Philo, its architect, gave so eloquent a
description of its merits ' that the most enlightened com-
munity in the world applauded him no less for his oratory
than for his talent as an architect.' [4]

In the days of Pericles, it is surely safe to assume that
any artist, even without the silver tongue of Philo, would
receive due recognition. Moreover, at least one inscription attests the existence of the official architect.[5] The
great public building at Olympia known as the Leonidæum

---

[1] Plutarch, *Life of Pericles*, xii. 5.   [2] Milizia, *op. cit.* i, p. 43.
[3] Plutarch, *Pericles*, xii. 5.   [4] Valerius Max. VIII. xii. 2.
[5] *Révue Archéologique*, 1905, ii.

(B. C. 350) was so called after its architect, Leonidas of Naxos, to whom a statue was also erected. He wrote a book on Proportion, and was a famous and wealthy man.

The nature of the architect's duties at that period seems to have been vague. Thus Scopas combined the functions of sculptor and architect,[1] while Philo carried out what we should now describe as civil engineering.[2] For the long wall of Athens Callimachus was ' contractor ' (ἐργολάβος). This, however, seems to have been an unusual practice. We may also include town-planning among the functions of the Greek architect in the days of Pericles, though Sir Reginald Blomfield considers that the Greeks in the fifth century had hardly begun to realize the possibilities of grouping buildings on axial lines.[3] In a recent book on town-planning [4] it is stated that, in the fifth-century cities of Piraeus, Thurii, Rhodes, Selinus, and Cyrene, a system of wide rectangular streets was provided, with the *agora* and chief buildings grouped at the intersection of the two main thoroughfares. Aristotle ascribes the introduction of this principle to Hippodamus of Miletus, who was born about 480 B. C., and also credits him with having been the first of all architects to make provision for the proper grouping of dwelling-houses. Hippodamus is said by Aristotle to have laid out the town of Piraeus (on a chessboard pattern), by Diodorus to have planned Thurii in South Italy (founded in 443 B. C., but not yet excavated), and by Strabo to have laid out Rhodes in B. C. 408, i. e., when he was over seventy years of age, which is, as Professor Haverfield has pointed out,[5] ' con-

[1] Pausanias, viii. 45.   [2] Plutarch, *Sulla*.
[3] Blomfield, *Greek Art and Architecture*, p. 71.
[4] Hughes and Lamborn, *Towns and Town-planning*, pp. 3-4. (Oxford, 1923.)
[5] Haverfield, *Ancient Town-planning*, pp. 31-2. (Oxford, 1913.)

ceivable but not altogether probable ', and, as the date of his birth is doubtful, ' certainty is unattainable ' on this point.[1] Strabo also states that Hippodamus built temples at Rhodes, so that it appears that he was definitely an architect rather than some kind of a civil engineer.

The town-plans of Selinus in Sicily and of Cyrene in North Africa may belong to the age of Hippodamus, the former being attributed by MM. Hulot and Fougères to Hermocrates, but Professor Haverfield does not accept this.[2] The lay-out of the newer town of Smyrna is assigned by Strabo [3] to the Macedonian age (330–130 B. C.) and to the labours of the Macedonians, Antigonus and Lysimachus. It seems conceivable that the chessboard pattern favoured for the plan of these Macedonian cities was suggested in part by the similar arrangement of a military camp, as it certainly was in later Roman days (see next chapter). It is even more probable that the rectilinear plan had its origin in the lay-out of the great cities of the Mesopotamian plain—Babylon, Nineveh, and Asshur.

Apart from actual town-planning, we know of other features of Greek civic life bearing on the work and duties of the architect. It was probably in the first half of the fourth century B. C. that various Greek cities instituted building by-laws, and appointed *Astynomi* or building inspectors to see that they were carried out.[4] Thus the regulations at Pergamum included clauses relating to party walls, dangerous structures, and the penetration of damp from one property to another adjoining at a lower level.[5]

[1] Strabo, XIV. ii. 9.

[2] *Ancient Town Planning*, p. 34.

[3] Strabo, XIV. i. 37.

[4] Haverfield, *op. cit.*, p. 37.

[5] *Ibid.*, p. 54.

Vitruvius quotes the Greek architect Pytheos, whose Commentaries have since been lost, to the effect that ' an architect ought to be able to accomplish much more in all the arts and sciences than the men who, by their own particular kinds of work and the practice of it, have brought each single subject to the highest perfection '. ' But this '—observes the canny Roman—' is in point of fact not realized '.[1] Yet it is evident that an architect was expected to be at least a Jack-of-all-trades, if not an Admirable Crichton. Sometimes veering towards the sculptor, sometimes towards the engineer, he was capable on occasion of designing theatrical properties and scenery [2] or the paraphernalia for public festivals.[3] We may gather that when Vitruvius tells us that ' the ancients ' expected an architect to be a man of good general education, he was referring to the Greeks.[4] And though some authorities [5] consider that among those described as ' architect ' in inscriptions were certain persons better styled ' contractor ' ($\dot{\epsilon}\rho\gamma o\lambda\dot{a}\beta os$), it is established that the architect was almost always a well-known and well-educated professional man, occupying a recognized position in society. This does not imply that the Greek architect was not expected to add the acumen of a business man to his other qualifications. At Ephesus, according to Vitruvius,[6] there was a law under which, if an architect's ' extras ' exceeded the contract amount by more than 25 per cent., he was held liable for them personally. In all probability architects accompanied each mission of civil and religious leaders that was sent to found a colony overseas, for the standard of design evident in buildings erected by newly-

[1] Vitruvius, i. 1.   [2] *Ibid.* vii. 6.
[3] Diodorus Siculus, v.   [4] Vitruvius, i. 1.
[5] Quoted in C. Lucas, *op. cit.*, p. 380.   [6] Vitruvius, x, preface.

arrived settlers was so high, and their features resembled so closely the characteristics of architecture in the mother-country, that other proof is hardly necessary. Vitruvius gives us a long list of Greek architectural writers, proving that in those days literature and art went hand in hand.

As regards the remuneration of the Greek architect, it has been stated [1] that he received ten times as much as a labourer. But a very careful and interesting study of ' Work and Wages in Athens ' by Dr. F. B. Jevons, though it throws some light on this subject, does not present such a rosy view of his status and pay.[2]　Dr. Jevons quotes three Athenian inscriptions of different periods. The first dates from the time of Socrates (5th cent. B. C.), the second relates to the building accounts of the Erechtheum (408 B. C.), and the third is dated 329–328 B.C. According to the first, a skilled artisan received 5 obols to 1 drachma a day, an unskilled labourer 3 obols a day, while no architect is mentioned (6 obols = 1 drachma = about $9\frac{3}{4}d$.). In the second, day labourers hired temporarily for any ' job ' received 1 drachma a day, piecework being paid on the same basis ; an architect received similar pay ; but a ὑπογραμματεύς (assistant clerk) earned only 4 obols. The third inscription is more detailed. At this period the unskilled labourer, finding his own food, earned $1\frac{1}{2}$ drachmas ; a sawyer was paid at the same rate ; a carpenter making doors was paid 1 drachma 5 obols ; the architect (ἀρχιτέκτων) received 2 drachmas ; but certain bricklayers and carpenters were paid as much as $2\frac{1}{2}$ drachmas. It seems that $1\frac{1}{2}$ drachmas was then the minimum wage for an adult, and that the few exceptions to this rule are payments to apprentices. It is clear that

---

[1] See C. Lucas, *op. cit.*, p. 374.
[2] In *Journal of Hellenic Studies*, xv, pp. 239 *et seq.* (1895).

the architect, though paid more than the inferior workers, did not rank as high as some of the skilled craftsmen. Dr. Jevons infers from these figures that there was a progressive rise in wages due to the increased cost of living, for there is evidence that the rise in the price of corn during this period bore a definite proportion to the increase in wages, and it is known that the corn standard at that time governed the cost of living. He points out too that ' the quantity of precious metals then in circulation was continually increasing, and that consequently their purchasing power must have been proportionately decreasing.'

He then cites a fourth inscription, which relates to Delos at the beginning of the second century B. C. and gives the official accounts of the Temple of Apollo there, with the various salaries paid to the staff. The vergers received from 1 to 3 obols a day, but probably they had time to ply another trade. The κρουνοφύλαξ (apparently the custodian of the well) received only 1½ obols a day, but Dr. Jevons thinks that he would also get ' tips ' from pilgrims. The secretary was paid 1⅛ obols, so we may infer that his also was a ' part-time appointment '. The ἀρχιτέκτων received 2 drachmas a day, a relatively large salary. Another ingenious calculation by Dr. Jevons results in the conclusion that at this period food alone cost 2 obols a day. Prices had dropped since 329 B. C. in the proportion of 5 : 3, and labourers' wages had probably dropped to 1 drachma a day, i. e., to the same point at which they stood in 408 B. C. Meanwhile the architect's pay had doubled, though it may have been no more than that of other skilled workers, and thus his status, as compared with that of the casual labourer, had evidently improved. But though many, perhaps most, architects worked for a regular salary as State or municipal officials, others carried on private practice.

With authentic evidence as to the social status of the architect, and with inferential knowledge of his duties, it remains to form some hypothesis as to the nature of his training in the Golden Age of Greece. ' Within their limits, in their mastery of what they set themselves to do '—writes Sir Reginald Blomfield—' the artists of the age of Pericles remain unapproachable '. [1] How did they attain this eminence ? We do not know whether they learned their craft in the *atelier* of a master, as pupils or apprentices, or whether there were schools in which they were trained, but the latter is unlikely. There are numerous cases of boys being trained by their fathers to follow their profession, and Plato in his *Laws* (Book I) recommends a sort of kindergarten method to such parents, advising that they should be supplied with miniature tools and employed on the erection of dolls' houses. Socrates, in one of his dialogues, says : ' In what employment do you intend to excel, O Euthedemus, that you collect so many books ? Is it architecture ? For this art you will find no little knowledge necessary.' Books were used by architects for other purposes than their own instruction. Thus architects wrote monographs explaining or defending their own buildings, describing new features of construction and design that they had introduced. In the fourth century B. C. the principles of design came to be a topic. Hippodamus of Miletus, the town-planner, made full use of literary methods of propaganda, and published ideal schemes of lay-out for towns.[2]

---

[1] Blomfield, *op. cit.*, p. 68.
[2] A. L. Frothingham, ' Greek Architects ', &c., in *The Architectural Record*, xxiii. pp. 85–8. (New York, 1908.)

But, returning to the question of training, close examination of the Parthenon and other masterpieces of the period has made it certain that such optical and aesthetic refinements as have been revealed therein could only have been achieved by long and patient study. Just as the marvellous success of St. Paul's dome must be ultimately attributed to the great brain of a man who had mastered mathematics, so it is only by scientific as well as artistic knowledge that the architects of the Parthenon could have created the most perfect building known to us. The lesson that we of to-day have to learn from Ictinus and Callicrates is that the greatest artist, whatever his dower of talent, can only achieve full mastery of his art by thorough and even tedious training.

As regards their actual methods of work, it appears probable that they had a greater freedom, in design and in making changes during the erection of a building, than prevailed later in Roman and medieval days. Sometimes they used a wax model ($τύπος$) of ornamental details, and occasionally a general model ($παραδείγμα$) of the whole building. The specification for the Arsenal at the Piraeus has been preserved and translated : it gives full instructions as to dimensions, materials, thicknesses of wall, and time of completion.

It has generally been held hitherto that the Greek artist strove consciously and persistently after beauty for its own sake, but a recent writer has endeavoured to persuade us to revise most of our ideas on this point.[1] In his view the evidence does not ' warrant a belief in any highly developed aesthetic gifts in his mentality,' or ' raise him in this respect conspicuously above the rest of the Ancients '

[1] F. P. Chambers, ' The Aesthetic of the Ancients ', in *R. I. B. A. Journal* (1925).

. . . ' Greek curiosity began and ended with an account of what the work represented, what it was made of, and what its size was. Herodotus is concerned with material value and dimensions ' . . . ' Evidently architecture, as architecture, did not interest the Greek ; it more nearly approached our concept of *engineering* ' . . . ' The only possible example of *taste*, in our sense, which Greek architecture provides is the architectural refinement ' . . . ' It is unfortunate that, except for one obscure reference in Vitruvius, there is no mention of refinement in the extant classics, and the whole subject is one where argument is at present useless ' . . . ' Evidently the Greeks could create what we have chosen to call Art, without the thought of an art.' I find it difficult to accept this estimate of Greek art. Even allowing for one's natural inclination to follow the unbroken stream of admiration which has long been lavished on the achievements of the Periclean age, one cannot feel that all this marvellous beauty was wrought unconsciously, that the builders of the Parthenon were only skilled engineers and the sculptors only clever anatomists. If this new theory is right, then we must certainly classify the Greek architects as technicians rather than as artists in the accepted sense of the word. Personally I prefer Sir Reginald Blomfield's firm statement, that ' the aim and ideal of the Greek was beauty of form, and this beauty, which he sought in the first instance as the expression of his religion, ultimately became almost a religion in itself '.

For the last chapter of the story of the Greek architect, the scene shifts to the coast of Egypt, and two more shadowy figures flit across our stage. Dinocrates, a skilful and ingenious architect of Macedonia, was employed by Alexander to lay out his wonderful new city. The means by which he attracted royal notice are worthy of the attention of every aspiring professional man. The usual letters of recommendation to influential persons having proved futile,

' he had recourse to his own efforts. He was of very lofty stature and pleasing countenance, finely formed, and extremely dignified. Trusting, therefore, to these natural gifts, he undressed himself in his inn, anointed his body with oil, set a chaplet of poplar leaves on his head, draped his left shoulder with a lion's skin, and holding a club in his right hand, stalked forth to a place in front of the tribunal where the king was administering justice.'

To cut the story short, as soon as the king noticed him and asked his identity, Dinocrates put forward a scheme :

' for shaping Mount Athos into the statue of a man, in whose left hand I have represented a very spacious fortified city, and in his right a bowl to receive the water of all the streams which are in that mountain, so that it may pour from the bowl into the sea.'[1]

In any well-regulated moral tale, this should have been the end of Dinocrates ; but it was not a moral age, and by this charlatan's trick he attained his end. Substitute horn-rimmed spectacles and side-whiskers for Dinocrates' disguise, and you have—*mutatis mutandis*—a very accurate portrait of the pushful architect of to-day. But Dinocrates was a man of real ability, and the plan that he drew for the new city, still commemorated by some of the streets of Alexandria at the present time, was perhaps the greatest achievement of ancient town-planning. Other works attributed to Dinocrates are the wonderful tomb of Arsinoë, and the later temple of Artemis at Ephesus, but Professor Lethaby doubts this.[2]

Sostratos, ' the friend and favourite of kings ',[3] at

---

[1] Vitruvius, ii, preface.
[2] In *Journal of Hellenic Studies*, xxxiii. 95.   [3] Vitruvius, v. 1.

a later period had the unusual privilege of designing one of the Seven Wonders of the ancient world, the Pharos at Alexandria.[1] We know very little about him otherwise, except that he hailed from Cnidos, and had made some reputation as an architect there. But evidently Ptolemy Philadelphos made his choice with discrimination, for, even if we allow for inaccuracy and exaggeration in contemporary writers, there can be no doubt that the idea and the erection of this great lighthouse represented a marvellous feat for any man. When the huge monument was completed, it bore on a panel a complimentary inscription in honour of Ptolemy, but, after a few years of Mediterranean gales had done their work, the cement surface of the panel peeled away, revealing, in bold letters carved in the stone and filled with lead, the words : ' Sostratos of Cnidos, son of Dexiphanes, to the gods the saviours, for the benefit of mariners.' Surely there is a professional grievance behind this story ? [2]

One more incident of this Hellenistic period relates to the status of the architect. Polybius states [3] that in B. C. 220 Ptolemy Philopater sent a hundred ' architects ' to Rhodes, which had been damaged by an earthquake. This statement has been used to prove that architects were then extremely plentiful in Alexandria, but it may well be assumed that among this hundred there were practitioners of the other arts. (The word used by Polybius is not ἀρχιτέκτων but οἰκοδόμος, which Liddell and Scott [4] define as ' builder, architect ', and the latest translator [5] has rendered it ' master-builders ' in this case.)

---

[1] Strabo, xvii.

[2] See also W. Deonna, ' Sostratos de Cnide et la vertu des formules invisibles ', in *Révue Archéologique*, ii. 175 (1921).

[3] Polybius, v. 9.   [4] *Lexicon*, latest edition.

[5] In the ' Loeb Library '.

Since this chapter was written, additional light on architectural practice in Greece has been furnished by Mr. A. H. Smith in a recent paper on *The Building Inscriptions of the Acropolis of Athens*. He describes the erection of a temenos or sacred enclosure on the Acropolis as a war-memorial, in 448 B. C. At first it was suggested that Callicrates should be employed as architect, but a member of the Boule proposed an amendment that there should be a competition. It was therefore resolved to invite designs : the drawings to be ' not less than 1 cubit large ' (equivalent to a scale of 1 inch to a foot), and to be publicly exhibited for ten days. They were then to be judged by popular vote. Other inscriptions show that architects were paid monthly, or on a ' prytany ' of 36 or 37 days (one-tenth of a year). In one case in 407-6 B. C. an architect was paid the skilled workman's wage of 1 drachma a day, but more than a clerk.

BIBLIOGRAPHY

Frothingham, A. L. ' Greek Architects, Contractors, and Building Operations,' in *The Architectural Record*, xxiii, pp. 81–96, and xxiv, pp. 321–38. (New York, 1908.)

Haverfield, F. *Ancient Town-planning*. (Oxford, 1923.)

Jevons, F. B. ' Work and Wages in Athens ', in *Journal of Hellenic Studies*, xv, p. 239. (London, 1895.)

Lucas, C. s.v. ' Architectus ', in Daremberg et Saglio, *Dictionnaire des Antiquités grecques et romaines*. (Paris, 1877, &c.)

Smith, A. H. ' The Building Inscriptions of the Acropolis of Athens ', in the *R.I.B.A. Journal* (18 December, 1926.)

III

ROME

THANKS to our possession of Vitruvius's famous treatise, we know a little more of the Roman architect than of his Greek predecessor, though even on this subject information is lamentably meagre. Vitruvius is generally supposed to have lived in the brilliant age of Augustus, and to have been able to devote his time to literary work because he was in receipt of a pension from that great patron of the arts.[1] Probably Félibien is more correct in his reading of the Latin,[2] and, if so, Vitruvius was paid a salary for designing artillery, in which case he would have little time for designing buildings. He describes in detail [3] a basilica that he designed at Fano, but beyond this history is silent.

Mr. F. P. Chambers has, however, recently propounded the novel suggestion that Vitruvius may have been an amateur as ' he omits to explain the arch and the vault, the great features of Roman architecture '.[4] The omission is curious, but there are so many references in Vitruvius to questions of professional practice, and so much information about other details of construction, that one may safely describe him as an architect with a strong bias in the direction of archaeology.

His work is divided into ten books, and was intended to cover the whole field of contemporary architectural knowledge, as, on the whole, it succeeds in doing. Beginning with a preface on the education of the architect, he deals in turn with sites, building materials, temples, the

---

[1] Milizia, *Le vite dei più celebri architetti*, i. 83. (1768.)
[2] Félibien, *La vie des plus célèbres architectes*, p. 69. (Paris, 1690.)
[3] Vitruvius, v. 1.   [4] *The Aesthetic of the Ancients*, p. 248.

FIG. 2. HADRIAN, EMPEROR AND REPUTED ARCHITECT

From the bust in the Museo Nazionale, Naples

Orders, the planning and grouping of public buildings, private houses, decoration and decorative materials, and water-supply ; concluding with two chapters that cover ground not traversed by the modern architect, viz., astronomy and its application ; and mechanical appliances for hoisting, for raising water, and for military purposes. He therefore supplies us with a manual of design and building-construction, interspersed so freely with references to the practice of ' the ancients ' that it may be said to include the history of architecture. It has been fashionable to make fun of Vitruvius for his pedantry and his prolixity, but probably the blame lies rather with those who have misused his invaluable and often entertaining work. The introductions to his various ' Books ' are certainly fulsome to our way of thinking, but were written in the language and manner of his time to the royal patron who made his writing possible. Together with much that is superfluous, they contain many illuminating allusions to architectural practice in his own day, more helpful for our purpose than the technical matters with which the bulk of his treatise is concerned. In his preface to Book V he admits the difficulty of writing on architecture for the general public, showing that he anticipated a circle of readers wider than his own profession ; and in the preface to Book VII he acknowledges his indebtedness to the numerous architects whose writings he has consulted.

' But for my part, Caesar, I am not bringing forward the present treatise after changing the titles of other men's books and inserting my own name, nor has it been my plan to win approbation by finding fault with the work of another. On the contrary, I express unlimited thanks to all the authors that have in the past, by compiling from antiquity remarkable instances of the skill shown by genius, provided us with abundant materials of different kinds.'[1]

Of the long list of authorities that follows, the majority are Greeks. Their writings have unfortunately perished, but it is interesting to find Ictinus and other practising architects among the authors. It appears that some of these works were manuals of the theory of architectural design, and more were descriptions of buildings actually executed. None of them seems to have dealt specifically, as Vitruvius does, with construction. He expresses his regret that, up to his day, Roman architects had written so little, and mentions one or two who might advantageously have done so. In an earlier passage,[2] after stating that he has never been eager to make money by his practice, and that ' only a little celebrity has followed ', he makes the ingenuous observation : ' but still, my hope is that, with the publication of these books, I shall become known even to posterity.' His hope has been realized !

Returning to his preface to Book I, we find his views on the education of the architect set forth with considerable fulness and freedom. He is convinced that technical training must be broad, and both theoretical and practical in character.

' Architects who have aimed at acquiring manual skill without scholarship have never been able to reach a position of authority to correspond to their pains, while those who relied only upon theories and scholarship were obviously hunting the shadow, not the substance. But those who have a thorough knowledge of both, like men armed at all points, have the sooner attained their object and carried authority with them.'

[1] The quotations from Vitruvius in this chapter are taken from the translation by Prof. M. H. Morgan. (Harvard Univ. Press, 1914.)

[2] Vitruvius, vi, preface.

His curriculum for the architectural student has often been quoted :

' Let him be educated, skilful with the pencil, instructed in geometry, know much history, have followed the philosophers with attention, understand music, have some knowledge of medicine, know the opinions of the jurists, and be acquainted with astronomy and the theory of the heavens.'

No modern architect would deny the importance of draughtsmanship and geometry, but the value of the other subjects is less obvious, and Vitruvius's own explanation must be given. The ' knowledge of medicine ' to which he refers means what we now call ' architectural hygiene ', and the ' opinions of the jurists ' represent what we term ' architectural law '. The ' history ' he mentions would be better defined as ' historical symbolism ; ' the philosophy (including also a knowledge of physics) ' makes an architect high-minded and not self-assuming, but rather renders him courteous, just, and honest without avariciousness '; finally, music and astronomy were required in those days for purposes which he explains, but which have lost their significance in modern times.

It may be objected that such a curriculum is of a general rather than a technical nature, and that it omits the two most important subjects in modern architectural training— design and construction. That Vitruvius did not mean to exclude these from his syllabus is apparent from the scope of his own treatise, which is largely devoted to them. Probably he intended his list of subjects to form a preliminary course of general education, to be followed by technical training on the lines of his textbook. He makes it clear that he attached great value to general education :

' I think that men have no right to profess themselves architects hastily, without having climbed from boyhood the steps of these studies, and thus, nursed by the knowledge of many arts and sciences, having reached the heights of the holy ground of architecture.'

We are left in complete ignorance of the means by which the young architect acquired his knowledge, whether in a school or from a practitioner ; nor do we know whether the Roman State, so highly-organized in many respects, required an architect to satisfy any test or obtain any diploma before he commenced practice. Lampridius tells us [1] that Alexander Severus (A. D. 222–35) established professors of architecture and numerous other subjects, to whose classes poor people could send their children in return for payment in kind. But that estimable emperor died young, so that his reforms may have had little effect. It seems probable that prior to that date architectural training was acquired by some means of apprenticeship in an *atelier*. According to an edict of Diocletian in A. D. 301, teachers of architecture were paid more per pupil per month than teachers of reading and arithmetic, but only half as much as those who taught Greek, Latin, rhetoric, and law. It seems clear that Roman architectural training devoted less attention to the study of optics, perspective, and theoretical mathematics than the Greek system had done : it tended, in fact, to make the architect less of an artist and more of a constructor.

It is known that building by-laws existed both in Rome and elsewhere. Thus in Rome itself the thickness of brick walls was prescribed in relation to their height, but outside the city boundaries the regulations were less stringent.[2] At Utica the magistrate had to certify that all bricks had been made at least five years before use.[3] The idea that

[1] Lampridius, *Alexandri Severi Vita*, xliv.
[2] Vitruvius, ii. 8.   [3] *Ibid.* ii. 2.

the architect in ancient times was an untrammelled genius, subject to none of the sordid restrictions that limit the individualist to-day, is a pure myth.

The scope of his duties appears to have been wide. It certainly included the work of what we now call a ' town-planner '.

The chessboard pattern of the typical Roman town suggests a military camp, and indeed the connexion may easily be traced, for many of the Roman cities—both in North Italy and in the provinces—were *coloniae* established as semi-fortified outposts and at first occupied by discharged soldiers. Timgad and Aosta are typical instances of this, and perhaps Caerwent—lying so near a ' barbarian ' frontier—may be regarded as another. But, even in towns which had no such military value, the same system was adopted, for the Roman mind was of an orderly type and loved military precision. Building by-laws have already been mentioned, but there do not appear to have been any town-planning regulations. The Roman *gromatici* (land surveyors) were recognized officials, and there were also the *mensores aedificium*, who were solely occupied in measuring and surveying buildings.[1] The architect, like Inigo Jones in later days, seems sometimes to have designed the trappings of triumphal progresses.[2] His close association with military and civil engineering is referred to later in this chapter, where the status of the official architect is discussed, and Vitruvius in his Chapter X deals with the engines of war which gave the engineer his name.

Some architects seem to have devoted themselves to one class of building; thus Hippias specialized in the

---

[1] Haverfield, *op. cit.*, passim.
[2] Panvinius, *De Triumpho*, p. 141.

designing of *thermae*.[1]   The private practitioner occasionally appears in the correspondence of the great masters
of Latin literature. Thus Cicero employed the architect
Cluatius to design a monument in memory of Tullia, and
writes thus to a friend about it : ' For my part I have no
doubt about the design (I like Cluatius's design), nor about
the erection (on that I am quite determined) ; but I have
some doubts about the place.' [2]   Cicero must have been
a valuable ' client ', for he built or bought at least twenty-
one houses in his lifetime, besides one which came to
him by inheritance. But, as he employed five different
architects, one may infer that he was not an easy man to
deal with. Pliny the Younger made a hobby of architecture, and the long descriptions of his various villas,
contained in his letters, are well known.[3]   But though
one can imagine him to have been a sympathetic and
discriminating client, his architects too must have experienced the troubles usually associated with work for
a gifted amateur. His enthusiasm for building was such
that Milizia includes him in his list of celebrated architects,[4] explaining that, ' though not an architect by profession, he was very learned, and built many edifices,
which he has described with great ability '. In his admiration for Greek architecture Pliny may safely be regarded as
an early example of the art connoisseur (Lucian and
Quintilian being other examples), whom we meet so
frequently in the history of eighteenth-century architecture
in England. The architect-emperor Hadrian is sometimes
included in the same category, but recent authorities are
inclined to award him professional rank, as will appear
later in this chapter.

[1] Lucan, *Dialog. Hipp.*   [2] Cicero, *Ad Atticum*, xii. 18.
[3] Pliny, *Letters*, ii. 17 ; and v. 6.   [4] Milizia, *op. cit.* i, p. 92.

A truly remarkable view of the functions of an architect seems to have been held by Crassus, as Plutarch relates :[1]

' Observing how natural and familiar at Rome were such fatalities as the conflagration and collapse of buildings, owing to their being too massive and close together, he proceeded to buy slaves who were architects and builders (ἀρχιτέκτονας καὶ οἰκοδόμους). Then, when he had over five hundred of these, he would buy houses that were afire, and houses which adjoined those which were afire, and these their owners would let go at a trifling price owing to their fear and uncertainty. In this way the largest part of Rome came into his possession. But though he owned so many artisans, he built no house for himself other than the one in which he lived ; indeed he used to say that men who were fond of building were their own undoers, and needed no other foes.'

This extract indicates that architects were sometimes drawn from the class of slaves, and we know of many who were freed slaves. On the other hand, both Cicero [2] and Vitruvius agree that architecture is one of the learned professions, for which men of good birth and good education are best suited. We know of at least one Roman architect who was a consul, and another who became a senator, and it appears that the status of the profession rose in the later days of the Empire. The names of rather more than a score of Roman architects prior to Constantine's day have been preserved. But we are told little more than their names and the titles of their principal buildings, little that sheds any light on their personalities or their methods of work. On the whole, Rome seems to have honoured her architects ; but occasionally they were forbidden to ' sign ' their buildings, and Pliny the Elder cites the case of Saurus and Batrachus, who retaliated

[1] Plutarch, *Crassus*, ii.   [2] Cicero, *De Officiis*, i. 42.

by carving a lizard and a frog on a temple that they had built.[1] This story seems almost too good to be true, and the average architect does not possess a name that is so readily translated into an appropriate emblem.

Our knowledge of professional etiquette in Rome is slight, but a paragraph from Vitruvius [2] shows that in his time there were black sheep of the same type that troubles us to-day :

' Other architects go about and ask for opportunities to practise their profession ; but I have been taught by my instructors that it is the proper thing to undertake a charge only after being asked, and not to ask for it ; since a gentleman will blush with shame at petitioning for a thing that arouses suspicion.'

The prototype of the modern architect who cannot avoid ' extras ' appears in another paragraph. After mentioning the sound methods adopted at Ephesus to deal with this nuisance (see p. 19), Vitruvius proceeds : [3]

' Would to God that this were also a law of the Roman people, not merely for public, but also for private buildings. For the ignorant would no longer run riot with impunity, but men who are well qualified by an exact scientific training would unquestionably adopt the profession of architecture. Gentlemen would not be misled into limitless and prodigal expenditure, even to ejectments from their estates, and the architects could be forced, by fear of the penalty, to be more careful in calculating and stating the limit of expense, so that gentlemen would procure their buildings for that which they had expected, or by adding only a little more. It is true that men who can afford to devote four hundred thousand to a work may hold on, if they have to add another hundred thousand, from the pleasure which the hope of finishing it gives

[1] Pliny, *Hist. Nat.*, xxxvi. 42.   [2] Vitruvius, vi, preface.
[3] Vitruvius, x, preface.

them ; but if they are loaded with a fifty per cent. increase, or with an even greater expense, they lose hope, sacrifice what they have already spent, and are compelled to leave off, broken in fortune and in spirit.'

Presumably there were many architects in Roman times who had lucrative practices ; this we may assume from the enormous amount of costly building that was done, and from the position that some of them occupied in society, but definite information is lacking. On the other hand, it appears from a passage in Vitruvius [1] that in his day the ' profession ' was overcrowded with ' the uneducated and the unskilful ', men who scorned to take up shoemaking, dyeing, or other useful occupations and rushed into architecture without even ' knowledge of the carpenter's trade ' . . . ' and this because the professionals do not possess the genuine art but term themselves architects falsely '.

The most interesting figure, after Vitruvius, among all the architects of the Empire is Apollodorus of Damascus, whose relations with the Emperor Hadrian afford some amusing episodes and give rise to many complicated problems: According to Dion Cassius,[2] Apollodorus was born about A. D. 60 and died about 70 years later. Rivoira describes him as ' essentially the architect-artist ',[3] and again as a Hellenistic architect with ' the incomparable Greek sense of elegance in art and decoration '.[4] He designed the Thermae of Trajan, which were carried out by Roman craftsmen, and the Forum of Trajan (A. D. 112–13). Publius Aelius Hadrianus, commonly called Hadrian, was born in A. D. 76, became emperor in A. D. 117,

[1] *Ibid.* vi, preface. [2] Dion Cassius, lxxviii. 16, 29 ; lxix. 4.
[3] Rivoira, *Roman Architecture*, p. 113. (Oxford, 1925.)
[4] *Ibid.*, p. 117.

and died in A. D. 138. Rivoira offers a remarkable statement [1] as to his

' ability as a master-architect. This has, indeed, been previously suggested [by Lanciani] but as yet the facts have never been established. Aelius Spartianus states that Hadrian was well versed in arithmetic, geometry, painting, and every department of art. His capacities as a geometrician and an artist are confirmed by other ancient authorities. From a passage in Dion Cassius, where he relates that Hadrian sent his plans for the temple of Venus and Rome to Apollodorus, we learn that he made his own designs for his buildings. There is therefore no room for doubt as to his architectural endowments. Among the structures . . . which he created and erected the most important is the Pantheon at Rome' (A. D. 120-4).

Besides the Temple of Venus and Rome already mentioned (A. D. 121–35), Rivoira also credits him with his own mausoleum and the bridge leading to it (A. D. 136), the Villa at Tivoli (A. D. 125–35), the Basilica of Plotina near Nîmes, and the monument to Pompey at Pelusium ; also with the rebuilding of the Saepta Julia, the Basilica of Neptune, and the Baths of Agrippa. The Thermae of Trajan were formerly included by Rivoira in this list, but in a later book [2] he discards this building. Another authority [3] attributes to him a number of important buildings in Athens, ' the favourite site of his architectural labours '. Finally, Rivoira ascribes to him the invention of ' a skeleton framework in vaults of circular form '.

This formidable catalogue from so eminent an authority must command our respect, but unfortunately we have learned to distrust many of the ascriptions of medieval

[1] Rivoira, *Lombardic Architecture*, ii. 100–2. (London, 1910.)
[2] Rivoira, *Roman Architecture*, pp. 120–1.
[3] *Encyclopaedia Britannica*, s.v. ' Hadrian '.

buildings to eminent ecclesiastics, and one cannot but view the work of this undoubtedly gifted monarch with equal suspicion. Spartian [1] makes mention of one Decrianus ' an engineer-architect and master-builder ', who moved the Colossus of Nero for Hadrian and carried out the emperor's ideas. He may have been one of that large class of architectural ' ghosts ' whose work has never received proper recognition. Hadrian's encounters with Apollodorus indicate that the older man was jealous of his imperial rival. On one occasion, according to Dion Cassius, the Syrian architect snubbed Hadrian, then a young man, in the presence of Trajan, by telling him to ' go away and paint pumpkins '. The second incident was more serious. Hadrian, after apparently swallowing the previous insult, sent Apollodorus his designs for the Temple of Venus and Rome. Apollodorus pointed out that, if the deities whose statues were sitting in the temple were to stand up, they would bump their heads against the roof. This tactless remark, unworthy of an experienced professional man, cost Apollodorus his head.[2] Rivoira, who is always anxious to ascribe all genius to Rome, is constrained to admit that ' it is not difficult to understand the unfavourable judgement ' passed on this building by Apollodorus [3] (rather suggesting that Hadrian was trailing his coat for the older man to tread on), and cannot imagine why he did not send him the designs of the Pantheon, ' as a tangible demonstration of what high achievements in construction and statics and of what daring conceptions a Roman emperor-architect and Roman builders were capable '. [4] Hadrian was

[1] Spartian, *Life of Hadrian*, xix. 12. [2] Dion Cassius, lxix. 4.
[3] Rivoira, *Lombardic Architecture*, ii. 100–2.
[4] Rivoira, *Roman Architecture*, p. 130.

unquestionably a versatile man, even a genius. It is possible that he himself designed everything that Rivoira ascribes to him ; on the other hand, the evidence is not absolutely convincing, and as a professional architect I hesitate to accept these great buildings too readily as the unaided work of an amateur.

Naturally the Roman system of government produced large numbers of official architects, indeed most of the great civic and national monuments must certainly be ascribed to them. Most of these men combined the functions of architect, civil engineer, and military engineer, even accompanying the legions in the field. They were entrusted, writes Rivoira,[1] with :

' siege works, with the manufacture and repair of the engines of war ; laying out and constructing camps whether temporary or permanent, roads, earthworks, bridges, gates, drains ; the erection of market-places (*fora*), temples, basilicas, the Imperial palaces and tombs, the public theatres, amphitheatres, and circuses, the public baths, &c.'

The lay-out and buildings of the garrison-town of Aosta, with its fortifications, gates, theatre, triumphal arch, amphitheatre, temples, sewers, and so on gives an idea of the scope of their work.

' Considering that the most important examples [of architecture] are to be found in the Imperial palaces and sepulchres, the basilicas, *thermae*, and other edifices intended for public use, the erection of all of which was entrusted to contractors paid either by the state treasury or by the emperor's privy purse, or by both, under the direct supervision of the state officials, we shall not be far wrong if we ascribe the origin of these works to state architects attached to the departments of roads, aqueducts, and military constructions.'[2]

[1] Rivoira, *Roman Architecture*, p. 86.   [2] *Ibid.*, p. 83.

It has often been remarked that Roman architecture displays all the characteristics of the great semi-military machine that brought it into being, an opinion which is accepted by nearly all critics. The sense of ordered power and rhythm which one feels in beholding the Pont du Gard or the Colosseum, almost causing the tramp of brass-clad legionaries to echo in our ears, is explained when we realize that Roman architecture, more than Greek, more than anything before or since, was the work of architect-engineers serving their great Empire.

From Greece they borrowed the Orders and most of their ornamental features, but one need not assume, as some have done, that they borrowed their architects and craftsmen from Greece too. Rivoira asserts that the names of such Greek architects as worked in Rome have all been preserved by Greek writers, who suppressed the names of Latin architects with equal care ;[1] but he also states that architects in the service of the state were forbidden to sign their buildings. Anonymity has long been the tradition in our own Civil Service, and it is probably due to the same cause that we know so comparatively little about the architects of a period which has left us an ample literature. But there are numerous inscriptions recording architects' names, e. g. of Julius Lacer on the famous bridge at Alcántara in Spain, on the pavement of the forum at Terracina (C. POSTUMIUS, C. F. POLLIO ARCHITECTUS) and in the theatre at Pompeii (M. ARTORIUS M. L. PRIMUS ARCHITECTUS). Tacitus mentions Severus and Celer, famous architects in the service of Nero, who planned the canal from Baiae to Ostia (never completed), the Claudian Aqueduct, the ' Domus Aurea ', the ' Macellum Augusti ', and the Thermae of Nero. Rabirius, who worked under

[1] Rivoira, *Roman Architecture*, p. 83.

Domitian, was praised by the poet Martial,[1] whose words may be quoted from a quaint old English translation :

> Rabirius modell tooke from heav'n to build
> Our wondrous pallace sure ; hee is so skill'd.
> For Phidian Jove a worthy fane to reare,
> Pisa must begg him of our Thunderer.

Rabirius designed Domitian's palace, the Temple of the Deified Augustus, and perhaps the palace and nymphaeum in the Gardens of Sallust. ' He was first and foremost an architect-engineer.' [2] Cossutius disregarded the rule as to anonymity, and we know that he was the architect of the Temple of Olympian Zeus at Athens because he himself recorded the fact in an inscription, Vitruvius also confirming this. But the chief features of Roman architecture are so characteristic, and so different from anything previously produced in Greece, that they proclaim their nationality, whether their architects' names have been preserved or not.

As regards methods of work, there is evidence that Roman architects drew plans of their buildings on parchment,[3] and also that models were frequently used.[4] Thus Aulus Gellius, in one of his *Attic Evenings*, speaks of a gathering in a friend's house at which a number of architects were present. They had been called in with a view to the erection of some new baths, and were displaying drawings on parchment for baths of various kinds. He selected, from among these, the one that seemed the best in plan and appearance, and asked what it would cost to build, everything included. Fig. 3 represents a plan carved on a marble slab, and now to be seen in the Museum at Perugia. It is said to date from the second half of the

[1] Martial, *Epigrams*, vii. 56.   [2] Rivoira, *Roman Architecture*, p. 113.
[3] Aulus Gellius, xix. 10.   [4] Cicero, *Ad Q. Frat*. ii. 6.

first century A. D., and to be the plans of a tomb near a guard-house, the upper plan showing the first floor to a smaller scale. The dimensions of the various rooms are given in figures. The instruments that architects used for drawing and for testing the angles of their buildings are sometimes found illustrated on bas-reliefs, and

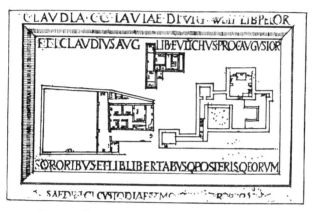

FIG. 3.   ROMAN PLAN ON MARBLE FROM PERUGIA
Drawn by M. S. Briggs from a photograph

Vitruvius describes [1] the levelling apparatus used for setting out aqueducts and other works. Some of these instruments were described by Dr. Ashby at a meeting of the British Association on 29 August 1925 ; among them the *dioptra* for measuring both vertical and horizontal angles ; and the *chorobate*, or water level, a rather clumsy instrument resembling in principle the modern dumpy level.

Fig. 6 is drawn from a fourth-century illuminated MS. of Virgil (No. 3225) in the Vatican Library at Rome, my

[1] Vitruvius, viii. 5.

own drawing having been made from Cardinal Angelo Mai's engraving, which appears to be much more accurate than the earlier engravings of Pietro Bartoli or Santi (*c.* 1635–1700). It is said to represent an architect directing the work of masons. The original MS. consists of leaves 8¾ by 7½ inches, of which this drawing represents only a part of a page. The miniatures are said by Dr. Middleton to be coarse and devoid of spirit,[1] but the Introduction to the Palaeographical Society's facsimile of some of the leaves describes them as ' some of the best and most interesting specimens of ancient painting which have descended to us '. Figs. 4 and 5 illustrate two more representations of Roman architects and builders. Fig. 5, from the Museo delle Terme, shows a Christian grave-slab from the Catacombs, with doves, chisels, level, plumb-line and square, indicating an architect's grave. Fig. 4, also from a Christian grave-slab, shows a man with a long tunic holding a stylus in his right hand and a drawing-board with a geometrical design sketched on it, suggesting an architect or marble-worker. (These are numbered 67675 and 67723 respectively in the Museo Nazionale.) A third slab,[2] from the sepulchral vault of Trebius Justus on the Via Latina, represents various workmen on a building in course of construction. Many other examples are to be found elsewhere.[3]

From various sources we learn that specifications were used in building, that competitive tenders were sometimes invited, that some government architects were stationed at quarries to supervise the cutting of stone, that Hadrian

[1] J. H. Middleton, *Illuminated Manuscripts*, p. 36. (Cambridge, 1892.)

[2] Rivoira, *Roman Architecture*, Fig. 94.

[3] See H. Stuart Jones, *Catalogue of Museo Capitolino*, pp. 73–7 ; and C. Lucas, s.v. *Architectus*, in Daremberg and Saglio's *Dictionnaire.*

Fig. 4 Grave-slab in the Museo Nazionale at Rome, said to represent an architect or marble worker at his drawing table.

Drawn by M. S. Briggs from a photograph

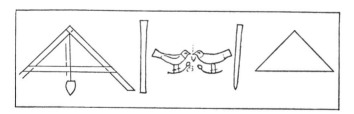

Fig. 5 Grave-slab in the Museo Nazionale at Rome, with symbolical doves, a pair of chisels, level and plumb-line, and square, indicating an architects' grave.

Drawn by M. S. Briggs from a photograph

took architects abroad with him to measure ancient buildings and then to reproduce them in his famous Villa at Tivoli, that architects—as members of a liberal profession—received an *honorarium* and not wages,[1] and that neither architects nor builders were responsible for defects

FIG. 6   ROMAN ARCHITECT AND MASONS AT WORK
From a fourth-century MS. of Virgil at the Vatican
Drawn by M. S. Briggs

in buildings which had been passed by the officials. An architect seems seldom to have acted as contractor.

Such, in brief, is the picture that remains to us in literature of the Roman architect up to the time of Constantine. The foundation of Constantinople led to an

[1] Curiously enough, painting and sculpture were not included as liberal occupations.

important event in the history of the architectural profession. In the words of Gibbon : [1]

' The impatience of Constantine soon discovered that, in the decline of the arts, the skill as well as numbers of his architects bore a very unequal proportion to the greatness of his designs. The magistrates of the most distant provinces were therefore directed to institute schools, to appoint professors, and by the hope of rewards and privileges to engage in the study and practice of architecture a sufficient number of ingenious youths who had received a liberal education.'

The edict in question, dated A. D. 334, appears in the *Codex Theodosianus* (Lib. XIII, Tit. 3), and a reference to the original Latin shows also that it was addressed to the African provinces of the Empire, and that the students were to be ' about 22 years of age '. Two further edicts, dated 337 and 344 respectively, refer, too, to the training of architects and craftsmen. A better Latin scholar than the present writer could find, in the two large pages of commentary on the edicts of 334 and 344, much interesting information about this experiment in the mass-production of architects to meet an emergency. Vegetius states that at the beginning of the fifth century there were 700 architects in Rome, possibly as a result of Constantine's measure just described.

Some two centuries later we find the following reference to the duties of an architect in a letter written to ' Aloisius the Architect ' at Ravenna by Cassiodorus, on behalf of his master, King Theodoric (455–526) :[2]

' This fountain then, as we before said, deserves a worthy habitation. If there be anything to repair in the *thermae* themselves or in the passages, let this be done out of the money

---

[1] E. Gibbon, *Decline and Fall, &c.*, chap. XVII.
[2] Cassiodorus, *Variae* (translated by T. Hodgkin), ii. 39.

which we now send you. Let the thorns and briars which have grown up around it be rooted up. Let the palace, shaken with extreme old age, be strengthened by careful restoration. Let the space which intervenes between the public building and the source of the hot spring be cleared of its woodland roughness, and the turf around rejoice in the green beauty which it derives from the heated waters.'

More explicit and informative is a later passage by the same writer :[1]

' FORMULA OF THE PALACE ARCHITECT.'

' Much do we delight in seeing the greatness of our Kingdom imaged forth in the splendour of our palace . . . Take then for this Indiction the care of our palace, thus receiving the power of transmitting your fame to a remote posterity which shall admire your workmanship. See that your work harmonises well with the old. Study Euclid—get his diagrams well into your mind ; study Archimedes and Metrobius.

When we are thinking of rebuilding a city, or of founding a fort or a general's quarters, we shall rely on you to express our ideas on paper. The builder of walls, the carver of marbles, the caster of brass, the vaulter of arches, the plasterer, the worker in mosaic, all come to you for orders, and you are expected to have a wise answer for each. But then, if you direct them rightly, while theirs is the work, yours is all the glory.

Above all things, dispense honestly what we give you for the workmen's wages ; for the labourer who is at ease about his victuals works all the better.

As a mark of your high dignity you bear a golden wand, and amidst the numerous throng of servants walk first before the royal footsteps that even by your nearness to our person it may be seen that you are the man to whom we have entrusted the care of our palaces.'

---

[1] Cassiodorus, *Variae* (translated by T. Hodgkin), vii. 5.

The translator's rendering of the above passage is not, perhaps, altogether ideal, but it supplies us with a more detailed picture of the architect than we have yet seen save in the pages of Vitruvius. We are justified in inferring that the State Architect in the sixth century occupied a high social and official position ; that he studied geometry and natural philosophy ; that he practised town-planning and military engineering ; that he acted as director of all the building craftsmen in all trades, and also as their paymaster ; and that in his day the idea of respecting ancient architecture had already appeared. The short document quoted above leaves no doubt that this architect was a recognized professional man in complete control of building operations. Another document quoted by Lanciani [1] states that when Theodoric came to Rome early in the sixth century he appointed a body of engineers and architects to superintend the restoration of public buildings, under the direction of an *architectus publicorum*.

According to Rivoira,[2] the architects of Ravenna at this period (when it was the capital city of Italy) came originally from the school of Milan, and then formed a school of their own. Among them was Aloisius or Aloiosus, already mentioned, who may have been the architect of Theodoric's mausoleum at Ravenna, and was not a Goth by birth.[3] More famous was Julianus Argentarius, a native of Ravenna, who, in Rivoira's words, ' has been made to figure in every capacity—a prefect, a treasurer of the Church of Ravenna, a wealthy merchant, a banker, a money-changer, everything in short, except his real character, viz. an architect of the first rank.' [4]

[1] Lanciani, R., *The Destruction of Ancient Rome*, p. 77. (London, 1901.)   [2] Rivoira, *Roman Architecture*, p. 261.
[3] *Ibid.* 197-9.   [4] Rivoira, *Lombardic Architecture*, i. 64-5.

This apparent desire on the part of writers to deprive the architect of his due is a sure indication that we are approaching medieval times, for, as the next chapter will prove, it was an article of faith among many Victorian critics that the great buildings of the Middle Ages were somehow designed and erected without an architect. Rivoira states that Julianus is responsible for San Vitale at Ravenna (526–47), Sant' Apollinare in Classe (533–49), possibly the Mausoleum of Theodoric, and also the Cathedral at Parenzo. The ascription of San Vitale to Julianus is important, and Rivoira supports it with quotations from Agnellus (. . . *parata est . . . constructa est . . . a fundamentis aedificavit, . . . ab Iuliano fundata et consummata fuisset*) and from a metrical couplet inscribed in silver letters within the church :

> *Tradidit hanc primus Iuliano Ecclesius arcem,*
> *Qui sibi commissum mire perfecit opus.*

Other architects of this late period included Cyriades, expert in architecture and mechanics, who became a consul and was employed by Theodosius to build bridges ;[1] Entinopus of Candia, who was concerned in the foundation of Venice ; Dalmatius bishop of Rhodes, who attempted to practise architecture without knowledge and with disastrous consequences ; and the two famous architects from Asia Minor—Anthemius of Tralles and Isidorus of Miletus—who designed and built for Justinian in A. D. 532 the great church of Sancta Sophia in Constantinople. Our knowledge of their work is derived from a book of Procopius, *De Aedificiis* ; but, as it was written to reinstate its author in the favour of the emperor, it abounds in exaggeration, inaccuracy, and fulsome

[1] Symmachus, *passim.*

flattery. According to Procopius, Justinian himself played a very active part in the direction of the work, spending much time on the building as it was in course of erection, and on more than one occasion offering inspired advice when his architects got out of their depth. The modern architect will be more inclined to ascribe the credit for this masterpiece to his professional brethren of long ago, for even Procopius admits their outstanding genius. Anthemius, we are informed, was an engineer and sculptor as well as an architect. He wrote a book on machines and 'invented various methods of imitating earthquakes, thunder and lightning '.[1]

'Everything leads us to think,' writes Rivoira,[2] 'that Anthemius, who is described by Procopius as the master-builder, must be regarded not only as the builder, in partnership with Isidorus of Miletus, of Justinian's church, but also as the originator of the plans for it. In fact it appears from Procopius that Isidorus was not the author of the design, but rather the associate of Anthemius, and an architect capable of carrying out plans already prepared. Of Anthemius we read in the Silentiary's poem that he was " skilled to draw a circle and set out a plan ". Gyllius had noticed the fact before me ; " *Quamquam Anthemius, qui aedem Sophiae architectus erat* ". So that everything leads us to believe that Anthemius studied on the spot the great buildings of Rome in order to base on them his plans for S. Sophia ; and this is all the more likely because one of his brothers, Alexander, followed the profession of medicine at Rome.'

Rivoira mentions other facts in support of his favourite theory that everything in the ' Dark Ages ' and afterwards had its origin in Rome, and observes in a later passage that Anthemius ' was not alone among Justinian's architects

[1] Milizia, *op. cit.* i. 119.
[2] Rivoira, *Lombardic Architecture,* i. 79.

in deriving suggestions from the great Latin mother-city '.[1] Soon after its completion, the mighty dome of S. Sophia collapsed in the earthquake of 558. This accident was attributed by architects to the defective construction of the great supporting piers, a result of parsimony.[2] Between the years 558 and 563 it was rebuilt ' with such increase of reinforcement as should enable it to defy, as it has done, other not less severe earth-movements ',[3] to the designs of Isidorus the Younger, who must have had an admirable knowledge of construction.

We may or may not believe Vegetius when he tells us that Justinian employed 500 architects in all ; it is more valuable to us to know that the architects of later Rome, as of the Augustan age, were versatile and well-trained men, whose success was due in part to their mathematical bias and their sound practical knowledge.

BIBLIOGRAPHY

(See works of Félibien, Lucas, and Milizia cited on pages, 10, 11 and 27). Brown, G. Baldwin. ' Vitruvius ' (*Burlington Magazine*, 1915).

Flagg, E. ' Vitruvius and his Module ' (*R. I. B. A. Journal*, 1924).

Frothingham, A. L. ' The Architect in History : Roman Architects ' in *The Architectural Record*, xxv. 179–92, 281–303. (New York, 1909.)

Morgan, M. H. *Vitruvius : Ten Books on Architecture*. (Harvard, 1914.)

Mortet, V. ' Recherches critiques sur Vitruve et son œuvre ' (*Révue Archéologique*, 1902, 1904, 1907, 1909).

Promis, C. *Gli architetti e l'architettura presso i Romani* [an attempt to ascribe Roman art to Greek sources].

Rivoira, G. T. *Lombardic Architecture*. (English translation, London, 1910.)

—— *Roman Architecture*. (English translation, Oxford, 1925).

Waterhouse, P. ' Veneranda Volumina ' [Vitruvius] in *Architectural Review*, xii. 47. (London, 1902.)

—— ' Vitruvius Transatlanticus' (*R. I. B. A. Journal*, 1915).

---

[1] Rivoira, *Lombardic Architecture*, i. 81.   [2] Agathias, v. 9.

[3] Rivoira, *Roman Architecture*, p. 276.

IV

THE MIDDLE AGES

THE personality of the medieval architect still remains tantalizingly elusive, in spite of the vast amount of literature describing medieval architecture. But some recent critics have succeeded in dispelling a good deal of the misunderstanding that has hitherto surrounded him. It is now generally agreed that his functions have been both misrepresented and depreciated by writers who ought to know better. A passage from Mr. March Phillipps's suggestive and interesting book, *The Works of Man*, is typical of the extreme view of those who would deny his very existence : [1]

' Added to much that is unique in it, Gothic has this, that it was built, so one may almost say, without the help of architects. In spite of the appalling difficulties to be over-come, and the daring innovations involved, any one could build Gothic. The people needed no teaching in the style. They seemed already to know all about it, and the architecture consequently rose, not slowly and by degrees, but spontane-ously with one impulse, rather like the uplifting of some tremen-dous chorus than the slow setting of stone upon stone.'

Now it is evident to any serious student of architecture that this wild statement contains more than one fallacy. The history of almost any great Gothic church shows that its growth was gradual, that its design was modified or altered during erection, and that to the masons employed upon it the ' slow setting of stone upon stone ' was slow indeed. But, on the other hand, we must remember that

[1] L. March Phillipps, *The Works of Man*, pp. 200–1. (London, 1901.)

romantic passages of this kind, like the glaring chapters of Ruskin, are read more widely than are the sober writings of architects, and that because of their literary excellence they have had an enormous influence upon the educated public on whose patronage and sympathy the reputation of the architect so largely depends.

Among the great mass of such people, as among architects themselves to a limited extent, it may safely be said that the following fallacies are commonly accepted : that there was no independent directing personage or 'architect' in the Middle Ages; that the controlling power was exercised by an artisan, the ' master-mason ', not by an educated professional man ; that no preliminary plans or working drawings were used ; that design was purely traditional, no ideas being borrowed from buildings of other styles or countries ; that the masons worked for the glory of God rather than for mere bread and butter ; that the master-mason lived on the building, not undertaking other work in the way that a modern architect runs a ' practice ' ; that he learned his trade at a bench, not in an office or a school ; that he was usually a monk, or a lay-brother attached to a monastery ; and that he gloried in his anonymity.

It cannot be denied that some of these fallacies have a foundation in fact ; but it is equally certain that they are inaccurate when used as sweeping generalizations (more often, be it noted, by literary men than by architects). Before proceeding to discuss these points in detail, some consideration should be given to the causes that have brought about such a distortion of facts.

The identity of the master-mason is often, admittedly, obscure ; but, as is explained later in this chapter, by no means always so. He was frequently a layman, and the monkish scribes who acted as chroniclers in the Middle Ages preferred to commemorate the abbot or bishop who corresponded to a modern ' Chairman of the Building Committee ; ' their concern was with the glorification of their Church or Order more than with the perpetuation of a mere artist's name. When an inscription states that an ecclesiastic ' built ' (*fecit*) a church, it means that he ordered it and paid for it. *Fieri fecit* is a more accurate description of the part he played. Too often nowadays we find a similar neglect of the man whose brain has created the design of the building.

There seems to have been a rift between the artist and the scribe in England and France, though in Italy a closer touch was maintained between literature and the arts, and every little commune delighted to honour its brilliant sons, whether they were laymen or clerics.

Returning to the first ' fallacy ' mentioned above, it may be stated without doubt that for every medieval building of any importance there was an architect. By an ' architect ' we mean, primarily, a man who designs and superintends the construction of a building. Whether his training is acquired in a workshop or an ' office ' is immaterial, nor does it matter in the least what title his contemporaries choose to give him. If he performs this dual function of design and superintendence properly, he is an architect. Can it be argued that there was any alternative in the Middle Ages ? It has often been stated that our cathedrals were the work of a school rather than of an individual. But that one cannot believe. An architect may have formed one of a group of craftsmen, just as in the great modern architectural offices in America there is a partnership of specialists in the various branches of architecture. He may have been trained to follow a tradition, but that in itself would not prevent him being an architect ; indeed the chief failing of certain architects in the eighteenth century was their insistence on tradition rather than on modern needs. Nevertheless, without going into elaborate details of argument, the popular belief in some form of travelling school or guild, more or less miraculously inspired, must be considered here. This theory may have been advanced to cheat the architect of his due, but in point of fact it fails to do so, as even a travelling guild may have had an architect in its ranks. Macaulay wrote : ' I believe that all the cathedrals of Europe came into existence nearly contemporaneously and were built by travelling companies of masons under the direction of a systematic organization. ' Professor Prior, who cannot be suspected of an undue bias in favour of the professional architect, comments on this passage : ' This guild, if it existed, must also have had a supernatural power of hiding its tracks, for in all our accounts and records are no references which can be twisted into a con- sciousness of a Freemason guild '.[1]   Still more recently,[2] Professor Hamilton Thompson (to whom all architects owe a debt of gratitude for his vigorous efforts to establish the status of their medieval ancestors) has poured copious ridicule on the legend of the Comacine masters, who have sometimes been credited hitherto with almost supernatural powers. Without denying the importance of Lombard architecture and its great influence, he points out that the legend was not invented until the seventeenth century, and he does not think that ' Comacinus ' necessarily refers to the island in an Italian lake. After referring to the laws of Liutprand and Rotharis, he derives the word

[1] E. S. Prior, *The Cathedral Builders*, p. 58. (London, 1905.)
[2] In a lecture before the Royal Archaeological Society, 1 May 1925.

Comacinus from the medieval Latin word *macinus*, meaning a mason, and assumes that all subsequent errors have been caused by misreading *co-macini*, which meant no more than ' associated masons '. Again quoting Professor Prior :

' Professors of architecture are driven to account for the atmosphere of medieval art on grounds of some superior power of design. They like to make it all out as the invention of a building school in France, or as the secret of some great masonic guild or class of unrecorded architects.'

He dismisses as valueless the irregularities discovered in some medieval buildings and hailed as indicating recondite principles of design, for such irregularities are due, he thinks, either to craftsmanship or to exigencies, not to conscious design.[1] Papworth, writing nearly fifty years ago, is equally emphatic, and does not believe that the ' travelling bodies of freemasons ', who are said to have erected all the great buildings of Europe, ever existed.[2] Street says of Spain : ' from first to last, I have found no reference to anything like freemasonry '.[3]

No thoughtful student of architectural history denies that local schools of architecture and craftsmanship (e. g. at Gloucester) contributed largely to the glory of building in the Middle Ages ; Professor Prior has convinced us all of that in a recent book.[4] What needs to be revised is the common idea that there was anything supernatural or mysterious either in their powers or their organization. It was an age of faith, a time of great enthusiasm—especially for religious building—but not necessarily an age

[1] Prior, *op. cit.*, p. 17.
[2] J. W. Papworth, ' Superintendents of English Buildings in the Middle Ages,' p. 222, in *R.I.B.A. Transactions*. (London, 1887.)
[3] G. E. Street, *Gothic Architecture in Spain*, ii. 265. (London, 1865.)
[4] E. S. Prior, *English Medieval Art*. (Cambridge, 1922.)

when the individual artist was replaced by a divinely inspired body of men. The ' school ' theory collapses simply because human nature declines to allow group-working to go beyond a certain point. No group or guild or committee could design a cathedral, and it is very unlikely that they could supervise its erection without delegating their powers to one of their number. Is it conceivable that workmen would obey orders from a group of twenty masters, or that such orders would not be mutually contradictory ? However well such a group or school might be organized, one person must eventually have been made responsible for design and one for super-intendence. Where, as seems to have been the general rule, he combined both functions, we have the modern architect in his medieval form.

This argument is in no way weakened by admitting that the title of ' architect ' was seldom applied to him. We are concerned here with the man rather than with his label. I have already said something of the origin of the title ' architect ' and of its use in Greek and Roman history (p. 3). During the Middle Ages it occurs very occasionally up to the time of its revival in the sixteenth century, and generally in its Latin form. The wide researches of Papworth failed to reveal a single instance of its use in England, and a reference to a *prudens archi-tectus* early in the twelfth century seems to imply no more than ' a wily fellow '.

In France the name is scarce, but occurs now and then in documents. Of these the most perplexing relates to the castle of Sault, and dates from *c*. 1000. Here the word is used in the plural, and the translator thinks that it implies a carpenter working on a roof, and thus resembles the word *architector* which is sometimes found in medieval

Latin.[1] Another document from the same collection is taken from the life of St. Arnulph, bishop of Soissons, 1091. An accident having occurred to the wooden steeple of the abbey church of St. Pierre at Oudenbourg near Bruges, 'architects' (in this case carpenters who specialized in wooden roofs) were called in, and were promised a special premium if the difficult task of reconstruction were accomplished safely. The exact wording of the relevant sentence of this remarkable document is as follows :

' *Congregati mane loci habitatores sub omni celeritate convocant architectos, statutis premiis, si illud revocarent, munerandos* . . .' [' The inhabitants having been assembled as quickly as possible, they summoned architects, who were to be rewarded with agreed payments if they were successful in restoring that work.']

Occasionally we come across the term *sapiens architectus* (e. g. at Cambrai,[2] 1080 ; at Compostela in Spain, *c.* 1080 ;[3] at Bamberg ;[4] and at Thérouanne[5]), which may mean an ' accomplished architect ', or may be derived from and have the same figurative sense in which it is used in 1 Corinthians iii. 10 (σοφὸς ἀρχιτέκτων in the Greek), where it is translated ' wise master-builder ' and has no technical significance. Apart from these doubtful or negative uses of the word, it occurs elsewhere, i. e. in connexion with the rebuilding of the abbey church of St. Remi at Reims, 1036 ; in a reference to the bishop of Osnabruck in the second half of the eleventh century (' Praeterea autem architectus praecipuus, caementarii

---

[1] V. Mortet (see bibliography at end of this chapter), pp. 168–75.
[2] F. de Mély, ' Nos vieilles cathédrales et leurs maîtres d'œuvre,' p. 297, in *Révue archéologique*. (Paris, 1920.)
[3] Street, *Gothic Architecture in Spain*, i. 192. (London, 1865.)
[4] Mortet, *op. cit.*, p. 69.   [5] *Ibid.*, p. 313.   [6] *Ibid.*, p. 41.

operis solertissimus erat dispositor ') ;[1] in a document describing the rebuilding of the abbey at Cluny, 1088–1114 ('. . . et assurgere compulit architectum nostrum timide commorantem ') ;[2] and in the account in Orderic Vitalis (viii. 24) of the erection of the tower of Ivry near Évreux by Master Lanfroi in 1094 (' Ferunt quod praefata matrona Lanfredum architectum . . . decollari fecerat ').[3] The Countess Albereda of Bayeux beheaded the architect after the castle was finished, in order that he might not construct another. Street quotes a reference in 1414 to an *arquitecto perito* (' accomplished architect ') in Spain,[4] and another who signed himself *architector* on the wall of a monastery.[5] From these quotations it is clear that we must search for the medieval architect under some other title. Laborious research for many years has now revealed the names of at least a thousand men in various countries who actually corresponded to the modern architect in their functions so far as comparison is possible, that is, men who carried out the design and superintendence of entire buildings. In spite of having excluded on the one hand the large number of clerics who organized building schemes, and on the other the imaginary guilds of craftsmen who must have had some directing head, we still have this considerable body of supervising and designing functionaries who bore other titles than that of ' architect ' in the Middle Ages.

For these personages the commonest designation in all countries is derived from the Latin word *magister*. In England it usually took the simple form of *master*, less frequently *master-mason*, occasionally perhaps *master of the works* (though there is some doubt as to whether that

[1] Mortet, *op. cit.*, p. 69.   [2] *Ibid.*, p. 271.   [3] *Ibid.*, p. 274.
[4] Street, *op. cit.* ii. 287.   [5] *Ibid.* ii. 287.

term signified an architect in this country). In French documents the word *maistre* or *maître* occurs constantly in this sense, but perhaps *maître d'œuvre* or *maistre des ouvrages* are more usual. *Magister* also occurs both in England and France, and *magister fabricae* in France. In Italy we find the form *maestro* ; in Spain *maestro* or *maestro mayor*, together with the Latin equivalents *magister operis* (frequently used), *magister fabricae*, and *magister et fabricator*. The German form is *baumeister*. On the whole, this word ' master ' is the commonest title for an architect in medieval Europe, and though, as will be explained shortly, he was, as a rule, specially trained in stone-craft, he is not usually described as a ' master-mason '. Conversely, the ' master ' was sometimes a mason rather than an architect in function. So there is no precise professional status about the word ' master ' in itself ; it implies rather a man who had qualified himself in some recognized calling. Professor Lethaby writes that, in the Masons' Guild,

' mastership was closely parallel to that of a master of arts in the university, that is, the Guild of Letters. By serving a seven-years' apprenticeship he became a bachelor or companion, and, on presenting a proper work-thesis, he was admitted master. Our curious courtesy title, " Mr. ", does not mean employer, but graduate of guild ; however the two meanings came together, as only a master might be an employer.' [1]

We thus reach the conclusion that, although contemporary documents make it clear that the architect of a medieval building was most frequently styled ' master ', that word cannot be taken as a specific title for an architect, nor does it necessarily indicate a master-mason.

[1] W. R. Lethaby, *Medieval Art*, p. 255. (London, 1904.)

Another puzzling term is *ingeniator*, which is properly translated ' engineer ', but is applied to many men who were in charge of large medieval building operations. This word, like *architectus*, may even have the figurative meaning of an ' ingenious man ', and was actually translated by a nineteenth-century writer in one case as ' bird-catcher ', but in general it seems to have been used mainly in England during the early Middle Ages to describe the architects or engineers of castles. Up to comparatively recent times, the architect undertook all branches of military and civil engineering, as later chapters of this book prove ; indeed the quotation given from Joseph Gwilt in 1825 (see p. 324) indicates that a hundred years ago the civil engineer was only just making his appearance as a separate entity. Professor Prior quotes [1] an exceptional use of *l'engineur* from the Salisbury records of 1262, where it is applied to a canon, Nicholas of York, who also appears as *architector novae fabricae* in the Durham records ; but in general we may assume that the word *ingeniator* and its equivalents is rare, that it is peculiarly English, and that, though it sometimes occurs in connexion with the records of cathedrals (e. g. Durham), it denotes an architect who specialized in military building.

Artifex is another word of doubtful significance. It is applied to William of Sens, who, according to Gervase's *Chronicle*,[2] was chosen by the works from many other *artifices* to undertake the rebuilding of Canterbury Cathedral in 1174. Everything in the records seems to indicate that both William of Sens and his successor, William the Englishman, occupied the position of the

---

[1] Prior, *Cathedral Builders*, p. 57.
[2] *The Historical Works of Gervase of Canterbury* (ed. W. Stubbs, *Rolls Series*. London, 1858).

modern architect. The former on one occasion fell fifty feet from a scaffold while directing operations, and sustained incurable injuries : meanwhile he continued to give orders to the leading mason (' cuidam monacho industrio et ingenioso qui cementariis praefuit opus consummandum commendavit . . . Magister tamen in lecto recubans, quid prius, quid posterius fieri debuit ordinavit'). In England the word *artifex* as applied to a medieval architect is rare ; usually it denotes a skilled craftsman. In France, out of thirteen *artifices* mentioned by M. Mortet,[1] he regards ten as architects proper, the remainder being craftsmen. According to an old document cited by De Mély,[2] the architect of St. Eutrope at Saintes (1085) was so described (' . . . Senior quidam peritus, Benedictus nomine, artifex '). But ' princeps artificum ' is generally used to describe the architect.

Operarius occurs frequently in France, occasionally in Spain, and sometimes may indicate an architect, but more often an unskilled workman or labourer, as one would expect. Sometimes it certainly refers to the treasurer or business-manager of the building.[3]

Mechanicus, a word employed in the fourth century to denote ' a theoretical and scientific architect and engineer of the highest rank ',[4] frequently occurs in the Middle Ages to describe ordinary artisans.

We now come to four words, all of which signify ' architect ' or ' mason ' according to circumstances : *lapicida*, *cementarius*, *lathomus*, and ' mason.' The first-named does not appear to have been used in England ; [5] in France it

---

[1] Mortet, *op. cit.*, pp. 485–513.
[2] F. de Mély, *op. cit.*, p. 353.
[3] Stein, H., *Les architectes des cathédrales gothiques*, pp. 23–4.
[4] Frothingham (see Bibliography at end of this chapter), p. 57.
[5] Papworth, *op. cit.*, p. 230.

is rare, in Spain and Italy fairly common.   Literally and often actually it means a ' stone-cutter ', but now and then documentary evidence makes it clear that the *lapicida* carried out a whole building.

Cementarius and *lathomus* are old words occurring in the Latin versions of the Bible, e. g. I Chronicles xxii. 15, and both are very frequently found in medieval records with their literal sense of ' mason ', but very often they denote the architect of a church or other structure, especially when preceded by *magister*.   Strictly speaking, the *cementarius* was a waller or setter of stones, hence engaged on rough masonry ; whereas the *lathomus* was a worker in freestone, a ' freemason ', whose chief work consisted in carving and in stereotomy ; but in practice the two words were almost interchangeable.   The English word ' mason ' (*maçon* in French, *masson* in old French) needs no further explanation here, and it is only necessary to repeat that the architects of most of our medieval buildings were originally drawn or promoted from the mason's craft.   The architect of the Sainte Chapelle at Paris, Pierre de Montreuil (d. 1254) is described on his tombstones as *doctor latomorum*,[1] a title even more suggestive of his status than the *magister latomorum* that one sometimes finds elsewhere ; but not more so perhaps than *magister carpentariorum vel latomorum* quoted by Mortet and rendered by him ' chief architect '.   Ruskin has a characteristic passage on the medieval architect's titles and functions, quoted here for its relevance to the previous paragraphs rather than for its untenable conclusion : [2]

' It became apparent to me that the master workman must have been the person who carved the bas-reliefs in the porches ;

[1] De Mély, *op. cit.*, p. 311.
[2] Ruskin, *Seven Lamps of Architecture,* Appendix I.

that to him all others must have been subordinate, and by him all the rest of the cathedral essentially arranged ; but that in fact the whole company of builders, always large, were more or less divided into two great flocks, of stone-layers and sculptors ; and that the number of sculptors was so great, and their average talent so considerable, that it would no more have been thought necessary to state respecting the master builder that he could carve a statue than that he could measure an angle or strike a curve.

' The name by which the architect of Cologne Cathedral is designated in the contracts for the work, is *magister lapicida*, the " master stone-cutter " ; and I believe this was the usual Latin term throughout the Middle Ages. The architect of the fourteenth-century portions of Notre-Dame, Paris, is styled in French simply *premier masson*.

' If the reader will think over this statement carefully he will find that it is indeed true, and a key to many things. The fact is, there are only two fine arts possible to the human race, sculpture and painting. What we call architecture is only the association of these in noble masses, or the placing them in fit places. All architecture other than this is, in fact, mere building.'

Assuming, however, that the modern architect was repre-sented in the Middle Ages by the master-mason, can we disprove the second fallacy, that the master-mason was an artisan rather than an artist or a professional man ? We are at once faced with the difficulty of distinguishing professional from manual work in such distant times. A recent authority [1] has written that :

' Except in Italy, when the Renaissance was already dawn-ing, it was impossible to distinguish between the medieval *artist* and *artisan* ; it may truly be said that the noblest piles, like Rheims, Chartres, and Amiens, were built from top to

[1] G. G. Coulton, *Social Life in Britain*, p. 468. (London, 1918.)

bottom by artisans, who received artisans' wages, the master-mason generally getting the same as the master-carpenter or master-smith. It has sometimes been argued, however, that what these lacked in money they earned in high esteem ; that they were as much respected as distinguished architects are in our own day ; in support of which, we are reminded that Charles V of France stood sponsor to the son of his master-mason, Raymond du Temple, and that the boy went to the University of Orleans (Lethaby, *Medieval Art*, p. 256). This, however, is an exceptional case, just as modern royalty has sometimes condescended to stand sponsor to a game-keeper's or gardener's child.'

This is hardly a fair or a full statement of the case. The amount of the master-mason's emoluments is difficult to determine, in view of the uncertain value of money in those days, and the mere fact that they were paid as wages proves nothing. The master-mason was paid much more than an ordinary mason, and often more than any other person employed on the building.

But careful study of a large number of the entries in contemporary documents relating to medieval wages in the building trade has not furnished me with any clear idea of the architect's status as compared with that of other workers of the higher grades, and I am of opinion that this matter requires even fuller investigation before we can use his rate of pay as an argument to prove his exact professional standing. There seems to be no consistent scale of wages, and they varied, not only in different districts and at different periods, but even according to the reputation of the master-mason. Assuredly there was no system of remuneration proportioned to the cost of the building, such as prevails to-day in architects' fees reckoned on a percentage basis.

So far as England is concerned, the figures collected by Papworth are of interest, though confusing because architects and master-masons are mixed up with comptrollers and other officials, and the Fabric Rolls of York, Exeter, &c., are illuminating. The Fabric Rolls of York Minster contain a long series of records of payments made to the principal workers on the building. Thus, in 1351, William de Hoton, mason, was granted a yearly ' pension ' of ten pounds of silver for life, together with a dwelling in the Close, provided that he undertook no other work. In 1368 there is a reference to Master Robert de Patryngton (*magistro sementario*), to whom

' for his good services rendered and to be rendered for the term of his life, we [the Dean, &c.] have granted . . . £10 a year, together with the houses within the close which William de Hoton occupied, Provided that he shall well and faithfully attend to the works, and shall not employ his time upon any other operations. And if he shall undertake any works elsewhere, and apply himself to them, neglecting, delaying, or leaving undone our works ; and after being a third time admonished on our behalf, shall not return to our works and diligently employ himself about the same, then his salary shall cease until he shall return and duly make up for his failures. If smitten with blindness or other bodily infirmity, whereby he may be disabled from bestowing his bodily labour upon the said works, then, so long as the infirmity shall continue, he shall receive 10 marks [£6 13s. 4d.] yearly, together with the houses aforesaid, bestowing his counsel and advice as far as he is able. In the event of his being unwilling to labour, or withdrawing himself altogether from the works, then the grant shall forthwith cease, until he shall fully return and attend to our works.'

Papworth adds that ' it was the general custom of the Chapter of York Cathedral to appoint the person who was next the head of the masons to the office of Master Mason whenever that office became vacant '. Writing elsewhere of the salaries paid to the various chief officers of the medieval Office of Works, he observes that : ' The Sunday, it appears, was paid for to those officers who had a yearly salary, the accounts often mentioning the 365 days at 6*d*. or 1*s*. a day.'

Professor Hamilton Thompson, writing of English master-masons in the fourteenth century, says that they ' were paid at a special rate, generally eightpence a day, while the principal masons under them received sixpence, and the inferior masons and workmen less. The ordinary mason's fee was reduced in the winter half of the year, but the master-mason was habitually paid at the same rate throughout the year for each day or half-day on which he worked in person.' [1]

But this question of the remuneration of architects in the Middle Ages has been summarized effectively by M. Lance.[2] His figures for France may not apply equally to England, but his conclusions as to the methods of payment adopted are of general interest, especially as he has translated all fees and salaries into French francs with the purchasing power of his own day (1872). In epitomizing his statements, I have further translated these figures from French francs into English pre-war pounds (reckoning 25 francs = £1) and have added in square brackets their equivalent rate to-day (adding 75 per cent. to the money value). The result is probably to depreciate the medieval salaries, as 25 francs in 1872 were presumably worth more than in 1914, but the figures given will allow some comparison to be made with modern times.

In the thirteenth century Eudes de Montereau, royal

[1] A. H. Thompson, *Cathedral Churches of England* (1925), p. 146.
[2] Lance, *Dictionnaire des Architectes français*, I, pp. xxi–xxvi.

architect, had a daily salary of 4 *sous*, an annual allowance of 100 *sous* for clothing, fodder for two horses, and food at court. Lance estimates the total value of these items at £600–£640 [=£1,000–£1,100 in 1925].

The usual arrangement with an architect in the Middle Ages was a daily salary plus an annual retaining fee (*indemnité*). In 1365–82 his daily pay at Troyes was 12s. [=21s.] ; in 1383 at Dijon it was 20s. [=35s.] ; and, also in 1383, at Limoges and Blois, 8s. [= 14s.]. In 1388 at Rouen an architect received 12s. a day salary, plus £144 a year for retaining fee and clothing allowance, making about £368 in all [=£650 in 1925]. The architect of a bridge at Rouen in 1396 received £235 a year [=£411 in 1925].

During the fifteenth century, when the state of France was disturbed, there is a corresponding drop in architects' earnings. Their daily wages ranged from 5s. 6d. to 11s. [=9s. 8d. to 19s. 3d. in 1925] according to the province, for rates of pay varied greatly in different districts. The highest *annual* stipend noted by Lance is that of the architect of the collegiate church of St. Quentin, £27 [=£47], plus a daily wage equivalent to £100 a year [£175] and a daily loaf of bread ; and the lowest that of the architect of the cathedral at Troyes in 1474, who had only £6 [£10 10s.] a year plus cloth for one robe.

Settled conditions in the next century contributed to better pay for architects, and by the middle of the century Serlio and other ' stars ' were drawing annual incomes of £400 to £800 [£700 to £1,400].

The only other country also for which information is readily available is Spain, thanks to the researches of Street,[1] who gives actual figures in six typical cases. But

[1] Street, *Gothic Architecture in Spain,* chapter XXI.

as these extend over a period of four centuries, and as the
value of the currency seems to be uncertain at any time
during the Middle Ages in Spain, it is difficult to form
any direct opinion as to the market value of the medieval
architect's services in that country. But one may infer
approximately what it was worth in one case, where
Maestro Raymondo came to an agreement with the Bishop
of Lugo in 1129 that if the value of money dropped during
the period of his employment (full-time) as master of the
works at the new cathedral, he should be paid in kind on
the following scale instead : six marks of silver, thirty-six
yards of linen, and seventeen loads of wood annually ;
' shoes and gaiters as he had need of them ' ; and each
month two *sueldos* for meat, a measure of salt, and a pound
of candles. After making all due allowance for changes
in habits since the twelfth century, we cannot feel that a
Spanish architect of those days was extravagantly overpaid.

So far we have been concerned only with annual or
regular salaries ; but specific fees for single commissions
and annual retaining fees are sometimes mentioned. I
have already noted (p. 59) the case of St. Pierre at Oudenbourg, where the fee to be paid on completion to the
' architects ' was agreed in advance. According to Lance,
Jean Gilde was paid 8 guineas [=14 guineas] in 1506 for
a plan of the cathedral towers at Troyes ; and Roulland
Leroux £71 [=£123] for drawings and supervision of the
tomb of Georges d'Amboise at Rouen in 1510. A contract with the architect was an ordinary arrangement, his
duties being set forth in considerable detail. Street prints
several such agreements, some in Latin and some translated ; while examples of English contracts are to be found
in Papworth and other authorities. In most of these it is
clearly stated whether the architect was to give the whole

of his time to the work in question, or whether he was permitted to undertake other work, this arrangement corresponding to modern conditions for official architects and architects in private practice respectively. Fees were also paid to consultants, and to architects serving as members of an expert advisory committee or *junta* (the latter especially in Spain). Thus Lance quotes the fees paid per day to consultants : in 1293 (for a verbal opinion only) 8s. [=14s. in 1925] ; in 1509 at Troyes, where pay was always low, 6s. [=10s. 6d.] ; and in 1517 at Paris, 10s. [=17s. 6d.]. I shall return to the question of ' private practice ' and consulting work later in this chapter. Occasionally travelling expenses, for the removal of the ' master ' and his family from one building to another when taking up a new appointment, are mentioned in the records. Jayme Fabre in 1318 was paid his travelling expenses from Mallorca to Barcelona every time he visited the Cathedral at Barcelona ; and he was not only living in Mallorca but carrying on work there at the time.[1] Lance also mentions several records of travelling expenses in France.

But though the voluminous figures published by Papworth and other authorities do not enable us to form any exact opinion as to the architect's remuneration, or indeed to infer more than that he was one of the better paid of the officials connected with a building enterprise, the frequent mention of special perquisites, privileges, and immunities that he enjoyed proves conclusively that his status was that of a professional man of to-day. Professor Prior [2] makes it clear that he was expected to be housed and dressed like a gentleman, and many specific instances bear out this assumption.

[1] Street, *op. cit.* ii. 266.   [2] Prior, *Cathedral Builders*, 87–8.

At York (as already mentioned), at Wells, and elsewhere he was provided with a free house. In 1257–8 Henry III rewarded John of Gloucester, the king's mason ' with his freedom for life from all tallage and tolls throughout the realm '.[1] In 1300 Arnolfo del Cambio was excused his income-tax in Florence. At York the master-mason drew his salary when absent on leave. Bonuses were paid on certain occasions, and frequently there were allowances of fuel, food, or for expenses of lodging and board. A horse was often provided.

' Master John of Gloucester is rewarded by the king in 1258 with gifts of land and houses for his excellent services at Gloucester, Woodstock, and Westminster. In 1255–6 five casks of wine are ordered to be returned to him for five which the king took at Oxford, an incident seeming to imply some personal intimacy ' . . . ' John of Beverley in 1275 had 12s. a day, which was increased to 16s. when he travelled, and the king gave him a tun of wine ' . . .[2]

In 1390 Henry Yevele, a King's mason, ' was exempted from serving on juries, and the manors of Frenisworth and Vannes in Kent were granted him in lieu of his pension of 1s. a day '. (The fact that he was eligible for service on juries presupposes a good social standing.)

The frequent mention of robes and other articles of apparel in the old record has a value in determining the status of the architect at a time when every man dressed strictly according to his social and professional rank. The master-mason usually received ' furred robes ' of Esquire's rank once or twice a year, or an allowance in lieu of robes. (A fur robe in the fourteenth century seems to have cost about 15s.) Where any allowance of food is

---

[1] Papworth, *op. cit.*, p. 209.
[2] Jackson, *Gothic Architecture*, i. 267–8.

described in detail, it is sometimes stipulated that it shall be of the same quality as that provided for the Esquires' table. Roger Keys, master of the works at All Souls' College, Oxford, 1442–4, was rewarded by Henry VI with the grant of a coat of arms. Another master-mason or architect became Lord Mayor of York. All these instances are taken from English records, but they can be matched by contemporary documents from France, Spain, Italy, and elsewhere. The tomb-slabs to the ' masters ' of great churches and even to their wives and families, several of which are described later in this chapter, supply further evidence of the architect's status. As Sir Thomas Jackson concludes :

' It would really seem that in the thirteenth and following centuries, far from being the humble unknown mechanic that has been supposed, the Master-Mason architect fared socially as well as the architect who represents him at the present day.' [1]

In addition to the various privileges cited above, the master-mason received fees for training apprentices. A contract,[2] dated 1488, between the Prior of Durham and one John Bell, mason, after outlining the master's duties in general, states that he is to train one apprentice for the prior and what he (the mason) is to be paid for so doing. It then proceeds that he

' also shall have *one apprentice of his own* for a term of ten years in the aforesaid mason craft, one after another during his life, to work and labour in the work of masonry of the said prior, &c., for the which apprentice he shall receive of the sacristan—every year of the three first years of his prentice head, 4 marcs (£2 13s. 4d.) and every year of the three next, 6 marcs (£4), and the tenth and last year, 7 marcs (£4 13s. 4d.), at eight times of the year by equal portions ;—and when it

---

[1] *Op. cit.* ii. 268.   [2] Quoted by Papworth, *op. cit.*, p. 219.

shall happen that the said John have continual infirmities or great age, so that he may not work or labour, nor exercise his craft and cunning, he shall then be content with 4 marcs yearly, to be paid at eight times of the year by the sacristan.'

It is easy to surmise why, in the Middle Ages, the directing personage on a building was a mason, and even why his training was so largely concerned with masonry, for a medieval building of any size consisted chiefly of masons' work. Plumbing, slating, glazing, and even carpentry were only accessory to the main structure. The architect had to master masonry above all the crafts, and it was by far the most difficult of them to understand, for every important structural problem involved in the building—the thrust of the vault, the counterpoise of the buttresses, the design of the tracery, the interpenetration of the mouldings—was a masonry problem. In an age when there were no text-books to speak of, knowledge of such intricate questions of mechanics and geometry could only be acquired from experience based on the experiments of others. In this view I am confirmed by Professor Prior, who holds that in the thirteenth century the master was always a mason, whose skill in setting-out stonework would give him skill in setting-out on a larger scale.[1]

It has been said that another difference between old and modern practice lay in the fact that the master-mason and the master-carpenter each prepared plans for their respective parts of the work.[2] It would form a fairer comparison to state that the master-mason (or ' architect '), after making the main design for the building himself, assigned the detail drawings for the roof and other wooden features to the master-carpenter, just as a modern

---

[1] *Op. cit.*, p. 59.
[2] Salzman, *English Industries of the Middle Ages*, p. 112.

architect, after making the main design for the building himself, often assigns the detail drawings of its roof and doors to his assistant or draughtsman.

But the functions of the master-mason or architect varied in different countries and circumstances. It is noteworthy that all the nine medieval architects mentioned by Vasari are also described as sculptors, two of them as 'architect, painter, and sculptor'; and one specially versatile person, Orcagna, adding poetry to this repertoire.[1] In another direction we find them undertaking military engineering — e. g. Lorenzo del Maitano (1275–1330), the *capo-maestro* of Orvieto Cathedral, also designed the fortifications of Todi;[2] Louis IX took an architect with him to Palestine to fortify Jaffa, and afterwards entrusted him with the building of a number of churches in Paris.[3] Street cites the case of Pedro Compte of Valencia, who not only designed the Exchange there in 1482, but also carried out some waterworks that we should certainly regard as engineering nowadays. He drew an annual salary as *Maestro Mayor* of Valencia, and was evidently an important person, as he also held the office of *Alcaide perpetuo*.[4] The status of the *ingeniator* has already been mentioned (p. 62).

Mention of the medieval engineer-architect naturally turns one's thoughts to medieval town-planning. So much stress has always been laid on the merely picturesque aspect of old towns that it will probably appear rank sacrilege to suggest that any of them may have been scientifically laid out by a professional man from a plan on paper. But it remains a fact that utilitarianism rather than a striving after the picturesque was the chief aim in the Middle Ages : and utilitarianism has given us our

[1] Vasari, *Lives of the Artists*, i.
[2] Sturgis, *Dictionary of Architecture*, s.v. ' Maitani '.
[3] Milizia, *op. cit.* i. 147.   [4] Street, *op. cit.* ii. 272

most beautiful old market-places as well as our most hideous Victorian factory-towns. Of the majority of medieval towns it may be said that they simply grew, in which case there is no need to seek for a designer. Others again have a Roman origin, such as Gloucester and Chichester where the main streets still follow the old lines ; or York, Lincoln, and Colchester, where the ancient plan has been more or less obliterated. But of such towns as were deliberately planned during the Middle Ages we know enough to classify them under different heads. First of all came the fortress-towns, such as Hertford, Bedford, Buckingham, Nottingham, and Stamford, founded by Edward the Elder between 913 and 924 as part of a scheme for defending southern England ; and those towns that huddle round and under some frowning Norman castle on a strategical site, such as Durham, Edinburgh, Windsor, Norwich, Shrewsbury, Chepstow, Radnor, Bridgnorth, and Ludlow. I can find nothing to show by whose hands these towns were planned, but one may safely assume that a military engineer was mainly responsible. This assumption does not rule out the possibility that he was an architect, for I have indicated already (p. 62) that *ingeniator* seems to mean a military architect. These early towns were planned for defence, and in other respects they display little more than a picturesque jumble of alleys and twisting streets.

In the thirteenth century, however, we come to more definite indications. St. Louis of France set the fashion of planning *bastides*, heavily fortified towns on a gridiron plan with a rectangular *enceinte* and a market-place. These fortresses soon spread over Europe, as far as Breslau and Cracow. Edward I built some fifty *bastides* in France, e. g. Montpazier ; and a century later part of

Calais was laid out on similar lines. But he probably utilized expert advisers, as well as ideas, from France. However, when he came to lay out English towns, there seem to have been native architects or engineers available, for in 1296 he ordered the citizens of London to elect

' four skilful men . . . persons competent to lay out the plans of towns . . . the most able and clever and those who know best how to devise, order and array a new town to the most profit of Us and the merchants, and who shall be ready and prepared to go for that purpose where we shall instruct them.'

(*Quatre prodeshommes des plus sachantz et plus sufficantz qui mieux sachent diviser ordonner et arrayer une novele vile . . . pretz et appareilles d'aller outre pour cete besoigne la ou nous leur enjoindrons.*) But these were only four out of fifty men to be appointed by various English boroughs, including places as insignificant nowadays as Dunwich and Winchelsea, and this small army of experts had to follow the king round the country as an advisory committee. Their first rendezvous was at Berwick, which he had just rendered ripe for town-planning by burning it down in the course of a campaign. Winchelsea had been planned in 1281 by three commissioners, of whom one was Warden of the Cinque Ports, another a financier, and the third one Itier of Angoulême, a Frenchman who had helped to plan the French *bastides*. He, presumably, was the technical town-planner or architect. Edward's Welsh fortresses were planned by the architect James St. George.

A claim has been made for Henry II as the parent of English town-planning, for he laid out the town of New Woodstock, where he often resided ' for the love of a certain woman named Rosamund ', but the records do not mention any architect, though the streets are laid out in gridiron fashion. Probably we may attribute the

plans of Eynsham, St. Albans, Malmesbury, and Tewkes-
bury to architects employed by neighbouring abbeys ;
and the credit of laying-out of Salisbury (New Sarum) is
certainly due to Richard le Poer, the bishop, who in 1220
transferred both the cathedral and the town to a new site,
but the name of the person who actually prepared the plan
is not recorded.[1]

In one respect, at any rate, the status of the ' architect '
in the Middle Ages often differed from present practice,
for there are numerous instances where he also acted as
builder and undertook contracts as well as design and
supervision of the work.   Papworth mentions several
cases in England, others are known in France and Spain.[2]
But although the practice seems to have been fairly
common, we need not assume that it would be justifiable
under modern conditions, or that, because the medieval
' master ' occasionally acted as contractor too, he therefore
ceased to be an architect.   In the few cases where we read
that he had to check the building accounts, it is quite
obvious that if he did, he could not have been acting
as contractor, and thus exercising this highly unpleasant
process on his own books !

The reader may object that, in my account of architectural work during the Middle Ages, I have eliminated the
' builder ' altogether, claiming the master-mason as an
architect, and regarding all other workers as craftsmen or
labourers.   In a sense this is true, for the Treasurer, Controller, Surveyor, or what not, was a member of the staff
of a monastery, a college, or the royal Office of Works,

---

[1] On the authors of medieval town-plans, see Tout, *Medieval
Town-planning* (Manchester, 1917) ; and Hughes and Lamborn,
Towns and Town-planning (Oxford, 1923).

[2] Jackson, *op. cit.* i. 267 ; Street, *op. cit.*; and Papworth, *op. cit.*
passim.

and though he dealt with financial matters, often ordered the material, and paid the workmen, he was not a ' builder ' in the modern sense of a commercial man who follows the architect's instructions. The position has been well defined by M. Lance in the Introduction to his great *Dictionnaire des Architectes français*.

' No intermediary existed then, as nowadays,' he says, ' between the architect and the craftsman ignorant of the task in hand ; there was no " builder " [*entrepreneur*] who was able to translate, from carefully-drawn plans and precise specifications, the designer's wishes to the workman. The architect himself was in direct touch with the workman, he dealt with him personally, bought the materials, drew out the details, measured up the work, and checked the accounts.' (My translation.)

But, Lance adds, the architect himself was often checked by experts called in from outside, who examined and reported on ' the job ', a practice that horrifies us to-day, but which acted as a safeguard from the ' client's ' point of view, and could only be objected to by dishonest or incompetent practitioners (*faiseurs*).

But the relation of the ' architect ', ' master ', or whatever he was called, to the other officials employed on a building still remains a perplexing question, for their name is legion. Papworth in his study of *The Superintendents of English Buildings in the Middle Ages* has dealt with this question in some detail, and his conclusions have not been seriously controverted since his paper was published in a revised form in 1887. Among a host of functionaries he devotes special attention to the Supervisor, the Surveyor, the Master of the Work, the Keeper of the Works or the Fabric, the Clerk of the Works, the Director, and the Devizor.

Papworth considers that the ' Supervisor ' was a

steward rather than a surveyor, and that his office closely corresponded with that of the comptroller or paymaster, though sometimes they are differentiated on one building. He quotes an instance of its use as early as 1100 (' Alduin de Malverne, Supervisor of the Bridge at Hereford ') and another of the fifteenth century.

The ' Surveyor ' makes his appearance in documents of 1417 and 1422. From *c*. 1520 the title is in common use. Fitzherbert in his work on *Surveyinge* in 1534 says that ' *Sarueyour* is a french name '. Several of the royal surveyors in the sixteenth century were ex-carpenters. During the reigns of Elizabeth and James I the head of the ' Office of Works ' ceased to be styled ' Clerk of the Works ' and became ' Surveyor '. Although the architect did sometimes hold the office of Surveyor in the royal service, Professor Prior says that generally in the thirteenth century the two offices were quite distinct, the duties of the surveyor consisting ' in providing the money, in collecting the materials, in the organization and payment of the craftsmen ',[1]—in fact, with all the business side of a building enterprise. The work involved in getting materials might include the felling of trees, the quarrying of stone, or even (as at Rievaulx) the digging of a canal to float stone to the site. Surveyors were also appointed to take charge of existing buildings : their posts were regarded as plums to be given to royal favourites. Professor Prior believes that surveyors usually had little if any training in the technique of architecture or the building crafts. But, because of their official position, they are more frequently mentioned in records than is the architect or ' master ' who actually designed the building and supervised its erection.

Prior, Cathedral Builders.

FIG. 7. ARCHITECT'S TOMB-SLAB, CAMPO SANTO, PISA.
Drawn by M. S. Briggs.
Conjectural reading : S(epulchrum) Magistro(rum) ope(ris)
s(an)c(t)e Marie Maioris.

FIG. 8. ARCHITECT'S INSCRIPTION IN THE CATHEDRAL,
FIESOLE. Drawn by M. S. Briggs.

The Master of the Work in England was usually a high official of a monastery, and his duties closely resembled those of the two functionaries already mentioned. In France and Spain, on the other hand, he was frequently the architect. But in Spain, according to Street, there was yet another official, the *Operarius*, who was usually the canon of a cathedral or collegiate church, whose duty it was to deal with the architect. His work would therefore resemble that of a comptroller or steward.[1] We also find the *Operarius* in France, e. g. in the cloisters of St. Trophime at Arles there is the epitaph dated 1183 of ' Poncius Rebolii sacerdos et canonicus regularis et operarius ecclesie sancti Trophimi '.

The titles of Keeper of the Fabric or the Works (*Custodes operationum*) and Director are all of doubtful significance, but probably all indicate officials connected with the finance and organization of building operations, as does the designation *custos ecclesiae*, which however may bear the interpretation of ' churchwarden ' in other instances. The ' Devizor ' seems to have been a subordinate officer concerned with similar duties, but the ingenious suggestion has been made that the title may be derived from the old French word *devis* or *deviz* (=' specification '), and hence that the devizor was an estimating clerk. A French document of 1497 refers to a ' *diviseur des bâtimens* '.[2]

The result of an examination of the references to these various officers is disappointingly vague, but it is now generally agreed among competent scholars that in England the architectural work involved in planning and erecting the building was not done by any of them (except occasionally by the Surveyor or the Master of the

---

[1] Street, *op. cit.* ii. 267.
[2] Quoted in Papworth, *op. cit.*, p. 200 *n*.

Work, where documents are clear enough to prove this). Their concern was solely with organization and finance. On all large ecclesiastical and collegiate buildings we find three principal personages—the donor or founder or instigator of the scheme, who admittedly may have given instructions as definitely as a modern ' client ' does to his architect, even including an amateur sketch-plan on occasion ; the comptroller, treasurer, surveyor, &c., who managed the business side of the work for him ; and the master, master-mason, or architect, who was a technically trained expert corresponding, *mutatis mutandis*, to a modern professional architect. Any one of these three was prepared to say of the work that ' he did it ' (*fecit*), so that when this statement is made we can only rely on further information in the records to decide whether as owner he ordered it, whether as business manager he looked after the funds, or whether he was the real architect who did the design and the erection.

Where, then, are we to place men like William of Wykeham, at one time regarded by critics as the first great English architect ? It is curious how completely opinion has changed in regard to this remarkable man. More than sixty years ago Papworth challenged his reputation with a wealth of documentary evidence, and now all recognized authorities have followed his lead. In two recent lectures Professor Hamilton Thompson has poured ridicule on the idea of Wykeham as an architect. He pictures him, ' after a hard day's work in the Government Office which he occupied, spending the leisure of his evenings—when artificial light was poor and difficult to obtain—in designing Winchester Cathedral or an Oxford College '.[1]

[1] Lecture to the Yorks. Archaeological Society. Reported in *The Builder*, 13 March 1925.

The terms of his appointment at Windsor stated his duties clearly, and prove that he was a business manager with a staff of clerks.[1] Of course he had good taste in architecture, like many patrons of the art, and his rapid promotion was perhaps largely due to his success in organizing building operations. But the real architect at Winchester was ' Master ' William Wynford (described sometimes as *lathomus* and sometimes as *cementarius*), whose portrait appears, together with portraits of the master-carpenter and the supervisor or paymaster, in a stained-glass window in Winchester College Chapel. The evidence in this case is far too lengthy to quote here,[2] but it seems quite conclusive, and is specially important in view of the claims made for William of Wykeham, whose services to architecture were magnificent, but whose position as an architect is no longer tenable. For similar reasons we must probably discount the claims of Alan of Walsingham at Ely, of Elias of Dereham at Salisbury, and of a host of others.

There is one more official whom we must not forget, the Clerk of the Works (*clericus operationum*), whose name survives to-day. What was his position in the medieval hierarchy of builders ? A livery was often granted to him, but his status is very uncertain. Sometimes he ranks high among the various officials ; on the other hand, he was paid only 8*d.* a day at Carnarvon Castle when the master-mason was drawing 2*s.* 2*d.* a day. In 1361 a royal clerk of works was made chaplain to the King, prebendary, and dean ; but when he reverted to his original occupation four years later his pay was only 1*s.* a day. An undated MS. of the time of Edward IV gives a list of officials

[1] Hamilton Thompson, Lecture to Royal Archaeological Institute, April, 1925.   [2] Papworth, *op. cit.*, pp. 202–8, &c.

in the royal Works Department including a clerk of works who received 2*s.* a day and had a staff under him, while the comptroller was paid only 1*s.* a day ; there was also a ' devisor of buildings ' who received the same salary as the clerk of works. This post was illuminated by Geoffrey Chaucer, who, with a little luck, might have had an architectural reputation equal to Wykeham's. As it is, his knowledge of architecture is displayed in his writings, e. g. in the *Knightes Tale* and the *Hous of Fame*. But Papworth does not think that he had any technical training or ability, and infers that the office was given to him, as to many others as one of the king's favourites. He was appointed Clerk of Works in 1389 for Westminster, the Tower, Berkhampstead, Kennington, Eltham, Clarendon, Sheen, Byfleet, Fakenham, &c., but held the post for only twenty months. Apparently the post existed almost exclusively in the royal service, and it was of considerable monetary value in most of the cases recorded.[1]

The ' master ' or ' architect ' presumably had assistants on all buildings of importance. In Spain the word *aparejador* is often used in medieval documents to describe an assistant, but it is not clear whether a clerk of works is meant.[2] The Latin word is *apparator*, and in France it sometimes seems to imply the architect himself (e. g. in a case at Rouen in 1362 cited by Stein), and sometimes clearly means his assistant (e. g. another case at Rouen, of about the same date, also cited by Stein, ' lathomum preparatorem seu gallice appareilleur '). The number of men employed on a large building often ran into many hundreds, sometimes over a thousand. Thus at Westminster Abbey there were as many as 700 workmen when Henry III was hustling the work so that it should be completed on

[1] *Ibid.*, pp. 196–9.   [2] Street, *op. cit.* ii. 275.

the ' opening day ' that he had decided on, and on the Round Tower at Windsor 720 men were employed during one week in 1344.[1] The masons, especially, moved from place to place on the larger buildings, so did not form the master-mason's permanent staff. They were hired by the clerk of works. Travelling craftsmen of this sort were regarded as ' foreigners ' by the local artisans, but for the smaller crafts local labour could often be utilized. The organization of building labour seems clearly to have been derived from the Roman system, and it lasted long after the Middle Ages, e. g. at Oxford, Hardwick Hall, Wollaton Hall, &c. The office of master-mason in England and Spain often passed from father to son, and in France there are numerous examples [2] of what I have called (in later chapters of this book) the ' architectural family '. I have heard the amusing suggestion made that rival towns and churches would bid for the services of a celebrated master-mason as furiously as modern football clubs haggle for the body of a famous half-back.

The common superstition that the cathedrals and other great buildings of the Middle Ages were erected without plans seems so incredibly absurd that one wonders how it could ever have arisen. The only explanation is that certain critics, in their desire to prove that the medieval master-mason bore no resemblance to the modern professional architect, have exaggerated every point of difference, and, in this case, have even invented differences where no difference existed. The arguments in favour of plans having been used are three : firstly, practical considerations, seeing that a plan expedites and simplifies all building operations ; secondly, that drawings are occasionally mentioned in documentary records ; and, thirdly,

[1] Salzman, *op. cit.*, p. 116.	[2] Mortet, *op. cit.* passim.

that a number of drawings have been preserved. In dealing with this question, we need not try to press the case for plans further than the evidence allows : we may admit at the outset that plans may not have been used on every medieval building in every period, that at first, if used at all, they were far less detailed than modern working drawings, and in fact that they differed very greatly from the plans that we use to-day. But even admitting so much, we may still conclude that the architects of the Middle Ages employed plans to help them in the design and erection of their buildings.

Indeed it is difficult to imagine any man nowadays attempting to build even a cottage without plans, if he is able to draw. He finds himself in all sorts of difficulties if he tries it : the staircase does not ' work ', the planning is wasteful of space and material, the effect internally and externally is unsatisfactory. In the case of a complicated building like a cathedral the need for some guiding design is far more urgent. But apart from the problems of construction involved during building, there are other reasons why plans should have been used. When a high ecclesiastic ordered a church, it would be infinitely easier for him to decide on a design if that design were graphically represented to him by his architect. Even the pen of a Chaucer, describing in prose or poetry the dimensions of a projected cathedral, would be less effective than a simple sketch in line. Then the comptroller, or whatever he was called, would find a plan helpful in ordering the materials required. Most architects will agree that the only possible explanation of this alleged method of building without plans would be the inability of the master-mason to draw them.

But we have sufficient evidence, in the shape of a few

drawings providentially preserved, to be quite certain that, from the thirteenth century onwards, at any rate, there were capable draughtsmen among the master-masons. Before describing the technique of their drawings, it may be helpful to suggest reasons why so comparatively few examples have survived. It is probable that a drawing was usually regarded in those days as no more than a utilitarian memorandum in a building process, or as a sketch-design prepared in advance. It does not seem likely that, in itself, it was ever regarded as a thing of beauty, and one can hardly imagine any master-mason hanging up a framed perspective view of one of his buildings in his drawing-office. A plan was, in short, merely the means to an end. Moreover, parchment was scarce, so that, when a plan had served its purpose, the ink lines were sometimes erased, and the skin used again for an illuminated manuscript. One plan so treated has been preserved, and will be described shortly.

But plans were not necessarily drawn on parchment. I have heard it stated that, some years ago, there was found in the roof of the choir of Glasgow Cathedral a piece of wood on which was marked the setting-out of the thirteenth-century crypt vaulting ; and that the incised lines on the chapter-house doors at Wells are probably the setting-out of the great inverted arches in that cathedral. M. Stein [1] writes that ' La " chambre aux traits " était le lieu où les maîtres d'œuvre dessinaient les plans des ouvrages à exécuter ou taillaient des modèles en légères planchettes que fournissait le chambrilleur ; ces plans et modèles s'appelaient des " molles ".' So in England we read of the mason's ' lodge ' (the workshop where the men rested and had their meals, and where they discussed

[1] H. Stein, *Les Architectes des Cathédrales gothiques*, p. 39.

trade secrets, hence the use of the word in freemasonry), to which was attached the ' trasour ', ' tracying house ', or drawing-office of the master-mason.[1] M. de Mély states that working drawings were made on the site, adjoining the building in progress, on slabs of plaster (*nappes de plâtre*), this fact explaining why the tombstones of the master-masons (see fig. 15 in this book) usually depict them with enormous pairs of compasses in their hands.[2] Another familiar appliance is the mason's square. One French effigy, illustrated in fig. 14, shows the architect holding in his hand a model of a church which he had designed, for models were used as well as plans.

In Gloucester Cathedral a Gothic recumbent effigy of Osric represents that Saxon ecclesiastic holding on his breast a model of his abbey-church. At Ravenna a fresco depicts an archbishop offering a model of St. Vitale to the titular saint of his church, in the sixth century. Our knowledge of plans before the thirteenth century is very slight. M. Mortet [3] has made a special study of the Chronicle of Gervase of Canterbury in regard to this point, and says that the way in which Gervase describes old churches leads one to think that he had in his possession plans of them, of which he made use in his writings. A passage is quoted to show what pains a celebrated architect like William of Sens took with the details of masonry, drawing out the mouldings full size on wood or parchment for the masons to work from :

' Formas quoque ad lapides formandos his qui convenerant sculptoribus tradidit, et alia in hunc modum sollicite preparavit.'

As examples of architectural drawings earlier than the thirteenth century, we are generally referred to the famous

[1] Salzman, *op. cit.*, p. 116.   [2] De Mély, *op. cit.*, p. 361.
[3] Mortet, *op. cit.*, pp. 212, 216, 217.

plans of the Monastery of St. Gall (commenced in 829) and of the Norman cathedral at Canterbury. The former has often been published, e. g. almost in facsimile, to illustrate a paper by the late William Burges on *Architectural Drawing in the Middle Ages*,[1] and again more recently.[2] It is drawn on a large sheet of parchment in thin red ink lines which appear to indicate not only all the external and partition walls, but also such furniture as benches, tables, and stoves. It is covered with inscriptions in black ink indicating the uses of the various rooms, and with certain dimensions, though the plan itself is not drawn to scale. The arches of the various cloisters and the crosses of the altars are drawn elevationally on the plan, a convention employed long before by Egyptian draughtsmen in depicting buildings in their tomb-paintings. Sir Reginald Blomfield dismisses it as a ' mere diagram plan ',[3] and so it appears to modern eyes. Mr. G. G. Coulton [4] regards it as ' a fancy drawing of an ideal monastery.' On the other hand, it is quite conceivable that at such a time, in the ' Dark Ages ', nothing more elaborate or geometrical than a determined sketch-plan of this type was used by the architect, for the elements of primitive Romanesque architecture were of the simplest.

Rather more advanced is the twelfth-century plan of Canterbury, representing the cathedral and precincts as they existed about 1165, and published in *Vetusta Monumenta* in 1755.[5] This drawing (inserted in the Great

[1] In *R. I. B. A. Transactions*. (London, 1860–1.)
[2] In Wasmuth's and Egger's books ; see Bibliography at end of this chapter.
[3] *Architectural Drawing and Draughtsmen*, p. 11. (London, 1912.)
[4] Quoted in D. H. S. Cranage, *The Home of the Monk*, p. ix.
[5] Also in *R. I. B. A. Transactions*, 1862–3, and in the ' Canterbury ' volume in *Bell's Cathedral Series*, and in Wasmuth as above.

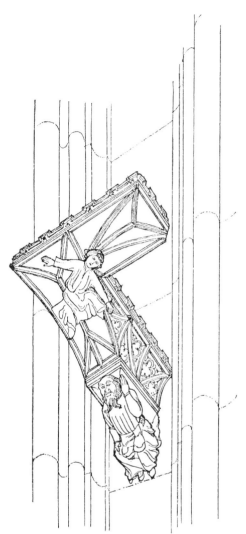

FIG. 9. THE 'MASON BRACKET' IN GLOUCESTER CATHEDRAL, AS
SEEN FROM BENEATH, SHOWING JOHN TULLY, MASTER-MASON (ARCHI-
TECT), from 1450 to 1457, IN THE ACT OF SALUTING, AND HIS YOUNG
APPRENTICE WHO WAS KILLED BY A FALL FROM THE TOWER. THE BRACKET
TAKES THE FORM OF A MASON'S SQUARE.

Drawn by M. S. Briggs.

Psalter of Eadwin and preserved in the library of Trinity College, Cambridge), is made in line and colour, and is another example of an ' elevational ' plan. Burges notes that Professor Willis made a close study of this drawing, and proceeds that :

' The way in which the plan and perspective are made to co-exist is by making a vanishing point in the centre of each court, so that there are three or four of these vanishing points in the drawing ' . . . ' All the water-courses and drains are shown, and upon the whole, considering the very original perspective, it may be pronounced to be a very accurate drawing ; indeed Professor Willis tells us that wherever a building is shown on this plan, Romanesque work is more or less found at the present day ' . . . ' I think, however, that we must consider this drawing of Canterbury more in the light of a survey for the purpose of showing the system of water-courses than as a document to be worked from.'

In the following century we find an elevation of the west front of a cathedral and several details,[1] discovered in 1838 under the writing of a MS. containing a list of the deceased members of the chapter of the cathedral at Rheims. As the last entry in the list is dated 1270, the drawings must be considerably earlier, and appear to have been first sponged out, then scraped over (to obliterate the lines) and finally cut into leaves. However, it has been found possible to trace the fragments, and thus to reveal something approaching more nearly to our idea of an architectural working drawing. The projection is in pure elevation, the straight lines are ruled, and the curves are struck from centres with an ink-compass. Still more significant, to my mind, is the fact that ornamental details are not ' repeated '—thus a few crockets are indicated on

---

[1] Illustrated in Burges, *op. cit.*

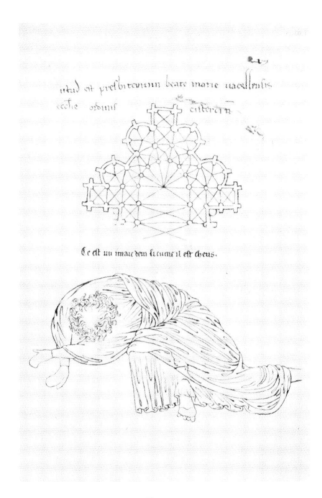

FIG. 10

A PAGE FROM THE SKETCH-BOOK OF VILLARD DE HONNECOURT

(*XIIIth century*)

one side of the main pediment of the portal, but none on the other. This seems to prove conclusively that the drawing was intended for some practical purpose rather than as a picture or record.

Far more elaborate is a drawing [1] of the west front of Strassburg Cathedral, stated to be of the thirteenth century, and executed in ink on parchment measuring 61·6×86 cm. This is drawn most carefully with instruments, and resembles a modern detail. Nearly all the ornamental features (including crockets, cusps, &c.) are delineated, almost the only exception being the carved capitals of the shafts (presumably left to the mason), and nearly every ' repeat ' of these ornamental features is drawn.

I am disposed to question the date of some other drawings attributed to the thirteenth century,[2] but there seems to be no doubt whatever that the famous sketch-book of Villard de Honnecourt [3] is of this period, and that it testifies to the high standard of draughtsmanship then prevailing. Moreover, it proves conclusively that this remarkable man travelled abroad in search of ' inspiration ', and that he sketched the plan and details of Rheims Cathedral with a view to reproducing them in the then unfinished church in his native town of Cambrai. Under a sketch of a window he has written : ' Here is one of the windows of Rheims Cathedral such as are placed in each bay of the nave between each pair of pillars. I was proceeding to Hungary on professional business when I drew this, because it pleased me best of all the windows.'

[1] Reproduced in Wasmuth's *Architektur-Zeichnungen*, plate 6. (Berlin, 1922.)

[2] *Dictionary of Architectural Publication Society*, s.v. ' Drawing '.

[3] See J. Quicherat, *Facsimile of the Sketchbook of Villard d'Honnecourt*. (London, 1859.)

Indeed, his little leather-bound book, preserved in the Bibliothèque Nationale at Paris, is one of the most valuable relics of the Middle Ages ; 33 of its original leaves remain, and on them are drawn 63 subjects, of which 35 represent figures and grotesques, 16 plans and details of architecture, 5 details of carpentry and masonry and geometry, and the remainder are miscellaneous. They are records of extensive travels in France, Germany, Switzerland, and Hungary, and in some cases are quite obviously sketches of features that seemed to him likely to prove useful in his practice at home. They prove, first of all, that he was an excellent draughtsman, not only of masonry details, as one would expect, but also of the human figure (see Fig. 10) and of ornamental work. There is one beautiful freehand sketch of a carved wooden bench-end that the most skilful modern draughtsman might be proud to own (see Fig. 11). The plans of cathedrals show all the lines of the vaulting (see Fig. 10), besides the walls and windows. Some of the diagrams of masonry display an intimate knowledge of geometry, and notes in writing on some of the plans indicate clearly that he was studying architecture and ornament with a view to utilizing it for buildings on which he was actually engaged or hoped to be engaged. It proves without doubt that the only medieval architect of whom we have so full a record was an accomplished draughtsman, a traveller, a student, and a man of wide artistic sympathies, in addition to being a competent master of stonecraft. It establishes the fact that the master-mason of the Middle Ages was the counterpart of the professional architect of to-day.

William Burges may be quoted in this connexion :

‘ First of all I must claim Wilars [Villard] for our profession, as some attempts have been made to hand him over to the

FIG. 11. A PAGE FROM THE SKETCH-BOOK OF VILLARD DE HONNECOURT

(*XIIIth century*)

sculptors and painters, because, forsooth, he drew the figure too well and frequently. There is one fact, however, which completely, so far as I can see, upsets this theory, and it is this—the tendency of an artist, either painter, sculptor, or architect, would be to sketch details which would come in useful to him. Thus the painter and sculptor would draw parts of the human body, bits of costume, anatomy, &c. ; while the architect, on the contrary would draw mouldings, capitals, foliage, &c. Now, in the sketches under considera- tion we do not find studies of hands, of feet, of anatomy, &c. ; but, on the contrary, there are a number of problems only useful to a man engaged in actual building. The sketches were first made with a leaden or silver pencil, either of which would perfectly mark on the vellum. If the subject were an archi- tectural one the straight lines were ruled, and the circles put in with a compass, one end of which had a leaden point. These lines were afterwards gone over with a blackish brown ink, no instrument being employed. Upon looking again at this MS. two months ago, I was struck more than ever by the extreme precision of the touch ; there is no faltering or wavering, but the line is just as thick and as firm where it ends as where it begins. Again, in drawing things in small, mouldings and foliage became simplified so as not to break up the breadth of the composition. Clearness is got by blacking hollows where they occur, and the grounds of ornament such as capitals, &c. The walls of the plans, however, are not hatched, and we shall find this practice obtaining even in the time of Thorpe, [*temp.* Elizabeth] the majority of whose plans are not hatched, although not devoid of colour.'[1]

Of drawings probably dating from the fourteenth century the most remarkable is the series illustrating the west front and one of the west towers of Cologne Cathe- dral, drawn to a scale of 4 or 5 ft. to the inch in ink on a sheet of parchment nearly 10 ft. long and a yard wide.

[1] Burges, *op. cit.*

Besides two plans of the tower at different levels, half the front and the whole of one tower are represented in elevation showing every detail with the utmost care. Fortunately these plans have been carefully traced and reproduced in facsimile on nine sheets of plates in an album, a copy of which is to be found in the R. I. B. A. Library in London.[1] The original, according to Baedeker's guide-book, is preserved in a massive oak frame in St. John's Chapel in the choir of the cathedral. Other fine German drawings which may reasonably be attributed to the same century are those of a church tower at Carlsruhe ;[2] of a plan of another tower ;[3] of the elevation of a church tower (probably at Thann near Colmar) ;[4] and an interior elevation of the cathedral at Ulm, signed by Ulrich Ensiger or Ensinger, who was architect of the cathedral in 1392-5. All these are illustrated by Moller.[5]

Among Italian examples of the fourteenth century, first place must be given to the five remarkable drawings preserved in the Opera del Duomo at Siena, which I have recently had an opportunity of examining. Unfortunately I found it impossible to obtain photographs of the most striking of these, nor can I find that they have been reproduced elsewhere. One of them is a competition plan (*concorso*) made in 1339 for the enlargement of the cathedral, according to the label on the drawing, and may be the work of Lando di Pietro. It is drawn in brown ink, apparently to a scale of about 10 feet to 1 inch, and shows all the vaulting. A few dimensions are indicated. There is another plan in the collection, similar in general

[1] Moller, G., *Facsimile der Originalzeichnung des Domes zu Koln*. (Darmstadt, 1837.)

[2] Moller, G., *Denkmaehler der deutschen Baukunst*, Plate 53. (Darmstadt, 1821.) [3] *Ibid*. Plate 47.

[4] *Ibid*. Plate 48. [5] See *Dict. of A. P. S.* s.v. ' Drawing '.

appearance to the one just described, but drawn to a slightly smaller scale with the vaulting lines delineated in red ink. A third drawing is described on the label as a design for the north façade of the Cathedral by Jacopo del Pellicciaio in 1384, and in Bertarelli's latest guide-book as a design by Jacopo del Mino for the façade of the Baptistery in 1382. It measures about 4 feet high, and is accurately finished in brown and red ink and wash. All the ornament is most carefully indicated, but the method of projection adopted is not perfectly elevational in the case of the great porches, which are drawn slightly in perspective to produce an effect of relief. Another drawing represents ' a design for the Cappella del Campo by Jacopo del Pellicciaio, 1350 ', and resembles the last-named as regards methods of presentation except that in this case strictly orthographic projection is used. But the most important drawing of all, a really astounding testimony to medieval draughtsmanship, is the ' design for the campanile of the Duomo by Lando di Pietro, 1339 '. Bertarelli explains that ' some regard this as Giotto's design for the campanile at Florence, others as a design by Michele di Landro for the campanile at Siena, in substitution for that now existing which was demolished as part of the scheme for a great new cathedral '. (My translation.) In any case, it is a most beautiful drawing, measuring nearly 7 feet high and about a foot wide, probably to a scale of about 4 feet to 1 inch. It is in strict orthographic projection, drawn with instruments in brown ink, slightly rendered to indicate relief, and coloured to show the natural tints of the marble facing. The whole of the statuary and the ornament is accurately shown. Unless this drawing is a forgery that has deceived all the critics, it supplies a complete answer to those who deny the existence of medieval plans. Sir Reginald Blomfield writes of two elevations on the west front of Orvieto Cathedral, that they are

' supposed to have been made by Lorenzo del Maitano of Siena soon after 1310, when he was appointed *capo-maestro* of the Duomo. These drawings, which were not carried out, are not really working drawings, inasmuch as they are set out in slight perspective, which, though not correct, is near enough to make one doubt whether they can be as early as 1310, and one's suspicions are heightened by the precision of the draughtsmanship and the fine drawings of the figures in the tympanum of the central archway.' [1]

Models also were used in Italy at this period ; thus Giotto made a model for the *campanile* at Florence, indicating on it the various sculpture and decorative details.[2]

From the beginning of the fifteenth century to the end of the Middle Ages a number of fine architectural working drawings have survived. Among English examples may be mentioned those of King's College Chapel, Cambridge, now preserved in the British Museum ; [3] the design for a gallery for Henry VIII,[4] and another design for the tomb of Henry VI which Henry VII intended to erect at Windsor,[5] these drawings also being at the British Museum ; a drawing of the old steeple (pulled down in 1421) of St. Michael's, Cornhill ; [6] and several others mentioned in the article on ' Drawing ' in the *Dictionary of the Architectural Publication Society*. But the German drawings form a really wonderful collection.

---

[1] Blomfield, *Architectural Drawing and Draughtsmen*, p. 12. (London, 1912.)

[2] Vasari, *op. cit.*   [3] Cottonian MSS. Aug. 1, vol. i. 2.

[4] *Ibid.*, vol. i. 4.

[5] *Ibid.*, Aug. 2, vol. i, also illustrated in Burges, *op. cit.*

[6] Illustrated in *Londina Illustrata* (1819).

FIG. 12. DETAIL OF PRINCIPAL PORCH, REGENSBURG CATHEDRAL

From a drawing of the XVth century

Their excellence may be inferred from Fig. 12, which represents a sketch design for the main portal of Regensburg (Ratisbon) Cathedral, and is typical of its period. Preserved in the Academy of Fine Art at Vienna, it is ascribed to the second half of the fifteenth century and is beautifully drawn in ink on a piece of parchment measuring 137·1 × 56·4 cm., consisting of two sheets pasted together. This was a usual practice where large sheets were required. Every detail of the mouldings, carved ornament, &c., is most carefully drawn, indicating that very little can have been left to the individual taste of the craftsmen.[1] There is a magnificent set of several drawings for St. Stephen's, Vienna, in the same collection ;[2] a design for the façade of a Rathhaus ;[3] an elevation of the towers of Freiburg Cathedral ;[4] and some highly finished detail drawings of a tabernacle in plan and elevation.[5] Comparable in excellence with these are two sets of designs for tabernacles reproduced by Moller, one of these being signed by the artist.[6] Every one of these drawings shows great skill in draughtsmanship, nothing is left in doubt, and the system of projection is in exact accordance with modern practice.

The whole question of architectural drawing has been treated somewhat fully here, and with plentiful references, as I wish to enable readers to prove to their own satisfaction that my statement that plans were used in the Middle Ages is founded on ascertainable facts. It is possible to strengthen the evidence from French and Belgian sources.[7] and there may be a few medieval plans

[1] H. Egger, *Architektonische Handzeichnungen alter Meister*, Plate 3. 'Vienna, N.D.)   [2] *Ibid*. Plate 4.
[3] *Ibid*. Plate 4.   [4] *Ibid*. Plate 2.   [5] *Ibid*. Plate 1.
[6] Moller, *Denkmähler*, &c., Plates 60, 61, and 66–70.
[7] *Dict. A.P.S.* s.v. ' Drawing '.

preserved in Spain.[1] There are also records of what we now call ' full-size details ' of mouldings and other ornamental features.

But, in addition to plans, the architect made use of a detailed specification (*devis*), on which the contract was based ; and sometimes he prepared preliminary estimates of cost. A design was frequently made to form an integral part of a building agreement or other similar document. Thus in 1451 one Guillermo Vilasolar was appointed *lapicida et magister fabricae* at Salamanca Cathedral, and one clause in his agreement provided that he should execute ' within the next coming year ' the tracery, &c., of six stone windows ' according to the design which I have delivered to you ', this master providing all the plant, tools, labour, and material required. For this work he was paid fifty pounds down, the balance of two hundred and eighty pounds being payable on completion.[2]

The contract made by Maestro Giorgio Orsini of Sebenico in 1450 with the Anziani for their Loggia dei Mercanti at Ancona was based on a preliminary design, and Orsini covenanted to ' make in the fashion shown on his drawing the statues carved life-size, with the horse great and fine, and with the arms of the *comune* in the places drawn on the said paper '.[3]

Street mentions one case where two Spanish architects were severely rated by their employers for departing from the agreed plans.

The common view that design was purely traditional, and that ideas were never borrowed from abroad, is disproved by a whole host of authenticated instances. The medieval architect certainly did not reproduce bygone

---

[1] Street, *op. cit.* ii. 273.   [2] *Ibid.* ii. 270–1.
[3] Albertini, *Cronaca Anconitana.*

' styles ' from copybooks, as we too often do and as architects have done from the sixteenth century onwards. His
mind was receptive rather than retrospective, and he
welcomed and experimented with new ideas as they came.
Sir Reginald Blomfield says that the workman, ' with an
immemorial tradition behind him ', would have no difficulty in interpreting general directions given to him by
his chief, without the need for detailed drawings, ' and
though he might modify his detail here and there, and
perhaps introduce some fancy of his own, he would not
conceive of the possibility of serious deviation from a
well-marked path '.[1] Though this statement contains
a measure of truth, I am inclined to think that the position
is more clearly defined by M. Stein :

' C'étaient des cas très rares que ceux où l'architecte nouveau,
abdiquant toute originalité, se bornait à copier les molles de
ses davanciers et à adopter pour le nef, par exemple, les plans
et les formes du chœur tracées par sa prédécesseur : au
contraire, on voit plutôt ces monuments conserver la marque
des diverses époques auxquelles se rapporte chacune de leurs
parties.' [2]

The sketch-book of Villard de Honnecourt (p. 93) affords
the most conclusive proof that architects even travelled
abroad with the express purpose of gleaning new ideas.

Nor is this our only evidence. Assuming that the architect or master-mason of Westminster Abbey was not a
Frenchman (and this Professor Lethaby seems to have
effectually decided), at all events it is probable that he
borrowed features from contemporary French architecture ; [3] while at Canterbury, long before, a French architect, William of Sens, was imported to design the new

---

[1] Blomfield, *Architectural Drawing and Draughtsmen*, p. 17.
[2] Stein, *op. cit.*, p. 39. [3] T. G. Jackson, *op. cit.* i. 272.

cathedral on the strength of the reputation that he had made for himself as an architect in his native land. Other master-masons were sent by their employers to sketch and borrow features from celebrated churches for use in their own buildings.

In 1220 Beaulieu Abbey asked for a safe-conduct for a French mason to build their apse, no doubt because the English masons could not manage the problems of vaulting.[1] And in 1414 the cathedral authorities at Valencia agreed that Pedro Balaguer, ' an architect ', should receive fifty florins from the fabric funds ' in payment of his expenses on the journey which he made to Lérida, Narbonne [in France], and other cities, in order to see and examine their towers and campaniles, so as to imitate from them the most elegant and fit form for the cathedral of Valencia '.[2] Conversely, architects from France found employment in most of the civilized countries of that time, including England, Italy, Spain, Bohemia, Hungary, Sicily, Sweden, Germany, Flanders, Cyprus, and the Holy Land. The pages of Street's book contain frequent references to the direct or indirect influence of French architects in Spain, and also mention the work of German, Italian, and perhaps even English masters there. Both Stein[3] and De Mély[4] print long lists of the French architects who obtained work abroad, this exodus continuing up to the end of the fourteenth century, after which it practically ceased.

In Italy, as early as 1026, the Bishop of Arezzo gave a sum of money to his architect to enable him to visit Ravenna and make a study of the monuments there with a view to introducing new ideas at Arezzo.

---

[1] Prior, *Cathedral Builders*, p. 64 *n*.   [2] Street, *op. cit.* ii, p. 8.
[3] Stein, *op. cit.*, pp. 103–16.   [4] De Mély, *op. cit.*, pp. 357–9.

The fifth ' fallacy ' mentioned at the beginning of this chapter, that the medieval mason was content to work for the glory of God alone, is probably due to the exaggerations of monkish chroniclers. A recent writer [1] has partially exploded this belief by stating that ' It is astonishing how few medieval documents testify directly to the artist's love of his work '. The medieval craftsman had no newspapers or ' class-consciousness ' to make him discontented ; none the less he was a human being, with the usual failings of his kind. The fact is that building in the Middle Ages was marred by many of the difficulties that beset us to-day. The craftsmen indeed worked very long hours, and they may have had fewer causes for grumbling because their horizon was, perforce, narrow. But they worked to con- tract ; they were summoned to work by a church-bell instead of a foreman's whistle ; they were fined for being late, for quarrelling, idling, losing their tools, and obstruct- ing other workmen. Wyclif says [2] of certain masons that

' . . . they conspire together that no man shall take less for a day than they fix, though they should by good conscience take much less, that none of them shall do good steady work which might interfere with other men of the craft, and that none of them shall do anything but cut stone, though he might profit his master twenty pounds by one day's work in laying a wall, without harm to himself.'

Nor were these shortcomings confined entirely to the lower ranks of labour. Thus, about the year 1200, the Abbot of St. Albans assembled

' a number of chosen *cementarii*, of whom Master Hugo de Goldcliff was the chief, a clever but deceitful workman (*artifex*) '. . . . ' It happened by the design of the said Hugh, in addition to stealth, fraud, impertinence, and above all,

---

[1] Coulton, *Social Life in Britain*, p. 466.   [2] *Ibid.*, p. 491.

extravagance, before the average of the work [the front wall of the abbey church] had risen to the boarded shed, the abbot grew tired, weary, and timid, and the work languished—the walls were covered up for the winter—they became fractured and fell with their own weight, so that the wreck of images and flowers became the laughing stock of beholders. The workmen therefore quitted in despair, nor did any wages reward their labours.'[1]

William of Colchester (who moved from Westminster Abbey after fifteen years work there to become master-mason at York in 1415, and designed the central tower of the Minster), in 1419, had to write a letter asking for the king's protection against

'certain stone-cutters, or masons,' who, ' being moved by a most wicked spirit of envy, wickedly conspiring for the death and ultimate destruction of M. William Colchester ' . . . treacherously assaulting the said William, did grievously wound him, and did so injure another person, his assistant, that his life is considered in serious danger.'[2]

Street tells a good story about the building of the beautiful bridge of St. Martin at Toledo about 1212.

' The architect, whilst the work was going on, perceived that as soon as the centres were removed the arches would fall, and confided his grief to his wife. She with woman's wit forthwith set fire to the centring, and when the whole fell together all the world attributed the calamity to the accident of the fire. After the bridge had been rebuilt again she avowed her proceeding, but Archbishop Tenorio, instead of making her husband pay the expenses, seems to have confined himself to complimenting him on the treasure he possessed in his wife.'[3]

I have quoted these trivial incidents here merely to emphasize that men and women were human beings,

[1] Papworth, *op. cit.* 208.   [2] *Ibid.* 215.
[3] Street, *op. cit.* i. 323 *n*.

even in the Middle Ages. If the result is a slight dent in the craftsman's halo, that does not prevent us admiring him for his undoubted enthusiasm and the splendour of his achievement.

The next misapprehension is that the architect was either a monk or a lay-brother attached to a monastery. In some cases he certainly was, but as often as not he was a layman, and was therefore ignored by clerical historians. The king's masons, for instance, were all laymen ; [1] and so also in many other instances. In a list of 137 Spanish architects, sculptors, and builders, from 1129 onwards, Street says [2] that nearly all were laymen and in independent practice. A typical example of the readiness of critics to style a cleric an ' architect ' occurs in the case of St. Hugh of Lincoln, of whom the chronicler merely says : [3] ' With wondrous skill he built [*construit*] the fabric of the Cathedral ; whereunto he supplied not only his own wealth, but even the sweat of his own brow ; for he oftentimes bore the hod-load of hewn stone or of building lime.' Can any cautious reader accept this as authentic evidence that St. Hugh actually designed Lincoln Cathedral, as he is often credited with doing ? Yet so little is recorded of Richard of Gainsborough, the master-mason whose effigy at Lincoln is illustrated on Fig. 16, that Professor Hamilton Thompson can only state that ' there is little doubt that he was the master under whom the Angel choir . . . was brought to completion '.[4]

In any building enterprise where a cathedral was concerned, the bishop appears to have occupied the position of a patron, or he may have instigated the undertaking :

[1] Jackson, *op. cit*. i. 267.　　　[2] Street, *op. cit*. ii. 265, 276–7.
[3] Coulton, *op. cit*. 272.
[4] Hamilton Thompson, *Cathedral Churches of England*, p. 140.

the actual conduct of operations was usually entrusted to
the dean and chapter. In the early Middle Ages, when
monasteries formed the chief centres of technical training
as well as of culture, it is natural that they played an active
and even predominant part in architectural work. Rivoira
mentions several men whom he regards as genuine clerical
architects, e. g., Hezzel, a monk formerly a canon of
Liége, who is said to have designed the abbey-church of
Cluny begun in 1089 ; [1] and William of Volpiano (961–
1031), a Benedictine monk born in Italy, whom he regards
as one of the chief originators of Romanesque or ' Norman'
architecture. To this man Rivoira attributes the abbey
of Fruttuaria in Piedmont (1003–6) ; the abbey of
St. Benignus at Dijon which was built 1002–18 (' . . . et
reverendus Abbas, magistros conducendo, et ipsum opus
dictando . . . ') ; and the abbey of Bernay in Normandy,
dedicated in 1013 (' . . . Haec enim auctore Guillelmo
abbate Fiscaunensi qui in locandis fundamentis non modi-
cum praestiterat consilii auxilium . . . ').[2] Yet even this
case is questioned by Professor Hamilton Thompson,
who says—' although he knew the sort of church he
wanted, and the kind of plan that would have to be followed
it did not follow that his ordering or direction of the work
went beyond general directions '. The same authority
cites the similar case of Gauzlin, Abbot of Fleury from
1025–9, who, ' when asked by the chief artificer what kind
of building he wanted, replied : " Such a building as
shall be a model to the whole of Gaul." (*Tale, inquit,
quod omni Gallie sit in exemplo.*) General directions of this
kind would not deprive a chief artificer of his initiative '.[3]

[1] Rivoira, *Lombardic Architecture*, ii. 104, 109.
[2] *Ibid.* ii. 30, 45–6, 67.
[3] Lecture to the Royal Archaeological Institute. Reported in
The Builder, 10 April 1925.

After comparing the views of several writers, of whom some would give all credit to the clerical architect and others none at all, I am disposed to follow the lead of M. Mortet, who has well described the position at the beginning of the Middle Ages in France, when clerical activity in architecture was most pronounced. He states that architects and other artists concerned in the building of monastic churches and other conventual buildings were to be found in the monasteries, especially in those of the Cluniac order at first, and of the Cistercian order later. There they drew up the rules of their art, the forms of which retained a traditional character as they developed. The importance of the various monasteries as centres of building activity varied greatly.

Sometimes one finds that the skill of certain serfs as craftsmen led to their being freed, e. g. at St. Aubin at Angers about the end of the eleventh century an artisan of that rank became a ' convert ' (*convers*) or ' lay-brother ' in recognition of some mural painting that he had done in the monastery. Art was regarded in those days as a branch of general education ; hence it is not surprising to find architecture flourishing in monasteries, where, among other subjects, hydraulics and military engineering (or architecture) were studied. The monks acquired such a reputation in these branches that they were often called out from their monasteries to erect a cathedral, e. g. Le Mans, or some other building, or to execute a tomb or a painting.

Much more rare are instances of *secular* canons undertaking building work on their own cathedrals, but Coutances is a case in point. At Auxerre they carried out the sculpture, paintings, and stained-glass ; at Avignon they taught the clergy how to paint, and encouraged the crafts of carving in marble, stone, and wood.

But the name of the lay-architect occurs frequently in documents of even these early days, as being in the service of monasteries, cathedrals, collegiate churches, priories, and seignories. Coming generally from the monastic schools, or from the cathedral or seignorial schools, the *maîtres d'œuvre* undertook contracts for either ecclesiastical or civil bodies. Thus we find them building churches, monasteries, fortresses, castles, and bridges. M. Mortet prints two interesting agreements between ecclesiastical bodies and lay-architects in support of his argument.

As time went on, we find that, outside the monasteries, where the services of the builder and architect were now less in demand, the architect or master-mason had established his position, and his status had increased in importance. Art had become *more personal* and was progressing rapidly. Traditions were changing; schools of architecture tended to develop on different lines. Study and technical training became more and more a matter of emulation and individual interest. But the monastic (or regular) and secular clergy by no means opposed this lay movement; they actually encouraged and took advantage of it. Even in the twelfth century the clergy constantly utilized lay help for the erection of their great stone buildings. Thus Suger appealed to architects and artists of all kinds from far afield to help him at St. Denis, at Canterbury William of Sens was selected from numerous French and English architects who offered consulting opinions, and at Andrès near Boulogne the abbot invited outsiders to beautify his church.[1]

I have translated and paraphrased these passages from M. Mortet's work at some length, because they seem to me to state the case for the monkish architect more fairly

[1] Mortet, *op. cit.*, pp. liii-lxxiii.

and more temperately than I have seen it stated elsewhere. But Professor Prior also gives us a very balanced judgement on this vexed question when he says that : ' . . . in the early Middle Ages the sanctity of the building craft was undoubted, . . . the early missionizing ecclesiastics undertook building as part of their pioneer work. . . . '[1] and, elsewhere, that by the end of the twelfth century the

' demand for skilled masonry had now created a craft of masons not directly amenable to ecclesiastical discipline, and these began to take the matter out of the hands of the church. In his education of the mason the ecclesiastic was gradually parting with that control of the form and spirit of art, which in the early times had been part of his missionary propaganda.' [2]

Briefly, we may safely conclude that monastic influence in architecture was all-powerful in France in the years preceding the Norman Conquest of England, and in the following century both in this country and abroad, but that in Italy laymen dominated the situation from the beginning ; that the middle of the twelfth century ($c.$ 1130–70) ' witnessed the gradual transfer of supremacy in architecture from monastic hands to the newly-risen class of lay artists ;'[3] that from $c.$ 1150–1250 the cathedrals of Northern Europe were mostly designed by men trained in the monasteries ; that, after that date, the importance of the monkish architect has been grossly exaggerated; and that the layman, whose appearance we have noted at a comparatively early stage, improved his position progressively as the centuries passed.

But, as we now reach the seventh delusion under which so many people have long laboured, that the medieval

---

[1] Prior, *Cathedral Builders*, p. 57.   [2] *Ibid.*, p. 38.
[3] A. L. Frothingham, *The Architect in History during the Dark Ages*, pp. 144–52.

architect received his training solely at the bench and not
in a school or office, we are constrained to award honour
where it is due and to admit that the monasteries not only
encouraged and practised admirable architecture throughout the Middle Ages but that they were largely responsible,
in the early centuries, for the training even of those laymen
who carried on what we call ' private practice ' in later
life.   Education was at that time so much in their hands
that it would be churlish to minimize or deny the debt that
we, as architects, owe to them.

A large part of the medieval architect's work being
masonry, he would naturally have to acquire an extensive
practical knowledge of that craft at the bench, but we may
also assume that he studied geometry in the ' tracyng
house ' or in the monastery cloister.   If Villard de Honnecourt is at all typical of his time, we can safely infer that,
either in the monastery or under some able lay architect,
he became a talented draughtsman of figures and ornament, and that he was also well versed in geometry and
mechanics.   He was a well-educated man, according to
medieval standards, understood Latin, and could write
neatly.   We may even infer that an architectural student
of those days was expected to travel and sketch, so far
as circumstances then permitted.   But it may startle some
people to know that he may have actually studied Vitruvius.
At any rate, Eginhard, Charlemagne's private secretary, did
so, and he refers to a model constructed by Eigil of Fulda
to illustrate a point in the text of that author.   ' Even as
late as 1100 we find a monk at Monte Cassino making a
compendium of Vitruvius for the study of the local school.'[1]

The eighth point to be discussed relates to the common
belief that the architect worked on only one ' job ' at

[1] Frothingham, *op. cit.*, p. 68.

a time, and resided on or near the building until it was completed. That fallacy also contains a measure of truth ; but, on the other hand, it does not apply universally. A modern general practice would be impossible without the post, the telephone and modern transport facilities. Medieval conditions therefore favoured the appointment of a resident architect, but there are many instances of men who undertook several commissions simultaneously, and of others who acted as consultants or specialists. Thus the architects of the great fan-vaults at Windsor and Westminster were appointed because of the reputation they had acquired at Bath.[1] Lorenzo Maitano was appointed master-builder at Orvieto in 1310, but remained in Siena, his native place, and did not move to Orvieto till 20 years later, when the cathedral must have been far advanced, having carried out work at Perugia, Todi, and Siena in the meantime.[2] In 1499 Martin de Chambiges was called to Paris as a consultant by Jean de Soissons, who paid him a fee for advice on the façade of the cathedral at Troyes.[3] The architect of Salisbury spire was paid a regular salary for his work there, though at the time of his appointment he was already engaged on work at Bath and Reading. The agreement with him, dated 1334, stipulated that, ' he should repair thither and make such stay as the necessity or nature of the fabric shall require ; and that, notwithstanding his prior obligations at Bath and Reading, he should not neglect or delay the works of the church '.[4] In England the architect was usually resident up to the thirteenth century, but not necessarily so in later periods.[5] The master-mason at

[1] Jackson, *op. cit.* ii. 110.
[2] Sturgis, *Dictionary of Architecture*, s.v. ' Architect '.
[3] Berty, *Les Grands Architectes de France*, p. 139.
[4] Papworth, *op. cit.* 209.   [5] Prior, *op. cit.* 59.

Kirby Muxloe Castle, 1481–3, ' visited it only from time to time. When he came he brought his apprentice and stayed for two or three weeks ; when he left, he put the work in charge of another mason known as the warden, who in these intervals was responsible to the clerk of the works and his comptroller '.[1]   In France, whereas each cathedral normally employed a permanent resident architect, smaller churches were content to dispense with the cost of his maintenance, and called in some master from a neighbouring building when expert advice was required. But as the salary and pension of a cathedral architect was often ridiculously small, sometimes no more than a sort of retaining fee, he usually sought to enlarge his income by undertaking other building work or by acting as a consultant.   He therefore had to leave as deputy in his place some representative of slightly inferior rank.   A few examples of this practice may be cited.   The celebrated Raymond du Temple, though architect both to the King of France and (from 1363 to 1404) to the cathedral of Paris, often slipped away from these two exacting posts to go into the provinces as a consultant, leaving an assistant in his place.   The same thing happened at Chartres early in the fourteenth century.   Pons Gaspar, architect of Mende Cathedral in the fifteenth century, did not reside in the town, but undertook to visit the cathedral work then in progress as occasion demanded ; it seems that his visits were infrequent, and that he trusted largely to a subordinate.   The mere fact that the architect often had to sign an agreement to devote his full time to the service of a royal or ecclesiastical master shows that otherwise he would undertake private practice.[2]

---

[1] Hamilton Thompson, *Cathedral Churches of England*, p. 142.
[2] On this see Stein, *Les Architectes des cathédrales gothiques*, 27–35.

Spain provides us with similar instances. Thus, about 1320–5 Jacopo de Favariis of Narbonne was appointed architect of the cathedral at Gerona on condition that he should come from Narbonne six times a year to examine the work. For this he was to have a salary of 250 *libras* a quarter.[1] A nearly contemporary case from Barcelona Cathedral has already been cited (p. 71). The Mole at Barcelona is said to have been built by Estacio, a famous ' hydraulic architect ' of Alexandria, in 1477 ; and the city authorities took counsel about it with ' the most learned professors of Syracuse, Rhodes, and Candia '.[2]

A particularly interesting aspect of professional work is revealed by the references in old Spanish documents to a *Junta* or consultative committee of eminent architects, established on several occasions to advise ecclesiastical or other bodies in cases of extreme difficulty. Three instances are given by Street. In 1416 a Junta of twelve architects was called together by the Chapter of Gerona Cathedral, and each member was asked separately for his views on the following points : (*a*) whether the nave of the cathedral (' commenced of old ') could safely be continued ; (*b*) if not, whether a nave with aisles would meet the case, or whether some other system should be adopted ; and (*c*) how the new nave, in whatever form was recommended, would best harmonize with the apse or *chevet* already completed with its chapels. The opinions of the experts were given on oath, and six months after the Chapter had considered the whole report in detail the ' Master of the Works ' was called in and asked to answer the same three questions. Two of the twelve architects had previously been appointed to collate the various opinions and draft a scheme. A week later, ' at a chapter-

[1] Street, *op. cit.* ii. 93. [2] *Ibid.* ii. 85.

meeting presided over by the Bishop, it was decided to carry on the ' work as proposed '. Street prints the whole of this lengthy report, of which he translates a part, and says that it ' equals in interest any with which I am acquainted, bearing on the profession of architect in the middle ages '.[1]

In the next case two architects who had been commissioned to prepare jointly a plan for the cathedral at Salamanca failed to agree on a point of dimensions. After the dispute had dragged on for some time, the Bishop and Chapter appointed in 1512 a Junta of nine architects, including one of the cathedral architects (the other having died in the meantime), and they eventually issued a joint report including a dimensioned plan and full details as to the methods of construction to be adopted. It is interesting to note that they were unanimous in their opinions, which were given on oath. Street prints this document also in full.[2]

The third case occurred at Zaragoza Cathedral in 1500, where there was some danger of the old Cimborio falling. The Archbishop appointed a Junta of five ' artificers and skilled engineers ' to advise him. After consulting with the cathedral architect, they presented a report in due course, and five years later one of the five experts was appointed to carry out the work thus recommended.[3]

There are occasional references to architectural competitions in Spain, of which Street mentions three, but of these he doubts the most important—the alleged competition among several architects for the building of Segovia Cathedral in 1522. The other two relate to a tomb and an iron screen respectively, not to whole

[1] Street, *op. cit.* i. 103, 106, and ii. 299–306.
[2] *Ibid.* ii. 94, 99–100, 319–33.   [3] *Ibid.* ii. 166.

FIG. 13. PORTRAIT OF EUDES DE MONTREUIL

Engraved from a XIIIth-century grave-slab, now destroyed,
in Thevet's ' Pourtraits et Vies ' (1584)

buildings, and may thus be compared to the famous competition for the bronze doors at Florence.[1] In 1355,
according to Vasari, the commune of Florence organized
an architectural competition for the lay-out of the Piazza
della Signoria, and from several designs submitted selected
that by Orcagna.[2]

And now we reach the last of the nine ' fallacies '
enumerated at the beginning of this long chapter, that the
medieval architect gloried in his anonymity. On this
point, as on many others, critics have often neglected to
reckon with human nature. There is nothing in his work
more galling to a modern architect than public indifference
to the authorship of some important building that he has
designed. Often he picks up his newspaper, on the morning after a great town-hall or hospital has been formally
opened, to find that though the speeches and dresses of
the bigwigs and profiteers who were present are chronicled
in detail, though a blurred picture of the Lord Mayor's
youngest daughter presenting a bouquet to Her Royal High-
ness defaces the last page, his own name is omitted. Are we
to believe that a medieval architect was immune from any
desire for reasonable recognition of good work well done ?

M. de Mély ridicules this assumption of inhuman
humility. He says that on occasion the medieval masters
claimed to have surpassed the marvels of antiquity, that
Natalis d'Autry-Issard, for example, regarded himself as
the rival (*l'émule*) of God ; just as painters like John of
Brunswick compared themselves to gods, and as Ingobert
said that he was equal and even superior to the painters
of Ausonia.[3]

Another French writer [4] prefaces his study of the

[1] *Ibid*. ii. 275. [2] Vasari, i. 211.
[3] De Mély, *op. cit*. 360. [4] Stein, *op. cit*. 5.

medieval architects of the French cathedrals with some
satirical reflections on the mental attitude of visitors to
great picture-galleries, pointing out that ' the more the
name of the artist is familiar to you, the more your
admiration increases ',

' Le public est attiré par un Rembrandt ou un Carpeaux,
non parce que les sujets représentés parlent à son âme ou
frappent sa mémoire, mais bien parce que le cartouche délicate-
ment posé à son intention par l'administration signale à son
attention un Rembrandt ou un Carpeaux. Par un phénomène
réflexe, les œuvres d'inconnus n'ont pas le don de piquer
la curiosité. . . .'

I have already explained why it is that the authorship of
so many medieval buildings, has been wrongly attributed
to ecclesiastical patrons and official paymasters, and that
the jealousy or indifference of monkish scribes is the usual
reason. As a result modern scholars have come to ignore
any significance in the legend *fecit* applied to a building,
relying on documentary evidence to show whether the
man who claims to have made it was the actual architect
or not. They agree, too, in calling the architect by his
modern name where the fact of authorship is established,
regardless of the title—monk or canon, master-of-the-
works or master-mason, *lathomus* or *ingeniator*—that is
applied to him by the old documents.

Yet in spite of all that we have lost by neglect, care-
lessness, jealousy, and fire, the number of names of
medieval architects that we now know for certain is
surprising. De Mély makes the astounding statement
that no less than *twenty-five thousand* names have been
preserved from the Middle Ages.[1] He records over

---

[1] De Mély, *op. cit.* 95. (It is not quite clear whether this number
includes painters and miniaturists.)

500 architects' names in France alone, after having sifted out from the list all those whose claims he considers ill-founded, and also some fifteen ' clerical ' architects. Papworth, writing more than sixty years ago, mentions the names of about 300 officials connected with English buildings, and adds that these are not ' a tithe ' of those available.[1] In the Introduction to the Historical Commission's monograph (1924) on Westminster Abbey, after stating that records prove the falsity of the common belief, that the architects of our great medieval churches are nameless, Dr. M. R. James says that in the case of Westminster recent investigations ' enable us to name, and in some degree to visualize, the whole line of the men who presided over the building from its inception '. Street, whose book is now over fifty years old, gives the names of nearly 100 architects or masters-of-the works in Spain.[2] When we remember that Germany and Italy, besides less important countries, are not included in these figures (though both have preserved lists of names) and that recent scholarship has greatly extended our knowledge of this subject, we may safely conclude that—in spite of their supposed anonymity—the medieval architects of Europe may be numbered nowadays not only by the hundred but by the thousand.

Besides documentary evidence, of which I have already said enough, we have carven records of various architects in various forms. Figs. 14 and 15 represent two fine tomb-slabs to the memory of Master Hugh Libergier (d. 1263) at St. Nicaise, Rheims, and Master William de Wermington at Croyland Abbey respectively. Fig. 16, reproduced from a recent measured drawing of my own, illustrates what is, so far as I know, the most interesting

[1] Papworth, *op. cit.* 216.   [2] Street, *op. cit.* ii. 285–99.

FIG. 14.   TOMB-SLAB AT ST. NICAISE, RHEIMS,
in memory of Hugh Libergier (d. 1263), architect of the church
Drawn by M. S. Briggs from a photograph
(The inscription reads:—' ✠ CI GIT MAISTRE HVES · LIBERGIERS · QVI·
COMENSA · CESTE · EGLISE · EN LAN · DE · LINCARNATION · M·CCXXX·IX ·
LE MARDI · DE · PAQVES ✠ TRESPASSA · LAN DE · LINCARNATION MCC·LXIII·
LE SEMEDI · APRES PAQVES · POVR · DEV · P[R]IEZ · PO[V]R LVI ✠ ').

FIG. 15. TOMB-SLAB OF MASTER WILLIAM DE WERMINGTON AT
CROYLAND ABBEY

Drawn by M. S. Briggs from an engraving in Le Boeuf's *Croyland
Abbey*

(The inscription reads :—' ICI : GIST : MESTRE : WILLM̃ : DE : WERMIG-
TON : LE : MASON : A : LALME : DE : KY : DEV . . . Y : P : SA : GRACE :
DOUNEZ : ABSOLUCION '.)

effigy of a master-mason in England. Richard of Gainsborough was, according to Professor Hamilton Thompson,
' evidently a man of position and substance ' . . . ' There
can be little doubt that he was the master under whom
the Angel choir of the cathedral [Lincoln] was brought
to completion, and it is probable that the alleys of the
cloister, with their traceried windows and wooden vaulting
of the last years of the thirteenth century, were of his
design '.   Sir Thomas Jackson describes him quite
definitely as the ' architect of Lincoln Cathedral '.[1]   The
inscription reads : ' HIC IACET RICARDVS . DE . GAYNS-
BVRGH . OLYM . CEMENTARIVS . ISTIVS . ECLESI[A]E . QVI .
OBIIT . DVODECIM . KALENDARVM . IVNII . ANNO . DOMINI .
MCCC.'   The drawing is composite, having been made from
the original tomb-slab now fixed vertically on the cloister
wall, from a plaster cast evidently made many years ago
before the slab had been so much defaced by traffic as
it is now, and from a modern floor slab about 40 years
old which has taken the place of the original but has
already become much worn.   The portions of my drawing
between the lines ABC and DD are taken from the original
and the cast, the remainder of the inscription from the
cast and the modern slab but apparently authentic, the
upper canopy-work and the lower part of the figure from
the modern slab which may be conjectural or from an old
drawing.   A mason's square is carved above the master's
right shoulder.   Other tomb-slabs are to be found at
Caudebec (where a plan of the church is engraved beside
the architect's effigy) ; to Pierre de Montreuil, *doctor latho-
morum*, architect of the Sainte Chapelle (d. 1254) at St.-
Germain des Près, Paris ; to Robert de Coucy (d. 1311) at
Rheims ; and to Conrad de Steinbach (d. 1329) at Nieder

[1] T. G. Jackson, *Architecture*, (London, 1925), p. 160.

FIG. 16.   TOMB-SLAB OF RICHARD OF GAINSBOROUGH, *cementarius*
(d. 1300), in the Cloisters at Lincoln Cathedral.   (See p. 120).
Measured and drawn by M. S. Briggs.

Haslach in Alsace. All these represent the architect in effigy, with the emblems of his craft and an inscription. There is said to be another at Châlons-sur-Marne, and two more of the thirteenth century are known to have been destroyed in Paris (one at Notre Dame to Jehan Raüy and another at the church of the Cordeliers to Eudes de Montreuil, but this last, which perished in 1580, has been preserved in a print by Thevet.) [1] See fig. 13 in this book.

At Strassburg is a fine statue of the architect Erwin de Steinbach (d. 1318) [2] and his reputed daughter ; at Winchester College Chapel Master William de Wynford is depicted in a stained glass window (cf. p. 84). In France there are inscribed tombstones of architects in Amiens, Clermont-Ferrand, and Metz Cathedrals, also at St. Ouen at Rouen, besides these mentioned with effigies.[3] At both Melrose and Paisley abbeys are quaint inscriptions by John Morow, who was architect of the rood-screen at Glasgow at the end of the fifteenth century (see fig. 17). In Spain there are similar memorials at Leon (*c.* 1066), Toledo (1290), and Segovia (1577).[4] In Rouen Cathedral the architect carved his name on the keystone of the vault ; other signatures are to be seen at Carenac, Elne, Moutiers, Saint Augustin-les-Limoges, and elsewhere. Sometimes he is commemorated by a monogram (as at Angoulême and Chartres) ; a chrono-gram (as at Brioude, Lisieux, Vaison, and Autry-Issard) ; a cryptogram (as at Névache and Cervières) ; or even by an enigmatic inscription composed of characters often mistaken for Arabic letters.[5] Italy possesses a very large

[1] De Mély, *op. cit.* passim. The effigy of Conrad de Steinbach is illustrated by De Mély.

[2] Illustrated in *La Renaissance*, 1919.

[3] De Mély, *op. cit.* passim.　　　　[4] Street, *op. cit.* i. 154, 258, 325.

[5] De Mély, *op. cit.* 361.

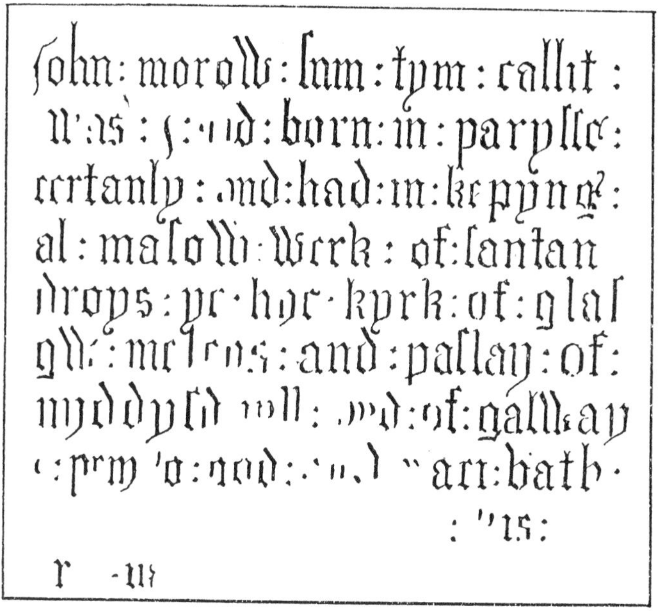

FIG. 17. INSCRIPTION IN MELROSE ABBEY TO JOHN MOROW OR MURRAY (d. 1485) MASTER-MASON (ARCHITECT) TO ST. ANDREWS, GLASGOW, MELROSE, PAISLEY, NITHSDALE, AND GALLOWAY.

Drawn by M. S. Briggs from Bell's *Glasgow*.

This inscription has suffered from the weather. It reads:

     ' JOHN : MOROW : SUM : TYM : CALLIT :
     WAS : I : AND : BORN : IN : PARYSSE :   [Paris]
     CERTANLY : AND : HAD : IN : KEPYNG :
     AL : MASOUN : WERK : OF : SANTAN   [St. Andrews]
     DROYS : YE : HYE : KYRK : OF : GLAS
     GOW : MELROS : AND : PASLAY : OF :
     NYDDYSDALE : AND : OF : GALWAY   [Galloway]
     I : PRAY : TO : GOD : AND : MARI : BATH :
     AND : SWEET : S : JOHN : KEP : THIS : DAY :
     KYRK : FRA : SKAITH.'

number of authenticated ascriptions carved on churches
and other buildings, from the eleventh century onwards,
e. g. at Pisa, and see fig. 8 ; and Portugal furnishes other
examples.[1] Incomplete as this short list is, it indicates
that the medieval architect was not always desirous of
concealing his identity.

In closing this study of his personality, it may be
repeated that an attempt has been made to restore to him
some of the credit that is his due. If, in qualifying
certain of the assertions made by prejudiced or careless
writers, some of the attractive mystery that surrounds
him has been removed, nothing can dispel the grandeur
of his achievement.   An age when architect and craftsmen worked in such close union that their identity is
almost indistinguishable has a lesson for us to-day, and
their buildings remain as an inspiration to us for all time.

.   .   .   .   .   .

In my book *Muhammadan Architecture in Egypt and
Palestine* I have related a few stories, probably legendary,
contained in the old chronicles of the Middle Ages.[2]
I reprint them here to enable readers to compare conditions in East and West, though it must be admitted that
they shed little light on the personalities of the Saracenic
architects or on the methods that they adopted in carrying
out their work.

The following two episodes are concerned with an
architect of the ninth century, who designed the great
mosque of Ibn Tulun at Cairo (*c.* 876–9) at a reputed cost
of £63,000. When Ibn Tulun, the amir or governor, was
informed that 300 columns would be required for his new

---

[1] See Frothingham, *op. cit.*, p. 145 *et seq.*

[2] M. S. Briggs, *Muhammadan Architecture*, &c., pp. 51, 56, 92–3,
107. (Oxford, 1924.)

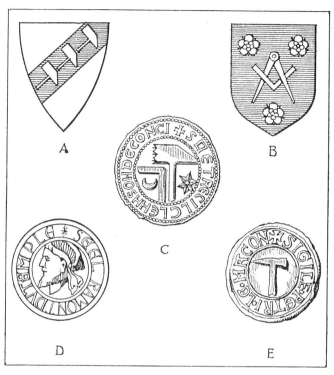

Fig. 18. Arms and seals of French master-masons, showing craft emblems, &c.

A. Conrad d'Obernhofen (arms of the corporation of master-masons of Strassburg 15th cent.) ; B. Robert Marquelet ; C. Gilles le Maçon (' s. metre gile le mason de conci ') ; D. Raymond du Temple ; E. Pierre le Maçon (' sigile petri le macon '). Drawn by M. S. Briggs after Lance, *Dictionnaire des Architectes français* (1872).

mosque if the ordinary method of construction were adopted, and that this would involve the destruction of a large number of provincial churches from which the Arabs rifled marble columns, he was very much troubled and declined to authorize the work. This difficulty came to the ears of Ibn Kathir al-Farghani, an unfortunate architect then languishing in prison. The governor had imprisoned him, and substituted 500 blows for a fee of 500 *dinars*, because a short time previously his horse had stumbled over a heap of mortar adjoining an aqueduct that this architect then had in hand for him. The prisoner saw in the amir's dilemma a chance of release. He wrote to Ibn Tulun and undertook to build him a mosque of the requisite size without employing a single column except the pair flanking the *mihrab*. He was brought before the governor and offered to draw a plan for him on the spot, if parchment could be brought to him. Ibn Tulun was surprised and delighted with the result, released the architect immediately, arrayed him in a rich robe, and paid him the sum of 100,000 *dinars* (over £50,000) to enable him to commence operations at once.

Should any reader of these pages be disposed to envy the architect's good fortune, it should be explained that he was master-builder as well as architect, so that this large sum of money was not by any means a fee for the design but rather a payment on account of the building. And at the price of a preliminary imprisonment to satisfy the whim of a cruel despot, it does not appear probable that the lot of a Cairo professional man in the ninth century was a happy one.

The second story also concerns Ibn Tulun. It is related that one day he was thoughtlessly toying with a piece of paper in the presence of his architect, that he was suddenly conscious of being observed in an act of frivolity ill-befitting so stern a ruler, and that he thereupon ordered the architect to take the spiral form that the paper had assumed in his hands as a model for the minaret of his new mosque. There is probably no truth in this legend, which may have been invented to explain the spiral form of the minaret in question, but it goes to prove that the forceful amir must have been a great trial to his professional advisers.

Towards the end of the eleventh century, the gates and a portion of the great walls of Cairo were reconstructed by three architect-brothers from Armenia. During the Crusades there was constant borrowing of ideas from Crusaders by Saracens and vice versa.

During the thirteenth and fourteenth centuries we find architects occasionally mentioned by Arab historians. Most of them seem to have been Turks or Tartars by birth. 'Abd al-Latif, a medieval chronicler, tells us how the architect drew his plans, or, more strictly speaking, how he ' set out ' the plan on the site :

' When any one wishes to erect a palace, house, or any other building, he sends for an architect. The latter then visits the site, thinks out in his mind how the site should be laid out and how the various parts of the building should be disposed to comply with the instructions he has received ; after that, he takes the various parts in turn, in order that each can be brought into use and inhabited as soon as it is finished without waiting for the whole to be completed. As one section is finished, he then takes in hand another, and so on, until the whole building is completely finished by uniting all the various parts, without any defects in the whole scheme, any wasted spaces, or any omissions that have to be remedied later.'

This somewhat prolix explanation does afford some

justification for the employment of an architect, and has not lost its value even to-day. Another paragraph from the same writer is interesting : ' The architect, with the help of a bag of plaster, marks out on the ground the boundaries and partition-walls of the building, according to the instructions of his client ; then the actual work of construction is begun.'

M. Gayet, an able critic, ridicules the possibility of setting out the complicated buildings of the medieval sultans by this rule of thumb method (which, after all, resembles our modern way of lining a tennis-court). He argues with reason that the extraordinary elaboration of the masonry throughout this period must have involved not only accurate and numerous drawings before building was commenced, but also a very thorough knowledge of geometry, in which the Arab mind has always excelled.

Lastly there is one constantly repeated story, which one hopes is no more than a legend, bearing on the magnificent mosque of Sultan Hasan in Cairo, begun in 1356. It is said that the sultan was so delighted with this building as it approached completion that he cut off the architect's right hand, lest he should ever design another and more beautiful mosque to rival it. This story may typify the spirit of the age, and it certainly indicates that an architect was in the habit of drawing plans, as indeed appears from the other anecdotes mentioned above. These trivial tales are probably exaggerated, if not fictitious, but they picture the architect as alternately the favourite and the victim of eccentric despots. Yet we know from their buildings that the designers of the Saracen masterpieces of the Middle Ages must have been well-trained, versatile, and artistic men, with an instinct for good craftsmanship and a love of intricate geometrical ornament.

BIBLIOGRAPHY

BAUCHAL, C. *Nouveau Dictionnaire biographique et critique des Architectes français* [Middle Ages to A.D. 1885]. (Abbeville, 1885.)

BURGES, W. ' Architectural Drawing in the Middle Ages ' in *R.I.B.A. Transactions*. (London, 1860–1.)

CEAN-BERMUDEZ, J. A. Noticias de los arquitectos y arquitectura de España, 4 vols. In Spanish. (Madrid, 1829.)

DE MÉLY, F. ' Nos Vieilles Cathédrales et leurs Maîtres d'œuvre ', in *Revue Archéologique*, xi, 290–362 ; xii, 77–106. (Paris, 1920–1.)

FÉLIBIEN, J. F. *La vie . . . des plus célèbres architectes*. (Paris, 1690.)

FERREY, B. ' Early Medieval Superintendents ' in *R.I.B.A. Transactions*. (London, 1860–1.)

FROTHINGHAM, A. L. ' The Architect in History, during the Dark Ages ', in *The Arch. Rec.* (New York, 1909), xxvi, 55–70, 140–52.

LANCE, A. E. *Dictionnaire des Architectes français*. (Paris, 1872.)

LETHABY, W. R. *Westminster Abbey and the King's Craftsmen*. (London, 1906.)

MORTET, V. *Recueil des textes relatifs à l'histoire de l'architecture et à la condition des architectes en France, au moyen âge, XIe–XIIe siècles*, in series *Collection de textes*. (Paris, 1911.)

PAPWORTH, W. ' Notes on the Superintendents of English Buildings in the Middle Ages ' in *R.I.B.A. Transactions*. (London, 1887.)

PRIOR, E. S. *The Cathedral Builders in England*. (London, 1905.)

QUATREMÈRE DE QUINCEY. *Histoire de la vie et des ouvrages des plus célèbres Architectes du XIe XVIIIe siècle*. (Paris, 1830.)

QUICHERAT, J. *Facsimile of the Sketchbook of Villard de Honnecourt*. (London, 1859.)

SCHLOSSER, JULIUS VON. *Quellenbuch zur Kunstgeschichte des abendländischen Mittelalters*. (Vienna, 1896.) *Schriftquellen für Gesch. der Karolingisch. Kunst*. (Vienna, 1892.)

' SCOTT, LEADER ' [pseudonym]. *The Cathedral Builders*. (London, 1899.)

STEIN, H. *Les Architectes des Cathédrales gothiques*. (Paris, N.D.) ' Comment on désignait les architectes au moyen âge in *Mém. de la soc. nat. des Antiquaires de France*. (1918.)

STREET, G. E. *Gothic Architecture in Spain* : chapter xxi, ' Spanish Architects of the Middle Ages '. (London, 1865.)

THOMPSON, A. HAMILTON. ' Cathedral Builders of the Middle Ages ' in *History*. (London, July, 1925.) *The Cathedral Churches of England*. (London, 1925).

TOUT, T. F. *Medieval Town Planning*. (Manchester, 1917.)

V

THE RENAISSANCE IN ITALY

IN the periods dealt with hitherto, it has been found
difficult to reconstruct the story of the architect owing
to the comparative scarcity of documentary records. With
the dawn of the Renaissance there is a sudden and complete change, the amount of material available being almost
embarrassing. The rift between the architect and the
scribe vanishes, for the revival of learning not only brought
about a brotherhood of all the arts and sciences, including
literature, but it often made the architect something of a
scholar. No longer was the chronicler a monk. If not
always an architect himself, he was keenly in sympathy
with architecture, and he was interested in everything
that made for the advancement of learning and for the
glory of his country and his *comuna*. In Italy the Renaissance of architecture provides such a galaxy of
talent that, even for this short study, it becomes necessary
to divide it into two sections. The simplest point of
division occurs at Vasari's death ; the early period
including the architects from Brunelleschi to Michelangelo, and the later stage (commencing with Palladio,
Alessi, and Vignola) concluding in the eighteenth century.
Not only is this a reasonable line of demarcation on the
ground of architectural style, but it is suggested by the
importance of Vasari's history,[1] which covers the ground
up to 1550 or so in a way which has never been equalled,
before or since, up to recent times.

[1] G. Vasari, *Le Vite de' più eccellenti Pittori, Scultori, ed Architetti*
(Firenze, 1550). The references in this book are to the English
edition in Bohn's Library (London, 1907).

FIG. 19. PORTRAIT OF GIORGIO VASARI

From the 1568 edition of his ' Lives of the Artists '

We are indebted to Giorgio Vasari for personal or authentic reminiscences of every great figure from about 1400 to 1560, besides the somewhat shorter lives and the historical introduction comprised in his ' First Part ' which carries the story back to the earliest times. Vasari was born at Arezzo in 1511, and died at Florence in 1571, having attained the supreme office of *gonfaloniere* in the latter city. Though he was, on the whole, a modest man, he always regarded himself as an accomplished painter and a skilful architect. Of the great work that has become a classic he says little in his autobiography, perhaps hardly realizing that it was destined to preserve his name to posterity when his paintings and buildings had been forgotten. We are concerned with him here as an author, but the picture reproduced on Fig. 23 of this book will give some indication of his doubtful ability as a painter, besides illustrating an interesting event, the presentation of the model of a church to Cosimo de'Medici by the architect Brunelleschi.

It is a singular fact that a man whose biographies of other artists occupy thousands of pages of print should leave us in the dark as to the inception of so monumental a work. For Mr. Carden, who has written a careful and authoritative biography [1] of Vasari himself, discredits that author's own account of its origin, and points out discrepancies in names and dates mentioned. Briefly, Vasari's story runs as follows : [2] When working at Cardinal Farnese's palace in Rome in 1546, he often remained there to join his patron's friends at supper. Among them were many *literati* and distinguished men. On one occasion an eminent guest, also a cardinal, spoke of the

[1] R. W. Carden, *The Life of Vasari*, pp. 72–6 (London, 1910).
[2] Vasari, v. 531–3.

need that there was for some authoritative biography of the leading artists to be written, with a detailed description and criticism of their works. Cardinal Farnese then asked Vasari what he thought of this suggestion. The ever-cautious Giorgio expressed his approval, provided that the writer should be assisted by some artist, as he evidently distrusted the critical ability of the amateur. Vasari was then asked whether he would undertake the collection of the necessary facts and material himself. This he agreed to do, the more readily because he had been preparing notes and memoranda for this identical purpose since his boyhood. Then, he proceeds, ' I put together all that seemed to be suited for the purpose, and took them to Giovio ', the cardinal who had first suggested the book, and who evidently intended to write it himself with Vasari's help. Having examined the manuscript, Giovio said :

' My dear Giorgio, I would have you undertake this work yourself, for I see that you know perfectly well how to proceed therein ; whereas I have not myself the courage to attempt it, not knowing the various particulars with which you are acquainted, nor possessing that judgement respecting the different manners of the artists which you have attained.'

Whatever may be the historical accuracy of this story, we know without doubt that Vasari slaved at his book for a year in 1546–7, that he submitted portions of it to literary friends for their criticism, and that finally it was published at Florence at the beginning of 1550. This first edition is a small quarto volume, without portraits or other illustrations, and is dedicated to Cosimo de'Medici. It seems to have had a success, for, in the preface to the second edition (1568), Vasari states that the booksellers have not a single copy left. He began the second edition on a more ambitious scale about 1562, and travelled over Italy to refresh his memory and to collect fresh information, besides revising all his previous work. He had a good deal of trouble with his printer at Florence, but it appears that the printer may have had some cause for complaint too, as Vasari sent his own portrait before his autobiography was ready for the press. The second edition fills three large volumes and over 1,500 pages without the lengthy introductions. It is illustrated with portraits of nearly all the artists, each engraving being framed in scrollwork to form an ornamental headpiece to the biography (see Fig. 19 in this book). Where no portrait was obtainable, the engraver left a blank space within the frame. Vasari apologizes for the indifferent merit of some of the portraits, saying that the engraving had to be done at a distance from him, so that he was unable to supervise the work personally. He dedicates the second edition of his book, like the first, to Cosimo de'Medici, and thanks him for ' the leisure which you have been pleased to secure to me ', enabling him to carry out this great work.

Vasari's *Lives*, indispensable to every student of art history, owe much of their value and interest to the fact that he knew all the great artists of his own day intimately. In regard to the earlier masters, he evidently had access to records or biographies of some sort, but does not acknowledge his ' sources ' in the manner of a modern historian. Thus he gives an admirable and vivid life of Brunelleschi, who died some fifty years before he was born, but makes no mention of a contemporary biography of that artist which has since been published. One cannot believe that all the mass of detailed information in the earlier part of the *Lives* is largely based upon hearsay.

As a critic and as a historian Vasari is inclined to be generous, fair, and discriminating. He is generally modest, seldom petty or spiteful. He has a knack of relating amusing incidents, which enliven his numerous pages, though sometimes one would prefer to know a little more about professional customs and methods instead of trivial gossip. Thus he discourses for ten pages about an eccentric dinner-club run by the painter and architect Rustici, which rivalled in extravagance and ingenuity the mad revels which are sometimes attributed to modern American millionaires. Nevertheless, it must be admitted that these passages make excellent reading. He is inclined to digress, and on one page remarks : ' But to return to Tribolo, from whom I have departed, I know not how. . .'[1]

As examples of his character-studies of men whom he knew personally, one may quote this picture of Girolamo da Carpi :

' Girolamo was a man of a cheerful character, very agreeable in conversation, in his works somewhat leisurely and slow, of middle stature, an immoderate lover of music, and perhaps rather more earnestly devoted to the pleasures of sense than was altogether desirable.' [2]

Of Jacopo Sansovino, Vasari writes that he was

' of the middle height, but rather slender than otherwise, and his carriage was remarkably upright ; he was fair, with a red beard, and in his youth was of a goodly presence, wherefore he did not fail to be loved, and that by dames of no small importance. In his age he had an exceedingly venerable appearance ; with his beautiful white beard, he still retained the carriage of his youth : he was strong and healthy even to his ninety-third year, and could see the smallest object, at whatever distance, without glasses, even then. When writing, he sat with his head up, not supporting himself in any manner,

[1] Vasari, iv. 210.   [2] *Ibid.* iv. 513.

as it is usual for men to do. He liked to be handsomely dressed, and was singularly nice in his person. The society of ladies was acceptable to Sansovino, even to the extremity of age, and he always enjoyed conversing with or of them. He had not been particularly healthy in his youth, yet in his old age he suffered from no malady whatever, insomuch that, for a period of fifty years, he would never consult any physician, even when he did feel himself indisposed. Nay, when he was once attacked by apoplexy, and that for the fourth time, in his eighty-fourth year too, he would still have nothing to do with physic, but cured himself by keeping in bed for two months, in a dark and well-warmed chamber. His digestion was so good that he could eat all things without distinction : during the summer he lived almost entirely on fruits, and in the very extremity of his age would frequently eat three cucumbers and half a lemon at one time.' [1]

A third example of Vasari's intimate character-studies may be taken from the most lengthy and remarkable of his biographies, that of his close friend and chief mentor, Michelangelo.

' He was of middle height, the shoulders broad, and the whole form well-proportioned. In his latter years he constantly wore stockings of dog-skin for months together, and when these were removed, the skin of the leg sometimes came with them. Over his stockings he had boots of Cordovan leather, as a protection against the swelling of these limbs, to which he then became liable. His face was round, the brow square and ample, with seven direct lines in it ; the temples projected much beyond the ears, which were somewhat large, and stood a little off from the cheeks ; the nose was rather flattened, having been broken with a blow of the first by Torrigiano, as we have related in the Life of that artist ; the eyes were rather small than large, of a dark colour, mingled with blue and yellowish points ; the eyebrows had but few

[1] *Ibid.* v. 425–6.

hairs ; the lips were thin, the lower somewhat the larger, and slightly projecting ; the chin well-formed, and in fair proportion to the rest of the face ; the hair black, mingled with grey, as was the beard, which was divided in the middle, and neither very thick nor very long. [1]

' Although rich, he lived like a poor man ; rarely did any friend or other person eat at his table, and he would accept no presents, considering that he would be bound to any one who offered him such : his temperance kept him in constant activity, and he slept very little, frequently rising in the night because he could not sleep, and resuming his labours with the chisel. For these occasions he had made himself a cap of pasteboard, in the centre of which he placed his candle, which thus gave him light without encumbering his hands.' [2]

These extracts may appear trivial, and without much bearing on the subject of this book. I give them here to indicate the intensely personal nature of Vasari's style, in the hope that any of my readers who are not familiar with the celebrated *Lives* may be induced to turn to the original and thereby gain an unrivalled picture of Italian artists in the sixteenth century. But Vasari is a keen and meticulous critic of the technique of all the fine arts. He gives lengthy descriptions of pictures, buildings, and statues : as well as innumerable anecdotes bearing on social life and professional practice.

After this brief general introduction to his great work, we must next examine its particular reference to the status and work of Italian architects in his day.

Of some 32 men mentioned by Vasari who practised architecture, either singly or with one or more other arts, we find that 11 were architects pure and simple ; 11 are described as ' sculptor and architect ' ; 6 practised architecture and painting ; 3 were versed in all three arts ; and

[1] Vasari, v. 346.   [2] *Ibid.* v. 339.

one is styled ' architect and engineer '. The prevailing and striking characteristic of this wonderful age was versatility, as will be shown later.

The education of the young architect depended very much upon the circumstances of his birth, upon his parents' ideas for his vocation, and as to whether he began his career primarily as an architect or not. In the 17 cases of which particulars are given by Vasari, we find that three architects (Raphael, Falconetto and Da Carpi), were the sons of painters ; three (Alberti, Rustici, and Jacopo Sansovino) ' of noble birth ' ; two (Bramante and Michelangelo) ' noble but poor ' ; four (Giuliano Sangallo, Antonio Sangallo the Elder, Bartolommeo Genga, and Sanmicheli) were sons of architects ; Andrea Sansovino was the son of a farm-labourer, Giuliano da Majano of a mason or builders' merchant, Lorenzetto of a bellfounder, Antonio Sangallo the Younger of a cooper, Tribolo of ' a poor carpenter ' ; and Peruzzi, though his parents are stated by Vasari to have been of noble birth if poor, is now believed to have been the son of a weaver.[1] These miscellaneous fathers appear to have had all the perplexities and prejudices of a modern parent as to the destiny of their sons. Thus we find Michelangelo's father actually beating him because he wished to be an architect, thinking the profession unworthy of his family.[2] The father of Giuliano da Majano was a mason by trade, and when his son showed some evidence of ability at school,

' resolved that he should be made a notary, his own trade of stone-cutting being, as he thought, too laborious and not sufficiently profitable. But this purpose was not carried out,

[1] *Ibid*. ii. 158 ; F. W. Bedford, ' Baldassare Peruzzi, in *R.I.B.A. Journal*, vol. ix (1902).

[2] A. Condivi, *Vita di Michelangelo*, i. 5 (Rome, 1553).

for, although Giuliano went for some time to the grammar-school, his thoughts were never there, and the consequence was that he made no progress whatever ; on the contrary he ran away several times, and showed that his whole heart was given to sculpture ; yet he commenced life by working as a joiner, but acquired practice in drawing at the same time.' [1]

Brunelleschi, like Giuliano da Majano, was intended for the law, Primaticcio and Jacopo Sansovino for business, Girolamo Genga for weaving, and Andrea Sansovino began life as a farm-boy. Antonio Sangallo the Younger and Tribolo were apprenticed to carpenters ; Giuliano Sangallo and Antonio Sangallo the Elder to woodcarvers ; Bramante, Raphael, da Carpi, Vasari, and Aristotile Sangallo to painters ; and there are only two, Bartolommeo Genga and Sanmicheli (both architects' sons) of whom we know without a doubt that they were intended for architecture from the beginning. It therefore follows that it is hard to generalize as to the system of architectural training then in vogue. It appears that some of the more fortunate youths had a measure of general education : thus Bramante, though intended to be a painter, ' studied arithmetic zealously ' ; [2] and Niccolò was nicknamed *Il Tribolo* (' thistle ' or ' tormentor ') because at school he proved ' a very devil ' and made no progress. [3] Jacopo Sansovino in early youth was sent,

' as is usual, to acquire the rudiments of learning, wherein he displayed much intelligence : he soon began to study drawing of himself, and gave evidence, in a certain sort, that nature had disposed him to the study of design rather than that of letters, since he went very reluctantly to school, and was most unwilling to undertake the difficult acquirement of grammar.' [4]

[1] Vasari, ii. 8–9.   [2] *Ibid*. ii. 427.

[3] *Ibid*. iv. 173.   [4] *Ibid*. v. 409.

FIG. 20. FILIPPO BRUNELLESCHI

From an old print

Bartolommeo Genga, an architect's son, pursued general studies till he began his professional training under his father at 18.[1] Those who were destined for the legal profession or for commerce seem to have been sent to school : thus, Michelangelo ' on attaining the proper age ' was sent to ' the school of grammar kept by Messer Francesco of Urbino,'[2] and others, like Alberti and Fra Giocondo, who turned to architecture from academic surroundings, evidently had a lengthy and extensive general education.

On the other hand, those who entered architecture from the ranks of building craftsmen seem to have had very little of what we call general education.

Vasari's own views on education may be quoted here :

' The knowledge of letters and the study of the sciences are, without doubt, of the utmost value to all, and offer the most important advantages to every artist who takes pleasure therein ; but most of all are they serviceable to sculptors, painters, and architects, for whom they prepare the path to various inventions in all the works executed by them ; and, be the natural qualities of a man what they may, his judgment can never be brought to perfection if he be deprived of the advantages resulting from the accompaniment of learning.'[3]

In none of Vasari's biographies of architects is there any mention of a school where architecture was taught, but most youths are stated to have been apprenticed or articled to an architect in practice. This was also the custom for painters and sculptors, and the form of articles drawn up between Michelangelo's father and the painter Domenico Ghirlandajo, when Michelangelo was apprenticed at the age of thirteen, is presumably typical :

' I record this 1st of April (1488) how that I, Lodovico di Lionardo di Buonarrota, bind my son Michelangelo to Dome-

[1] *Ibid.*   [2] *Ibid.* v. 229.   [3] *Ibid.* ii. 40.

nico and Davit di Tommaso di Currado for the next three ensuing years, under these conditions and contracts : to wit that the said Michelangelo shall stay with the above-named masters during this time, to learn the art of painting, and to practise the same, and to be at the order of the above-named ; and they, for their part, shall give him in the course of these three years 24 florins ; to wit, 6 florins in the 1st year, 8 in the 2nd, 10 in the 3rd, making in all the sum of 96 pounds.'

But Michelangelo's father was a man in a good position, and though doubtless the architects' sons mentioned above were well trained by their father, other youths who were less fortunately placed had to pick up their knowledge as best they could, until their talents by good luck came to the notice of one of those noble patrons of the arts who could do so much for the career of a poor lad. Whatever their original intentions, these youths eventually entered architecture as a rule because they showed a taste for drawing. Other studies which they pursued appear to have been geometry, perspective, mathematics, and mechanics.

A few quotations from Vasari indicate the varied ways in which the chief architects of the Italian Renaissance acquired the rudiments of their technical training. Thus, Brunelleschi's father ' perceiving that the mind of the boy was constantly intent on various intricate questions of art and mechanics, made him learn writing and arithmetic, and then placed him in the Guild of the Goldsmiths, that he might acquire design from a friend of his.'[1] In boyhood Andrea Verrocchio ' gave considerable attention to science, more especially to geometry,'[2] and later approached architecture by way of goldsmiths' work and sculpture. Bramante ' found his principal pleasure in

---

[1] Vasari, i. 416.   [2] *Ibid*. ii. 250.

architecture and the study of perspective ; he departed therefore from Castel Durante, and proceeded to Lombardy, repairing first to one city and then to another, working in each meanwhile as he best could '.[1] Of Baldassare Peruzzi it is recorded that he frequented ' the workshops of goldsmiths and others, who practised the arts of design '.[2]

Andrea Sansovino and Michelangelo studied in the garden of Lorenzo de'Medici's palace at Florence, where the interest of that powerful patron secured a career for them in later years. Michelangelo, who entered architecture only as an old man, began his career as a successful ' faker ' of drawings and statues to represent antiques, resorting to ingenious tricks to make a drawing look old and to give bronze the appearance of having been long buried beneath the earth.

The best account that Vasari gives us of an architect's professional training relates to Bartolommeo Genga, already mentioned, who was himself an architect's son. He was sent to school to learn Latin and remained there until he was eighteen. Then his father

' perceiving that he was more decidedly disposed to the arts of design than to letters, gave him permission to study these arts under his own care for about two years, and these being then concluded he then sent him to pursue the studies of design and painting in Florence.' [3]

He remained in Florence three years, and returned to his father's office at Urbino, where he helped him with the drawings for a church. His father then, and only then, came to the conclusion that Bartolommeo showed an aptitude for architecture rather than painting, and after giving him some months training, including perspective,

[1] *Ibid*. ii. 428.　　　[2] *Ibid*. iii. 158.　　　[3] *Ibid*. iv. 409.

sent him to Rome ' to the end that he might behold the wonderful buildings, both ancient and modern, which abound in that city '.[1]

After four years measuring and drawing in Rome, he finally returned to Urbino, where he commenced practice under the patronage of the Duke. It will thus be seen that his training lasted over nine years, and that it was not completed until he was 27 or 28 years of age.

In another passage Vasari tells us how, in his opinion, an architect should be qualified for his work.

' Architecture is to be adequately pursued only by such men as possess an excellent judgment, a good knowledge of design, or extensive practice in some such occupation as painting, sculpture, or woodwork, and have been thereby led to the habit of measuring figures, edifices, and bodies of similar character in their several members ; such as, for example, are columns, cornices, and basements, and to examine all these in their relative proportions, even to the most minute particulars of such parts as serve for embellishment alone, and for no other purpose.' [2]

Although Vasari elsewhere commends Michelangelo for breaking away from the bondage of Vitruvius and his kind,[3] the passage quoted makes it clear that an architect was expected in those days to be a close student of the antique. It is a remarkable fact that almost every famous architect whose life is described in detail by Vasari, even the poorest of them, somehow contrived to spend long periods, often many years, in measuring and drawing the antiquities of Rome, and even in making ' restorations ' of the ruins. Brunelleschi went there with Donatello at about 25 years of age, sold a farm to provide funds, and when these were exhausted took up gem-setting in Rome

---

[1] Vasari, iv. 410.   [2] *Ibid*. iii. 458.   [3] *Ibid*. v. 272.

Fig. 21. DONATO BRAMANTE

From an old print

to maintain himself while measuring.[1] Overwork in the bad climate of the Campagna put an end to his studies ; this being a frequent occurrence in Vasari's lives. Bramante was not able to get to Rome till he was over fifty, when he had saved enough to settle there for the sole purpose of study.[2] Fortunately he also picked up a large practice there. Raphael's paintings display his wide knowledge of Roman architecture. Cronaca obtained his name (' chronicle ') from his constant talk in Florence about Roman antiquities.[3] Falconetto spent twelve years studying the ruins of Rome, financing himself by working for other painters two or three days a week ; [4] he also travelled to Pola to study the Roman buildings there. Sanmicheli, an architect's son, was sent to Rome in his sixteenth year, and his studies there were so much appreciated that they obtained for him an appointment in charge of the cathedral at Orvieto, ' with a most honourable stipend '.[5] Other names might be added to this list. A quotation from Vasari shows how hard students worked in his day in Rome : [6]

' And to the end that each of us might have drawings of every work, we did not copy the same thing on the same day, but different ones, and when night came we copied each other's drawings for the purpose of saving time, and also to advance our studies ; nor did we ever breakfast in the morning, except on what we ate while standing, and that very frugally.'

Simone Mosca, whose home was at Settignano, managed to obtain employment in Rome as assistant to Antonio da Sangallo, and spent all his available holidays in measuring and sketching the ruins.[7] For Rome was

[1] *Ibid*. i. 422–4.   [2] *Ibid*. ii. 430.   [3] *Ibid*. ii. 80.
[4] *Ibid*. iii. 436–7.   [5] *Ibid*. iv. 419.   [6] *Ibid*. v. 505.
[7] *Ibid*. iv. 385.

the Mecca of the ambitious student, as of the practising architect, and every youth aspired to become assistant to an architect in Rome.

The revival of Roman architecture, commonly called the Renaissance, was due primarily to Filippo Brunelleschi, who, when he first beheld the city, ' stood like one amazed, and seemed to have lost his wits '. So he and his friend Donatello, though the latter was a sculptor, together began measuring the ground-plans of Roman buildings and taking profiles of their cornices with wild enthusiasm.

' And as Filippo was free from all household cares,' writes Vasari, ' he gave himself up so exclusively to his studies, that he took no time either to eat or sleep ; his every thought was of Architecture, which was then extinct : I mean the good old manner, and not the Gothic and barbarous one, which was much practised at that period.'[1]

Brunelleschi had two objects in mind when he began his studies, firstly to revive the use of Roman architecture, and secondly to discover among the ruins some method of constructing the dome of the cathedral at Florence, a problem which was baffling all the architects of that city, and which he, at the early age of twenty-five, had thus determined to solve. So, with the one purpose in view, he and Donatello excavated and measured and drew so assiduously that the local populace suspected them of being treasure-seekers ; and, on the other hand, Brunelleschi devoted special attention to examining ancient brick buildings, studying the principles of their vaulting, and the methods by which bricks and stones were cramped together by metal fastenings. Meanwhile his long study of the ruins had the result that ' he became capable of entirely reconstructing the city in his imagina-

[1] Vasari, i. 423.

tion, and of beholding Rome as she had been before she was ruined '.[1]

Brunelleschi's love for beautiful old things was so intense that on one occasion, when he was told by Dona- tello of an antique marble vase at Cortona, he rushed off there from Florence just as he was, ' in his mantle, his hood, and his wooden shoes, without saying where he was going, and went on foot to Cortona ' [some 72 miles] ' for that purpose '.[2]

A similar story is related of Falconetto, who frequently visited Rome ;

' the journey thither was consequently so familiar to him that he would undertake it on any occasion, however slight, while his youth and vigour remained to him. On this subject people still living relate that, being one day in dispute with a foreign architect, who chanced to be in Verona, respecting the propor- tions of some ancient cornice, I know not what, in Rome, Giovan-Maria, after many words had passed, remarked, " On this point I will soon make myself certain ", and departing at once to his house, he set out without more ado to Rome ' [nearly 300 miles away].[3]

Evidently there were connoisseurs and *virtuosi* among architects in those days. Vasari was certainly one of them, and he collected drawings and antiques with the same discrimination that inspired Sir John Soane (see p. 331) a century ago. Michelangelo's success dated from the occasion when he palmed off a spurious ' antique ' bronze of his own manufacture on an unsuspecting cardinal. In Brunelleschi's day, as we have seen, the hunt for antiques had barely begun, but it developed into a craze, and in the sixteenth century Primaticcio, then working in France, was dispatched by the king to Rome to buy and copy

[1] *Ibid*. i. 424. [2] *Ibid*. i. 425. [3] *Ibid*. iii. 441.

antiques.[1]   One edition after another of Vitruvius's book was published, and when the wits of Florence ridiculed Baccio d'Agnolo's architecture in sonnets, he remained unruffled because ' he knew that he had imitated good examples.' [2]   Most significant of all, perhaps, is Vasari's reference to ' a house with the appearance and form of a Ruin ', designed by Girolamo Genga (1476–1551) to the order of the Duke of Urbino, of which the biographer observes that ' This also is an object very pleasant to see '.[3]

When one reads of this overwhelming passion for the antique, one cannot help speculating on the attitude of Italian architects of the Renaissance to the buildings of the Middle Ages scattered over the length and breadth of Italy.   Vasari himself was a critic of catholic taste, and though his preference, as we have seen, was all for ancient architecture, he chronicles the lives and describes the work of medieval masters without undue bias.   There are a few references in his pages to works of restoration. Thus, when the Palazzo Vecchio at Florence, designed by Arnolfo del Cambio in the thirteenth century, had to be restored for structural reasons and modernized to meet changed requirements in 1538, the Duke resolved to carry out the necessary alterations ' without destroying the old works, in which there was certainly something good '.[4]

On the other hand, according to Lanciani,[5] the architects of the Renaissance were guilty of shocking vandalism in Rome.

' This system of wholesale plundering, of promiscuous usage of Pagan and Christian materials, of ruining many edifices for the benefit of one, inaugurated by Constantine, was

---

[1] Vasari, v. 372.   [2] *Ibid*. iii. 460.
[3] *Ibid*. iv. 403.   [4] *Ibid*. i. 501.
[5] R. Lanciani, *Wanderings through Ancient Roman Churches*, pp. 99–106.   (London, 1925.)

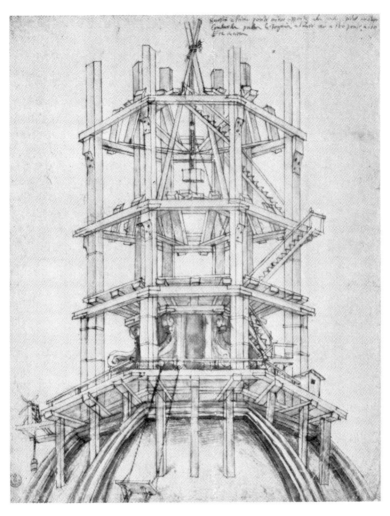

FIG. 22. A DRAWING OF SCAFFOLDING

By an unknown artist of the XVIth century in the Uffizi Gallery,
Florence (see p. 164)

followed by his immediate successors, and even more merci-
lessly by the architects of the Renaissance, such as Fra Giocondo
of Verona, the two Sangalli, the two Peruzzi, Raphael, Michelangelo, to whom the care of rebuilding St. Peter's was entrusted.'
. . . They 'had no more compunction about burning into
lime antique statues and portrait-busts and historical inscriptions than of levelling to the ground temples, baths, porticos,
triumphal arches, &c., provided such misdeeds made easier
and cheaper their task.'

The masons of Julius II broke into three pieces a
ninth-century historical inscription of great value : one
piece was lost, a second used in paving the nave, a third
in the altar. One of Giotto's frescoes was only saved
because Pierino del Vaga happened to pass just as its
destruction was imminent. The architects of the *fab-
brica* of St. Peter's were authorized by a papal brief of
1540 to excavate in the Forum and the Via Sacra for
antiques and other ' materials '. Terrible damage was
done in this way during ' that fatal decade, 1540–49 '.
86 cartloads of travertine were taken from one building
in the Forum. In 1546 Paul III, the Pope who gave
the authority just mentioned, instructed his confidential
manager to transfer this priceless plunder to his own
house, not to St. Peter's. Thus we see another side of the
picture.

But not all famous architects of this period limited their
activities to architecture. We are constantly impressed
by their versatility. Leonardo da Vinci is sometimes regarded as the Admirable Crichton of the Italian Renaissance. He was ' painter, poet, sculptor, architect,
mechanist, mathematician, philosopher, and explorer.
He also studied botany and anatomy, was an admirable
performer on the lyre, and the first scientific writer on his

special art of painting '.[1] Yet his surviving work is not to be compared with that of Michelangelo or Peruzzi, and as an architect he did little. Most of the great artists of the Renaissance were many-sided men, with the intense intellectual curiosity and love of learning for its own sake that distinguished their period and country. Many of them dabbled in music and poetry, several of them wrote books (though not so freely as in the next period), and most of them combined the artistic and the practical to an extent noteworthy for us to-day. There was no hard line between ' science ' and ' art ' : mathematics, mechanics, and geometry were an essential part of the architect's equipment, and even in his re-searches into antiquity he was as much concerned with the composition of Roman stucco and the bonding of Roman masonry as with the proportions of cornices and the de-tails of mouldings. He passed with apparent ease from one craft to another, and his ability to do so can only be explained by inexplicable genius. Occasionally one finds an ambitious man with a fixed object in mind : thus the versatile Brunelleschi is said to have decided quite early in life to revive Roman architecture and to complete the unfinished Duomo at Florence. Rapidly running through painting, mechanics, goldsmith's work, gem-setting, architecture, carving, classical studies, inlaying, geometry, the Scriptures, and Dante, he attained both his objects at the last.

Even more startling is the career of Fra Giocondo, a learned friar who, in the course of a long life, almost boxed the intellectual compass. Having excelled in philosophy, theology, and Greek, he made a model for a bridge while still acting as a pedagogue, became proficient in per-

[1] H. Ricardo, ' The Cardinal Medici's Pleasure House ' in the *R.I.B.A. Journal.* (London, 1911.)

spective, studied the Roman ruins and wrote a book on them, edited Cæsar and Vitruvius, edited Pliny's letters, built two bridges at Paris, carried out other architectural work in France, took a hand in the erection of St. Peter's, designed a whole system of drainage for the Venetian lagoons, and finally evolved a town-planning scheme for the Rialto district of Venice. Knowing that he also practised agriculture and gardening, one can only gasp at this catalogue, and then accept Vasari's apt statement that he was ' a man of universal attainment '.[1]

Sometimes we find music mentioned among the many accomplishments of these versatile architects ; others are praised for their conversational powers. Others again had scientific tastes, thus Pelori, ' a good and able architect ' when he liked, frittered away his time in fanciful designs, in measuring old buildings, and in inventions of various kinds. ' He gave much attention to mathematics and cosmography, constructing quadrants, the mariner's compass, instruments for measuring, and other things of similar kind, with his own hand.'[2] Rustici wasted his time in freezing mercury, keeping hedgehogs, and flirting with the occult. For this prevailing versatility had its drawbacks. A man who was able to practise several arts with equal ease often failed to progress in any one of them as far as his ability could have taken him. Vasari points out that Tribolo, whose explosive personality we have already noted in this chapter, abandoned sculpture, ' in which it may be truly said that he was an artist of high excellence, and surprised all who beheld his works, for the vain attempt to restrict the course of rivers, in which he met with no success,'[3] this being a reference to his ill-starred career as Commissioner of Roads and Rivers to

[1] Vasari, ii. 394.   [2] *Ibid*. iii. 172.   [3] *Ibid*. iv. 215.

the State of Florence. On the other hand, it was Michelangelo's perfect confidence in his own abilities that took
him into architecture as an old man. When he started
painting the ceiling of the Sistine Chapel he designed all
his own scaffolding, because that which Bramante had
erected was unsuitable, and had no hesitation in telling
the Pope that Bramante ' did not know how to construct
it '.[1] At that time, we must remember, Bramante was
architect of St. Peter's, and Michelangelo only a famous
painter and sculptor. Again, when Michelangelo was
commissioned by the Pope to prepare a model for the
façade of S. Lorenzo at Florence, the leading architects of
the day, several of whom had submitted designs for this
work, objected to the appointment of an ' amateur '. But
he ' determined to prepare the model himself, and not to
accept any guide, or permit any superior in the matter of
the architecture '.[2]

Yet even in that marvellous age men were capable of
astonishment, and when Brunelleschi, acknowledged already as a master of many crafts, showed his first carved
crucifix to his friend Donatello, the latter was so surprised
that he dropped out of his apron on to the floor the eggs and
other comestibles that he had brought for their frugal meal.[3]

About 1423 we come across the mention of a woman-
architect, probably an amateur, ' of the Gaddi family
who ventured to place her knowledge in competition with
that of Filippo ' [Brunelleschi].[4]

The range of the architect's duties during the early
and middle Renaissance in Italy was astoundingly wide,
but little is said about town-planning by Vasari and other
writers, chiefly because town-planning was not then much

---

[1] Vasari, v. 255.   [2] *Ibid*. v. 268.
[3] *Ibid*. i. 419.   [4] *Ibid*. i. 446.

FIG. 23. BRUNELLESCHI PRESENTING THE MODEL OF THE CHURCH OF
S. LORENZO TO COSIMO DE' MEDICI (see p. 165)

From the painting by Vasari in the Palazzo Vecchio, Florence

in fashion. It was in the Baroque period that it suddenly
blossomed out on the grand scale. As early as 1355 it is
recorded that Orcagna won a competition for the lay-out
of the Piazza della Signoria in Florence ; [1] Poggio Im-
periale was laid out by Giuliano da Sangallo (1443–1517)
at a much later date, but apparently with a view to defence ; [2] and Fra Giocondo's lay-out of part of Venice
has just been mentioned. These instances are, however,
comparatively infrequent in Vasari's pages, and we may
conclude that, though architects undertook what little
town-planning was required, the idea of an ordered dis-
position of streets and squares to produce a monumental
effect had hardly emerged.

But the position as regards works of engineering,
especially military engineering, is very different. In
those days the functions of the engineer, military or civil,
had not been detached from those of the architect, and
the art of fortification formed an important part of his
duties. It is hard to realize that the same man might be
designing fortifications one day and painting Madonnas
or carving crucifixes on the morrow. Brunelleschi,
Michelozzi, Bramante, the Sangalli, Peruzzi, the Genghe,
Michelangelo, and, especially, Sanmicheli, all carried out
such work. Yet of those who figure in Vasari's pages in
this connexion, only one, Cecca, is described as an
' engineer ', though he began life as a joiner. Giuliano
da Sangallo was still occupied ' with his studies in
design, and the blood of youth was still dancing in his
veins ' when an hostile army appeared in Florentine
territory ; whereupon Lorenzo de'Medici

' saw himself compelled to despatch an engineer to Castellana
for the purpose of constructing bastions and defences of

[1] *Ibid.* i. 211, and cf. p. 115 in this book.   [2] *Ibid.* ii. 494.

various kinds, and who should also take charge of the artillery, to the management of which few men were at that time competent. He therefore sent Giuliano, whom he considered to be a man of intelligence, promptitude, and resolution.' . . . ' Arrived at Castellana, therefore, Giuliano fortified the place within and without, constructing good walls and strong outworks, with all other defences necessary to the security of the town. He remarked that the artillerymen handled their guns very timidly, standing at a distance from them while loading or raising them, and firing them with evident fear ; he set himself therefore to remedy this evil, and so contrived that no further accidents happened to the artillerymen, although several of them had previously been killed by the recoil.' . . .

Giuliano's successful solution of this and other military problems resulted in the abandonment of the siege, gained for him ' no small praise in Florence, and obtained ' him the goodwill of Lorenzo, who received him most favourably and loaded him with commendations '.[1]   At this point Vasari remarks that Giuliano, hitherto a joiner or wood-carver with a taste for drawing, ' afterwards turned his attention to architecture '. Thus we find an untrained civilian put in charge of artillery and defences, yet succeeding so well that the ducal interest afterwards enabled him to enter a profession from which circumstances had previously barred him.

The military adventures of other architects were not all so creditable. When the Pope was planning the siege of Florence in 1529, he commissioned Tribolo (a native of Florence, born in 1500) and another man to collaborate in making a relief-model of the city and its neighbourhood, showing thereon not only the surrounding hills, mountains, rivers, and churches, but also ' the squares and

[1] Vasari, ii. 489–90.

streets within the town, together with ' the walls, bastions, and other defences '. This model, which the treacherous Tribolo had actually suggested to the Pope, involved for its makers much dangerous spying by night, ' measuring the roads, and ascertaining the exact number of braccia between one place and another, with the heights and levels of the summits of all the churches and towers '.[1]

For the sake of lightness the model was made of cork ; its size was four *braccia* (about 7 feet 6 inches), it was made to scale, and it could be taken to pieces. When finished, it was packed up and conveyed secretly ' out of Florence '—(this is significant)—in bales of wool to the Pope, so that he could direct the siege from a distance, just as a modern general directs his campaign at a distance with the aid of a large-scale ordnance map. At all events, the whole incident is thoroughly discreditable to a professional architect.

Peruzzi was also invited to assist the Pope in the preparations for this siege. According to Vasari he actually went to the camp outside Florence, and then patriotically declined to have anything further to do with it ; but a letter of Peruzzi's, since discovered and published, shows that he actually did take part in the operations against the city.[2]

Michelangelo was working on the famous Medici Chapel in Florence when the city was besieged in 1529, and lent the authorities the sum of 1,000 crowns towards the cost of the defence. He was in charge of the fortifications,

' and as he made one of the Council of War, called the Nine, he turned all his mind and thoughts to the perfecting and strengthening of the defences. But at length, and when the

[1] *Ibid*. iv. 179–81. [2] *Ibid*. iii. 168 *n*.

enemy's troops had closed round the city, while all hope of aid was gradually disappearing,'—as he—' felt himself to be in a position not suited to him ', he ' resolved for the safety of his person, to leave Florence and repair to Venice '.

He departed secretly with two friends, and worked at Venice for some time, but later was prevailed on to return to his native city and, ' moved by love of his native place, he did eventually return, but not without danger to his life ', and rendered valuable help in the later stages of the siege.[1]

But it was Sanmicheli above all others whose achievements in military architecture have enhanced his reputation. Vasari rightly compares his frowning gateways at Verona and elsewhere with the work of the Romans,[2] and he does seem to have inherited the genius of his great ancestors for expressing in stone the power of the armed State. He was mainly employed by Venice, and designed fortifications for the Venetian possessions in the Adriatic and Mediterranean as well as in the mother-city. On the island of the Lido, known to us nowadays as a gay bathing-beach, he erected a fortress on piles, the site being marshy in itself and exposed to the full force of the sea. Vasari describes the elaborate precautions taken by the architect to ensure a stable foundation, and then proceeds to relate how its strength was tested. The Signori

' ordered an immense quantity of artillery, and that of the very heaviest to be found in the Arsenal, to be brought to the fortress, and having caused all the embrasures above as well as below, to be filled with cannon, even more heavily loaded than common, they had all fired off together. Then the uproar, the thunders, and the earthquake that were heard and felt were such and so vast, as to make it appear as if the '

[1] Vasari, v. 275–7.   [2] *Ibid.* iv. 428.

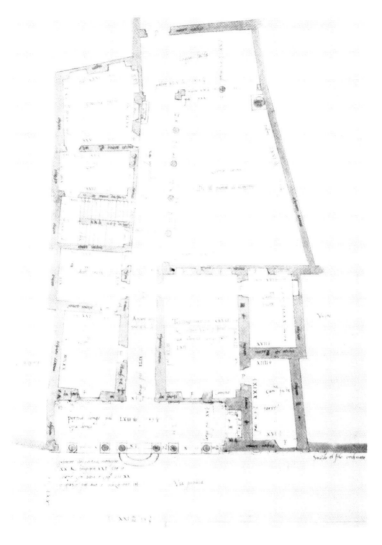

FIG. 24. A PLAN BY BALDASSARE PERUZZI

In the Uffizi Gallery, Florence (see p. 164)

whole world were falling to pieces, while the mass of the building itself, with all its mouths of fire, presented the aspect of a great volcano, or rather of a very hell. But the fabric remained firm in its seat nevertheless, exhibiting all its wonted strength and solidity, to the utter shame of the malignant critics, who were proved to be utterly destitute of judgment.' . . . ' The envious detractors had nevertheless caused so much terror in Venice, that many gentlewomen who were pregnant at the time were removed from the city in the fear of some frightful catastrophe.' [1]

Architects also practised ' civil ' engineering, thus Michelozzi constructed an aqueduct and a road at Assisi, Camicia built ' mills ' for the King of Hungary, Baccio Pintelli designed the Ponte Sisto at Rome, Antonio da Sangallo arranged the water-supply at Orvieto and Terni, and Fra Giocondo, as already noted (see p. 149), acted as bridge-builder and town-planner among his many occupations.

In regard to what we now call ' garden architecture ', mention must be made once more of the name of Tribolo, whose antics have earned for him undue prominence in this chapter. The formal lay-out of gardens was a novelty up to the sixteenth century, and when Tribolo began work at Castello he was mainly concerned with carving the ornamental fountains, while the arrangements for water-supply were in the hands of an engineer or builder who ' had neither invention nor knowledge of design '. However, shortly after the engineer had brought the water up to the fountains, he suddenly died, whereupon Tribolo undertook the remainder of the engineering work involved, including the diversion of a stream and the construction of an aqueduct.[2] Garden architecture in the sixteenth

---

[1] *Ibid*. iv. 426–7.   [2] *Ibid*. iv. 191–5.

century, in Italy as elsewhere, included the construction
of elaborate ' waterworks ' destined to surprise and drench
the guests, usually from the floor, as a merry quip on the
part of their host.

The passion for symbolism and display that marked
Italian society in this brilliant period led to the addition
of another kind of design for the architect. He was constantly employed in the invention of masques, triumphal
arches, and all the gorgeous trappings of festivals arranged
to commemorate a victory, a deliverance, or the visit of
a royal personage. Such work required a vivid imagination and great mechanical ingenuity as well as high artistic
ability. Vasari devotes many of his most diverting pages
to descriptions of this pasteboard architecture, and there
is one intensely amusing story in the life of Tribolo the
troublesome, relating how the *Girandola*, a great set-piece
of fireworks intended to burn for a full hour, suddenly
flared up when it was lighted, thus diminishing the
reputation of poor Tribolo, who had insisted that such
things should be designed by an architect and not by
' simpletons '.[1]   It is interesting to note that when
Antonio da Sangallo designed a triumphal arch, he
directed the sculptors and painters who were concerned
in its decoration.[2] Brunelleschi, too, did work of this sort,
and Peruzzi sometimes worked as a scene-painter.

The status of the architect in this period depended
solely on his ability. His social position in Italy could be
what he made it, and there was no limit to the heights he
might attain. Architects held high positions as magistrates
and councillors ; they were held in honour by Popes,
cardinals, and the great princes of the Medici house.
Raphael, we are told, lived ' the life of a prince, not that

[1] Vasari, iv. 211–13.   [2] *Ibid*. v. 415.

of a painter ; ' [1] on the other hand, Antonio Sangallo was afflicted with a wife (married in haste against the wishes of his family) who ' lived rather in the manner of a most splendid lady than of an architect's wife ', and made extravagant demands upon his otherwise ample income.[2]

The privileged position occupied by famous practitioners may be inferred from the way in which they sometimes spoke to their noble patrons. Thus, when Giuliano da Sangallo requested to be dismissed from his post at St. Peter's because of the Pope's lack of interest in the progress of the building, Julius replied with some heat that Sangallo was not the only architect on earth.

' Whereupon Giuliano made answer that for truth and faithful service never would he find an equal to himself, whereas it would be easy for him to find princes who would maintain their promises with more fidelity than the Pope had shown towards him.' [3]

Rustici, an architect of independent means, told the Syndics of the Merchant's Guild at Florence that they were ' a herd of stupid oxen '.[4] Michelangelo, the most truculent of them all, frequently lost his temper with the Pope, and on one of these occasions threw a plank at his Holiness' head from the top of a scaffold.[5]

Michelangelo insisted on having a clause inserted in his contracts that he should not be interfered with. Once, when the assembled cardinals, constituting what we should call the ' Building Committee ' of St. Peter's, objected that insufficient lighting had been provided, Michelangelo replied :

' —I neither am nor will be obliged to tell your lordship or any other person what I intend or ought to do for this work ;

[1] *Ibid*. ii. 63.   [2] *Ibid*. iv. 24.   [3] *Ibid*. ii. 502.
[4] *Ibid*. v. 62.   [5] *Ibid*. v. 251.

your office is to procure money, and to take care that thieves do not get the same ; the designs for the building you are to leave to my care.' [1]

Nor must one forget the case of Verrocchio, who stipulated that, wherever he was working, but ' more particularly for monks or friars, . . . the door of the cellar, or whatever place the wine was kept in, should be left constantly open, that he might go to drink whenever he pleased, without asking leave from anyone.' [2]

An architect obtained his work then, as nowadays, either by personal interest or in competition. Personal interest was largely confined to the Pope and his cardinals, and to princely patrons like the Medici. One often reads of architects living in close touch with such celebrities and even following them into exile when their stars waned. Luigi Cornaro ' conceived so great a liking ' for the architect Falconetto ' that he caused him to dwell in his own house, where he entertained him honourably for the space of twenty years ' [that is, for the remainder of Falconetto's life], and, during that period, ' feeling a desire to behold and to examine those antiquities of Rome which he had seen in the drawings of the artist, took the latter with him to that city, where, having Falconetto constantly in his company, he took care to examine every building minutely '.[3]

Bartolommeo Genga, like his father, was permanently attached to the service of the Duke of Urbino, who provided for his five children after his death.[4] Other architects, as we have seen, relied on the patronage of the famous family of Medici. Alberti utilized the good offices of a friend who was secretary to the Pope.[5] Cronaca was

[1] Vasari, v. 304. [2] *Ibid*. ii. 257–8. [3] *Ibid*. iii. 439.
[4] *Ibid*. iv. 414. [5] *Ibid*. ii. 43.

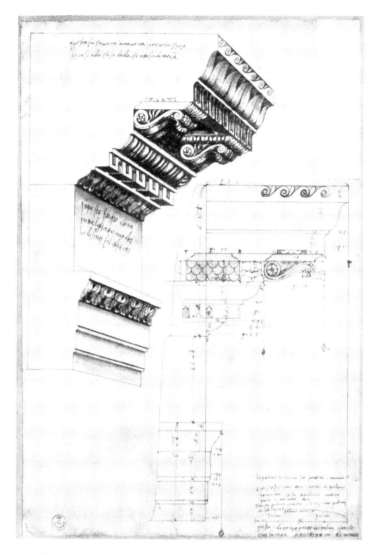

FIG. 25. A MEASURED DRAWING BY ANTONIO DA SANGALLO
In the Uffizi Gallery at Florence (see p. 163)

successful in a competition for a church chiefly because he was a friend of the great Savonarola.[1] Competitions seem to have been arranged usually by invitation, and were often resorted to not only for large buildings, and schemes, but even for parts of buildings, such as the dome and the bronze doors at Florence, and the cornice of the Farnese palace at Rome. As nowadays, competitions often gave rise to bickering and bad feeling among the architects concerned. The story of Brunelleschi's adventures in the great competition for the dome at Florence forms one of the most interesting passages in Vasari's *Lives* [2] but is unfortunately too lengthy for quotation here.

The practice of architecture in Italy at that period was beset with the same difficulties and worries that often mar it to-day, so that a sensitive man with the artistic temperament was sometimes driven to despair. The intensely personal nature of the architect's work that had so largely replaced the semi-communal organization of the Middle Ages led to rivalries and jealousies, usually caused by the struggle for fame and consequent remuneration. So, though Vasari pictures an age where art was genuinely worshipped for its own sake, he mentions a host of petty squabbles, some of them among really great men, like Michelangelo. Most of these architects had to rely entirely on their earnings for their livelihood. Occasionally we came across the mention of architects of independent means, such as Rustici (see p. 134), and Franceso di Giorgio, ' a man of fair possessions ', who were therefore more or less their own masters. Falconetto who had ' a great and most exalted mind ', coupled with the patronage of Messer Luigi Cornaro, had so soaked

[1] *Ibid.* iii. 87.   [2] *Ibid.* i. 424–35.

that mind with the achievements in architecture of the Romans that he preferred to spend his time in drawing fanciful designs for grandiose schemes and ' would not deign to prepare designs for private dwellings of the gentry . . . although very frequently urged to do so '.[1] But his case was exceptional, and for most architects the scramble for a livelihood was inevitable. Professional rivalry inevitably resulted, and occasionally professional men discovered and duly pulverized an amateur in their preserve,[2] though, as we have seen, the door leading into architectural practice was generally ajar. Sometimes the architect was dilatory, sometimes over-hasty. Thus Bramante's hustling of the foundations of the Belvedere at the Vatican, to please an exacting master, afterwards led to a failure and Raphael also is typical of the architect who is too ready to meet unreasonable requests, in fact, at the Vatican he was

' so courteous and obliging, that for the convenience of certain among his friends, he commanded the masons not to build the walls in a firm uninterrupted range, but to leave certain spaces among the old chambers on the lower floors, to the end that they might store casks, pipes, firewood, &c., therein,' [3]

and again the result was disastrous. Michelangelo's troubles in old age with the authorities at St. Peter's may be compared with those that darkened Wren's latter days at our own St. Paul's ; and Jacopo Sansovino was once thrown into prison, fined, and degraded at the instance of detractors, but afterwards released and reinstated in favour when it was discovered that the collapse of a vault which had led to this accusation was in no way his respons-ibility. But of all the pictures that Vasari gives us of an architect's cares, there is none more vivid than that of

[1] Vasari, iii. 441.   [2] *Ibid*. i. 451–3.   [3] *Ibid*. iii. 45.

Brunelleschi working on the dome at Florence, dealing with labour troubles, locking out strikers, organizing canteens in the dome to save time lost by workmen descending for dinner at midday, inventing and improving scaffolding and tackle.[1] Yet Brunelleschi, though hampered by all these sordid details and capable of dealing with every one of them, was one of the foremost artists that Italy has ever produced.

An architect in general practice sometimes undertook ' consulting ' work, either in his own State, or in other parts of Italy : and there is frequent mention of architects who undertook work abroad—e. g. Michelozzi designed a hospital at Jerusalem for the Medici ;[2] Andrea Sansovino worked for the King of Portugal for nine years ;[3] Sanmicheli designed fortresses in Dalmatia, Corfu, Cyprus, and Crete ;[4] Primaticcio settled in France,[5] and Fra Giocondo worked there ;[6] and Bartolommeo Genga designed fortifications, a town-plan, and many palaces and churches in Malta, for the Knights of St. John.[7]

Though the professional status of the architect was not quite so clearly defined as it is to-day, there seems no reason for concluding that he often undertook the work of the builder too. Even so early as 1423, we find that Brunelleschi succeeded in paralysing all the work on the cathedral at Florence by shamming illness and remaining in bed. The ' master-builders ' and the ' purveyor of the works ' came to see him there, unable to proceed without him, and thus making it clear, as Brunelleschi intended, that he and he alone possessed the master-brain on that great undertaking.[8] On another occasion Giuliano

[1] *Ibid*. i. 442–4.   [2] *Ibid*. i. 506.   [3] *Ibid*. ii. 121.
[4] *Ibid*. iv. 422.   [5] *Ibid*. v. 371.   [6] *Ibid*. iii. 388–9.
[7] *Ibid*. iv. 413–14.   [8] *Ibid*. i. 438.

M

da Sangallo took builders (*maestri muratori*) and masons (*scarpellini*) to Loreto.[1] Sometimes the architect was not above a commercial speculation, thus Aristotile Sangallo ran a cement-factory for his architect-brother.[2]

It is very difficult to ascertain how an architect was paid on individual commissions, though there are a few references by Vasari to annual salaries. Brunelleschi, after finally getting rid of his rival Ghiberti on the cathedral at Florence, received 100 florins down and a permanent appointment in charge of the building with a salary of 100 florins.[3] It is clear that while some artists declined ill-paid work, others were content to put their art before money. They even declined tempting offers to change their employment or their place of abode. But on the whole the capable artists lived well, in so appreciative an age, and the great masters became rich men. When Michelangelo declined to accept any fees for his work at St. Peter's, he was already old and wealthy. Perquisites, allowances, and ecclesiastical or state offices sometimes enhanced a salary or fees. Thus Jacopo Sansovino, as architect to the Venetian state, had a house as well as a salary. Giuliano da Sangallo declined a large present of money from the King of Naples when he left that monarch's service, but suggested that a few ' antiques ' would be acceptable instead ; nor did he reject the horses and clothing included in the original offer. Architects employed by the Popes often held some office connected with the papal court, and Raphael was intended for, and would have received, a cardinal's hat, but ' meanwhile did not abandon the light attachment by which he was enchained, and one day on returning to his house from

---

[1] Vasari, ii. 496.   [2] *Ibid*. iv. 472.
[3] *Ibid*. i. 441.

Fig. 26. A RESTORATION OF THE BATHS OF DIOCLETIAN AT ROME

From a drawing by Giuliano da Sangallo in the Uffizi Gallery at Florence

one of these secret visits, he was seized with a violent fever ', and so died hatless.[1]

The architect's assistant appears now and then in Vasari's pages, marrying his master's daughter,[2] acting as ' ghost ' to an incompetent chief,[3] and sometimes obtaining generous recognition, as when young Cronaca designed the magnificent cornice of the Strozzi Palace for Brunelleschi after a sketch that he had made in student days in Rome.[4] One of Bramante's assistants was a carpenter, perhaps employed by him to make models.[5] Many architects were assisted by sons or younger brothers who themselves became famous in later years. A hereditary practice, passing from father to son or nephew, was no rare thing, and the ' architectural families ' of Sangallo, Genga, Peruzzi, Falconetto, d'Agnolo, Sanmicheli, and Sansovino may be mentioned.

The large number of drawings preserved from this period enables us to judge of the architect's ability and methods of draughtsmanship without much difficulty. For the purpose of brief criticism here they may be classified under four general heads : studies from the antique, free sketches, working drawings, and imaginary designs. Figs. 22, 24, 25, 28, illustrate examples of each type, all taken from the wonderful collection in the Uffizi Gallery at Florence. Fig. 25 is a reproduction of one of a series of measured drawings of antique fragments made by Antonio da Sangallo the Elder (1455–1534) and represents an entablature found in the Piazza Navona in Rome. There are other decorated cornices in the same series and a beautiful study of an Ionic capital. This architect's measured drawings are among the most interesting that

---

[1] *Ibid*. iii. 59–60.   [2] *Ibid*. iv. 218.   [3] *Ibid*. iv. 388.
[4] *Ibid*. iii. 81–3.   [5] *Ibid*. ii. 442–3.

we possess from this period ; but there are others of outstanding merit, by unknown artists, in the ' Sketch-book of Andreas Coner ' at the Soane Museum. Drawings of whole buildings, such as the Colosseum, have also survived. If it were possible to illustrate here a number of examples,[1] it would become evident that Italian masters of the Early and Middle Renaissance were skilled in perspective. This appears notably in some of Bramante's drawings ; as also in Fig. 22, from a remarkable sketch in the Uffizi Gallery, by an unknown master of the sixteenth century, representing the scaffolding for the lantern of the Duomo at Florence (cf. Fig. 27) ; and in another study partly in plan and partly in elevational perspective, by Bramante according to Geymüller or by Peruzzi according to later critics, for the completion of St. Peter's at Rome. Fig. 24 is from Peruzzi's working drawing for the Palazzo Massimi in Rome. In the same collection is a bold sketch to a large scale for details of the building ; also a plan and details of the church of S. Domenico at Siena. Both plans are drawn to scale, dimensioned, and annotated. There is a large-scale detail elevation of the interior of the church of S. Lorenzo at Florence, by Brunelleschi, probably the earliest Renaissance drawing extant. Fig. 28 is a conjectural restoration for the great hall of the Baths of Diocletian by Giuliano da Sangallo (*d.* 1516), and is given here as an example of imaginative design, though there are many other drawings which, perhaps, better deserve that title. But it was in the last period of the Renaissance that architects gave free rein to their fancy, and produced whole albums of masterly designs for buildings which they never could expect to carry out.

[1] For a representative collection of examples see Blomfield's *Architectural Drawing* (1912), Brogi's *Disegni di Architettura* (1904), &c.

It has sometimes been assumed that models were used as a *substitute* for drawings, but there are many references in Vasari making it quite clear that this was not generally so. For example, the picture reproduced in Fig. 23 clearly shows the architect presenting the model to his patron, while the plan lies beside him ready for subsequent action. A model gives to a layman the clearest idea of a building in three dimensions, and though we know that Brunelleschi was regarded as an expert in perspective, on this occasion he is evidently relying on a model and a utilitarian plan rather than on a skilful perspective drawing. Fig. 26 illustrates the model of the lantern for the Duomo at Florence, made by Brunelleschi to enable it to be finished according to his ideas after his death, and now preserved in the Museo dell' Opera del Duomo. It is of worm-eaten wood, and is made, as nearly as I can calculate, to a scale of 3 feet to 1 inch, measuring about 21 inches from the base of the lantern to the underside of the ball. A small portion of the dome is shown stripped of its covering, thus enabling the ribs and staircases to be seen. The same museum contains two wooden models of the dome, said to be even earlier. Bramante is said to have made ' innumerable ' models,[1] but we also know him as an excellent draughtsman. On one occasion Michelangelo's assistant made five alternative sketch designs for a church, and then a clay model of the design selected by his clients. This model was ' of eight palms ' in length and took the assistant ten days to make.[2] Michelangelo himself made a model in a fortnight for the completion of St. Peter's, at a cost of 25 crowns. Vasari contrasts it with the model made for the same purpose by Antonio da Sangallo, which cost 4,000 crowns

[1] Vasari, ii. 437.   [2] *Ibid*. v. 329.

and took several years to make.[1] Sangallo's model was
37 palms in length and the actual building was intended
to have a length of 1,040 palms. Hence the scale of
the model was approximately 1 : 28, or rather less than
½ inch to 1 foot. Both models are preserved at St. Peter's.
For his models of the dome at Florence, elaborately made
to scale in wood with all internal and external details,
Brunelleschi was paid in 1423 only some 50 lire, while at
the same time Ghiberti was paid 300 lire for his rejected
model, a difference ascribed by Vasari to sheer favouritism.[2]
It appears that important permanent models, serving as
a guide to the builders, were made of wood, and that those
used to give a client a general idea of the effect of a building
were modelled in clay. Mention has already been made
(p. 153) of Tribolo's cork model of Florence, constructed
in sections to facilitate transport. There are other
instances of relief models of towns [3] and of fortifications :
thus the Venetian state kept a model of the fortifications
of Venice which was periodically brought up to date.[4]
Fra Giocondo made a model for a bridge at Verona.[5]
and Bartolommeo Genga completed a church from a
model left by his father.[6] Michelangelo's full-size competition model of the cornice for the Farnese Palace at
Rome was fixed on the building to give an idea of the
ultimate effect.[7]

   Though architects before the days of Palladio and
Vignola were not prolific authors, they produced a number
of books, mainly concerned with Vitruvius and the Orders.
One of them, Cesare Cesariano, ' had written a commentary on Vitruvius, but falling into despair at finding

[1] Vasari, v. 293.   [2] *Ibid*. i. 437.   [3] *Ibid*. iii. 172.
[4] *Ibid*. iv. 440.   [5] *Ibid*. iii. 387.   [6] *Ibid*. iv. 404.
[7] *Ibid*. v. 296.

FIG. 27. BRUNELLESCHI'S WOODEN MODEL OF THE LANTERN OF THE
CATHEDRAL DOME AT FLORENCE

himself disappointed in the remuneration he had expected to receive for that work ', eventually lost his reason.[1] Alberti and Fra Giocondo were the chief writers in this field, Francesco di Giorgio published a book on engineering, Andrea Sansovino wrote on ' distances and measurements ' and another treatise on floor-construction, and Peruzzi commenced a work on the antiquities of Rome, afterwards incorporated in Serlio's volumes.

The admirable biographies contained in Vasari's *Lives* are not the only records we possess of Renaissance architects in Italy. Contemporary portraits have been preserved of most of them, their chief buildings still stand, and their tombs are to be found in St. Peter's, the Pantheon, and the churches that they designed. For it was a great age for an architect to live in ; he was appreciated and honoured.

Yet the temperament of the artist often abhorred publicity, and it is perhaps necessary to correct misapprehension on this point by quoting in conclusion one of Vasari's most intimate and reflective passages.

' Art ', he writes, ' demands the whole man, with all his thoughts, for herself. He who resigns his life to her may well disregard society, seeing that he is never alone nor without food for contemplation ; and whoever shall attribute this love of solitude to caprice or eccentricity does wrong. The man who would produce works of merit should be free from cares and anxieties, seeing that Art demands earnest consideration, loneliness, and quietude ; she cannot permit wandering of the mind.' [2]

.   .   .   .   .

For the later and ' Baroque ' periods of the Renaissance our information is largely derived from Milizia, a scholar

[1] Vasari, ii. 428.   [2] *Ibid.* v. 355.

whose work on the lives of famous architects first appeared in 1768.[1] Though not himself an architect, he is a keen and unsparing critic, much more so than Vasari. He seldom condescends to give us the amusing and trivial incidents of life as Vasari does ; nevertheless on one occasion he tells us that an architect, who was old enough to know better, died of eating too much iced melon.[2] By summarizing facts from his lengthy volumes, one is enabled to make comparisons between conditions obtaining in the period 1550–1750 and those already described.

As one might expect, in that essentially aristocratic age, architects usually came from the upper and professional classes ; thus, of some 30 typical examples, only four appear to have been the sons of artisans, whereas nine were architects' sons, three the sons of painters and sculptors, and the remainder ' well-born '. More than a third of them were Lombards, the proportion of Florentines and Tuscans being much less than in earlier days, and the number of Romans being small ; one architect, Vanvitelli (Van Witel), came to Italy from Holland. Many entered the profession from other walks of life ; thus, out of 50 or 60 lives examined, seven men entered architecture from other branches of art, three from the study of letters, one or two from the law, one was a builder, another a mason, another an engineer in the army, and three came from the Church (though Milizia states [3] that Juvara, one of them, assumed the ecclesiastical habit solely with a view to studying architecture). Father Pozzo, the author of the maddest architectural designs that ever

[1] F. Milizia, *Vite degli Architetti più celebri* (Roma, 1768). The references given here are to Mrs. Cresy's translation. (London, 1826.) (See also list of earlier authorities in Bibliography on pp. 188–9.)

[2] *Ibid.*, ii. 193.   [3] *Ibid.* ii. 307.

appeared in print, began as a Jesuit cook, then successively practised painting, perspective, and architecture.[1] Curiously enough, the other chief extremist of the Baroque period, Filippo Guarini, was a Theatine monk.

Up to the middle of the seventeenth century, training continued to be chiefly by means of pupilage or apprenticeship, supplemented by exhaustive measuring and sketching of Roman antiquities. Subjects of study, besides drawing, included especially mathematics, geometry, perspective, and mechanics, but literary subjects are frequently mentioned. Architectural studies were sometimes commenced at 12 years of age. Milizia relates that one Teodoli, a marquis by birth and an architect by profession, ' being desirous of taking pupils, selected young men of the best capacity, whom he instructed with the greatest possible kindness.' . . . ' His theory was good, and his manner of teaching excellent.' [2]

A few typical instances may be quoted, showing how the chief architects of this period acquired their training. Alessi studied drawing and architecture under Caporali, an architect who had edited Vitruvius, then spent six years among the Roman ruins, and commenced practice at the age of thirty. Vignola first studied painting and perspective, then turned to architecture, and worked on the Roman antiquities until he was thirty. Palladio commenced architectural studies at the outset, and made three visits to Rome to sketch and measure, but also gave some attention to literature. Tibaldi, a mason's son, began as a painter, went to Rome to study architecture at twenty, and seems to have commenced practice about three years later. Domenico Fontana, ' having acquired the rudiments of geometry ', went to Rome at the age of twenty

[1] *Ibid.* ii. 253.   [2] *Ibid.* ii. 329.

to join his brother who was studying architecture there. Vicenzo Scamozzi was trained by his father, an architect, also studied mathematics, and proceeded to Rome to study the antiquities at twenty-five. Giacomo della Porta and Carlo Maderno both began as stucco workers ; the former was trained in architecture by Vignola, the latter by his uncle. Aleotti was at first a builder, then studied architecture and geometry, and became an architect. Rainaldi commenced his education with geometry and literature, then passed into architecture. Bernini, like his prototype Michelangelo, entered architecture from sculpture ; his great rival Borromini spent a short time in the same work, but then was sent to Rome to his uncle Carlo Maderno who taught him architecture and geometry.

In the last stage of the Renaissance, the influence of the architectural academies was strongly felt in Italy. The earliest of these, the Accademia di S. Luca in Rome, was reorganized in 1577 as a centre of artistic culture and a means of intercourse between artistic and learned men. It had its own statutes, privileges, professors, and lecturers ; and was intended to further the education of painters, sculptors, and architects. The close connexion between these three arts remained unbroken, in spite of the development of architectural scholarship, and Father Pozzo—the eccentric draughtsman already mentioned—once said that : ' He who has mastered painting and perspective will be a good architect.' Certainly Bernini's powers as a sculptor, like Michelangelo's before him, appear to advantage in his designs and his drawings. The architect now had to supplement his training in a master's studio with attendance at lectures in the Academy at Rome. Among those who studied there were Pietro da Cortona, Algardi, Carlo Fontana, Maderno, Bernini, Borromini, and Vanvitelli. Rome thus became more than ever the Mecca of the ambitious architectural student from other parts of Italy. Other academies were established in Bologna (the Accademia Clementina), Venice, Naples (the Accademia di S. Carlo, founded in 1755), Turin (the Compagnia di S. Luca, founded in 1652 and later merged in the University), and Milan (1776) ; as well as smaller academies in Lucca, Modena, Parma, and Ferrara.[1] Among the architectural staff of the academy at Bologna was Francesco Bibiena, of the famous family of theatrical architects, who taught geometry, perspective, mathematics, and surveying.[2] A chair of civil architecture was established at Padua in the eighteenth century. In connexion with the Accademia di S. Luca at Rome, an architectural scholarship or prize was established in 1702, to be followed by similar foundations of less importance. It is extraordinary that all this movement towards the standardization of architectural training, inevitably placing a heavy emphasis upon the Rules of the Ancients, should so nearly have synchronized with the cheerful unconventionality of the Baroque masters, to whom all rules are supposed to have been equally abhorrent. Probably the explanation is that, at first, close contact with painters and sculptors tended to make the architect strive for the bold and picturesque rather than the correct ; and that when the professors really got a strangle-hold on design in the eighteenth century they killed it so successfully that their work has been forgotten.

Milizia relates one pleasing anecdote about an archi-

[1] On these Academies see ' Architectural Education in Italy in the Past ', by G. Giovannoni and P. d'Achiardi, in the *Proceedings of the International Congress on Architectural Education*. (Published by the R.I.B.A., London, 1925.)

[2] Milizia, *op. cit.* ii. 263.

tect's assistant. Domenico Fontana, being occupied with other work, entrusted the design of a church to his pupil or assistant Rainaldi. The design was shown to the Pope, who admired it. Fontana gave the full credit for it to Rainaldi, whose fortune was thereafter assured.[1]

The status of the architect was now clearly defined, and though he sometimes dabbled in painting and sculpture, he generally confined himself to one art. No longer is there any chance of confusing him with the builder, for the two occupations are differentiated, as when we are told that Silvani, the architect, aged ninety-six, ascended the winding stair of a campanile in company with the builder, aged 100.[2] Yet one architect came to grief over his alleged maladministration of clerical building funds.[3] The design of fortifications, theatrical properties and scenery, gardens and bridges, formed a part of the architect's normal duties, and he continued to be a versatile man. One may safely award the palm for many-sidedness to Guidotti of Lucca, who practised architecture, painting, sculpture, and body-snatching ; studied mathematics, astrology, law, music, and poetry ; and finally broke his thigh in a flying accident, after covering a quarter of a mile on wings of his own design at a public display.[4] But one can detect a certain change in the nature of the work done by architects at this period. Military engineering is less often mentioned than in Vasari's *Lives* ; whereas civil engineering, as we understand it, continues to form a part of general practice. Thus Ammanati, Buontalenti, Domenico Fontana, Silvani, and Girolamo Rainaldi all designed bridges—some of great beauty ; Domenico Fontana constructed the great aqueduct, 22 miles long,

[1] Milizia, *op. cit.* ii. 197.   [2] *Ibid.* ii. 172.
[3] *Ibid.* ii. 84.   [4] *Ibid.* ii. 150.

known as the Acqua Felice, at Rome ; also a canal ; and was assisted in all this work by his elder brother Giovanni who specialized in hydraulic engineering.

The characteristics of the Baroque period in Italy were splendour, freedom, ostentation, and the introduction of planning on the grand scale with the admitted aim of producing a monumental effect. Bernini's wonderful Piazza di S. Pietro, the ' Spanish Steps·', and the Scala Regia at the Vatican are all cases in point ; while the villas of Genoa, Tuscany, Frascati, and the Brenta show the same ideas applied to domestic architecture in country surroundings. Hence one finds town-planning, formal garden design, and theatrical architecture assuming an increased importance in the architect's repertoire. It was an artificial and an aristocratic age, less spontaneous and more stilted than the previous period. The ideal ' client ' was now invariably the Pope or one of his cardinals, though the great nobles continued to erect palaces of increasing magnificence. Bernini and Borromini, among other leading architects, both had enormous general practices, and struggled with each other for professional supremacy. It does not seem that many architects specialized in any one type of building : the exceptional case of Giovanni Fontana has been cited, and to this may be added the remarkable monopoly of theatre design enjoyed in their day by the Bibiena family. But general private practice appears to have been the rule, and there are few instances in Milizia of the salaried appointments that were so common in earlier days.

It need hardly be said that a successful architect in Rome at this period enjoyed both riches and honours. The Grand Duke of Tuscany was so much attached to his architect Buontalenti ' that he commonly took him in his own carriage, not only to evening amusements, but about the city during the day ' [1]   After Domenico Fontana had succeeded in erecting the obelisk in the Piazza di San Pietro at Rome

' the artificers, intoxicated with joy, carried Fontana on their shoulders in triumph to his own house, amidst the sound of drums and trumpets and the plaudits of an immense crowd.' . . . ' For this undertaking Fontana was created a knight of the Golden Spur, and a Roman nobleman : he had a pension of 2,000 crowns, transferable to his heirs, ten knighthoods,'

and other substantial rewards ; while two medals were struck in his honour, his name was inscribed on the base of the obelisk, and a large book was published describing his achievement in detail. ' But what is the value of these obelisks ? ' asks Milizia, and after a sententious reference to ' difficulties surmounted ' he sarcastically adds that ' from this species of vanity some advantages have certainly arisen ; as the invention of machines, the employment of men, fame and riches to the artists '.[2]

It is, however, in the life of that great architect Lorenzo Bernini that the tale of vanity and riches attains its climax. Bernini's career, as well as his accomplished work, is typical of the gorgeous, artificial Baroque spirit of seventeenth-century Rome. His biography, first written by his son Domenico, has been undertaken by so many subsequent writers that the main facts of his triumphal progress are familiar to most students of art, but one or two incidents may be quoted to show the social position that he occupied, at a time when social position was one of the main ends in life. While he was still a young man, his patron Cardinal Barberini became Pope as Urban VIII, and addressed him as follows : ' It is fortunate for you that

---

[1] Milizia, ii. 69.   [2] *Ibid*. ii. 78–9.

FIG. 28. PORTRAIT OF BERNINI

In the Uffizi Gallery, Florence

the cardinal Maffeo Barberini is become Pope ; but we are still more so, that the Cavaliere Bernini should live during our pontificate.'[1] Cardinal Mazarin ' wrote to him repeatedly, entreating him in the warmest terms to enter the service of the King of France, promising him 12,000 crowns a year. But the Pope would not consent to it, saying that " Bernini was made for Rome, and Rome for Bernini ".'[2] On a subsequent occasion Urban VIII suggested to one of his cardinals that he should pay a visit to Bernini's own house to see the work that he was doing there. ' O Holy Father,' replied the cardinal, ' why such condescension ? You lower the papal dignity.' ' Very well then,' said the Pope, ' we will go and play with the children in our nephew's house.' ' That will be doing rightly ', said the master of ceremonies. ' In fact,' said the Pope with a smile, ' you approve of our becoming a child, but condemn our going to admire the greatest of men.' And on the same day His Holiness went with sixteen cardinals to visit Bernini.[3]

It was actually at the Pope's instigation that Bernini was affianced to the daughter of an ' honest secretary ' though hitherto he had felt no inclination to the married state, ' not from any aversion to the sex, but from his great love for his profession '. However, from his wedding onwards, ' he conducted himself with the steadiness and propriety becoming his new character '.[4] But his visit to Paris in 1665 reads like some Eastern romance. Louis XIV himself wrote to Bernini in terms of flattering eulogy, congratulating him on the designs he had just made for the Louvre, and begging him to honour Paris with his presence. At the same time Louis addressed

[1] *Ibid*. ii. 204.   [2] *Ibid*. ii. 207.
[3] *Ibid*. ii. 207.   [4] *Ibid*. ii. 208.

a letter to the Pope, requesting him to release Bernini for a period ; and eventually the great architect, now sixty-eight years of age, set out on his travels.

'The preparations for his journey resembled a triumphal march.' . . . Tuscany and Turin treated him with the utmost splendour ' as he passed through.

' At Lyons, all the professors of the arts, and persons of the first rank, went out to meet him ; and in every country he went through the people so flocked in the streets to see him that he was accustomed to compare himself to an elephant, or some *lusus naturae*. The nunzio went out of Paris with relays of horses to receive him, and he was conducted to the royal palace like one about to dispense happiness to the nation. The whole court and nobility vied with each other in paying him attention, and the king evinced to him every possible mark of friendship and generosity.' [1]

Yet all this splendid reception led to nothing, and Bernini's colossal design for the Louvre was never carried out. On the whole, we may regard this with equanimity, even with thankfulness. Dr. Christopher Wren, then a young man studying architecture in Paris, made an effort to see Bernini and sketch his designs for a collection of drawings of French buildings that he was making.

' Bernini's Design of the Louvre I would have given my skin for ; ' writes Wren to his friend Dr. Bateman, ' but the old reserved Italian gave me but a few minutes view, it was five little Designs on paper, for which he hath received as many thousand pistoles. I had only Time to copy it in my Fancy and Memory, and shall be able by Discourse and a Crayon to give you a tolerable Account of it.[2] During the eight months that he was in France, he had five *louis d'or* a day ; and finally a present of 50,000 crowns, with an annual pension of 2,000

[1] Milizia, ii. 217.
[2] L. Milman, *Sir Christopher Wren*, p. 83. (London, 1908.)

crowns, and one of 500 for his son, whom he took with him. Such magnificent rewards do honour to the fine arts, but this shows more ostentation than reason, because it was not extended in the same degree to those who were natives of France.'[1]

Yet Bernini, unquestionably the greatest architect of his age in Italy, and perhaps an even greater sculptor, was no sycophant. He was accustomed to visits from crowned heads and clerical notables while he was at work, but ' he never moved from politeness to any one ; and whoever went to him, lords of the first quality and cardinals, they always seated themselves in silence and watched his labours '. Sometimes, especially when engaged on a work of sculpture, he would relapse into a brown study for hours at a time and had to be watched lest he should fall. On such occasions he would say, ' Do not touch me, I am in love ', and this was true. Like his great predecessor Michelangelo, whom he resembles both in technique and temperament, he was a tremendous worker and loved his work. ' Could we sum up together all his idle moments,' writes Milizia, ' setting aside his hours for sleep and refreshment, they would not, in the course of so long a life, amount to a month '.[2]

Bernini's rival, Francesco Borromini, was created a *Cavaliere di Cristo* by Urban VIII and awarded 3,000 crowns and a pension. He also received the Cross of St. James and 1,000 pistoles from the King of Spain, for designs made (but never carried out) for a royal palace.[3] Alessandro Algardi was created a *Cavaliere di Cristo* by Innocent X, who also ' presented him with a collar of gold worth 300 crowns '.[4]

---

[1] Milizia, ii. 218.   [2] *Ibid*. ii. 220.
[3] *Ibid*. ii. 190.   [4] *Ibid*. ii. 185.

It is difficult to arrive at any estimate of the rate at which architects were paid for their work at this period, but there seems to be no doubt that successful members of the profession became wealthy men. For nine years' work on the *baldacchino* at St. Peter's Bernini received 10,000 crowns ;[1] his fees for his visit to Paris have already been mentioned. At his death he left property worth 400,000 crowns ;[2] a fortune which may be compared with 200,000 crowns left (to a church) by Pietro da Cortona,[3] 80,000 crowns left by De' Rossi,[4] and 100,000 crowns earned by Pellegrino Tibaldi during nine years' residence in Spain.[5] Whatever may have been the purchasing power of the crown in those days, the figures cited above must represent large sums when we find that a well-born and successful architect named Constantino de' Servi (1554–1622) was tempted to England to work for the then Prince of Wales for a salary of 800 crowns a year,[6] while Filippo Juvara (1685–1735) was appointed chief architect to the King of Sicily, ' with an annual allowance of 600 crowns ', and also presented with ' the rich abbey of Selve, worth 1,100 scudi a year '.[7] Any surmises on these financial questions are complicated by uncertainty as to whether an annual salary was paid for an architect's whole time, or whether it allowed him to accept other work or perquisites. Juvara himself was an abbot while practising architecture and drawing a salary ; another architect became a bishop.[8] Buontalenti, whom we remember as a Baroque designer with good taste and a playful fancy, added to a varied architectural practice an appointment as ' engineer of all Tuscany ', and in this

[1] Milizia, ii. 205.   [2] *Ibid*. ii. 219.   [3] *Ibid*. ii. 175.
[4] *Ibid*. ii. 234.   [5] *Ibid*. ii. 61.   [6] *Ibid*. ii. 144.
[7] *Ibid*. ii. 308.   [8] *Ibid*. ii. 51.

capacity designed bridges and fortifications, to say nothing of theatrical scenery and the accessories of public festivals. But, for his invention of ' a method of preserving ice and snow, the Grand Duke gave him all the duties upon those articles '.[1]

It is quite certain that practically all the great architects of the seventeenth century in Italy carried on ' general practice ' in the modern sense, and something has already been said of their multifarious activities. A practice often passed from father to son, or from uncle to nephew, and among Italian architectural families of the late sixteenth, seventeenth, and early eighteenth centuries may be mentioned those of Palladio, Lunghi, Fontana, Rainaldi, De' Rossi, and Bibiena. The leading architects in Rome and other great Italian cities were often invited abroad, but in spite of substantial bait in the form of salaries they did not always respond. Among those who entered the service of foreign courts may be cited Alessi and Juvara who worked in Portugal ; Tibaldi, who spent nine years in Spain ; Scamozzi, who designed the cathedral at Salzburg ; Constantino de' Servi, who was employed in Persia, England, Holland, and elsewhere ; Coccopani, who carried out works of military engineering for the emperor at Vienna ; Guarini, who built churches at Paris, Prague, and Lisbon ; Mattia de' Rossi, who did some work in France ; Galilei, who resided seven years in England, but did little there ; and Ferdinando Bibiena, who was summoned first to Barcelona and then to Vienna to arrange the staging of royal festivals.[2]

Francesco Bibiena (1659-1739) was invited to London, but unfortunately declined the invitation ; otherwise we might possess in this country an example of his theatre-

[1] *Ibid*. ii. 69.   [2] *Ibid*. ii. *passim*.

craft.[1]   Vignola is said to have supplied a design for Kelston Manor House, Somerset (rebuilt in 1760), but there is no record that he visited England himself.[2]   Italian architects often supplied drawings or models for buildings abroad without supervising their erection.   Thus Carlo Fontana sent models for a cathedral to Fulda in Germany, and for royal stables to Vienna.[3]

Besides the ordinary routine of general practice, there are references by Milizia and other writers to consulting work, competitions, and arbitrations.   Vignola was invited by the King of Spain to act as assessor in the competition for the Escurial, for which twenty-two architects of various nationalities had submitted designs by invitation.   Whereupon Vignola,

' with that exquisite discernment so peculiar to him, selected whatever was most elegant from each, and, writing his own ideas, produced so beautiful a whole, that Philip II immediately decided on it, and invited Vignola to Spain to execute it ; but his advanced age and attachment to Rome prevented him from undertaking the journey, and the design was not carried into effect.' [4]

Milizia offers no opinion as to Vignola's professional conduct as an assessor in this case, but then Milizia was not an architect ; at the present day such a proceeding would not be tolerated.   On another occasion Vignola was employed to settle a boundary dispute, and did so ' with judgement and integrity '.[5]

Considering that the greater part of Rome was rebuilt, and magnificently rebuilt, during this period it is interesting to see how the architects concerned treated the monu-

[1] Milizia, ii. 262.
[2] M. S. Briggs, ' Vignola ' (in *The Architectural Review*, London, 1915).
[3] Milizia, ii. 265.   [4] *Ibid* ii. 22.   [5] *Ibid*. ii. 23.

ments of antiquity which consecrated (or encumbered) so much of the ground. In spite of the frantic enthusiasm for the antique that was assumed in the early days of the Renaissance, we have seen (pp. 146–7) that marble columns and priceless sarcophagi were treated with scant respect by the great ecclesiastical builders and the architects whom they employed. In the Baroque period, when every other architect perpetrated a book on the Orders, very similar conditions prevailed. Sixtus V commissioned Domenico Fontana to convert the ruins of the Colosseum into a wool factory : this noble work was duly put in hand, but was abandoned at the Pope's death in 1590.[1] In the work of Sixtus V at St. Peter's, according to Lanciani, we find ' the same contempt for the memories of the past, and the same prodigious activity and liberality in the substitution of new monuments...' He is responsible for ' the melting of the bronze doors of the old basilica, for the destruction of the invaluable mosaics of the apse of Innocent III, and for the removal of the seven porphyry steps which the pilgrims *ad limina* were wont to ascend on their knees '.[2]

Bronze doors and beams, bronze *ciboria* and roof tiles, were stripped ruthlessly from old churches and temples, especially from the Pantheon, which supplied a large part of the 80 tons or so of bronze used in Bernini's famous *baldacchino* at St. Peter's. It is unfair to attribute all the blame for this vandalism to the architects, who were probably only carrying out the orders of clerical employers, but one cannot help feeling that they were partly responsible. Nor were all these priceless relics used as

[1] *Ibid*. ii. 83–4.
[2] R. Lanciani, *Wanderings through Ancient Roman Churches*, 99–106. (London, 1925.)

materials to satisfy the megalomania of the papacy. Sarcophagi from St. Peter's were rifled of their sacred contents and then used as water-troughs ; the bones of medieval popes were thrown on to rubbish heaps ; mosaics, tombstones, ' souvenirs ' of every age and kind were scattered over Italy or given to favourites of the Curia.

For this splendid age, with all its achievements in architecture and town-planning, its generous patronage of every art and its honour to successful artists, had its seamy side. The sordid tales of nepotism and intrigue that defile the history of the popes in the seventeenth century are matched by occasional references to equally unsavoury disputes among architects. Professional rivalry was sometimes acute, and when Borromini was appointed architect at St. Peter's under Bernini's direction, ' he soon became ambitious, then envious, and finally the enemy of his master, endeavouring to supersede him in all his offices '.[1] Lastly, though a long and successful career had brought him fame, he came to the conclusion that his reputation was still inferior to Bernini's, fell into a state of melancholy, and had to be put under supervision, but succeeded in getting possession of a dagger one night and committed suicide.

Another typical story relates how an architect made his fortune. Domenico Fontana, having left his native village in Lombardy at the age of twenty to study architecture in Rome, was employed by Cardinal Montalto to design a chapel in S. Maria Maggiore, and a small palace adjoining :

' but Pope Gregory XIII, having deprived the cardinal of his income, thinking that his building was an evidence of too

[1] Milizia, ii. 190.

great riches, it was suspended for want of funds ; but Fontana being attached to the cardinal and to the building, sent for 1,000 crowns, which he had saved by his own industry, with which he was enabled to continue the chapel.   This act of generosity made the fortune of Fontana.   Soon after Cardinal Montalto became Sixtus V and Fontana the pontifical architect.' [1]

The number of books produced by architects of this period is considerable, but the bulk of them are concerned with the Orders and their application.   The writings of Vignola, Palladio, and Scamozzi on this somewhat dreary topic were translated into foreign languages and spread all over Europe.   Thus Vignola come to be the mentor of French architects and Palladio of our English predecessors. In spite of the antiquarian interest of these vellum-bound folios with their fine engravings, they have wrought incalculable harm to the spontaneous development of individual design in this country and others.   A torrent of them poured from the printing-presses of Italy, France, England, Germany, Belgium, and Spain, from the six- teenth to the eighteenth century.

' Vitruvius became the architects' Bible,' writes Sir Thomas Jackson, ' . . . The effect has been to bring the Art into bondage to formula, to enslave practice to theory, to extinguish origin- ality, and to make architecture into a mechanical pursuit— in fact, instead of the architecture of freedom and imagination, to give us the architecture of the book.' [2]

Yet an age and a country that was guilty of so much pedantry also gave us the buildings of Bernini and Borro- mini, who certainly made use of the Orders, but in a way that must have caused Vitruvius and his later editors to

[1] *Ibid.* ii. 72.
[2] Sir T. G. Jackson, *Architecture*, p. 248. (London, 1925.)

turn in their graves. And we must admit that books on the Orders were not the only output of architectural scribes of that day. A measure of comic relief is provided, quite unintentionally, by Domenico Fontana's pretentious folio recounting his heroic exploit in erecting the obelisk in the Piazza di S. Pietro at Rome. In the following century Carlo Fontana, by order of the Pope, wrote a lengthy description of the Vatican including St. Peter's : this was not entirely a historical study, as recommendations were made for replanning the area surrounding the Vatican group of buildings. Other architects wrote on mathematics, perspective, hydraulics, and philosophy, as well as on architecture. Carlo Lambardo produced a small book on the floods of the Tiber ; Ignazio Danti wrote a life of Vignola ; Palladio, a good classical scholar, published an annotated edition of Caesar's *Commentaries* ; and F. M. Preti in his *Elementi di Architettura* (1780) actually condescended to refer to ' Gothic construction, magnificence, and unity '.[1]

But the chief attraction of architectural books of the period is the high standard of the engravings that illustrate them, and even, in many cases, form their entire contents. Palladio's own drawings of ancient Roman buildings have both an artistic and an antiquarian value ; the Bibiena family's designs for theatres are magnificent examples of draughtsmanship. Domenico Fontana's book, already mentioned, on the obelisk at St. Peter's, contains a wonderful engraving showing the obelisk being actually raised into position, the complicated scaffolding and shoring being made to enhance the decorative effect of the composition. During the seventeenth century the same high level of illustration was not maintained, but, in the

[1] Milizia, *op. cit.* ii. 376.

FIG. 29. A DESIGN FOR AN ALTAR-PIECE, BY BERNINI

From the drawing in the Uffizi Gallery at Florence

eighteenth, there was a brilliant succession of architectural draughtsmen in Italy, including (in addition to the Bibiena family, mentioned above) Canaletto, Mauro Tesi, Panini, and, above all, Piranesi. The Library of the R.I.B.A. contains a fine and representative collection of the work of these artists, and the illustrations in Sir Reginald Blomfield's book, *Architectural Drawing and Draughtsmen*, give an idea of the brilliant technique and exuberant fancy that characterizes them. But few of these draughtsmen were practising architects, and it will be noticed that the names of Bernini and Borromini are not included. Bernini's style of draughtsmanship (see fig. 29) betrays the sculptor. His bold use of light and shade, his free handling of the human figure, alike reveal the predominant bent of his taste. In regard to actual working drawings. Sir Reginald Blomfield writes that those ' made by such men as Bernini and Borromini are inferior to the drawings of Bramante, Peruzzi, and the two Sangalli. Those that I have seen are not worth reproducing '.[1] In addition to the R.I.B.A. collections already mentioned, students of Italian draughtsmanship at this period should refer to the drawings preserved at the Soane Museum, including works by Francesco Bibiena and Panini. In the Museo dell' Opera del Duomo at Florence there is a set of six wooden models made by leading architects between *c.* 1586–1635 for the completion of the west front of the cathedral. Some of these are coloured, and the scale varies from about $1\frac{1}{2}$ to $3\frac{1}{2}$ feet to 1 inch.

At the conclusion of this, the first of three chapters dealing with architects of the Renaissance, one can hardly avoid a comparison with conditions during the preceding

[1] Sir R. Blomfield, *Architectural Drawing and Draughtsmen*, p. 59. (London, 1912.)

centuries, and the most striking contrast between the two periods, so far as we are concerned here, lies in the emergence of the architect's personality. I have already argued at some length that the medieval master-mason was in fact the prototype of the modern professional architect, that differences of status and training were largely due to prevailing social conditions, and that his much exaggerated anonymity was usually a matter of compulsion rather than choice. But, as the Renaissance dawns in Italy, we find all doubt as to authorship, even as to the most trivial details of an architect's career, swept right away by Vasari and others, who took pride in recording the achievements of all the great artists of their time and their country.

Do we lose or gain by this additional knowledge? In a recent and striking study, a well-known novelist and critic has considered this question.[1] He is primarily concerned with literary anonymity, but on one page he says that 'the Cathedral builders left their works unsigned' That is relatively but not absolutely true, as I have pointed out, and even in this present commercial age few architects sign their buildings. Mr. Forster's main argument is, however, that, in the case of what he calls 'creative' literature, anonymity of authorship is a positive advantage to the reader, whereas in 'informative' literature we gain by knowing the author's name, so that we may judge whether his facts are to be relied on and take proceedings against him if they are not. Now it seems to be held by some critics that Gothic architecture acquires an additional glory because they are ignorant, or pretend to be ignorant, of its designers' names. They argue that its beauty is largely due to its spontaneous and traditional evolution,

---

[1] E. M. Forster, *Anonymity* (1925).

as contrasted with the formal and sometimes pedantic work of the Renaissance, with which architects and their pattern-books of the Orders were so actively connected. That argument has something in its favour : formalism and pedantry are not the most attractive of qualities. But to my mind we *lose* nothing by knowing a little of the names and lives of our great architects of all periods ; otherwise this book would never have been written. One's admiration for Michelangelo's ceiling at the Sistine is not affected one way or the other by having read Vasari's detailed account of its painting ; nor does one judge Cellini's art by any of the moral standards that he so conspicuously ignored in his life. But it is important that our criticism of all forms of art should be well-founded and that writers on architecture, even if they do not wish to reveal the names or the personalities of architects, should not ascribe authorship to supernatural or ecclesiastical sources when they are aware that some trained man must have been responsible. It is, therefore, for justice and truth that I plead in this book ; though I think that most of us experience an added interest in studying an old building if we can picture the methods by which it came into being. The marks of the adze on the oak, the curious masons' marks on the stone, the effigies of master-masons with the emblems of their craft beside them, seem to bring the Middle Ages more vividly before us. And certainly, if one had to choose between Vasari's *Lives* and Palladio's *Orders*, there is no doubt which work most of us would select. So far from the human interest preventing our critical appraisement of an architectural masterpiece, it should heighten our interest without in any way affecting our judgement.

BIBLIOGRAPHY

(Abbreviations : *A.R. = Architectural Review* ; *J. = R.I.B.A. Journal.*)

(a) COLLECTIONS.

Baglione. *Vite de'* . . . *architetti dal pont. di Greg. XIII–Urbano VIII* (1642).

Milizia, F. *Le Vite dei più celebri architetti* (1768).

Passeri. *Vite di* . . . *architetti che hanno lavorato in Roma, morti 1641–73* (1772).

Soprani and Ratti. *Pittori, scultori, ed architetti Genovesi* (1768).

Temanza, T. *Dei più celebri architetti e scultori Veneziani* (1778).

Vasari, G. *Le vite de' più eccellenti pittori, scultori, ed architetti* (1550). [For bibliographical notes see pp. 130–6 in this book. The most complete modern edition of Vasari in English is that published in 1912–16 by Messrs. Macmillan and the Medici Society, translated by G. de Vere, in ten volumes.]

(b) MONOGRAPHS.

Alberti, L. B. By A. Venturi (1923).

Alessi, Galeazzo. By M. S. Briggs (*A.R.* 1915).

Bernini, Gian Lorenzo. By Baldinucci (1682) ; by D. Bernini (1713) ; by M. S. Briggs (in *Burlington Mag.*, 1915) ; by Max v. Boehm (1912) ; by Fraschetti (1900) ; by F. Pollac (1909) ; by R. Norton (1914) ; by M. Reymond (N.D. recent).

Bianco, Bartolommeo. By M. S. Briggs (*A.R.* 1915).

Borromini, F. By E. Hempel (1915) ; by A. Muñoz (1920).

Bramante, D. By A. Malaguzzi-Valeri (1924) ; by M. Reymond (N.D. recent).

Brunellesco (or Brunelleschi), F. By F. Baldinucci (1767–74) ; by C. von Fabriczy (1892) ; by A. Manetti (1887) ; by M. Reymond (N.D. recent) ; by Leader Scott (1901) ; by P. S. Worthington (*J.* 1909) ; by A. Venturi (1923).

Buonarotti, Michelangelo. By D. Frey (1923) ; by H. F. von Geymüller (1904) ; by C. Holroyd (1903); by R. Rolland (N.D. recent) ; by J. A. Symonds (1893).

Cortona, Pietro da. By A. Muñoz (1921) ; by Fabbrini (1896).

Laurana, L. By A. Colasanti (1922).

Leonardo da Vinci. By Anon. (*A.R.* 1914).

Ligorio, Pirro. By C. A. Harding (*J.* 1923).

Longhena, Baldassare. By M. S. Briggs (*A.R.* 1916).

Lurago, Rocco. By M. S. Briggs (*A.R.* 1915).

Maderno, Carlo. By A. Muñoz (1921).

Michelozzi, Michelozzo. By F. R. Hiorns (*J.* 1912).

Palladio, Andrea. By B. F. Fletcher (1902).

Peruzzi, Baldassare. By F. W. Bedford (*J.* 1902) ; by J. H. Worthington (*J.* 1913) ; by W. W. Kent (1925).

Rainaldi, Carlo. By H. Hempel (1921).

Ricchini, F. M. By M. S. Briggs (*A.R.* 1915).

Sangallo, G. and A. da. By R. Falb (1902) ; by P. S. Worthington (*J.* 1921).

Tibaldi, Pellegrino. By M. S. Briggs (*A.R.* 1915).

Vasari, Giorgio. By R. W. Carden (1910).

Vignola, G. Barozzi da. By I. Danti, in preface to Vignola's *Le Due Regole*, &c. (1583) ; by M. S. Briggs (*A.R.* 1915) ; by F. R. Hiorns (*J.* 1911).

VI

THE RENAISSANCE IN FRANCE

A COLLECTION of biographies of French architects, from the Middle Ages to his own day, was
written by Quatremère de Quincy nearly a century ago,[1]
yet though it tells us much of his own not very valuable
opinions about their buildings, it fails to present us
with a vivid picture of their lives and methods of work.
Sir Reginald Blomfield considers that Quatremère de
Quincy was ' one of the most ferocious and dogmatic
pedants that ever lived '. But the *lacuna* in English architectural literature concerning the French Renaissance
has been amply filled during the past fifteen years by the
publication of important books by the late Mr. W. H.
Ward,[2] Sir Reginald Blomfield,[3] and Sir Thomas Jackson,[4]
in all of which the position of the French architect has
received attention, Sir Reginald Blomfield especially
having treated the subject in great detail.

Even for the purpose of this brief study it is convenient
to divide the period into three stages : the first lasting
up to the appearance of the professional architect about
1550, the second from that date up to the foundation of
the French Academy of Architecture in 1671, and the

[1] Quatremère de Quincy, *Histoire de la Vie et des Ouvrages des
plus célèbres architectes, 1100–1800.* (Paris, 1830).

[2] W. H. Ward, *Architecture of the Renaissance in France.* (London,
1911.)

[3] Sir R. Blomfield, *A History of French Architecture from the reign
of Charles VIII till the death of Mazarin,* 2 vols. (London, 1911) ;
and *A History of French Architecture from the death of Mazarin till
the death of Louis XV,* 2 vols. (London, 1921.)

[4] Sir T. G. Jackson, *The Renaissance of Roman Architecture,*
vol. iii, ' France '. (Cambridge, 1923.)

third to the end of the eighteenth century. As was the case in England, medieval architecture and medieval methods persisted at least a century later than in Italy. The medieval master-mason is therefore found in France up to 1550 or so, and of his status during the preceding century, when so many wonderful buildings were erected in France, singularly little is known. The problem is greatly complicated by the fact that there was a constant influx of Italian artists into France for fifty years from 1494, when the French invasion of Italy made the king and his courtiers familiar with the buildings of the Renaissance in the latter country. Among these artists were several architects, notably Fra Giocondo, Domenico da Cortona, and Serlio. It has been contended that the influence of these men on French architecture was slight, that the amount of building executed by them was almost negligible, and that such architectural masterpieces as the *châteaux* on the Loire only became strongly influenced by Italian *motifs* at a time when most French architects studied and measured for themselves in Rome.

This is the view advanced by M. Palustre [1] and other patriotic French writers ; whereas M. Dimier, an enthusiastic admirer of Primaticcio, would ascribe all the credit to the artists who came from Italy. Sir Reginald Blomfield, who has little admiration for work of the early Renaissance in France, grudgingly concedes the authorship of a few designs to the Italians, but is loth to admit that the French master-masons had any architectural qualifications whatever, and concludes that the great buildings erected during the reign of François I were mainly the work of masons and other craftsmen directed by the king himself or by other architectural ' amateurs '. Sir Thomas Jackson, on

[1] Palustre, *La Renaissance en France*, vol. i. (Paris, 1892.)

the other hand, says that we owe the buildings of the early French Renaissance to ' master-masons of the medieval type '.[1]   Finally, Mr. Ward, whose lengthy survey of this period was published almost simultaneously with Sir Reginald Blomfield's first two volumes, takes a moderate and judicial view about midway between the four others already mentioned, but does not support his statements with many references to original documents. Thus we are faced with a startling divergence of opinion among three distinguished English architectural writers, all of them practising architects, and we find equal disagreement among French critics.   Nor do they (except Mr. Ward) display any doubt or diffidence in stating their opinions.   What, then, are we to conclude ?   To whom do we owe the designs of the great *châteaux* of the Loire, of Blois, of Fontainebleau, of St-Germain ; of churches such as St-Eustache at Paris, and St-Pierre at Caen ?   Were they the work of Frenchmen or Italians ; of architects, masons, or royal amateurs ?   In this period, at any rate, we are spared the suggestion that they were designed by inspired ecclesiastics ; but here, almost as much as in the case of the Middle Ages, there is need for commonsense in facing so controversial a problem.

At the end of the fifteenth century, when the invasion of Italian artists began, the directing personage on a building in France was, as I have been at some pains to prove in Chapter IV of this book, the master-mason, who did what drawing of designs was needful, and worked under or with a Treasurer or Comptroller representing the building owner, individual or corporate.   He usually, but not invariably, resided near his work ; often undertook only one ' job ' at a time ; and was largely trained

[1] Jackson, *op. cit.*, p. 75.

at the bench. ¶He was reasonably well paid, and occupied
a good social position. Occasionally, in the Middle Ages,
he acted as the contractor or ' builder ', and Sir Reginald
Blomfield, quoting the original documents relating to
François I's early work at Fontainebleau, seems to have
proved conclusively [1] that Gilles Le Breton, the mason,
undertook the masonry contract there in 1528 ; that other
building tradesmen signed contracts for carpentry, slating,
tiling, and so on ; and that the work was controlled by
an Italian who is generally called *valet-de-chambre* and
only once *architecteur*, but whose duty it was to check
the accounts of the building and transact the secretarial
business connected therewith. He received an annual
salary of 1,200 *livres*, probably equal to as many pounds
sterling in ' pre-war ' values [2] But, even if we accept
these apparently uncontrovertible facts, we have no proof
that Gilles Le Breton is thereby absolved from all share in
the design of the Fontainebleau buildings. Another
interesting case, also quoted by Sir Reginald Blomfield,[3]
refers to Chambord, where in 1556 Jacques Coqueau, the
master-mason, ' received his wages for preparing drawings
and specifications for carpentry and masonry and superintending the work '. Now the same author appears to
ascribe the original small-scale model for Chambord to
Domenico da Cortona, an Italian architect, who must
have made it thirty or forty years before ; but this model
did not include the central staircase which remains its
most striking feature, and is apparently the work of the
master-mason. Even if the Italian supplied the preliminary idea of the design, it is clear that at Chambord

[1] Blomfield, *French Architecture . . . till the death of Mazarin*, i. 13.
[2] On comparative money-values see Jackson, *op. cit.*, p. 80 *n.*, and
his preface, p. vii.   [3] Blomfield, *op. cit.*, p. 30.

the master-mason was a resident architect with considerable power of initiative, and that to him we owe one of the architectural marvels of France.[1]

Sir Reginald Blomfield [2] and Sir Thomas Jackson [3] agree in stating that the ' business ' of a master-mason often descended from father to son (e. g. in the families of Le Breton, Chambiges, and Grappin) ; and the latter authority says that this fact seems to imply something material to inherit, such as a builder's yard and plant. He does not, however, envisage, as he might, the possibility that the goodwill of an hereditary architectural practice is also a thing worth handing down.

Returning to the question of design, we may now compare the different opinions of the eminent writers already mentioned, to see how far they agree as to the position of the master-mason. M. Palustre and his disciples hold that in Gilles Le Breton, the Chambiges, and Pierre Nepveu we are to recognize architects who need not fear comparison with those of any country. Sir Thomas Jackson assumes that the first architects of the early Renaissance in France held exactly the same position as the master-masons of the Middle Ages. He insists that there must have been one man who designed the building and probably also supervised its construction.

' The general conception of the design was due to the master-mason, from whom it received the individual stamp which made it an original work ; and the details were filled up under his general supervision by the workmen, whose training taught them exactly what to do to realize his intention.... It is evident that after general instructions had been given to the master-mason, as to what the employer wanted, accompanied or not by a model on a small scale, he was left to carry the work out

[1] Blomfield, *op. cit.*, p. 55.   [2] *Ibid.* p. 33.   [3] Jackson, *op. cit.*, p. 87.

in a traditional way. Philibert de l'Orme in fact tells us so. . . .
He says the employer consults some master-mason, who draws
and submits some single plan, and when this single plan is
accepted, he is left to his own devices in executing the work.
The owner naturally would often visit the building, as François I
seems to have done, and would make suggestions sometimes
useful, more often perhaps injudicious and troublesome. But
practically the master-mason, as Philibert describes him, was
the architect.' [1]

Mr. Ward is rather less definite in his conclusions, but
seems to favour the theory that Italian artists designed
most of the buildings of this period. He says that few
of these men ' were architects in the strict sense of the
word ', but were masters of some one art or craft, and
were able to draw.

' The bulk of the work necessarily fell on the native *maîtres
d'œuvres* and their men. The French master-masons and
master-carpenters held positions which approximated, according to circumstances, to those of architect, clerk of works, or
contractor, and occasionally combined these functions. The
race of medieval craftsmen who built the Gothic castles and
cathedrals, originating the designs and making their own drawings, was dying out. With some brilliant exceptions, such as
Martin Chambiges of Beauvais and Roland le Roux of Rouen,
the *maîtres d'œuvres* had sunk to the rank of working contractors and were neither able nor called upon to initiate
designs.' [2]

Thus Mr. Ward, without denying that the noble patron
or employer often played an active part in the design of
a building by suggesting the incorporation of ideas or
details culled from Italy, assumes that somebody acted
as architect : either an Italian master who had graduated

[1] Jackson, *op. cit.*, pp. 89–90.   [2] Ward, *op. cit.*, pp. 7–8.

in some ancillary craft, or else one of the ' brilliant exceptions ', that he mentions among the master-masons.

Sir Reginald Blomfield is more dogmatic but not more
convincing.

' Can we ', he writes, ' in these earlier examples trace the
hand of an architect ? If, for example, a building shows con-
spicuous individuality and an architectural quality of its own,
the conclusion must be that an architect was at work here, no
matter what the guise under which he appears in documents,
whether *valet-de-chambre*, maker of models, or master-mason.
On the other hand, the fact that a man repeatedly appears in
the accounts for certain buildings as " master of the works "
would not prove that he was an architect, if those buildings
are precisely similar to many others of the same period, and
do not, in fact, show any personal quality of design. It may
be that Le Breton at Fontainebleau was an architect in all
respects on the same footing as De l'Orme at Anet.' [1]

Elsewhere he writes that the master-masons, including the
families of Chambiges, Le Breton, Grappin, and Bachelier
—that is, some of the most brilliant men of their time—
were

' at their best competent building tradesmen, men who not
only contracted for work, but worked with their own hands
in the shops and on the building ; but who, so far as it can be
ascertained, did not in any way fill the rôle that was played
by Bullant and De l'Orme a generation later.' [2]

At Fontainebleau, where an army of French building
craftsmen and Italian decorative craftsmen had been
employed since 1528, the same writer says that no architect appears in the accounts till 1541, when Serlio of
Bologna, *peintre et architecteur*, is granted a salary of
1,600 *livres* (say £1,600) a year plus an allowance for

[1] Blomfield, *op. cit.* i. 2.   [2] *Ibid.* i. 33.

travelling expenses of 20 *sous* (say £1) a day.[1] Sir Reginald
Blomfield then notes that Serlio, although holding this
apparently important position and drawing this handsome
salary (subsequently reduced to 400 *livres*) was not consulted in the design of the Salle du Bal, the most important
room in the palace. After indicating what part of the
building was designed by Serlio, he proceeds to attribute
the initiative here, as in many other great royal palaces,
to François I himself, who certainly had a passion for
building.

' The fact was, that it was not till the middle of the sixteenth
century that the French noblemen realized the necessity of
serious and detailed designs for buildings, beyond the models
prepared to the dictation of the employer.   There is an
ominous sentence in Du Cerceau to the effect that the King
(François I) was so well versed in building that it is hardly
possible to call any one else the architect of his palaces.' [2]

But we have heard this sort of thing before in previous
chapters : and it will arise again in Chapter VII.   The
abbot or the bishop in the Middle Ages had the word
fecit carved after his name on the building he had inaugurated but not designed ; the sycophantic architect
of the eighteenth century, in the grovelling dedications
to his folios advertising his own designs, was prepared
to attribute divine qualities to the noble patron who paid
for printing the book.   We must not forget that Du Cerceau
himself dedicated the second volume of his chief book to
the Queen of France,[3] and that he had every reason for
flattering the royal family and its forbears.

It appears to me that in this case Sir Reginald Blomfield
is hardly just to his own profession, though generally he

[1] In our ' pre-war ' currency. See foot-note 2 on p. 193 in this book.
[2] Blomfield, *op. cit.* i. 20.   [3] *Ibid.* i. 145.

is one of its stoutest defenders. All through the early chapters of an otherwise great book he seems to be possessed with the idea that the buildings erected in France between *c.* 1500 and *c.* 1550 attain so low a standard that they do not deserve the name of architecture. It may be for this reason that he attributes them to royal amateurs or to uneducated masons ; but with his main assumption he will surely find many critics, including the present writer, utterly at variance. He says of Blois, Fontainebleau, Villers-Cotterets, and St-Germain that they are

' great agglomerations of building details which, when sifted by critical analysis, resolve themselves into a few very common-place motives strung together without serious thought of composition, without that anxious consideration of scale which alone justifies the claim of buildings to rank as architecture. If therefore Chambiges . . . and other worthies are to be considered as architects and the founders of the French Renaissance, one can only say that they were very poor architects with very little sense of the possibilities of their art. I do not believe myself that they either were or were considered to be anything of the sort. They were just working builders.' . . . [1]

Yet the same writer admits that the irregular planning of all these four buildings is partly due to the fact that they rest on medieval foundations.[2] Equally severe criticism is made of other buildings of the period, some of which are said to be ' irregular and haphazard ',[3] others exhibiting ' little individuality ',[4] and almost all indicating that no architect was employed. At Écouen, for example, where the *château* (1532–42) seems to me to reveal the hand of an architect in its orderly *ensemble*, where Sir Reginald Blomfield actually commends its ' extreme simplicity of plan ' and the ' admirable placing of the

[1] Blomfield, *op. cit.* i. 26. [2] *Ibid.* i. 44–6.
[3] *Ibid.* i. 46. [4] *Ibid.* i. 60.

building on its rock above the town ', he adds that, ' all these matters were probably settled by ' the owner of the building, ' a man of violent temper ', rather than by the master-mason, Charles Billard. [1] Why ?

So also at the Château of Madrid (1528) near Paris, now destroyed, we are told that ' the control of the architect is conspicuously absent ,[2] a statement which is certainly open to question. In this building, as at La Muette (1541–8) and at Ancy-le-Franc (1537–46), the symmetry, balance, and formal planning seems to me to indicate the hand of the architect in every line. In fact La Muette was carried out by Pierre Chambiges, who agreed to carry out the work ' as specified and as shown in the *portrait*.' [3] Finally we come to those beautiful *châteaux* in Touraine which attract so many visitors from this country. It cannot possibly be claimed that the charm of such buildings as Chenonceaux, Chambord, Azay-le-Rideau, or Villandry lies in their ruined and tumbledown condition (though admittedly that is a great attraction to minds of a certain type), because they are very well preserved and one only longs for the formal gardens that once surrounded them. No, the charm of Azay-le-Rideau, for example, lies principally in the originality and grace of its design, as studied a bit of grouping as ever an architect achieved. There is nothing accidental or haphazard about it ; and yet we know nothing of its designer. Villandry (1540) is a very different building, severe and formal in spite of its steep roof and its dormers ; just what an enemy of the Renaissance would call ' an architect's design ', but its author is unknown.

Yet Sir Reginald Blomfield concludes his paragraph about these *châteaux* with this chilly sentence : ' A cool

[1] *Ibid*. i. 62.   [2] *Ibid*. i. 56.   [3] *Ibid*. i. 59–60.

and critical study of these buildings will show that they are not the last word of a consummate art, but the half articulate efforts of beginners striving to express themselves in an unfamiliar language.'[1] The swing of the pendulum is a recurrent phenomenon in architectural criticism, and the passage just quoted may not have permanent value. But the purpose of my present study is history rather than criticism ; I have quoted three distinguished modern writers at considerable length in an attempt to reconcile their views and to ascertain the truth about the French architects of the first half of the sixteenth century.

We must now turn to the Italian architects and other artists already referred to several times in this chapter. At first they were mainly concerned, as in England under the Tudors (see Chapter VII), with minor decorative work or with tombs, and, though much of this work is of high artistic importance, it does not affect the story of the architect. Italian monuments were ' plumped down in the midst of incongruous surroundings ',[1] and so were the Italian artists. From Naples, for instance, twenty-two artists of all kinds were imported, and these included two women.[2] There were colonies of Italians at Amboise, Tours, Blois (the centres of the *château* building, be it noted) and elsewhere ; while at Fontainebleau a large number were employed. Of all these, only the following have any serious claim on our attention here : Domenico da Cortona (nicknamed *Il Boccador*), Primaticcio, Fra Giocondo, Vignola, and Serlio. Domenico da Cortona, a pupil of Sangallo, arrived with the first ' invaders ' in 1496, but for thirty-five years or so we only hear of him

[1] Blomfield, *op. cit.* i. p. 39.   [2] *Ibid.* i. 4.
[3] Jackson, *op. cit.*, 11.

as *valet-de-chambre* to the queen, as a furniture-maker, and as a maker of architectural models. The last-named occupation is the most interesting to us here, and at once suggests the question whether he made these models to the instruction of somebody else, or whether he himself was an architectural designer. In the first event, who gave him the instructions? Surely not amateurs like François I and his courtiers, as Sir Reginald Blomfield seems to assume? Could his employers have been the French master-masons? These are questions that seem at present insoluble. At all events he is definitely said to have supplied the models for Chambord,[1] which was begun in 1519. Other early models were made by him for castles at Tournay and Ardres, also for bridges, wind-mills, and other works whereby he lost much money [2] In 1531 he was appointed architect for the new Hôtel de Ville at Paris, for which he made the designs. Over the doorway was carved the words ' Domenico Cortonensi architectante '. While so employed, he received a salary of 250 *livres* per annum, and had as his coadjutors a carpenter and Chambiges the master-mason. The last fact is significant but perplexing. ' In 1534 the municipal authorities had to remonstrate with " the architect " and his assistants for all going off to dinner and leaving the building to look after itself.' [3] It is uncertain whether he had any hand in the design of the *château* at Blois ; but he was living in the town at the time (1515–20) when the north wing was being built. Mr. Ward attributes to him the design of the remarkable church of St-Eustache at Paris.[4] ' Il Boccadoro ' is a tantalizing and elusive figure.

Primaticcio (1504–70) has been the subject of violent

[1] Blomfield, *op. cit.* i. 29.   [2] *Ibid.* i. 9.
[3] *Ibid.* i. 10.   [4] Ward, *op. cit.*, p. 86.

controversy. He appears at Fontainebleau in 1536 with a salary of 20 or 25 *livres* a month, and seems to have been a ' leading hand ' under Il Rosso, the master-decorator, and to have worked impartially in various capacities until 1559, when, on the accession of François II, he was appointed Surveyor-General to the Crown. Yet there seems to be no evidence that he actually carried out any architectural work. [1]

Fra Giocondo (*c.* 1453–1515) has been credited with many buildings in France, but the only one for which we have certain evidence is the Pont Notre-Dame in Paris. Sir Reginald Blomfield says that the ' legend ' of his employment at Gaillon ' has long been exploded ',[2] but Mr. Ward, without quoting any evidence, says that he ' very probably acted as consulting architect' there ; [3] and elsewhere suggests that he may have been ' the inspirer of the whole Loire school '.[4] He was in France from 1495 to 1505, and drew an annual salary of 562 *livres* while employed in the royal service. Vignola only stayed a few months in France and seems to have done no architectural work there.[5] Mr. Ward attributes the *château* of Madrid near Paris to Girolamo della Robbia, a pupil of Sansovino.[6]

Sebastiano Serlio (1475–1554) is a more important figure in our story. We know little of his architectural work in France : he held a well-paid appointment at Fontainebleau, and may have designed the *château* of St-Germain, which, like that of La Muette, seems to bear the stamp of Italian sobriety. But, like so many architects, he achieved immortal fame by producing a book of the Orders, and

[1] Blomfield, *op. cit*. i. 14–17.   [2] *Ibid*. i. 42.
[3] Ward, *op. cit*., p. 20.   [4] *Ibid*., p. 17.
[5] *Ibid*., p. 120.   [6] *Ibid*., p. 64.

thereafter the French masons were thoroughly drilled in the ' Manner of the Ancients '. It is refreshing to find Sir Reginald Blomfield admitting that ' with increased knowledge came a tendency to preciosity ', and a consequent neglect of local tradition in the use of materials.[1] Fortunately, tradition died hard in France as in England, and the massed attacks of the Vitruvians never entirely killed the steep roofs and dormer windows which are among the many attractions of French buildings of the early Renaissance.

In this half-century, then, we find both French and Italian architects. Their status is very uncertain, but it is clear that the Frenchmen were survivors of the medieval system, and the Italians heralds of a new dawn, when the light of the Orders came to illumine the dark world of Gothic ignorance. Sometimes we have a taste of that astounding versatility that we have seen in Italy ; thus Hugues Sambin (1520–1602) who began as a joiner like his father, later became borough-surveyor of Dijon, built a slaughter-house, a drinking-place, and windmills there, diverted the river, improved the fortifications, carved a ' Last Judgement' and many other subjects, arranged a triumphal progress, designed the Hôtel de Ville at Besançon, and published a book of *Termes*, containing eighteen astonishing plates of terminal figures.[2] But such versatility appears to have been exceptional.

I have already said something of the methods by which buildings came into being. Models have been mentioned, and seem to have been largely used at this period. They were generally of wood. The model made by Domenico da Cortona for Chambord was 4 feet long,[3] and, as the

---

[1] Blomfield, *op. cit.* i. 67.   [2] *Ibid*. i. 36–7.
[3] *Ibid*. i. 30 *n*.

main front of the *château* measures some 512 feet, must
have been made to a scale of rather more than 10 feet to
an inch. Plans were also used, but we know very little
about them, and I have been unable to discover any records
of drawings preserved to-day which would enable us to
judge of the draughtsmanship of the period. Sir Reginald
Blomfield observes that it is doubtful whether measured
drawings were made of old buildings which were altered,
or whether working drawings to scale of new buildings
were made ; [1] but, on the other hand, we have no evidence
to the contrary.

A *devis* or detailed specification formed the basis of
every building contract. The famous example from
Fontainebleau, dated 1528, has been preserved. The
section containing the masonry and brickwork is a document of some 25 pages and about 16,500 words. ' It
contains a complete description of the building, the
numbers and sizes of rooms, the staircases, chimneys,
thickness of walls, and the materials ; with details. . . . ' [2]

I can find no reference to the architect's staff, and very
little to the method by which young architects acquired
their training. Mention has been made of the masters
under whom some of the Italians studied before coming
to France ; and doubtless a similar system prevailed
among the French ' master-masons '. But Mr. Ward
says that ' from the third decade of the [sixteenth] century
onwards, one young Frenchman after another set forth
thither [i. e. to Rome] to pursue his studies before settling
down to his career '.[3] By the middle of the century, then,
France had come into line. Books of the Orders were
available, students went to Italy to measure the ruins of

---

[1] Blomfield, *op. cit.* i. 46. [2] *Ibid.* i. 24.
[3] Ward, *op. cit.*, p. 115.

Rome, and at last the professional architect, under his present name, appears in his modern form.

.   .   .   .   .   .

From our point of view it is unfortunate, as Sir Reginald Blomfield has remarked, that ' France had no Vasari '. The annals of the seventeenth century included the names of a number of first-rate architects, yet of these only two were mentioned by Perrault in his lives of illustrious men of the period,[1] and one of them was the author's own brother. However, Sir Reginald himself has gone far to remedy this lack by publishing the four great volumes in which he traces the architecture of the period with a patient scholarship and critical ability that is sometimes wanting in works of this nature.[2] An architect himself, he has never lost sight of the personal aspect of his subject, and he is keenly interested in the methods by which the buildings under discussion were produced.

Yet even his monumental work fails to enlighten us on certain details of the architect's training and professional career. During the period *c.* 1550–1670, some ten names stand out : those of Philibert de l'Orme (*c.* 1515–70) ; Jean Goujon (*c.* 1005–10—*c.* 1564–8) ; Jean Bullant (1515–78) ; Pierre Lescot (*c.* 1510–78) ; Jacques Androuet du Cerceau (*c.* 1510–15—*c.* 1585) ; Étienne Martellange (1569–1641) ; Jacques Lemercier (1583–1654) ; Pierre le Muet (1591–1669 or 1680) ; Salomon de Brosse (before 1562–1626) ; and François Mansart (1598–1666). Eight of these were quite certainly architects in our sense of the word, Du Cerceau was an architect who spent most of his life in making drawings and imaginary designs, and Goujon, who is chiefly known as a very talented sculptor,

[1] Perrault, *Les hommes illustres qui ont paru en France pendant ce siècle*. (Paris, 1698.)   [2] See footnote 3, p. 190.

is assumed by Sir Reginald Blomfield to have acted as ' ghost ' to the architect Lescot.[1]

Architecture seems to have run in families in France at this period. We have already seen how the business or practice of the earlier master-masons became hereditary ; and now we find families such as those of De l'Orme, Du Cerceau, Métezeau, De Brosse and Lemercier ; to be followed in the later period by those of Mansart, Gabriel, and Blondel. Sometimes the founder of an architectural family was its most famous member, in other cases an architect's son or nephew surpassed his father or uncle. So, of the seven architects from our original ten of whom there is any record, we find that four were sons of men engaged in some branch of architecture or building, one of a distinguished lawyer, one of a painter, and one of a soldier.

Information about their training is disappointingly meagre, but the case of De l'Orme is interesting. According to his own statement, ' from his earliest youth he had devoted himself to new inventions, consulting the most learned men in Europe in geometry and the sciences necessary for architecture '.[2] It must be remembered that he was the son of a builder in a small way, living in Lyons not in Paris, yet he managed somehow to get to Italy and began measuring ancient buildings, ' which ', he says

' I did with great labour, charges, and expenses, so far as I was able, not only in ladders and ropes, but also in excavating foundations, which I was not able to do without being followed by a number of men, some to earn their two centimes a day, others to learn, for they were workmen, cabinet-makers, carvers, and the like, who wished to know what I was doing, and get the benefit of what I discovered.'

[1] Blomfield, *French Architecture . . . till the death of Mazarin*, i. 117–18.   [2] *Ibid.* i. 75.

FIG. 30. PHILIBERT DE L'ORME

From his collected works, 1567 edition

In my last chapter I pointed out how many Italian architects of this period owed their subsequent career to some
lucky encounter with a cardinal or nobleman while engaged
on their studies from the antique in Rome. So De l'Orme
too had the good fortune to attract the attention of a
passing Cardinal with his retinue, and by this meeting
laid the foundation of his large practice in later years.
According to De Quincy, the cardinal—

' witnessing the zeal and progress of the young artist, received
him into his palace, and took pleasure in furthering his education ; he also induced him to abandon the use of the French
foot when measuring old buildings, and to adopt in its place
the ancient Roman foot, of which he gave him the exact dimensions from an old marble [block] on which they were preserved.' [1]

Yet though De l'Orme came into prominence by way of
his archaeological studies, and though in middle life he
published a famous book on architecture to which I make
reference later, his ' considerable reputation as an architect ', according to Sir Reginald Blomfield, is due to his
' careful study of building construction and his unusual
skill in it ',[2] rather than to his artistic ability. ' He did
actually revolutionize building methods in France, and
it is here that he stands apart from, and indeed ahead of
his contemporaries, for Lescot, the elegant Court gentleman, left these matters to his builders, and Bullant, fine
artist as he was, approached architecture too exclusively
from its artistic side '.[3] But in another passage the same
writer observes that De l'Orme ' fell into the pitfall that
has tripped up many an architect, the snare of archaeology,
and an over rigorous science '.[4] Bullant states definitely,

---

[1] Quatremère de Quincy (see Bibliography at end of this Chapter),
ii. 30.
[2] Blomfield, *op. cit.* i. 77.   [3] *Ibid.* i. 91.   [4] *Ibid.* i. 106.

in his book on architecture, that he measured buildings
in Rome ; Du Cerceau, Martellange, and Lemercier are
said to have done the same, but the evidence is incon-
clusive ; Le Muet first appears as a model-maker in
France, and François Mansart is supposed to have been
trained by his brother-in-law, a French official architect,
so it is unlikely that they studied in Italy. There seems
to be no record as to whether the remaining three of our
ten architects travelled in Rome or otherwise.

But the publication of book after book on the Orders, in
French as well as in Italian, may have rendered the
enthusiasm for study in Italy a little less keen by the
middle of the sixteenth century ; students were probably
content to acquire their knowledge second-hand. Again
quoting Sir Reginald Blomfield :

' As was, perhaps, natural with men intoxicated with their
new-found learning, the use that they made of their gleanings
in Italy was rather pedantic. The orders loomed large and
formidable in the forefront of architectural study. To design
the orders in strict accordance with the proportions found in
the remains of Classical Rome, and with the rules laid down
by the authorities of the time, was the first ambition of every
architect.' [1]

Apart from the Orders, we know very little about the
nature of an architectural student's curriculum. Lescot
did drawing at school when he ought to have been minding
his books ; at twenty he was studying architecture, painting, and mathematics. Goujon, whose artistic ability is
unquestioned, wrote in an introduction to Vitruvius in
1547 that a knowledge of perspective, geometry, and the
books of Vitruvius is essential for an architect. The
French mind is practical by nature, and it is not surprising

[1] Blomfield, *op. cit.* i. 166.

that the first good book on building construction, full of new ideas, came from Philibert de l'Orme,[1] in spite of his archaeological training. We may safely assume that a young architect in France at this period studied the Orders, perspective, geometry, and mathematics ; and possibly mechanics and other branches of science too.

I can find very little definite information as to the date when these men commenced practice, and the question is complicated by the fact that so many of them held official appointments which do not seem to have precluded private practice. An analogous case would be that of a ' draughtsman ' in our own Office of Works to-day, who occasionally designed a house and eventually gave up his appointment to devote himself to private work. But it seems certain that François Mansart, of whose youth we know next to nothing, began his huge practice in his early twenties and was a flourishing architect within a few years.

Work was obtained almost always through private interest, as a competition, open or limited, is hardly ever mentioned. When the scheme for the Pont Neuf at Paris was mooted in 1577, ' various projects were submitted to Henry III. When the King had selected a scheme the details were worked out by the King's architect ',[2] Baptiste du Cerceau, son of the famous architectural draughtsman ; and afterwards a committee of experts, corresponding to the Spanish *junta* described in Chapter IV, was appointed to watch over the progress of the work. Still, this can hardly be called a ' competition ' in the modern sense ; and the case of the Hôtel de Ville at Lyons is little more satisfactory. In 1646 the city fathers of Lyons decided that a new town hall should be built.

[1] See p. 219. [2] Blomfield, *op. cit.* i. 153.

They therefore gave instructions that plans were to be obtained from their own city surveyor and from certain other architects (apparently by invitation). The surveyor was then to proceed to Paris with all the plans ; and was to consult with various notable architects there, especially with Desargues, one of the competitors, and to obtain the opinion of the Governor of the province. It is difficult to imagine any arrangement affording more opportunities for intrigue ; and the result was, as might be expected, a deadlock. The Governor favoured one design, the city fathers another, and the surveyor waited his opportunity. The design of Desargues was finally accepted, the surveyor carried it out ; but he altered it in execution so unsatisfactorily that he was dismissed in 1661 and is said to have ' died of chagrin ' in 1668.[1] It may be added that Desargues was a celebrated mathematician, competing against practising architects, of whom Lemercier was one. An architect sometimes consulted others ; and when Salomon de Brosse was preparing sketch-designs for the Luxembourg (1616) he sent the one which the queen preferred to Italy ' and even to other countries ', in order to obtain opinions and criticism from the most prominent architects of the day.[2]

Of all architects' clients during this great building epoch, perhaps Cardinal Richelieu was the most profitable, for his enormous income was matched by his powers of imagination. His town house in Paris, later known as the Palais Royal, is said to have cost 10,000,000 *livres* ; but he surpassed it when he commissioned his architect, Lemercier, to prepare plans for a vast *château* in Touraine, big enough to house the whole court ; and next instructed him to lay out a whole town to serve the *château* and to

[1] Blomfield, *op. cit.* ii. 147.   [2] De Quincy, *op. cit.* i. 144.

house its menials. All this work, including the town of ' Richelieu ', was duly carried out and may still be seen.[1]

Another costly house of this period was Maisons, still standing some 10 miles from Paris but shorn of its magnificent park and surroundings. François Mansart was the architect. He was a fastidious person, already well-established in practice, and after going down to view the site with his client he undertook the work only on condition that he had absolute *carte blanche* in regard to expense. Everything was to be of the best. He seems to have gained his point, for the cost of the building is said to have been 12,000,000 *livres*. Yet the total size of the building (two storeys high) is only about 240 feet by 90 feet. He appears to have suffered for this extravagance in later years, for, after having been appointed architect to the great church and monastery of Val-de-Grâce in Paris and having carried the building 9 feet above ground, he was superseded by Lemercier, partly as a result of political intrigue but partly because the promoters of the scheme were becoming frightened of his recklessness.[2] Though a great architect, he suffered from two generous a supply of the artistic temperament, and this was his undoing. He had an opportunity of acting as architect for the Louvre but could not even decide which of his own sketch-designs should be submitted to the king. ' This condition appeared harsh to a genius accustomed to independence, and so he preferred to sacrifice such a favourable occasion for the exercise of his talents, rather than give up his freedom to change his ideas if any better occurred to him '.[3] Another story relates that Bullant the architect used to read for

[1] Blomfield, *op. cit.* ii. 113–16.   [2] *Ibid.* ii. 129–31.
[3] D'Argenville, quoted by Blomfield, *op. cit.* ii. 133.

hours to the workmen employed on his buildings, but this seems to be an ill-founded legend.[1] Some of the greatest building enthusiasts of the period were the ladies of the Court, respectable and otherwise. Of the second group the most important was Diane de Poitiers, who seems to have had as much of a passion for building as Henri II had for her. A holiday in Touraine leaves one with the impression that her initials appear in every *château* there. Her rival, the queen Catherine de Médicis, must have been a permanent thorn in the flesh to all the architects whom she employed. Sir Reginald Blomfield writes that

' She was obsessed by the mania for building prevalent in France in the earlier part of the century, and the worst of it was that her taste was extremely bad and extremely obstinate. Having little real insight into the arts, she insisted on interfering at all points in the design of her buildings, overrode the suggestions of her artists, and insisted on their carrying out her ignorant caprices.'[2] She built a number of houses, of which her fifth contained ' among other things a lofty Doric column with a newel staircase formed inside, intended to form an observatory for her astrological efforts.'[3]

But one beneficial result of the increasing part played by women in building schemes was an improvement in the standard of domestic comfort and hygiene, sadly needed in the seventeenth century. In this movement the leader was the Marquise de Rambouillet, a clever woman, who

' seems to have seen that these arrangements might be much improved, that private rooms should be provided as well as public, that service staircases were indispensable, that cabinets

[1] Blomfield, *op. cit.* i. 93. [2] *Ibid*. i. 140. [3] *Ibid*. i. 104.

de toilettes, salles des bains, and the like, ought to be near bedrooms instead of at the other end of the garden, that the cavernous chimney openings of the sixteenth century took all the heat up the chimney when they did not let all the smoke back into the rooms, and when the Hôtel de Rambouillet was to be built she endeavoured to realize these ideas.'[1]

So far so good, but Sir Reginald Blomfield discounts the next anecdote.

' Des Réaux has a pleasing story of youthful genius, and describes how the Marquise, discontented with the design proposed for the Hôtel de Rambouillet, suddenly called for drawing-paper, and then and there made the design of the house, which was followed in every detail.' . . . ' There is simply no evidence worth the name to support the legend of the reform of architecture by the Marquise de Rambouillet. All architects of experience know how much they can learn from the taste and individuality of their clients, and there can be no doubt that the Marquise was original enough to have views of her own as to the decoration and general arrangements of her house, and able and determined enough to see that they were as far as possible carried out. But to lay it down that a young lady of twenty-two, with some little accomplishment in drawing, revolutionized the great and slow moving art of architecture, *ex mero motu suo*, is asking too much of the credulity of historical students. Molière bitterly remarked, " Les gens de qualité savent tout sans avoir rien appris ". The Marquise de Rambouillet's claims to architectural genius rest on no better foundation.'[2]

On the whole these architects of the seventeenth century appear to have been competent professional men and there is little doubt as to their status. Both De l'Orme and the younger Du Cerceau had an interest in stone-quarries, but the only definite instance that I have noted of an

[1] *Ibid*. ii. 141-2. [2] *Ibid*. ii. 142-4.

architect acting as a contractor occurs in the case of Salomon de Brosse, who bought quarries for the stone-work at the Luxembourg and provided all the plant and materials for that building, which he also designed. There was some trouble about the payments for the work, and eventually he was superseded by another contractor.[1]

The desirability of separating the functions of architect and builder was made manifest by frequent cases of embezzlement and dishonesty, and the example of De Brosse, exceptional at so late a date, affords an excellent instance of the need for such differentiation of function. For better or for worse, the architect in France was now recognized as an expert in design on the fashionable Italian lines, and gradually the master-mason architect, clinging tenaciously to the French Gothic tradition, was frozen out of existence.

It must often have puzzled visitors to France to account for the very distinctive character of her Jesuit churches, and Sir Reginald Blomfield explains this in an interesting chapter.

' The practice was for the architect of the Order to prepare designs and specifications, which were faithfully adhered to in essential points, whether the building took five years to build or fifty. These plans and specifications were handed over to the local people for execution. The Jesuit architect visited the work from time to time to settle difficult points of construction or business, but does not appear to have superintended the work from start to finish.' [2]

This method does not seem to have been altogether successful, for Martellange, the most famous of these Jesuit architects, had a good deal of trouble with contractors over practical and financial questions, and one

---

[1] Blomfield, *op. cit.* ii. 55.   [2] *Ibid.* ii. 21.

is inclined to suspect him of being somewhat of an amateur. Lemercier, though a general practitioner, was in close touch with the members of the Order in Paris, and built a large number of important churches.

But specialization by architects was rare. Most of them undertook all classes of building, and several of those already mentioned must have had enormous practices. A good deal of what we now call 'engineering' was included in their work. Thus Philibert de l'Orme who, as we have seen, came into the limelight as a student of Roman antiquities, was appointed at thirty years of age 'Conductor-general of buildings and fortifications in Brittany. His duties consisted of visiting twice a year all the ports and fortifications of Brittany, and of inspecting military and naval stores '.[1] In this capacity he seems also to have seen some active service and to have taken part in a siege. I have already mentioned Baptiste du Cerceau's design for the Pont Neuf. Another architect, Lemercier, was sent in 1620 (at the age of thirty-seven) with an 'engineer' to report on a bridge near Rouen. This is one of the first cases we have yet encountered of any distinction being made between engineering work and architecture, both of which had hitherto been done by architects. Another instance occurs in the design of the Place Royale, now the Place des Vosges, and the Place Dauphine, both in Paris, by the brothers Châtillon about 1607. Sir Reginald Blomfield, apparently quoting Sauval, describes them as 'engineers;'[2] but Mr. Ward calls Claude Châtillon 'architect and engineer', which is probably the truth. These squares were laid out as part of a scheme for improving Paris inaugurated by Henry III, and form admirable early examples of town-

[1] *Ibid.* i. 58.   [2] *Ibid.* ii. 45.

planning on modern lines. Another striking example is the little town of Richelieu, already mentioned, which is symmetrically laid out on a rectangular plan and well planted.

' No description can convey the old-world charm of this delightful little town, far away from the main track of travellers and tradesmen, and slumbering peacefully amid its planes and lime-trees. In its way it is unique, a page of the seventeenth century preserved to us intact, and more suggestive of the spirit and purpose of the architecture of the time of Richelieu than any other building that has reached us.' [1]

It was designed by the architect Lemercier, who may also have laid out the small fortified town of Brouage near Rochfort, planned like Richelieu on rectangular lines.[2] Lemercier was also employed on the fortifications of Paris. Besides town-planning, architects now undertook the lay-out of gardens for the larger town houses and the great *châteaux* that were springing up all over France. Much of this work is admirable, showing that, long before the days of the famous Le Nôtre, garden-design was successfully practised.

Though architects still carried out works of engineering and town-planning, they no longer flirted with the other arts, and on one occasion Poussin the painter had a great quarrel with Lemercier the architect about the decorations of the Louvre.[3] The position of Jean Goujon the sculptor is obscure ; but Sir Reginald Blomfield is convinced that in reality he was a talented architect who acted as ' ghost ' to Lescot ; that is, that Lescot, himself a courtier with influence in high places, obtained the work and drew the salary, but employed Goujon to do it for

[1] Blomfield, *op. cit.* ii. 85.   [2] *Ibid.* ii. 86–7.
[3] *Ibid.* ii. 90–1.

him.[1] Such a practice, despicable as it seems in cold print, is doubtless to be found in all periods, certainly at the present day, and seems inevitable.

Mention of a salary raises the whole question as to how architects of this period were remunerated. In spite of Sir Reginald Blomfield's learned researches, and the profusion of figures that he cites in the course of his two volumes, I find myself utterly at sea as to the real position of the salaried architect; moreover there is only one mention, and that quite vague, of any payment by fees as opposed to an annual salary. A salary is frequently mentioned. It appears that 1,200 *livres* was usually paid to an architect of good standing in the employment of the Court. Bullant received this sum in 1557 as Controller of building operations, Primaticcio at Fontainebleau in 1563, Lescot as architect to the Louvre in 1550 and again in 1568, Jacques du Cerceau the younger as Controller and Architect of Royal Buildings in 1602, Jacques Lemercier as one of the architects of the royal palaces in 1618. But this was not an invariable rate of payment. Louis Métezeau in 1608 drew 2,400 *livres* as *architecte du Roy*, but he was also *concierge et garde des meubles du Palais des Thuileries*. Le Muet received 3,000 *francs* for his work at the Val-de-Grâce in 1655, but this salary was later reduced to 1,000 *francs* per annum. In 1618 Salomon de Brosse received 2,400 *livres* as one of the royal architects, subordinate architects received 1,200 and 800 *livres*, and Pierre le Muet (*jeune garçon*) was retained by her Majesty to work on models and elevations of houses at a salary of 600 *livres*. The largest salary of all occurs in 1585, when Baptiste du Cerceau is said to have had 6,000 *livres* a year as *ordonnateur-général* of royal buildings, but he gave it up rather

[1] *Ibid.* i. 117.

than become a Catholic. It is impossible to attempt any accurate estimate of the value of these salaries in modern purchasing-power, opinions differing widely as to the value of the livre.[1] And even more perplexing is the position of the salaried architect. Was he paid for the whole of his time, or was he at liberty to undertake private work too ? Most of the leading Court architects of the sixteenth and seventeenth century built churches, town houses, and *châteaux* while in the royal employment. Again, could an architect who was paid for work on one specific palace draw another salary simultaneously for work on another palace ? These questions have an interest beyond their merely financial aspect, and if an answer could be found to them it would clear up many difficult points about work in France at that period.

Apart from any private work that he was at liberty to do, it appears that occasional perquisites occasionally found their way into the pockets of the state architect. Thus Philibert de l'Orme, who was accused by his enemies of making 20,000 *livres* a year in all, held four sinecure abbacies which brought him in 3,300 *livres* a year, and was also made a Canon of Notre-Dame, though the Canons objected to his beard (see fig. 30). Such cases seem to have been exceptional, but it is significant, perhaps, that Lemercier receives special mention for declining bribes from contractors, and for being an honest man.[2] But we have seen that Baptiste du Cerceau declined a large salary rather than give up his religious convictions ; and another famous Protestant artist, Jean Goujon, as penalty for having attended a Lutheran service in 1542, was condemned to walk through the streets in his shirt

---

[1] Jackson, *Renaissance of Roman Architecture : France*, p. 96 *n.*
[2] Blomfield, *op. cit.* ii. 92.

and to attend the burning of the preacher.[1] Salomon de Brosse, though of the same faith as Goujon, managed at a later date to design churches impartially for both Catholics and Protestants.[2]

It is hardly necessary to say that the more eminent of the French architects of this period occupied a good social position. The inordinate vanity of François Mansart, according to Mr. Ward,[3] ' prompted him to a display more suitable to a duke. He caused a pedigree to be drawn up, according to which his ancestors had been architects to every king of France, from Hugh Capet in the tenth century downwards, and drove about in a coach drawn by horses trained to a rhythmic step '. Yet Sir Reginald Blomfield, who admires François Mansart as much as he detests Jules Hardouin Mansart, says that the former ' had no capacity for self-advertisement '.[4] The pedigree and the rhythmic horses seem to belie that statement.

Of the ten architects chosen to represent this period, five at least published books. De l'Orme intended to compile a vast encyclopedia of architectural knowledge, but did not live to complete it. His first published work was *Nouvelles inventions pour bien bastir et à petitz frais*, and was chiefly concerned with the construction of timber roofs (hence ' the Philibert de l'Orme truss ' in modern text-books), domes, and arches by building them up in thicknesses instead of cutting them out of heavy scantlings. Fig. 31 is taken from this book, and is typical of his drawings of constructional details. In 1567 he published a great folio entitled *L'Architecture*, in nine books. In this volume he deals successively with sites, masonry, building materials, the Orders according to Vitruvius and other

[1] Jackson, *op. cit.*, p. 120. [2] De Quincy, *op. cit.* i., p. 244.
[3] Ward, *op. cit.* i. 226. [4] Blomfield, *op. cit.* ii. 119.

authorities, and finally with the construction of chimneys and the avoidance of down-draught.

' But his work is something very much more than a technical treatise. Scattered up and down his pages are queer personal reflections, passages of autobiography, strains of thought which suggest an intense, if somewhat bizarre, personality. A sense of personal grievance underlies every page of his book, and a temper always under imperfect control blazes out in the concluding paragraphs in which he describes the good architect and the bad one, the man without hands and eyes, blind, stupid, wicked, and incompetent.' [1]

Jean Bullant produced a treatise on sundials in 1561, another on geometry in 1562, and a book on the Orders according to Vitruvius in 1564 which appeared in a second edition in 1568 ' for the use of all workmen using the compass and the square '. This book went into two further editions. Martellange, after retiring from the practice of architecture, probably spent the last years of his life in assisting other men in writing books on stereotomy and perspective. Le Muet, though a busy practitioner, published his *Manière de bien bastir* in 1623. This work appeared in a second and enlarged edition in 1647, and contained many of his own designs for large houses. He also produced two books on the Orders ; the first, according to Vignola, in 1642 ; and the second, according to Palladio, in 1645. Salomon de Brosse in 1619 found time to edit Bullant's book on the Orders for a new edition. Jacques Androuet du Cerceau, however, was the chief architectural book-maker of the period. A work on ' Triumphal Arches ' appeared in 1549, another on ' Temples ' in 1550, a book of ' Grotesques ' and ' Fragments from the Antique ' in the same year, ' Com-

[1] Blomfield, *op. cit.* i. 86.

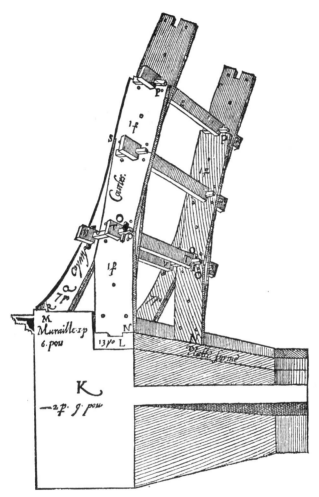

FIG. 31. DETAIL OF A ROOF-TRUSS BY PHILIBERT DE L'ORME
(from ' *Nouvelles Inventions pour bien bastir et à petitz frais* '. 1561).

positions of Architecture ' and ' Optical Views ' in 1551, the two volumes of his ' Book of Architecture ' in 1559 and 1561 respectively, a small treatise on the Orders in 1583, *Édifices Antiques Romains* in 1584 and, most important of all, *Les Plus Excellents Bastiments de France* in two large volumes in 1576 and 1579. This last publication was never completed. The two volumes which appeared were designed as the second and third of a series which was intended to cover all the principal houses of France, but the first part of the work, which should have illustrated the chief buildings of Paris, had to be delayed owing to political disturbances in the capital and was finally abandoned. But there is no question that the drawings by Du Cerceau preserved in the two published volumes reach an astoundingly high level of draughtsmanship. Fig. 32 in this book gives an idea of the kind of line adopted and of the bird's-eye perspective that he generally employed. There is a very fine collection of his original drawings in the British Museum, and many of them have been admirably reproduced in a publication by Mr. Ward.[1] Summing up the quality of his work, Sir Reginald Blomfield says that

' He had at his command a line of unfaltering precision ; . . . he could, if he wished, draw almost anything ' . . . and again, ' His drawings are very clear and of scientific accuracy, but they leave one cold ; they are tight, if one may say so of a drawing, unsuggestive, unresponsive. Du Cerceau worked conscientiously at his versions of buildings, indifferent apparently to anything but the exact statement of the building as it was. He seems to have been intensely honest in these drawings of buildings.' . . . [2]

[1] W. H. Ward, *French Gardens and Châteaux in the Sixteenth Century*. (London, 1909.)

[2] Blomfield, *Architectural Drawing and Draughtsmen*, p. 32. (London, 1912.)

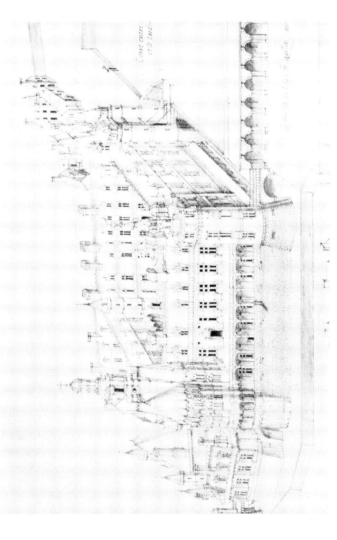

FIG. 32. THE CHÂTEAU OF GAILLON

From a drawing by J. A. du Cerceau

It is just this quality of intense honesty (coupled, as it appears to me, with an ability for selecting the most telling point of view of a subject) that makes Du Cerceau's drawings such a welcome change from the numerous books of the Orders published at the same period. He represents buildings recently erected, and, as many of them have now perished or have been altered beyond recognition, his record is invaluable ; the other books reproduced with wearisome monotony but with very doubtful accuracy the crumbled fragments of a bygone age. Du Cerceau, an architect turned draughtsman, has left us a priceless heritage ; the books on the Orders are at best amusing because of their slovenly rendering of the antique originals. It is clear that such pattern-books were intended, like their English counterparts of the eighteenth century, for the use of the ' Ingenious Artificer ' (see p. 321) and the architect who could not afford a trip to Rome. They must have had a great vogue.

In regard to the actual working drawings used on the building, information is scanty ; undoubtedly plans and perhaps details were so used, a wooden model serving sometimes as a general guide to the architectural draughts-man. The specification (*devis*) is frequently mentioned. Sir Reginald Blomfield describes a specification (written about 1610) by the Jesuit architect Martellange, but considers that it is ' loosely worded ',[1] and far more vague than that used at Fontainebleau in the time of François I (see p. 204).

.   .   .   .   .   .

The foundation in 1671 of the Academy of Architecture has been taken, in this study, as a dividing point of the period, for it marked the close connexion between

[1] Blomfield, *French Architecture till the death of Mazarin*, ii. 23.

architecture and the State that existed under Louis XIV and his powerful minister Colbert. ' Through Colbert's elaborate organization ', writes Sir Reginald Blomfield,[1] ' all the best artistic ability of the country was mobilized in the King's service and was under his direct, almost personal, control '. An Academy for painters and sculptors had been established in 1648, intended ' not only to promote the arts of painting and sculpture, but also to instruct and train students ',[2] who had to pay fees. In a short time the students began to complain of laxity in the administration, and in 1662 they mutinied and established rival schools of their own, which may be regarded as the embryo of the famous French *atelier* system.

The first members of the Academy of Architecture were all practising architects. It seems to have grown out of a small consultative committee appointed to superintend the building of the Louvre, but it had for its principal object the instruction of artists. Its members met weekly to discuss problems of design or construction, and acted as a kind of Court of Appeal for all questions that perplexed architects. On the one hand it laid down a code of orthodox practice in regard to the Orders, but it performed a more useful and apparently more congenial service in settling abstruse problems met with in building —e. g. concerning the strength of foundations and the construction of domes. The members drew a fee of 11 livres apiece (say 3 or 4 guineas in modern values) for each meeting that they attended. Their work had an influence in consolidating professional status, for architectural practice was attempted even at that time by the master-builder and the ' gifted amateur '. In 1699 the

[1] Blomfield, *French Architecture from Mazarin to Louis XV*, i. 6.
[2] *Ibid.* i. 7.

Academy was finally organized, consisting thereafter of seven architects of the first class, seven (later ten) of the second class, a third class of a somewhat inferior grade, a professor, and a secretary.

The travels of students in Italy were not recognized officially until 1666, when the French Academy at Rome was founded, consisting of twelve young artists, among them two architects. They were to be subject to strict discipline and they lived in collegiate fashion. ' They were to get up at five in the summer and six in the winter, and go to bed at ten, not omitting to say their prayers. They were to devote two hours a day to the study of arithmetic, geometry, perspective, and architecture.' This applied to painters and sculptors as well as to architects. ' The architects were to make plans and elevations of all the fine buildings in Rome and its neighbourhood '.[1]

They also acted as collectors of pictures and antiquities on behalf of their royal patron ! For it must be remembered that this French Academy at Rome was established primarily in the interests of the State, to create a supply of well-trained young artists for the royal service. A winner of the *Prix de Rome*, on returning from Italy, was guaranteed employment by being appointed to the charge of some historical building. But the directors of the Academy at Rome became sycophants or art-dealers, neglecting their main duties, and the number of students decreased to six in 1723 and was only eight in 1735. Possibly owing to this lack of guidance, they sometimes studied buildings very alien to the orthodox ideals of the founders, and Oppenord's extravagances were apparently derived from his sketches of Borromini's wildest aberrations.

Yet as we read the lives of famous French architects

[1] *Ibid.* i. 27–8.

between 1660 and 1800 we find little evidence of the
Academy's educational activities. I have selected the
following as the twelve chief architects of the period in
question : Louis le Vau (1612–70) ; Claude Perrault
(1613–88) ; Anthoine le Pautre (1614–91) ; François
Blondel (1618–86) ; Libéral Bruand (1635–97) ; Jules
Hardouin Mansart (?1645–1708) ; Jacques Jules Gabriel
(1667–1742) ; Jean Jérôme Servandoni (1695–1766) ;
Ange Jacques Gabriel (1710–82) ; Jacques Germain
Soufflot (1713–81) ; Jacques Denis Antoine (1733–1801);
and Jacques Gondouin (1737–1818). Of these twelve,
only three are known to have studied in Rome at all, and
one of them, Servandoni, was a painter in his youth. Of
three more nothing is known, but it is fairly safe to
add their names to those of the six who were never in
Italy. The circumstances of their early life are worthy
of attention. Of the dozen architects mentioned, six were
the sons of men connected with architecture or the building crafts, two of lawyers, and the remainder were sons
of a painter, a gardener, a carrier, and a tradesman
respectively. Curiously enough, both the lawyers' sons
(Perrault and François Blondel) entered architecture at
the mature age of fifty-two. Perrault was a learned man,
and in many ways his career resembles Wren's. He was
trained for medicine, took a doctor's degree in medicine
and philosophy, and was also well versed in literature
and mathematics. His brilliant success as an architect
may be ascribed to a combination of great natural ability
and an extremely thorough scientific education. But
neither he nor Blondel had anything like an architectural
training ; another famous architect began life as a mason,
yet another as a painter ; and of all the twelve architects
now under consideration, we only know that one was

probably taught by his architect-father, and that two more studied at the Academy in Rome.

The ' architectural families ' of Hardouin, Gabriel, Mansart, Bruand, Blondel, and Le Vau continued a tradition already mentioned in this chapter as characteristic of the Renaissance in France. Although the title *architecte* was still sometimes loosely applied to persons engaged in b··ilding in other capacities, the status of the architect was becoming more definite ; but even in this period ' from time to time the architects of Louis XIV undertook contracts on their own account '.[1] This improvement in status was certainly due in part to the work of the Academy as I have already remarked, and the title of *Architecte du Roi* was now confined to architectural members of the Academy. Practice seems to have been commenced at a very early age in some cases ; thus Libéral Bruand appears to have been only twenty-one when he was instructed to design the huge hospital or asylum of La Salpêtrière to accommodate 4,000 or more inmates.[2] But there are other instances that are explained rather by the social conditions of the period than by any precocity of genius. The sons of wealthy contractors were sometimes sent into the service of the king as architects, and not always for very worthy reasons. So when we hear that J. J. Gabriel entered this service as one of the royal building officials with a salary of about 6,000 francs a year (say £1,500 a year in our pre-war values) *at the age of twenty*, we must not forget that his mother, widow of a builder, had paid 80,000 francs (say £20,000 in pre-war money) to her cousin J. H. Mansart, then chief architect to the king, for arranging the matter.[3]

His son, A. J. Gabriel, was a very distinguished archi-

---

[1] Blomfield, *op. cit.* i. 115.   [2] *Ibid.* i. 131.   [3] *Ibid.* ii. 56.

tect, and had a large practice, as well as highly lucrative appointments, before he was thirty. J. H. Mansart may not have been quite so complete a charlatan and *entrepreneur* as Sir Reginald Blomfield maintains, but he was certainly a smart and pushful young man. He adopted the surname of his famous predecessor and great-uncle François Mansart, and wormed his way into the royal favour *viâ* the servants' hall and the boudoirs, so that at thirty he was entrusted with perhaps the biggest building in history, the Palace of Versailles. But he too was son of a Court artist, and flocks of his relations, the Hardouin family, soon appeared as contractors and parasites of the Court.

Even if one does not take the blackest possible view of J. H. Mansart and his contemporaries, the fact remains that Louis XIV's building department became a vast family party. Of the Gabriels it is said [1] that ' what the architect designed, his brother or his uncle contracted for, and some other relation checked the accounts, and it must have been almost impossible for an outsider to break into the ring-fence of this early Office of Works '.

The versatility that characterizes all the chief architects of the Renaissance is evident in France at this period too. I have already mentioned Perrault and Blondel as men who both entered architecture at the belated age of fifty-two, after distinguished but somewhat miscellaneous careers outside. For that reason they can hardly be considered typical of their class. Perrault slipped out of architecture as easily as he came in. After eighteen years of practice, he returned to science when fortune ceased to smile upon him, and died a few years later from the effects of dissecting a decomposed camel. Blondel spent

[1] Blomfield, *op. cit.* i. 48.

FIG. 33. JULES HARDOUIN MANSART

By Rigaud, engraved by Edelinck

his life between the ages of twenty-nine and fifty-two as captain of a galley, travelling tutor to a nobleman's son, professor of mathematics, diplomatist, and civil engineer. In the latter capacity he repaired a bridge, and afterwards was sent to the Antilles to report on positions for fortresses there. This experience, coupled with his extensive journeys in Europe elsewhere, is apparently his only qualification for his appointment as Director of the Academy of Architecture in 1671, except his first real design in the previous year, for the alteration of the Porte St-Bernard. Blondel is therefore something of a pedant, and once wrote that ' the worst punishment that God could inflict on mankind would be to condemn us to live without architects '. A sense of humour was evidently not his strong point. On the title-page of his *Cours d'Architecture* he modestly describes himself as ' Membre de l'Académie des Sciences, Professeur du Roi en Mathématiques, Maréchal de Camp aux Armées du Roi, Maître de Mathématiques de Monseigneur Le Dauphin '. This is an extraordinary nosegay of titles to proffer to the architectural student, whose need is not primarily for field marshals or mathematicians.

But though Blondel, as something of an amateur and a pedant, was inclined to give too scholastic a bias to architecture, it is clear that the architect still carried on all branches of civil and military engineering. The sacred books of Vitruvius and his disciples still remained the architects' bible in all matters of taste, but the Academy itself had become as much of a school of Engineering and Building as of the Fine Arts. It was consulted on such questions as irrigation, fortifications, road making, canals, and bridge construction ; and even on technical processes in manufacture. J. J. Gabriel built no less than eight bridges, including the remarkably fine one over the Loire at Blois ; and J. H. Mansart built one at Moulins, which, as Sir Reginald Blomfield is careful to point out,[1] was washed away five years later. Town-planning now advanced rapidly : fine examples being found in Paris (Place des Victoires, Place Vendôme, &c.), Nancy, Bordeaux (Place de la Bourse), and Rennes ; the last two being designed by J. J. Gabriel. The lay-out and embellishment of huge formal gardens by architects reached a level of great magnificence during this period. Servandoni, the son of a humble carrier of Lyons, wandered from his studies in Rome to Portugal, and designed a theatre in Lisbon.

' In 1724 he appeared in Paris with a great reputation as a designer of stage scenery and effects, and was entrusted with the *mise en scène* of the Opera.' . . . ' Within the next eighteen years he set on the stage more than sixty operas, with scenery ranging from the Palace of Nineveh to the Mosque of Scanderbeg.' [2]

Later he arranged a spectacle out-of-doors to celebrate a royal marriage, partly on the river and including illuminations, which was witnessed by 80,000 people. In 1749 he visited London to direct the illuminations (said to have cost 100,000 guineas) for the Peace of Aix-la-Chapelle.[3] But Servandoni had a general architectural practice, so affords yet one more example of versatility.

As in the preceding period, an architect obtained his work in competition, by private interest, or through influence at Court. The most important competition, if it can be so called, was that for the completion of the Louvre in 1665, to which I have already made reference [4]

[1] Blomfield, *op. cit.* i. 90.
[2] *Ibid.* ii. 109.
[3] *Ibid.* ii. 111.
[4] See pp. 175–7.

in connexion with Bernini's visit in the following year. The story is so well known that a brief summary will suffice here. In 1665 Louis le Vau was architect to the Louvre and part of the east front that he had designed was 8 or 10 feet above the ground. The minister Colbert, then the most powerful man in France, was not pleased with the design, so had a wooden model made of it, and then called on the architects of Paris to offer their suggestions for its improvement. This was an opportunity for displaying loyalty to a professional colleague, yet they had no scruples in submitting designs as requested. But they were fairly dealt with by Nemesis in the person of Claude Perrault, a complete amateur who had translated Vitruvius and who utilized the services of his brother, Colbert's secretary, to submit anonymously a design which far surpassed those of the Paris architects. In this competition there was an assessor, who seems to have been an amateur of no practical experience who had perpetrated an extremely inaccurate book on the Orders. He was paid 4,000 francs (say £800 ' pre-war ' money) for his award,[1] but evidently Colbert placed no reliance upon it, for the designs were all sent to Poussin the painter in Rome, so that he might obtain the opinion of leading Italian architects upon them. Meanwhile Bernini's friends were intriguing at Court, and, while the French architects' drawings were on their way to Rome, Louis invited him to come to Paris and bring designs for the new Louvre. Though every precaution was taken, Charles Perrault managed to gain admittance to the room where Bernini's designs were locked up, then denied that he had done so, and afterwards proceeded to poison Colbert's mind about Bernini in his brother's interest.

[1] *Ibid.* i. 69.

In this effort he was ably seconded by the disgruntled architects of Paris, who presumably felt that, of the two evils, a French amateur was on the whole preferable to an Italian rival. Bernini's royal reception has already been described (p. 176); but, though his designs were accepted, an elaborate specification written, and the foundation-stone actually laid, the brothers Perrault finally succeeded in getting rid of him by proving conclusively how utterly he had ignored practical considerations in his scheme. Then Bernini faded away, and Claude Perrault came into his hard-earned own.[1]

It is a sordid story, like so many others of that period. But probably competitions were sometimes better organized. One was held about 1667, for a triumphal arch in Paris. Perrault, Le Brun, and Le Vau were invited to submit designs; other architects sent in drawings without being invited; and Perrault was successful.[2] In 1668 five architects sent in competitive plans for the enlargement of Versailles.[3] There was a competition in 1732 for the west front of St-Sulpice at Paris, won by Servandoni with a model, which remained on exhibition for a year so that the public might have a chance of criticism.[4] (This method has recently been suggested in the English Press as a result of recent controversy about memorials in public places.) There was a very important competition in Paris in 1748, for a memorial to the king and to celebrate the Peace of Aix-la-Chapelle. All the architectural members of the Academy were invited, many other architects submitted designs without being invited, and in all some fifty schemes were received. Apparently the nature of the memorial and its position was left entirely to com-

[1] Blomfield, *op. cit.* i. 68–70.   [2] *Ibid.* i. 85.
[3] *Ibid.* i. 186.   [4] De Quincy, *op. cit.* ii. 288, 293.

petitors, who suggested about twenty different sites. Boffrand sent in three different designs. Cost was completely disregarded. As all schemes involved the destruction of existing buildings, a second competition was promoted and fifteen Academicians competed, ' but the King, finding there were good points in all the designs, desired to combine them in one, and handed over the work to his *premier architecte*, A. J. Gabriel '.[1] The result was the fine Place de la Concorde, According to De Quincy,[2] several architects sent in designs in the competition for the Panthéon at Paris, Soufflot being successful.

But for the most part architects depended on private influence in obtaining their work, and petticoat intrigue often played its part. The amazing career of J. H. Mansart may be briefly outlined as an example of contemporary conditions. Mansart is the villain of Sir Reginald Blomfield's great study of Renaissance architecture in France, and he is there described as ' perhaps the most successful architect that ever lived ',[3] success in this case being interpreted in its most worldly sense. I have described his early entry into Court favour, and ' in 1675 he was forcibly imported into the Academy by Colbert '.[4] In the following year, when he had only begun one building of any size, the king instructed him to prepare designs for the colossal palace at Versailles, which, with all its subsidiary buildings and lay-out, eventually cost the fabulous sum of ten or twelve millions sterling, according to Sir Reginald Blomfield's reading of recently published official figures.[5] The same writer considers him to have been little more than a clever, pushful, and unscrupulous adventurer, who exploited the services of more competent

[1] Blomfield, *op. cit.* ii. 185.   [2] De Quincy, *op. cit.* ii. 340
[3] Blomfield, *op. cit.* i. 181.   [4] *Ibid.* i. 183.   [5] *Ibid.* i. 188–9.

but less enterprising architects for his own glorification. In justice to Mansart, it must be said that this view is not shared by all contemporary or modern critics. Even in an admittedly venal age, it is difficult to believe that any man could have reached the heights that he did without any real artistic ability, for Versailles was not his only great work; the second church of the Invalides is a masterpiece. Putting aside divergent opinions of his character and ability, we may at least follow his rise to fame and material prosperity as it is reflected in the salary that was paid to him by the king. In 1676, the year in which he commenced Versailles, he received 500 francs; in 1678 his official emoluments reached 10,000 francs; in 1681 he received 8,000 francs plus 20,000 francs to build himself a house; in 1683 his salary alone amounted to 15,000 francs. From that time onwards his income was almost fabulous; so much so that (according to Saint Simon, who cordially disliked him) the sum of 3,000,000 francs was offered for the succession to his post.[1] If we accept Sir Reginald Blomfield's calculations, this sum is equivalent to about £600,000 in pre-war values, and therefore, about £1,000,000 at the present day. It need hardly be said that these princely salaries were accompanied by every kind of honour, and that Mansart occupied a high social position. I may add that he seems to have had many other sources of income beyond his official emoluments.

It is rather a relief to turn from this record of blatant success to consider the means by which building was carried on. It appears that a model and a specification (*devis*) formed the usual basis of a Crown contract, with what we should call a ' schedule of prices '. On completion, all work was measured by the king's masons and

[1] Blomfield, *op. cit.* i. 48.

carpenters, but it does not appear that payment was made on the architect's certificate. The architect inspected the work during construction.[1] Materials were found sometimes by the contractors, sometimes by the Crown authorities, who often obtained them at a price lower than that of the open market. The accounts contain a mass of information as to prices then current. It appears that glass and iron were scarce, and that lead had to be brought from England. Eight-inch cast-iron pipes were used in large quantities at Versailles, and then cost 20 francs a fathom. Labour was employed on a large scale, thus Mansart had 2,800 men working under him at Versailles. Most of the work there, on the aqueduct of Maintenon, and on some other of the larger schemes carried out by Louis XIV and Mansart, was pressed on with feverish haste, and, when sufficient labour could not be found, troops were pressed into the service. Accidents were naturally frequent, but some form of compensation was usually paid to workmen injured in the discharge of their duties.[2] Payments to contractors are, of course, frequently mentioned, but I have seen nothing to indicate that the ' builder ', i. e. general contractor, then existed. In some parts of England nowadays the ' builder ' means the contractor for brickwork, masonry, and concrete, who has no authority over the carpenter, plumber, slater, painter, &c. ; probably some similar form of contracting by separate trades then existed in France, the *liaison* between them being supplied by the architect, the clerk-of-works, and the comptroller or surveyor. J. H. Mansart's staff of draughtsmen and assistants was provided for him by the Crown, so that their salaries did not come out of his own princely pocket. In 1699 Pierre le Pautre was

[1] *Ibid*. i. 44–9.   [2] *Ibid*. i. 50–2.

appointed to his *Bureau des Plans* (drawing office) at a salary of 2,000 francs a year, with six other draughtsmen (*dessinateurs*), one of whom received 3,000 francs, a very handsome salary. Sir Reginald Blomfield is convinced that some of these men acted as ' ghosts ' (*architectes sous clef*), and that Mansart himself could not possibly have had time to do his own designing. Certainly he had a very competent staff, including artists and craftsmen of all kinds as well as draughtsmen. Most of his assistants were eventually promoted to higher posts in the royal service, and they seem to have been well treated. Their travelling expenses were paid by the State.[1]

J. J. Gabriel in 1708 had a salary of over 20,500 francs a year, and a large staff of draughtsmen, of whom many afterwards rose to fame.[2] J. H. Mansart himself is said to have been trained in the offices of François Mansart and of Libéral Bruand.[3] The ' pupils ' of Louis le Vau are mentioned by Sir Reginald Blomfield in two instances,[4] but there is nothing to show that a regular system of indenture for articled pupils was then in existence.

The high standard of draughtsmanship then prevailing is exhibited in books of the period. It is not to be wondered at that only three of the twelve architects whom I have taken as typical of their age found time to write books, for, though books were extensively used as sources of ' inspiration ', most of these men were, as we have seen, far too busy to dissipate their energies in the unremunerative pastime of writing. Anthoine le Pautre's contribution was limited to a folio of his own designs,[5] executed or merely conceived. Blondel edited Savot's *Architecture*

[1] Blomfield, *op. cit.* i. 158, 186–7 ; ii. 18 *n.*, 27, 71–2.
[2] *Ibid.* ii. 57.   [3] Ward, *op. cit.* ii. 316.
[4] Blomfield, *op. cit.* i. 66, 121.
[5] A. le Pautre, *Œuvres d'Architecture* (1652).

FIG. 34. A DRAWING BY DANIEL MAROT

française (1664), became first director of the Academy, and published his lectures as a *Cours d'Architecture* (1672). He also wrote several other volumes on architecture, mathematics, the Calendar, watchmaking, on Pindar and Homer, and—on bomb-throwing ! Perrault's scholarly translation of Vitruvius was apparently his first introduction to architecture, and was followed in 1683 by a book on the Orders. But the most remarkable publications of the later Renaissance in France were the large collections of architectural engravings made by Jean le Pautre and by Jean and Daniel Marot. The former included 780 engravings ; an example from one of the Marot collections is illustrated on fig. 34. The work of these three men, all of whom had been well trained in architecture but who preferred draughtsmanship to actual practice, is of the very highest artistic standard and deserves the attention of every student. Sir Reginald Blomfield writes that,

' Marot made it his business to supply " pensées " as he called them, for architects, painters, sculptors, jewellers, gardeners, and others. In other words, his books were pattern-books, naked and unashamed. If, as appears to be the case, there is no escaping these parasites of modern architecture, one could only wish they were up to the standard of Marot and Le Pautre.' [1]

With these notes on the details of practice I conclude my study of the architect during the later Renaissance in France. Architecturally it was a magnificent period, but, in the instances that I have given of intrigue, nepotism, pedantry, grovelling toadyism, and criminal extravagance, one can detect the germs of that decay which, before the end of the eighteenth century, brought down the whole crazy fabric in a crash of ruin.

[1] Blomfield, *Architectural Drawing and Draughtsmen*, p. 46.

BIBLIOGRAPHY

(a) COLLECTIONS.

d'Argenville, A. J. D.   *Vies des fameux architectes* (1787).
Bauchal, C.   *Nouveau dictionnaire . . . des architectes français* (1887).
Berty, A.   *Les grands architectes français* (1860).
Blomfield, R. T.   *The Italians at Fontainebleau* (*Arch. Review* 1902).
Dilke, Lady.   *French Architects . . . of the Eighteenth Century* (1901).
Lance, A.   *Dictionnaire des architectes français* (1872).
Quatremère de Quincy.   *Histoire de la vie . . . des plus célèbres architectes, 1100–1800* (1830).
Vachon, M.   *Une famille parisienne de maistres-maçons : Les Chambiges* (1907).
(See also the works of Palustre, Ward, Blomfield, and Jackson cited in the foot-notes on pp. 190–1.)

(b) MONOGRAPHS.

De l'Orme, Philibert.   By H. Clouzot (1911) ; by M. Vachon (1887) ; by Sir R. Blomfield.   (*Architectural Review* 1904–5.)
Du Cerceau Family, the.   By H. von Geymüller (1887).
Gabriel, A. J.   By E. de Fels (1912) ; by H. Bartle Cox (1926).
Goujon, Jean.   By P. Vitry (N.D. recent).
Lescot, Pierre.   By Sir R. Blomfield (*R.I.B.A. Sessional Paper*, 1911).
Martellange, Étienne.   By E. L. G. Charvet (1874).
Primaticcio, F.   By L. Dimier (1900).
Serlio, Sebastiano.   By E. L. G. Charvet (1869).

VII

THE RENAISSANCE IN ENGLAND

THE student of architectural biography of this period is confronted with an enormous mass of material, much of which is admirable in quality and profoundly interesting. Mr. Beresford Chancellor's *Lives of the British Architects* [1] summarizes very capably the chief biographies, and monographs in the form of books or articles [2] deal with individual architects. Nevertheless, in spite of painstaking research on the part of some of our best scholars, we know less of English architects prior to the time of Inigo Jones than of their contemporaries in France and Italy. Thus we have no definite knowledge of the designers of Hampton Court, first under Wolsey and then under Henry VIII, though elaborate records and accounts of the works have been preserved.[3] It seems possible that the chief credit may be due to ' Mr. Henry Williams, priest, surveyor of the works ', as payments for the building were made in his presence monthly.[4] In a recent letter to *The Times* (24 June 1925), Mr. Ernest Law, whom I have just quoted, adds that the Royal Surveyor of the Works was the old title for the official architect as late as the days of Wren, and puts forward the interesting theory that Wolsey's architects at Hampton Court and at Christ Church, Oxford, must have been the same man, for the great halls in the two buildings are almost identical, especially the roofs. Italian craftsmen

---

[1] Published 1909.
[2] See Bibliography at end of this Chapter.
[3] Ernest Law, *History of Hampton Court* (1924), p. 28.
[4] *Ibid.*, p. 106.

were largely employed during the sixteenth century in England, but their work seems to have been confined entirely to decorative details, and it does not appear likely that any of them merited the title of 'architect' as generally accepted. But the influence of the Italian Renaissance is clearly manifested in a book by John Shute which was first published in 1563 and had an important effect on the trend of design in this country. It is curious that only five copies of this book are known to exist, and that none of them is preserved in the British Museum, the best being in the R.I.B.A. Library.[1] The full title is :

' *The First & Chief Groundes of Architecture* used in all the auncient and famous monymentes : with a farther and more ample discourse uppon the same, than hitherto hath been set out by any other. Published by Jhon Shute, Paynter and Archytecte. Imprinted at London in Fletestrete near to Sainct Dunstans churche by Thomas Marshe, 1563.'

The opening chapter is headed ' The discourse from time to time hovve this science of Architecture increased.' It begins with ' the fludde of Noe ', discusses the building of the Egyptians, Greeks, Etruscans, and Romans ; and on the third page outlines :—' What the office and Ductie is of him that vvyll be a Perfecte Architecte or Mayster of buyldings ', and then quotes or paraphrases Vitruvius on this at some length. The writer concludes that Vitruvius :

' nameth himselfe to be an Architect, wherein he thinketh him selfe parfait, But I the setter forth of this treatise in English, acknolage myself not to be a parfaict Architecte, (as he saith) nor yet Gramarian, and though I have put myself in prease, it is not through the depe knowlaige aboue rehersed, but I do

A facsimile, with an introduction by L. Weaver, was published in London in 1912.

it for to put in use an entraunce or beginning to them which be therein Ignoraunt, and desyre further Knowledge in these things, as hereafter appereth by the declaracion hereof.'

The rest of the book is taken up by plates of the Orders, explanatory letterpress, and some account of antique temples and their intercolumniation. Shute has made extensive use of Serlio as well as of Vitruvius, and mentions the former in the colophon with which his ' smal trauailes ' conclude. It appears fairly certain that the author studied in Italy from 1550 for some time, but not, as sometimes stated,[1] that his book was reprinted twice after 1563. I mention Shute now as an architect, and shall return later to the question of architectural authors and draughtsmen of this period.

Next comes the problematical personality of that John Thorpe whose famous book of drawings, preserved in the Soane Museum,[2] has given rise to so much speculation and controversy in recent years. It is a small folio of 280 pages, and contains plans and elevations of a large number of houses built between *c.* 1570 and *c.* 1600. Some of these are drawn to scale ; others are merely rough sketches ; some illustrate buildings which he is believed to have designed ; others represent even more certainly work for which he was not directly responsible. We do not even know how many of the pages were actually drawn by his own hand, still less can we be sure that any of them are plans of his own buildings. Mr. Gotch thinks that he drew most of them personally,[3] but Sir Reginald Blomfield doubts this and, moreover, is of opinion that they are probably only surveys drawn

[1] W. J. Loftie, *Inigo Jones and Wren* (1893), p. 93.
[2] Bought by Sir John Soane in 1810.
[3] Gotch, *Early Renaissance Architecture in England* (1901), p. 226.

after completion of the buildings rather than working plans drawn in advance.[1] Sir Thomas Jackson, writing more recently than either of the other eminent authorities just quoted, inclines to Mr. Gotch's view. He thinks that

' the book is an album or notebook in which are collected studies for his [Thorpe's] own use, such as the five orders and the chapel at Westminster . . . together with a number of designs of his own . . . and others in which he was interested. In one case he writes against a drawing " a front or a garden syde for a nobleman ". Again, two of the elevations are copied from '

Du Cerceau and another from a Flemish architectural book (1577) by Vredeman de Vries. Various striking discrepancies between Thorpe's plans and the buildings that they represent

' prove that the plans are not surveys of existing buildings, for, if they were, there would be none of these inaccuracies. They are just such departures from the original plan as would occur while the building was in progress : they happen constantly in our own practice, and must have been more frequent when there were no complete working drawings, no detailed specifications, no quantities, and no building contract beyond the vaguest description of what the building was to be like. Such a plan as Thorpe's would have been enough for the master-mason to set out the walls, and the general design would be explained by model, or word of mouth, as the building progressed, a great deal being left to the master-mason and workmen who followed the traditions of the craft in which they had been brought up.'[2]

In other words, medieval building methods still persisted in Elizabethan days in England, but it appears that

---

[1] Blomfield, *Short History of Renaissance Architecture in England*, (1900), pp. 33–8.

[2] Jackson, *Renaissance of Roman Architecture : England* (1922), pp. 94–6.

working drawings and detail drawings were sometimes employed, as we shall see when we come to consider the Smithson Collection, nearly contemporary with Thorpe's book of drawings.

All that we know otherwise of John Thorpe is that he was employed at Ampthill (a royal house) as surveyor ; that a writer in Peachman's *Gentleman's Exercise* of 1612 describes him as ' an excellent geometrician and surveior ' ; that in 1600 he was ' one of the clerks of Her Majesty's works ; ' [1] that in the same year he visited Paris, where he either built or surveyed a house in the ' Faber St. Jarmin ' for Marie de Médicis and another house for ' Monsieur Jammet ' ; and that his son John followed in his professional footsteps. Sir Reginald Blomfield observes that ' it is not even certain that he was an architect at all '. At all events his status is tantalizingly obscure, and one would gratefully welcome further light on his remarkable book of drawings.

Of the remaining names of so-called ' architects ' during the reigns of Elizabeth and James I, only two or three can be accepted. The epitaph in Wollaton Church, near Nottingham (see fig. 36), of Robert Smithson, who died in 1614, describes him as ' gent, architector, and survayor unto the most worthy house of Wollaton with divers others of great account ', which may mean either that he was the ' resident architect ' at Wollaton, or that he did in fact design and build the house. He is also described as the ' free master-mason ' of the works at Longleat.[2] Thus, though we now meet with the term ' architect ', we cannot be sure that any great change in status has taken place since the Middle Ages. Huntingdon

[1] Letter from Sir H. Nevill, dated 16 May 1600, in the Salisbury Papers.   [2] Blomfield, *op. cit.*, p. 39.

Smithson (*d.* 1648), son of the last, is said 'to have been sent to Italy by his patron in order to gather materials and designs',[1] and his work at Bolsover certainly shows an extensive knowledge of German detail also. But the Smithsons are chiefly noteworthy for the book of their drawings that has survived, in the possession of Col. Coke of Brookhill Hall.[2] The authorship of these is very doubtful; it appears that not only had both Robert and Huntingdon a hand in it, but also older and younger members of this 'architectural family'. Seventeen out of the ninety-nine sheets of drawings are dated (from 1599 to 1632), but none of them bear distinctive initials, the draughtsman describing himself merely as 'Mr. Smithson'. But however many persons may be represented by this generic term, 'he' was unmistakably a competent architect.

'A very remarkable and clever designer he was', writes Mr. Gotch,[3] 'unsurpassed, I venture to say, as a planner of houses. Every fresh example of his drawings increases one's admiration of his ingenuity, and almost every one of his plans has a touch of the grand manner about it.'

It is therefore the more to be regretted that a number of these drawings were destroyed by fire when the house of a friend to whom Colonel Coke had lent them was burned down.

Of Ralph (or Rudolph) Simons (or Symons or Symonds) Sir Reginald Blomfield thinks that he designed as well as built much of the work at Cambridge that is commonly ascribed to him, between *c.* 1584–1605.[4] Three plans

[1] E. B. Chancellor, *Lives of the British Architects* (1909), p. 46.

[2] On the Smithson Drawings see papers by M. B. Adams and J. A. Gotch in the *R.I.B.A. Journal*, vol. xiv, 366–72 (1907), and vol. xvi, 41–66 (1908) respectively.

[3] Gotch, *op. cit.*, p. 48.   [4] Blomfield, *op. cit.*, p. 42.

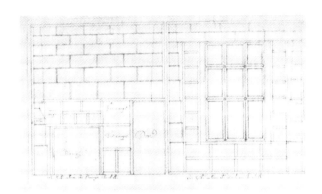

FIG. 35. DETAIL DRAWING OF A STUDY, WITH BOOKCASES
From the Smithson Collection (see p. 249)

FIG. 35 a. PLAN OF A HOUSE
From the Smithson Collection (see p. 248)

and three elevations, signed by him and by one Wigge, are preserved at St. John's College. He departed from Cambridge rather suddenly in 1605, owing to a dispute

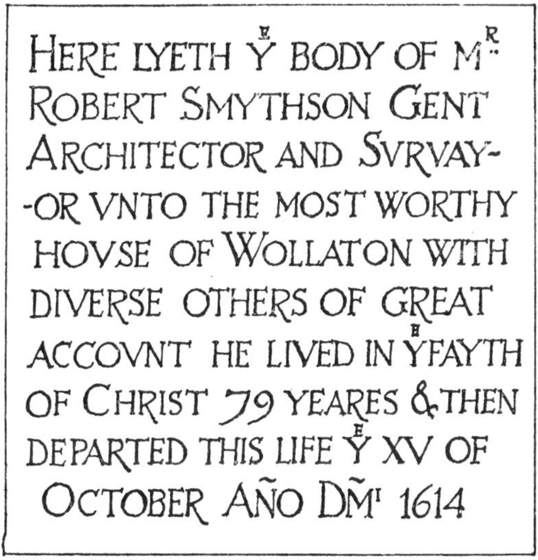

HERE LYETH Y̆ BODY OF M͡ᴿ ROBERT SMYTHSON GENT ARCHITECTOR AND SVRVAY- -OR VNTO THE MOST WORTHY HOVSE OF WOLLATON WITH DIVERSE OTHERS OF GREAT ACCOVNT HE LIVED IN Y̆FAYTH OF CHRIST 79 YEARES & THEN DEPARTED THIS LIFE Y̆ XV OF OCTOBER AÑO DM͡ᴵ 1614

Fig. 36. Inscription to Robert Smithson, Wollaton Church.
Drawn by M. S. Briggs.

over some building accounts, leaving Wigge (? his partner) to face the music and eventually to spend some years in jail.[1]

Mr. Sirr[2] quotes a very interesting letter of 1596, in which one Robert Stickells applies to Sir Robert Cecil that any candidate for a royal surveyorship, himself

[1] *Ibid.*, p. 42.
[2] On Thorpe and other architects of this period see the three papers by Mr. H. Sirr mentioned in the Bibliography at end of this chapter.

included, ' be put on his trial, either in the mathematical sciences, or in the rules of architecture, of shipbuilding, or of fortifying, house building, or any such ingenious cause '. This indicates on the one hand that the versatility of the Renaissance had reached England, on the other that the functions of a royal surveyor were far from being limited to architecture as we know it. Incidentally, we find mathematics again mentioned in the same breath as architecture, a phenomenon of regular occurrence up to the end of the eighteenth century or thereabouts.

A careful study of the numerous drawings in the Thorpe and Smithson Collections, valuable as they are, does not clear away all doubts and difficulties as to the functions of an architect in England during the reigns of Elizabeth and James I. I have already summarized the conflicting views of leading writers on the drawings of John Thorpe. It may be added that the leaves of the album containing them are of thick drawing-paper ; that some drawings are highly finished in ink, others roughly sketched in pencil ; that some are drawn to scale and others are not ; and that many are drawn in an inaccurate but effective perspective. In those days plans were called ' platts ' and elevations ' uprights '. There are hardly any sections among Thorpe's drawings, but one, taken through the great hall of a large house, delineates the hammer-beam roof carefully. Whatever else may be uncertain, it seems impossible to doubt that a large number of these plans were working-drawings and others sketch-designs. The alterations made on them show modifications and improvements effected either during building or during the designing period before building was commenced. Moreover, there are many details shown on these plans that no surveyor would think of indicating on a mere record plan.

Thus the treads of the staircases are numbered, and in a few cases flues are shown. Some of the plans have corresponding elevations, others have elevational perspectives, but many have neither elevations nor perspectives. Mr. Gotch [1] uses this as an argument to prove that, ' it is almost certain that in some cases only a plan was provided, without elevation ', but on the same page he quotes the contract made with Messrs. Symons and Wigge in 1598 for the second court at St. John's College, Cambridge, where ' platts and uprights ' are specifically mentioned. It is pretty certain that at this date a good deal was left to the discretion of individual craftsmen, thus the details of ornamental plaster ceilings were provided from pattern-books or models by itinerant craftsmen, and some enrichments were cast in a mould. In 1615 one Walter Gedde published a pattern-book entitled *A Book of Sundry Draughtes. Principally serving for Glasiers ; and not Impertinent for Plasterers and Gardiners : besides sundry other Professions.* This book, which I have discussed elsewhere,[2] is specially interesting because it shows that plasterers, glaziers, and gardeners made use of standard geometrical patterns in the design of ceilings, leaded windows, and parterres respectively. The various building ' trades ' still worked separately, and the building owner arranged a contract with each of them. But there is the puzzling case of Robert Timmins ' architect and builder ', who is said to have designed Blickling Hall in Norfolk, and was interred in the adjoining church in 1628.

The Smithson Collection consists of 99 sheets of draw-

[1] J. A. Gotch, *Early Renaissance Architecture in England* (1901), p. 199.
[2] M. S. Briggs, *Short History of the Building Crafts* (1925), pp. 278–9.

ings, many of the sheets comprising more than one drawing, and is now preserved on loan in the Library of the R.I.B.A. Mr. Gotch considers that about eighty sheets of drawings may definitely be assigned to the Smithsons. Partly because this collection is not so well known as Thorpe's album, I have reproduced three of the drawings here (figs. 35, 35a, and 37). But I have also selected these three examples, typical of the collection as a whole, to show that they are, to all intents and purposes, what we call architectural ' working drawings '. Fig. 35a (numbered ' seventy-eight ' in the original collection and in Mr. Gotch's 1922 catalogue published by the R.I.B.A.) is one of a set of four drawings of a large unnamed house, and is the first floor plan to a scale of 12 feet to 1 inch. The remaining drawings show the ground floor, second floor, and roof plan. The dimensions of the principal rooms are figured, flues are indicated, and an elaborately decorated scale appears on the original plan, but not on my reproduction. The lines are in brown ink, the names of the rooms in red ink, and a little tint is used on the walls. Nearly all the Smithson drawings, including these plans, are on paper but three are on parchment. I find it difficult to believe that any mere survey drawings would show flues, or the plan of the roof.

There are other sets of plans as elaborate as these in the collection. Many of them have little ' flyers ' or flaps of paper pasted over certain details. The object of this practice, familiar in modern architectural practice, is to substitute a modification of the original scheme, in which case one usually pastes the flyer firmly down; or to show an alternative, in which case the flap is hinged to show the detail underneath, in the same way that stamps are mounted in a modern album. Flaps are also used on the

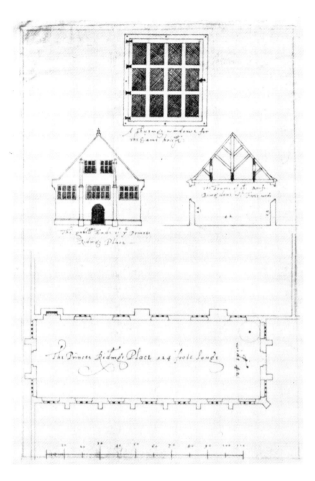

FIG. 37. WORKING DRAWINGS OF A RIDING SCHOOL

From the Smithson Collection (see p. 249)

Smithson drawings to show external shutters, and underneath one finds a leaded window. Some plans are drawn to the scale in use to-day, viz. 8 feet to 1 inch.

Fig. 37 (original number 21) shows a plan, elevation, and section to a scale of 24 feet to 1 inch of ' The Princes Ridinge Place ', together with a detail drawing of one of the windows to a larger scale, all drawn in brown ink and dimensioned. Fig. 35 (original number 12) is part of a sheet of three drawings to a scale of $\frac{2}{5}$ foot to 1 inch, of three sides of a small study lined with bookshelves and other fittings. These last two examples, by no means unique in the collection, prove that architects at that early date prepared carefully finished detail drawings in ink, and did not leave everything to the craftsmen. For instance, the Smithson collection contains a large number of detailed designs for mural monuments, screens, windows, gateways, chimney-pieces, doorways, and fountains—the very details which we are often told were done without an architect's direction. Here, too, we find designs for bedsteads, finials, panelling, cartouches, bridges, cisterns, strapwork, summerhouses ; plans of famous formal gardens, drawn to a scale of from 48 to 60 feet to an inch ; a survey of Warwick Castle ; the prosaic details of a brewhouse ; and, most remarkable of all, No. 55 iii, ' The Platforme [plan] of a frame : for the Teachinge of a yonge Horse : Before Hee come To the Ridinge : '. Some of these details clearly indicate the pins and joints required in the carpentry work. Finally we find a few drawings of older Gothic buildings (among them Henry VII's Chapel at Westminster, King's College Chapel at Cambridge), and an elaborately drawn detail of a wheel window.

But the study of medieval architecture was unusual at this

date, when everything novel from Italy was hailed with enthusiasm. I have mentioned John Shute's contribution to the literature of the period, and there were many other architectural writers—French, Flemish, and Dutch especially—who compiled fanciful pattern-books providing English architects and craftsmen with a more or less inaccurate rendering from Italian sources of the immortal Five Orders and their trimmings. Up to the time of Inigo Jones, English architects of the early Renaissance relied mainly on these heterodox authorities for inspiration in the new manner, not travelling much in Italy, and to this cause may be ascribed much of the florid and coarse detail in Jacobean architecture.

The most interesting architectural book of this period is, however, the work of a layman, Sir Henry Wotton, and was published in London in 1624. It is entitled *The Elements of Architecture . . . from the best Authors and Examples*, and is a small volume of about 100 pages, without illustrations. He leans heavily on Vitruvius, as one would expect, and follows him fairly closely in his Part I, dealing in turn with the site, its aspect, materials, forms, and elements in design, foundations and subsoil drainage, walls, pillars and pilasters (including rules for the Orders), arches and vaulting, doors and windows, staircases, chimneys, drains, the use of plans and models, internal planning, and roofs. Part II is devoted to painting, sculpture, and architectural ornament ; to gardens, fountains, and ' Conservatories of rare Beasts, Birds, and Fishes ; ' concluding, surprisingly, with some very apt reflections on the difficulty of establishing a standard of architectural criticism. Finally he takes the opportunity of announcing his next book, ' Namely, a Philosophical Survey of Education ', about which he hopes to write

' without publike offence though still with the freedome of a plaine Kentish man. In the meane while I have let these other Gleanings flie abroad, like the Bird out of the Arke, to discover what footing may bee, for that which shall follow '.

Sir Henry Wotton (1568–1639) followed the profession of a diplomatist, whom he once defined as an ' honest man sent to lie abroad for the good of his country '. He was stationed at Venice for many years. His *dicta* on architecture have often been quoted, and his little book is full of amusing passages ; as when he speaks of entasis badly designed as

. . . ' a practice growne (I know not how) in certaine places too familiar, of making Pillars swell in the middle, as if they were sicke of some Tympany, or Dropsie, without any Authentique Paterne or Rule, to my knowledge, and unseemely to the very iudgement of sight'.

But we are concerned here with his views on the status and functions of an architect in his day. He himself was an early type of the *dilettante* nobleman who in later years came to regard architecture (more precisely the Orders) as an essential item in every gentleman's *répertoire*. Long sojourn in Italy had saturated him with the spirit of the Renaissance and the maxims of Vitruvius. He apologizes quite frankly for producing ' a Pamphlet of this subject under my poore name ', and explains that he wrote it to divert his mind while ' troubled with a miserable stopping in my breast and defluxion from my head. It was printed sheete by sheete as fast as It was born, and It was born as soone as It was conceived '. I have outlined the scope of the book, and my outline will show the reader what Wotton regarded as the chief elements in architecture.

On his pp. 8–9 he speaks of the need to examine building materials with great care, but adds that,

' I must heere remember that to choose and sort the materials for every part of the Fabrique, is a Dutie more proper to a second Superintendent, over all the Under Artisans called (as I take it) by our Author, Officinator lib. 6 cap. 11, and in that Place expressely distinguished, from the Architect, whose glory doth more consist, in the Designement and Idea of the whole Worke, and his truest ambition should be to make the Forme, which is the nobler Part (as it were) triumph over the Matter.'

But in this passage Wotton seems much more concerned to state the practice in Vitruvius' day than in his own, an attitude somewhat characteristic of his class and age. A later paragraph is more informing :

' Let no man that intendeth to build, setle his Fancie upon a draught of the Worke in paper, how exactly soever measured, or neately set off in perspective ; And much lesse upon a bare Plant thereof, as they call the Schiographia or Ground lines ; without a Modell or Type of the whole Structure, and of every parcell and Partition in Pastboord or Wood. Next that the said Modell bee as plaine as may be, without colours or other beautifying, lest the pleasure of the Eye preoccupate the Iudgement ; which advise omited by the Italian Architects, I finde in Philippe de l'Orme, and therefore (though France bee not the Theater of best Buildings) it did merit some mention of his name.

' Lastly, the bigger that this Type be, it is still the better, not that I will persuade a man to such an enormity, as that Modell made by Antonio Labaco, of Saint Peters Church in Rome, containing 22 foot in length, 16 in breadth, and 13 in heighth, and costing 4,184 crownes ; The price in truth of a reasonable Chappell : Yet in a Fabrique of some 40 or 50 thousand pounds charge, I wish 30 pounds at least layd out before hand in an exact Modell ; for a little misery in the Premises, may easily breed some absurdity of greater charge, in the Conclusion.'

And finally one may quote, from Shakespeare, a passage in the *Second Part of King Henry IV*, written in 1598 :

> When we mean to build,
> We first survey the plot, then draw the model ;
> And when we see the figure of the house,
> Then must we rate the cost of the erection ;
> Which if we find outweighs ability,
> What do we then but draw anew the model
> In fewer offices, or at last desist
> To build at all ?   Much more, in this great work,—
> Which is almost to pluck a kingdom down
> And set another up,—should we survey
> The plot of situation and the model,
> Consent upon a sure foundation,
> Question surveyors, know our own estate,
> How able such a work to undergo,
> To weigh against his opposite ; or else
> We fortify in paper and in figures,
> Using the names of men instead of men :
> Like one that draws the model of a house
> Beyond his power to build it ' . . .[1]

So we leave the Elizabethan architect, a problematical personage, welcoming the new light from Italy, using plans much as we do to-day, yet clinging in some ways to the methods of the Middle Ages.

.   .   .   .   .   .

From about 1620 to 1720, the history of architecture in England is so completely monopolized by the gigantic figures of Inigo Jones and Wren that hardly any other architects, save that pathetic figure John Webb, find

[1] *Henry IV, Second Part*, Act I, Scene iii, 41–59.

a place even as ' supers ' on the stage. Hence it becomes necessary here to break the rule that I have endeavoured to observe hitherto, of considering period-types rather than individuals, and in this case to deal, however briefly, with the separate careers of these three men. Such a treatment is the more desirable because during the last few years a great deal of attention has been devoted to their work,[1] with the result that many existing assumptions have had to be abandoned.

Inigo Jones (1573–1652) was the son of a Smithfield clothworker, whose chief claim to fame lies in having been fined for using bad language to a lady. Mr. Beresford Chancellor considers that the elder Jones, who bore the same unusual name Inigo, ' seems to have been at first in easy circumstances, but the violence of his passions, as well as the " untamed vehemence of his language ", attributes that seem to have been inherited to some extent by his son, were perhaps responsible for his later financial troubles '.[2]

Mr. Ramsey hazards another speculation, that his father was ' of supposedly Welsh descent, and this strain of Celt may account for his imaginative and artistic qualities '.[3] His father's career has something more than a comic interest for us, as the fact of his bankruptcy in 1589 presumably has a bearing on Inigo the younger's

[1] See especially, J. A. Gotch, ' Inigo Jones : Some Surviving Misconceptions ', in the *R.I.B.A. Journal*, 16 August 1924 ; S. C. Ramsey, ' Inigo Jones ', *R.I.B.A. Journal*, 20 September, 1924 ; W. G. Keith, ' Inigo Jones as a Collector ', *R.I.B.A. Journal*, 19 December 1925 ; and J. A. Gotch, ' Some Newly Found Drawings and Letters of John Webb ', *R.I.B.A. Journal*, 24 September 1921 ; also the recent books and articles cited in the Bibliography at the end of this chapter.

[2] Chancellor, *op. cit.*, p. 53.

[3] S. C. Ramsey, *Inigo Jones* (1924), p. 13.

early training. Very little is known of this period of the great architect's life. Even John Webb, his pupil and relative, is forced to admit that ' there is no certain account in what manner he was brought up, or who had the task of instructing him '. A slender tradition relates that he was apprenticed to a joiner in St. Paul's Churchyard. The anonymous author of the memoir in his book *Stonehenge Restored* (1725) remarks that he was ' early distinguished by his inclination to drawing and design, and was particularly taken notice of for his skill in the practise of landscape-painting ', and adds yet another tradition that he went up to Cambridge, but these may be only the legends that commonly spring up a century after the death of a great man. Webb's statement that Inigo Jones was ' a great geometrician ' may be exaggerated but is at least credible ; he was certainly a good draughtsman ; and he must have had a fair education, otherwise he could never have ' held his own, as he did, in the pedantic court of James I ' . . . ' His work on Stonehenge bristles with classical allusions '.[1]

With our present lack of evidence, this is all that can be said of his early training. Next we come to his first visit to Italy, which must have taken place sometime before 1603. Mr. Ramsey, without citing his authorities, states that the tour lasted four or five years, that most of his time was spent in Venice, and that he probably went with a view to studying painting. The last supposition has much to recommend it, for we hear of Inigo Jones as a designer of theatrical scenery long before he appears as an architect proper. The idea of study in Italy does not seem to have taken hold of English architects at this period as it did a century later. John Shute (*d.* 1563)

[1] Chancellor, *op. cit.*, p. 55.

author of the first English book on the Orders, spent two or three years there. But travel had become part of a nobleman's education, and it is stated by the anonymous writer in *Stonehenge Restored* that Inigo Jones made his first Italian visit at the expense of the Earl of Pembroke, by Wren that he was financed by the Earl of Arundel. But it has since been pointed out that these two noblemen were born in 1580 and 1586 respectively, so that they could hardly have acted as his patrons. On the other hand, it seems to me conceivable that he might have been sent as a sort of tutor-draughtsman-cicerone to youths of this type making the Grand Tour ; and in later life they certainly both helped him in his career. Mr. Chancellor suggests a very simple solution of this problem : that he went to Italy at his father's expense. Nowadays it is possible for a bankrupt to live in considerable affluence, and it may have been so in the spacious days of Queen Elizabeth too, but on the whole it seems unlikely. If Inigo Jones did in fact spend some time in Venice in the last years of the sixteenth century he made a wise choice, for, though Palladio—whose works inspired him in later life —died a few years before, that great master's buildings are situated in Venetia. He himself writes thus of his travels :

' Being naturally inclined in my younger years to study the arts of design, I passed into foreign parts to converse with the great masters thereof in Italy, where I applied myself to search out the ruins of those ancient buildings which, in despite of time itself and violence of barbarians, are yet remaining.' [1]

But though we know so little of this first visit to Italy, there is sufficient documentary record of his second visit to enable us to form some idea of his methods of study.

[1] At the beginning of his book, *Stonehenge Restored*.

This second visit commenced sometime in 1613 : in early summer according to Sir Reginald Blomfield, in February or March according to Mr. Chancellor, some-time before September according to Mr. Gotch who points out that the earliest entry in his annotated copy of Palladio bears that date. The last-named authority states that he returned to England in January 1615. He may possibly have made a flying visit to England in January 1614, but in any case it is clear that he spent from fifteen to eighteen months altogether in Italy. Notes in his Palladio show that he was in Vicenza on 23 September 1613, and again on 13 August 1614, in Tivoli on 13 June 1614, and also in Rome and Naples during that year. It must be remem-bered that at this time Inigo Jones was forty years of age, a man who had already established a reputation for himself as a skilful and imaginative designer of those masques and revels so dear to the heart of his splendour-loving age. He had held an appointment as Surveyor of the Works from 1610 until the death of Prince Henry in 1612, with a salary of 3*s.* a day, and it may be that when this appointment lapsed he decided to turn his attention seriously to architecture. His previous tour in Italy probably gave him a desire to study the work of Palladio more thoroughly on this second visit, and he may have been financed on this latter occasion by the Earl of Arundel, for whom he seems to have collected ' antiques '.

In the Library of Worcester College, Oxford, there are a number of books formerly belonging to Inigo Jones and containing his autograph. The list is significant, because it contains so many Italian works of an early date that one may assume that he bought them and used them during his first and second visits. Besides the copy of Palladio (dated 1601), which I have already mentioned and shall return to again, they include De l'Orme's *Architecture* (1567 edition), Vasari's *Lives* (Florence, 1568), Alberti's *Descrittione di Tutta Italia* (Venice, 1588), Scamozzi's *L'Idea della Architettura Universale* (Venice, 1615), Sarayna's *De Origine . . . Civitatis Veronæ* (Verona, 1540), Summonte's *Historia . . . di Napoli* (Naples, 1601), *De Rebus Praeclare Gestis a Sixto V. Pont. Max.* (Rome, 1588), and *Le Cose Maravigliose dell' Alma Città di Roma* (Rome, 1588). From this list it may surely be assumed that Inigo Jones was a serious student. The annotated copy of Palladio, is, like Villard d'Honnecourt's and Inigo Jones's own sketch-books, one of the most valuable examples of architectural study that we possess, and its interest has been enhanced by recent research. Mr. W. G. Keith, who for some time has been studying the magnificent Burlington-Devonshire collection of Palladio's original drawings in the R.I.B.A. Library, has recently published a remarkable article entitled *Inigo Jones as a Collector*,[1] in which he proves with a wealth of patient argument that the bulk of this great collection was made, not by Lord Burlington in the eighteenth century as has been hitherto supposed, but by Inigo Jones himself in Italy, and purchased by Lord Burlington at a much later date. So now we must believe that ' Inigo Jones, having acquired Palladio's drawings, proceeded to record those in his possession as he identified them with the plates in his copy of the *Architettura*. Where he noted any variations between Palladio's original sketches and the published versions, he amplified the entries to that effect '.[2] Thus we find him making a second visit to Italy with a definite object, to study the work of Palladio and possibly to augment the collection of that master's drawings which

---

[1] In the *R.I.B.A. Journal*, 19 December 1925.   [2] *Ibid.*, p. 103.

he had already made. Many modern architects have followed the same course : their first visit to Italy has been a tour of general sightseeing and study, but they have returned again and again to that magic land to follow up some specific line of research.

At Chatsworth is the sketch-book that Inigo Jones used on his second Italian tour in 1613–15. All but one of the seventy or eighty drawings that it contains are studies of the human figure, showing that even at this stage he was not devoting himself exclusively to preparation for an architectural career. They are bold sketches in pen and ink, accompanied with notes on antique drapery, the topography of ancient Rome, ' the proportions of children ' the mixing of colours, the use of architectural ornament, and the design of ships' poops. A facsimile of this book is in the R.I.B.A. Library.

Inigo Jones was quite certainly a scholarly man, but, except for some ' very bad verses ',[1] his only contribution to literature was a work entitled *The Most Notable Antiquity of Great Britain, vulgarly called Stone-Henge, on Salisbury Plain, restored*, which was published after his death by John Webb in 1655, and reprinted in 1725. He writes as follows of the circumstances which led to its inception :

' King James, in his progress in the year 1620, being at Wilton, and discoursing of this antiquity, I was sent for by William, then Earl of Pembroke, and received there his Majesty's commands to produce out of mine own practice in architecture and experience in antiquities abroad, what possibly I could discover concerning this of Stone-Heng.'

John Webb, in editing the book, says that it is ' wrote with so much accuracy and skill, that 'tis uncertain which most deserves our commendation, his Industry or his

---

[1] Chancellor, *op. cit.*, p. 91.

Sagacity ', and sums up the main conclusions of the work in these words : ' After much reasoning, and a long series of authorities, he concludes at last, that this antient and stupendous Pile must have been originally a Roman Temple inscribed to *Coelus*, the senior of the Heathen Gods, and built after the *Tuscan* order.' This view of Jones's efforts in research will hardly be accepted by modern archaeologists. I have departed from a strict chronological sequence in order to deal with his two visits to Italy, and must now retrace my steps to discuss the events that separated them. Some time after his first return from Italy, and apparently about 1603, he was invited to enter the service of Christian IV, King of Denmark and brother-in-law of James I of England, on the strength of the reputation that he had acquired in Italy as a student of the antique. It is uncertain what he did in this capacity : possibly he acted as draughtsman to the king who was something of an amateur in architecture.

In 1605, the University of Oxford made preparations to entertain the king with three plays in the hall of Christ Church. They obtained the services of a controller of the works and two of the royal carpenters, and ' also hired one M[r] Jones, a great Traveller, who undertook to further them much, and furnish them with rare Devices, but performed very little of that which was expected. He had for his pains, as I heard it constantly reported, £50 '.[1] From this date onwards for seven years or so he was painting scenery and designing apparatus for theatres and masques. He resumed this work abreast of architectural practice in 1621, and continued it until stage plays were prohibited in 1640 by an ordinance of Parliament. In

[1] Leland, quoted in Blomfield, *Renaissance Architecture in England*, i. 99 (1897).

this field of activity he displayed the amazing versatility which characterized architects of the Renaissance, as we have seen, in Italy and France. He designed not only the scenery, the costumes, and other artistic details of a production ; but devised all kinds of mechanical contrivances for shifting scenery and improving lighting effects. And here we see the full effects of the Renaissance bursting on our country, just at the time when Shakespeare's plays were taking England by storm. The splendours of masque and theatre, the copious allusions to mythology in literature and art, were part of the spoil that Jones and his contemporaries brought back from their Italian journeys. The movement was formal in some ways, but nevertheless brilliant and gay.

There is a fine set of Inigo Jones's drawings for these masques at Chatsworth,[1] consisting of studies of costumes and for scenery, both architecture and landscape. They display bold draughtsmanship and a fertile imagination. Nine of the costume designs are in colour, the remainder in pen and ink, many with a wash of sepia or ink. The fees paid to him for his work in this connexion have been recorded in several instances : thus he received £40 for arranging a New Year's masque probably in 1609 ; and for the masque of *Oberon*, presented on New Year's Eve, he received £16 as its ' devyser '. But the preparation of these displays involved a large amount of work, and he was certainly not overpaid. Next he occasionally appears in connexion with small works of repair to State buildings, and in 1614 was appointed Surveyor of the Works to James I, with a salary of 8s. a day ' for entertainment ',

[1] Admirably reproduced and described in the Walpole Society's Volume for 1924 ; see also P. Cunningham, *Inigo Jones* (Shakespeare Society, London, 1848).

£80 a year for ' recompence for avails ' (i. e. for his services), and 2*s.* 8*d.* a day for travelling expenses. Details of his livery are preserved in a MS. in the British Museum. His annual allowance for this purpose was ' 5 yards of broad cloth for a gown, at 26*s.* 8*d.* a yard ; one fur of budge for the same gown, price £4 ; 4½ yards of baize to line the same, at 5*s.* the yard ; for furring the gown 10*s.* ; and for making it, 10*s.*' He also had a house in Scotland Yard. The salary mentioned above, even with allowances, was a comparatively small one, and there is evidence that it was not always paid regularly. The fees that he received for designing masques and other occasional work were also inconsiderable, and it does not appear that he had yet undertaken any architectural work of importance. His father was a bankrupt only a few years before he died, so can hardly have left him a fortune. Yet Webb records the following remarkable example of disinterested sacrifice on his part :

' The office of His Majesty's works of which he was supreme head, having through extraordinary occasions, in the time of his predecessor contracted a great debt, amounting to several thousand pounds, he was sent for to the lords of the Privy Council, to give them his opinion what course might be taken to ease his Majesty of it, the exchequer being empty, and the workmen clamorous. When he, of his own accord, voluntarily offered not to receive a penny of his own entertainment, in what kind soever due, until the debt was fully discharged. And this was not only performed by him, himself ; but upon his persuasion the Comptroller and Paymaster did the like also, whereby the whole arrears were discharged.'

Inigo Jones was a real courtier, prospering when the king was in favour, but loyal enough to share adversity with him. In 1640 he lent £500 to his royal master, then a fugitive ; in 1643 he was deprived of his office and fined £545 as a Royalist ; in 1644 he underwent the siege of Basing House and was then imprisoned and fined again. He naturally occupied a good social position, and became a justice of the peace. At his death in 1651 he left £100 for a monument, £100 for funeral expenses, and £10 to the poor.

He was ' in practice ', as we should say, from about 1616 to 1643, and again from 1646 to his death in 1651. During his period he carried out other work ; such as the masques already mentioned, and in 1631 he was ordered to arrange the king's collection · of Greek and Roman coins and medals, a strange commission for an architect. A large part of his work during this thirty years or so of practice was connected with his office as Surveyor of the Works, such as the designs for Whitehall in 1619. In 1617 he is said to have designed the Queen's House at Greenwich ; and also the Gothic chapel of Lincoln's Inn. In 1618 he was asked to prepare a plan for the lay-out of Lincoln's Inn Fields, of which Lindsey House survives. Then came York Stairs in 1621, the portico of St. Paul's Cathedral and the church of St. Paul's, Covent Garden, in 1631, Wilton House in 1648, and Coleshill in 1650, besides a host of other buildings, many of which have since been destroyed. A ridiculous number of houses have been attributed to Inigo Jones on the slightest evidence ; his only rivals in this direction are the brothers Adam, to whom tens of thousands of ceilings and chimney-pieces must have been credited by careless scribes. But the case of Inigo Jones has become serious of late years, for no less an authority than Mr. J. A. Gotch [1]

[1] J. A. Gotch, ' Inigo Jones : Some Surviving Misconceptions ', in the *R.I.B.A. Journal*, 16 August 1924.

has attributed some of the principal buildings on which his reputation rests to his pupil, John Webb. Briefly, Mr. Gotch holds that Jones designed the Banqueting Hall only, not the whole Palace of Whitehall ; that Webb designed King Charles's block at Greenwich ; and, that Pratt, perhaps with Webb's co-operation, designed Coleshill, but he adds that ' Inigo Jones was consulted during the operation '. The argument is long and learned, far too detailed to reproduce here ; but before depriving Inigo Jones of any of his glory we must remember that he was an impulsive artist, who may well have handed a hasty sketch to a trusted and skilled draughtsman like Webb to develop ; it is difficult to believe that a man about whom so much has been written, from Webb's time onwards, can have been credited with much work that was due to the genius of another, however modest and self-effacing that other may have been.

There is a very large collection of drawings attributed to Inigo Jones at Worcester College, Oxford, and another at Chatsworth ; but Mr. J. A. Gotch,[1] after a careful study of the handwriting on them, attributes a number of them to John Webb. They include plans, elevations, sections, and details, drawn in ink with hatching or wash to indicate sectional parts and openings. They are mostly dimensioned, annotated, and drawn to scale. The plans of Whitehall Palace are to a scale of 60 ft. to 1 inch, those for Somerset House 40 ft. to 1 inch, while for smaller buildings the scale for plans varies from 10 ft. to 15 ft. to 1 inch, showing that no fixed scale was used. The same applies to detail drawings, which vary from 2 ft. to 5 ft. to an inch. These plans show carved ceilings, plaster vaulting, &c., but not the lines of floor joints nor the

---

[1] In the *R.I.B.A. Journal*, 29 March 1913.

difference between brick and stone. Nor are sash bars indicated on the carefully drawn elevations. Some of the sections show roof-trusses, and there is one elaborate sheet of details of all the roof carpentry of the Banqueting Hall. There are other elaborate details of panelling, ceilings, book-cases, and plaster cornices. Inigo Jones also used models, and a warrant of 27 June 1619 authorizes the payment to him of £37 for making two models, one for the Star Chamber and the other for the Banqueting Hall.

John Webb (1611–72) has, for a long time, been treated by architectural historians as a foil to his brilliant master Inigo Jones. His patient humdrum career is contrasted sharply with the triumphal progress of the great artist-courtier who preceded him, and with the astonishing rise to fame of his gifted successor Wren. His early life was spent as a faithful draughtsman, carrying out Jones's bold ideas ; and his old age was clouded by disappointment when Wren stepped into a high office that Webb had a right to regard as his proper due. But now we have to revise our ideas of Webb,[1] as I have already indicated. No longer must we regard him as a nonentity, as an architectural ' ghost ' in fact, but as an architect of the first rank, to whom we owe the great scheme for the palace at Whitehall, and the designs for King Charles's block at Greenwich and for Lamport Hall ; as well as other works that have never been in doubt. He came of a Somersetshire family, was born in London, and was educated at the Merchant Taylors' School where he seems to have spent three years from 1625–8. This is the first instance where we have a definite record of an English architect's early education. Webb thus had a good grounding in general subjects before he entered the office

[1] See Mr. Gotch's papers, already cited, in the *R.I.B.A. Journal*.

of his relative Inigo Jones as a pupil at the age of seventeen. It is interesting to note that Jones is said to have taught him mathematics as well as architecture ; a detail which supports the view already advanced in these pages, and confirmed by the case of Wren, that there was a close connexion between mathematics and architecture in the past. There seems to be no evidence that he travelled in Italy, but Mr. Keith's recent researches into the history of the Burlington-Devonshire collection of drawings show that John Webb copied at least 17 of these for his own purposes from Palladio's originals. He may have done this while serving his articles, to improve his knowledge of ancient architecture, or at a later date as an exercise in design or even as an archaeological pastime. At any rate, these drawings remain to us and show his methods of study. There are, of course, details of the Roman Orders and other antique fragments, and copies of some of Palladio's own designs. One very interesting sheet (No. 63 in the Worcester College collection) contains no less than twenty-one plans, drawn to a very small scale in ink, with the Italian names of rooms, &c. translated into English. Obviously he was studying the principles of planning and of architectural composition. He remained as assistant with Inigo Jones until the death of the latter in 1652, having married his niece in the meantime, and was appointed his executor. This is not the place to pursue the vexed question of their relative responsibility for the Whitehall and Greenwich designs, nor to attempt any precise estimate of his importance as an architect. Everything goes to show, however, that his share in Inigo Jones's work was considerable, and that his talents have probably been underestimated in the past.

When Jones died in 1652, Webb was forty-one, and he

carried on independent practice till he retired some years before his own death in 1672. During this period he did a good deal of work for the Crown, but his salary was often overdue and on one occasion he was £1,000 out of pocket. The Crown also owed him £1,500 as Inigo Jones's executor. Webb was a Royalist, and claimed, when he applied for post of Surveyor-General to the Crown in 1660, that he had sent to King Charles at Oxford plans of fortifications, at great personal risk. In spite of this, he was passed over in favour of Sir John Denham, an amateur, in 1660 ; and again on Denham's death when this coveted post went to Wren. But it is a mistake to think of Webb as a poor and unfortunate architect. He had a large and aristocratic practice. His reputation has suffered mainly because of his own modesty and his intense loyalty to his master.

The recent discovery of nine letters, written by Webb to Sir Justinian Isham between 1654 and 1657, and a number of drawings that accompanied them, have shed a flood of light on an architect's methods at that period.[1] They all relate to the building of Lamport Hall in Northamptonshire. Webb's office was in Scotland Yard, Westminster. At the time when he undertook the work at Lamport Hall, he was engaged on at least three other large country-houses in Northamptonshire, Leicestershire, and Kent. His visits to the ' job ' in progress were infrequent, travel being difficult in those days, but partly, perhaps, because Webb was a busy and successful man. In one letter he says :

' I beginn my journey hence, god willing on munday next for Belvoir castell, intending to bee with you either the latter end

[1] J. A. Gotch, ' Some Newly Found Drawings and Letters of John Webb ', in the *R.I.B.A. Journal*, 24 September 1921.

of the next weeke, or at farthest the weeke following, certaine time I cannot pitch uppon, in respect I know not how long I shalbe detained at Belvoir.'

Webb dispatched the necessary working drawings and details at intervals to his client, who, being a man of taste and ability, saw that they were carried out according to the instructions that Webb sent with them. Both drawings and letters were sent by carrier from London. In one case at least the drawings were sewn up in a cardboard case. The drawings are carefully delineated to scale in ink and wash, a fine line being used. Dimensions and notes are frequent. The collection includes a number of detail drawings, many of these being full-size sections of mouldings. There is a set of four fine elevations of the interior of the music room to a scale of 4 ft. to $1\frac{1}{8}$ inch. The elevation of the exterior is drawn to a scale of 5 ft. to an inch. The letters make mention of practical points relating to construction and materials, and presumably a specification was used, but little practical information appears on the drawings. As examples of Webb's style as a letter-writer I quote two passages :

' As for yor ffrench workman I desire alwaies to employ our own countrimen, for by emploiment those grow insolent & these for want thereof are deiected, supposing they are not accompted able to performe when indeed it is only want of encouragement makes them negligent to study because a better conceite of foreiners as had then of themselves. I say this not in disaffection to strangers for I love them, as I should expect the like from them if I were abroad but only that our own natives may be used to good workmanshippe and enioy the benefitt their country affords, howsoever if the man be able in gods name employ him rather than bee at charge to bring one from London especially if you intend statues in the neeches as I designed, but then also let him cast them for you out of

Antique moulds for ffrench fashions are you know fantasticall.'
. . . ' That we shall have a warr with ffrance is doubted but wee
feare them not.'

The second passage indicates that Webb advised his client
as to the purchase of pictures :

' Normandy glass is here at 45s ye case. Whether you buy
it in London or not I would have it cutt at yor owne house
otherwise you wilbee cosened, & it may bee carried safe inough.
I have beene with Mr Wase, whose paintings & prises ye
enclosed note will shew you : that of Vandikes is a pretty thing
but hath beene much spoiled, though indifferently repaired.
The Lucretia is by a genuine hand, it hath beene likewise very
much spoiled, & not so well made good. The copy after Titian
quoad a copy is tollerable but I should suppose it not so pleasing to yor Ladye because of ye naked woman in it. That after
Guercino though it be very hard yett mee thinks might well be
placed over ye dore in yor roome betwixt ye first window &
Ceeling, at wch height much of ye hardness would bee taken off.'

A contemporary of Inigo Jones and Webb was Nicholas
Stone (1586–1647), a sculptor and ' architect ', whose
career presents many points of interest for us and has
recently formed the subject of exhaustive research.[1] He
is chiefly remembered for the great number of sculptured
monuments that he designed and carried out, but he is
also definitely described in sundry documents as an architect. He was born near Exeter, apprenticed to a mason in
London, and then worked in Holland under the Dutch
sculptor Hendrik de Keyser, whose daughter he subsequently married. In 1619 he was appointed Master-
Mason for the new Banqueting House, Whitehall, under
Inigo Jones whom he calls ' the ofisor of his Mat^{tes} workes '.
He was employed on this work for three years, receiving

[1] See Bibliography at end of this chapter.

4*s*. 10*d*. a day for the first two years and 3*s*. 10*d*. in the third, but carried out other building and statuary at the same time. In 1626 Charles I appointed him ' Master Mason and Architeckt for all our buildings and reparations within our hous and castle of Windsor ', with wages of twelve pence *per diem* and other allowances, including 2*s*. a day ' riding allowance ' on many occasions. In 1631 he carried out work at Oxford for the Earl of Danby, comprising three gateways in the Physic Garden and the rebuilding of part of the Tudor house at Cornbury Park. He paid 33 visits to this work while it was in progress, acted as architect and directed the working, receiving in all £1,000 for his services. Stone built the portico of St. Paul's from Inigo Jones's designs in 1633, but in the previous year had reported to ' Your Lopps ', the Commissioners, on the defective state of the foundations. In 1634 the Goldsmith's Company decided to rebuild their Hall. They obtained ' 2 or 3 several plats ' [plans], but whether Stone or Jones prepared these, or whether they were obtained in competition is not stated. At any rate, Stone was appointed Surveyor to the work with a quarterly salary of £10. He carried out some architectural work and much more sculpture after this date. Among works attributed to him are the porch of St. Mary's Church at Oxford and the York Water-gate (' York Stairs '). The striking points about his career are that he practised architecture as well as sculpture, and acted simultaneously as architect and master-mason. It is clear, too, that he received retaining fees or salaries for government work with full liberty to carry on private practice.

His son Nicholas (1618–47) was trained as a sculptor but died young. He and his brother Henry (1616–53) spent four years travelling in Italy between 1638 and 1643.

Nicholas (junior) has left a lengthy diary of their tour, in the form of a small leather book preserved in the British Museum, and also a sketch-book which is now in the Soane Museum. Though neither of these two were architects, this record of their travels gives a vivid account of students' work in Italy at that date, with such prosaic but none the less interesting details as expenses of travel, and board, and amusement. I transcribe the following entries relating to books purchased by the brothers.

	liuers.	cratts.	sold.
1638. 2 Sept. FIORENZA. The book of prints of the show upon the water entertainment of the Great Dukes mother in the yeare 1608.	01	05	00
the 3 parts of the Booke of the life of paint. Sc. Ar.[1]	04	00	00
The booke of Euclides geometria.	03	04	00
the booke of the ruines of Roome.	04	00	00
Eosopes fables in Italian.	00	10	00

	iuliotts.	biocs.	qua.
— from 29 Sept. for Ouid in Italian.	06	00	00

	crowns.	iulios.	biocs.
1639. 24 May for a booke of perspectiue of Vignolo.	01	5	00
— 14 Sept. for 2 bookes of temples anticke.	01	4	0
— 28 Sept. for a booke of the fountaines of Rome.	0	3	0
— 19 Oct. for Archytecture of Vitruvius.	01	8	00
1640. 10 July. for a booke Le Imagini degli Antichi.	0	9	0
— 11 July. for ye workes of Julio Camill.	0	5	00

[1] This evidently refers to Vasari's *Lives*.

Then come purchases of Vignola on perspective, Vitruvius, Camillo, the fountains of Rome, &c., obviously second copies so that each brother might have his own ; and a number of expensive books (including Alberti) bought in 1642 shortly before the end of the tour. The most startling entry in all the diary is dated 20 March 1640, ' for a place to stand to se the Jew burnt in Campo Fiora. o. 1. o '.

.   .   .   .   .   .

We now arrive at the career of Sir Christopher Wren (1632–1723), which has rightly formed the subject of many volumes of biography, and can only be briefly summarized here. The recent bicentenary of the great architect's death was made the occasion for publishing tributes to his fame (mentioned in the Bibliography at the end of this chapter), and for the foundation of a society with the expressed object of perpetuating his memory. In those celebrations, much stress was laid upon the versatility of his genius : here I must confine myself strictly to his train-ing for the profession that he eventually adopted, to his status as an architect, and to the methods by which he carried out his work. Thus limited, the great mass of biographical material that is available shrinks to more convenient dimensions. For at the outset we are faced with the fact that Wren never was trained for architecture. Like Perrault in France (see p. 226) he dropped into it, more or less accidentally, from scientific pursuits in which he had already attained eminence. His early career there-fore only affects this study in so far as it prepared and influenced him for the marvellous success that he subse-quently attained. Two things at least are certain about his scientific training : that its very breadth and extent enabled him to grasp the principles of architectural design and construction the more quickly when the time came, and that the fact of his having received no specialized education in architecture is no argument whatever against specialized education for architects at the present day. Wren is generally considered to be the greatest architect England has ever produced ; but that was in spite of rather than because of his training. From early childhood he was recognized as a prodigy and a genius ; nothing could stop him. The mere catalogue of his inventions and preoccupations in his youth takes one's breath away and seems almost inhuman.

But his success was not wholly due to his own efforts. He came of a family distinguished for devotion to Church and King. His father the Dean of Windsor, and his uncle the Bishop of Ely, though both suffered for their Royalist sympathies during the Commonwealth, were largely instrumental in obtaining his first commissions for him, and both had a taste for building too. His very reverend father is said to have prepared designs and detailed estimates in 1634 for a building at Windsor to cost over £13,000. This work was done for the Queen, but was never actually executed. Heredity, environment, and opportunity alike favoured Wren's chances.

His scholastic career, as I have just said, takes one's breath away. After some preliminary tuition in mathematics from a clergyman, Christopher Wren entered Westminster as a ' Town Boy ' at the age of nine, and left there shortly before he became thirteen. He seems to have been a small and delicate child with a tendency to consumption but nevertheless lived an extraordinary busy life and died at an advanced age. Even at this early stage he was precocious, displaying marked ability in his school work, especially in mathematics. After leaving Westminster, he became assistant to Sir Charles Scarborough (1616–94), a Court physician with mathematical tastes. In this way he was employed for some years in preparing anatomical specimens ; but his duties were miscellaneous. It was probably early in this period that he wrote a letter (dated 13 September 1645) in Latin verse to his father, dedicating to him an instrument called *Suum Panorganum Astronomicum* and a tract *De Ortu Fluminum*. The letter is somewhat stilted, even having regard to the language of the time. In another Latin letter of 1647 to his father he mentions an invention of his : ' a Weather clock namely, with Revolving Cylinder ; ' and proceeds :

' The other day I wrote a treatise on Trigonometry which sums up as I think, by a new method and in a few brief rules, the whole Theory of Spherical Trigonometry. An Epitome of this I re-wrote on a brass Disc of about the size of one of King James' Gold Pieces, and having snatched the Tool from the Engraver, I engraved much of it with my own Hand which Disc Sir Charles had no sooner seen than he insisted upon having a similar one of his own.'

Another letter to his father describes an Easter holiday spent at a country-house. Cunningham speaks of the ' barren eloquence ' and ' puerile pedantry ' of Wren's letters and speeches in earlier days, but that is an unnecessarily severe judgement.

His long association with Oxford began when he entered Wadham College as a gentleman-commoner, in 1646 and in his fourteenth year according to his son's biography, *Parentalia* ; in 1650 according to Sir Reginald Blomfield ; in 1649 according to Sir Lawrence Weaver who gives evidence from Sir Thomas Jackson and the Warden of Wadham in support of his statement. He took his B.A. in 1651, his M.A. in 1653, and soon afterwards

became Fellow of All Souls. During his sojourn in Oxford
he produced no less than fifty-three inventions, covering
many branches of science and industry. These were concerned, among other things, with astronomy, physics,
anatomy, embroidery, etching, mining, military fortifications, printing, musical instruments, writing in the dark,
weaving, sailing, submarine navigation, whale fishing, 'new
designs tending to strength, convenience, and beauty in
building ', and ' a pavement harder, fairer, and cheaper
than marble '. The last two items show that his wide
range of curiosity embraced building in its ambit, but
probably the skill that he acquired in scientific experiment, in accurate drawing, and in laboriously constructing
delicate models stood him in even better stead later in
life. On 11 September 1654, John Evelyn, with whom Wren
was so closely associated after he turned to architecture,
visited Oxford, and writes thus in his Diary : ' After
dinner I visited that miracle of a youth Mr. Christopher
Wren, nephew of the Bishop of Ely ' ; and again, two
days later, speaks of the remarkable collection of instruments and inventions that he saw in Dr. Wilkins's rooms
at Wadham, ' most of them of his owne and that prodigious
young scholar Mr. Chr. Wren, who presented me with
a piece of white marble, which he had stain'd with a lively
red very deepe, as beautiful as if it had been natural '. In
1657 he was appointed Gresham Professor of Astronomy
in London. At first he declined the honour, for he was
only twenty-four ; then accepted it and delivered a somewhat pedantic inaugural address. In 1660 he took a prominent part in the foundation of the Royal Society, of
which he became President in 1680. Even in his dissect-
ing-room days, he was in constant touch with the leading
London scientists of the day. In 1661 he became Savilian

Professor of Astronomy at Oxford, a post that he continued to occupy until protracted absences from Oxford
after he had amassed a large architectural practice led to
complaints and his ultimate resignation. Of his scientific
attainments there is no question. Generous appreciation
of his talents was voiced in his own day, and echoed at
the bicentenary celebrations of 1923. In science as in
architecture, though he had little time for research after
he reached the age of thirty-five, he was and is recognized
as a genius. It may be, as Sir Lawrence Weaver suggests,
that he was ' too universal ', that he diffused his energies
over too extensive a field, and that had he concentrated
on architecture at an earlier stage his work would have
reached an even higher level than it did. Such speculation
is tempting, but beyond the limits of my book. It is
enough for us to know that Wren brought to architecture
a mature and brilliant brain, sharpened by frequent contact with the brightest intellects of his day and tempered
by abstruse problems in scientific research.

The circumstances of his entry into architectural practice
are illuminating. When in 1661, at the instance of John
Evelyn, the King appointed him assistant to Sir John
Denham, Surveyor-General of His Majesty's Works, Wren
had had no training whatever in architecture. Doubtless
his inquiring mind had led him into speculation on the
nature of building materials, even into the geometry of
architecture : he certainly had learned to draw ; but
beyond these rudimentary qualifications he was a complete
amateur, and Sir Reginald Blomfield is probably justified
in describing his appointment as ' a discreditable job '.[1]
At this date the real work of the Surveyor's office was done

[1] Sir R. Blomfield, *The Touchstone of Architecture* (Oxford, 1925),
p. 178.

not by Denham (a mediocre poet drawing a salary for nothing in particular), but by John Webb, a man who, as we have seen, was deficient in the mysterious quality known as ' push ' in modern slang. Wren succeeded to the Surveyor's post a little later, on Denham's death, and Webb was left out in the cold, though the reversion of the appointment had been promised to him. It was a bitter blow, to be displaced by a young amateur with influential friends, and Webb must have felt it keenly.

Shortly after entering the service of the State, Wren was offered a commission to visit and report on the fortifications of Tangier. It is interesting to note that this invitation was actually written by his cousin Matthew Wren, son of the Bishop of Ely, and that we have here another little family job. Cunningham suggests that the invitation was the result of a Court intrigue to get rid of Wren, the climate of Tangier being notoriously bad, but in that case Matthew's conduct was not the act of a loyal kinsman. At any rate, Wren declined the honour, and the good pay that went with it, urging reasons of health as his excuse. Then came several private commissions : the designs for the Sheldonian Theatre at Oxford (1662), for Gilbert Sheldon Archbishop of Canterbury ; and in 1663 plans for the Chapel of Pembroke College, Cambridge, for his uncle Matthew, who had previously tested his abilities (as the best of uncles will) on the north transept doorway at Ely. Sir Reginald Blomfield says of these two works that the Sheldonian Theatre ' is about as bad as it can be ', and that ' similar solecisms of design appear ' in Pembroke Chapel, the pilasters in front being some twelve diameters high. With the former criticism most people will agree, but the charm of the Pembroke belfry or lantern tempts one to overlook minor shortcomings in the rest of the facade. In 1663 Wren was invited by the Dean and Chapter to serve on a Commission for the restoration of Old St. Paul's, though he did not in fact issue his report until 1666. In 1665 he was instructed by the authorities of Trinity College, Oxford, to prepare designs for a new quadrangle.

At this stage in his career, actuated perhaps by a desire to learn something of architecture which he was now practising, or tempted out of England to escape the Plague, business being then at a standstill, he suddenly set off on a lengthy sketching-tour in France. He left for Paris early in July, and remained for some eight months in that city and its neighbourhood. He had an introduction to the British Ambassador, Lord St. Albans, and one may assume that every facility for study was put at his disposal. Our knowledge of the work that he did during these eight months is based on a long letter written to his friend Dr. Bateman and quoted in *Parentalia*, his son's recollections (see Bibliography at end of this chapter). ' I have busied myself ', he says, ' in surveying the most esteem'd Fabricks of Paris, and the Country round ; the Louvre for a while was my daily Object, where no less than a thousand Hands are constantly employ'd in the Works ' ; . . . He then describes the principal buildings and sights of Paris, their decoration and furniture, the great royal *châteaux* at Fontainebleau and St.-Germain, the ' incomparable Villas of Vaux and Maisons ', and a dozen other great country-houses. He describes his famous interview with Bernini (see p. 176), and the meetings of the Academy. Of Versailles he says,

' Not an Inch within but is crouded with little Curiosities of ornaments ; the Women, as they make here the Language and Fashions, and meddle with Politicks and Philosophy, so they sway also in Architecture ; Works of Filgrand, and little Knacks are in great Vogue ; but Building certainly ought to have the Attribute of eternal ; and therefore the only thing uncapable of new Fashions.'

All the buildings mentioned above, and many others, he ' survey'd ; and that I might not lose the Impressions of them, I shall bring you almost all France in paper, which I found by some or other ready design'd to my Hand, in which I have spent both Labour and some Money. . . . I hope I shall give you a very good Account of all the best Artists of France ; my Business now is to pry into Trades and Arts, I put myself into all shapes to humour them ; 'tis a Comedy to me, and tho' sometimes expenceful, I am loth yet to leave it. . . .'

At the end of this letter he gives a hint of a projected book, of which the completion and publication was presumably prevented by the rush of building work which came to him shortly after he returned from his travels :

' My Lord Berkeley returns to England at Christmas and I propose to take the opportunity of his Company, and by that Time to perfect what I have on the Anvil—Observations on the present State of Architecture, Art and Manufactures in France.'

Walpole remarks of this tour that Wren ' visited France and unfortunately went no farther '. It is natural to speculate on the reason for this, and to wonder what sort of an effect a visit to Italy would have had on his designs. Wren cannot have been a very poor man at this time, he had at least eight months at his disposal, and we know from the example of Inigo Jones that the idea of study in Italy was no novelty. But perhaps we have gained something after all, for had Wren concentrated on antique and Palladian precedent as laboriously as some of his followers did, the imaginative genius which marks so much of his work would have been sterilized. On the other hand, my

own opinion has long been,[1] and still is, that Wren's work
(e. g. the picturesque outline of his steeples and the bold-
ness of his grouping) has in it far more of the Baroque
spirit of seventeenth-century Italy than is generally
admitted ; and it is possible that further acquaintance
with Bernini and other practitioners of that style in Italy
would have resulted in a new variant of Baroque in England,
preserved from excess by Wren's splendid sanity and more
attuned to English tastes than are some of its wilder
manifestations elsewhere.

That Wren did not attach much importance to study
in Italy appears from a letter that he wrote to his son
Christopher about 1698, when the latter was in France with
' young Mr Strong ', son of the master-mason of St. Paul's :

' If you thinke you can dine better cheape in Italy you may
trie, but I thinke the passing the Alpes and other dangers of
disbanded armies and abominable Lodgings will ballance that
advantage : but the seeing of fine buildings I perceive temptes
you and your companion Mr Strong, whose inclination and
interest leades him, by neither of which I can find you are
moved ; but how doth it concern you ? You would have it to
say hereafter that you have seen Rome, Naples, and other fine
places, a hundred others can say as much and more ; calculate
whether this be worth the expence and hazard as to any
advantage at youre returne.'

Undoubtedly Wren was strongly influenced in his design
by what he saw for himself on his French tour, but it is
equally certain that Italian and Dutch architecture made
a great impression on his mind. These several influences
have been traced in two admirable essays [2] published in

---

[1] M. S. Briggs, *Baroque Architecture* (London, 1913), pp. 210–11.

[2] A. Stratton, ' Dutch Influence on the Architecture of Sir C. Wren ' ;
and W. H. Ward, ' French and Italian Influence on Sir C. Wren's
Work '.

the *R.I.B.A. Wren Bicentenary Volume* (1923). Wren must have imbibed all his knowledge of Italian and Dutch work, and extended his first-hand acquaintance with French architecture, from the numerous books published in various languages on these subjects. The catalogue of Wren's library, which was sold in 1748, shows that he possessed copies of all the standard Italian and French authorities ; as well as many of the slipshod and rather Baroque treatises on architecture published in Holland and Flanders. Sir Reginald Blomfield writes that ' a hasty wrestle with Serlio's very inaccurate *Architettura*, and Fréart's still more inaccurate *Parallel of Architecture*, recently translated by his friend John Evelyn, appears to have concluded his technical studies ',[1] and this in the year preceding his Paris visit. We know that Wren was a scholar, and may infer that he used books frequently in his work throughout his long career.

Passing from these fragmentary facts and speculations about his professional training, we next have to consider the scope and nature of his amazing practice. I have pointed out already that his early work was due mainly to family influence ; but it is erroneous to infer that Wren himself took a passive share in moulding his career. The Great Fire of London provided his first great opportunity. It broke out on 2 September 1666, some months after his return from France, and burned for several days. On 7 September John Evelyn visited the ruins, ' clambering over heaps of yet smoking rubbish ', the ground being so hot that it even burnt the soles of his shoes ; and on the 10th, ' went againe to the ruines, for it was now no longer a Citty '. On the 13th Evelyn, who was an architectural amateur of some pretensions, ' presented his

[1] Sir R. Blomfield, *The Touchstone of Architecture*, p. 179.

Majesty with a survey of the ruins, and a plot for a new Citty, with a discourse on it. . . .' Writing to a friend, he says that, ' It was the second that was seene, within 2 dayes after the Conflagration : But Dr. Wren had got the start of me.'

So we see that Wren himself was largely responsible for the phenomenal stream of work that kept him busy from 1666 for some thirty years, after which his activities diminished until he retired. Though his plan for rebuilding London was never carried out, he was appointed architect for St. Paul's, for fifty parish churches in the City, and for various new public buildings to replace those which had perished. Thereafter his official post brought him such enormous commissions as Greenwich and Chelsea Hospitals, Hampton Court Palace, and a host of lesser works. He did much building at Oxford and Cambridge, Morden College at Blackheath, and some of the charming private houses that have been attributed to him. But when a Bill was passed in 1712 ' for building and endowing fifty new churches in London and Westminster ', Wren was appointed one of the Commission to arrange for other architects to prepare designs : his own day of designing was done.

Besides the design and erection of new buildings of almost every type, Wren's work included, as I have just noted, a great town-planning scheme, and much restoration of old buildings. The plan for rebuilding London was a magnificent conception. It would have made London one of the most beautiful cities in the world, with main streets 90 feet wide, a broad quay lined with stately buildings along the Thames, and churches placed to the greatest advantage on commanding sites. This sense of ordered planning for effect is characteristic of

FIG. 38. SIR CHRISTOPHER WREN

PRESENTING HIS NEW PLAN OF LONDON TO CHARLES II

From an old print in the R. I. B. A. Library

the seventeenth century in Europe, and England lost an opportunity of laying out her greatest city on lines which would have served as a model to the world. Wren does not seem to have prepared any other scheme on this scale, but his projects for the lay-out of the Palace at Winchester (never carried out), Hampton Court (only partially completed), Greenwich and Chelsea Hospitals show that he possessed to the full the Baroque sense of ordered magnificence. Except for the Tangier incident already mentioned, he did no important work of military or civil engineering ; nor did he carve statues, paint pictures, or write books.

Wren's attitude to the architecture of the past, and especially to Gothic, is a matter of some interest. At some period in his life he dabbled in archaeology, preparing conjectural restorations of the Mausoleum of Halicarnassus and of the shrine of Artemis at Ephesus. But his bias towards classic architecture was accounted for partly by practical considerations, and it is amusing, in view of the writings of Ruskin and his school, to find that one of Wren's chief objections to Gothic was that it so often implied bad construction. Sometimes he called it ' Gothick ', sometimes ' Saracen ' ; but again and again he refers to the structural shortcomings of medieval buildings. Thus, in reporting on the condition of Salisbury Cathedral in 1669, he begins by admitting that : ' The whole Pile is large and magnificent and may be justly accounted one of the best Patterns of Architecture in that Age wherein it was built . . .' but concludes his lengthy report with these significant sentences :

' There is scarce any Gothick Cathedral, that I have seen, at home or abroad, wherein I have not observed the Pillars to yield and bend inwards from the Weight of the Vault of the

Aile ' . . . ' for this Reason, this form of Churches has been rejected by Modern Architects abroad, who use the better and Roman Art of Architecture.'

His report on Westminster Abbey (1713) is profoundly interesting, and opens with an historical account of the fabric, in which Wren suggests that Gothic architecture was derived from Saracen rather than Roman sources, as a by-product of the Crusades. He describes Henry VII's Chapel, perhaps with intentional irony, as ' a nice embroidered Work ', and finally submits his own recommendations and designs for restoration, ' such as I conceive may agree with the original scheme of the old Architect, without any modern Mixtures to show my own Inventions '. Yet at St. Paul's he proposed that the interior walls should be ' new flagg'd with Stone of larger size than before ; and in doing this it will be as easy to perform it, after a good Roman manner, as to follow the Gothick Rudeness of the old Design '. Later in this report he suggests that, ' a spacious Dome or Rotundo, with cupola, or hemispherical roof, and upon the Cupola (for the outward ornament), a Lantern with a spiring top ', to take the place of the famous soaring spire of Old St. Paul's.

Wren evidently did not share his friend Evelyn's utter contempt for medieval architecture : [1] his restoration work was carried out after exhaustive preliminary study and was not fanatically destructive. Sometimes, as at Kilmainham Hospital, he preserved Gothic features that might have been sacrificed. Most surprising of all, he even

[1] John Aubrey, whose *Lives* of his contemporaries between *c.* 1669 and 1696 has recently been republished, was a zealous antiquarian who thought Gothic architecture barbarous, nevertheless he made careful drawings of windows, porches, &c., and endeavoured to formulate a systematic chronology of Gothic styles or periods. This attitude was rare in Wren's day.

built in the ' Gothick ' manner himself on occasion ; either where local tradition required it, as at Tom Tower, or merely *per divertimento*, as in some of the City churches. But the references to St. Paul's in the report quoted above show that he was always hankering after Roman forms, and in the Library which he erected in the cloister of Lincoln Cathedral we see that his own taste, and incidentally the requirements of a well-lighted apartment, triumphed over any scruples about harmony with medieval surroundings. Doubtless he was justified in criticizing defects in Gothic construction, but his scornful remarks about the rubble-cored piers of Old St. Paul's sound odd to us, who know how he himself constructed the new piers under the great dome of its successor.

In his attitude to old buildings, then, he seems to have preserved an equivocal position ; but in his remarks about the Orders there is no such wavering :

' Modern authors who have treated of Architecture seem generally to have little more in view, but to set down the Proportions of Columns, Architraves and Cornices in the several Orders, . . . and in these Proportions finding them in the ancient Fabricks of the Greeks and Romans (though more arbitrarily used than they care to acknowledge) they have reduced them into Rules, too strict and pedantick, and so as not to be transgressed, without the Crime of Barbarity, though in their own Nature they are but the Modes and Fashions of those ages wherein they were used. . . . Curiosity may lead us to consider whence this Affection arose originally, so as to judge nothing beautiful but what was adorned with Columns, even where there was no real Use of them.'

In this astoundingly ' modern ' passage we can see the essential greatness of Wren's mind. With all his love for the ' good Roman manner ', he was far above the level of

those pedants who stifled the interest of English craftsmanship in the later eighteenth century by reducing every
architectural form and detail to rules based on the precepts
of Vitruvius and Palladio. The same reasonable outlook
appears in his advice to the Commissioners for Queen
Anne's fifty churches, advice based on his own experience
and practice. Practical common sense always distinguished
his judgement on artistic questions.

It need hardly be said that Wren was a tremendous
worker. Not only had he to carry on a large number of
important buildings simultaneously, but his appointment
as Surveyor involved many minor duties such as supervising repairs to Government offices, finding lodgings for
State officials, and at one time, pulling down Dissenting
meeting-houses as fast as they were erected. Thus he led
a party of soldiers and carpenters to pull down the Quaker
meeting-house at Horsleydown in Southwark, after the
Five Mile Act of 1670.

Presumably his ' office ' was located in his official residence in Scotland Yard, one of the perquisites of his own
appointment. It is probable that he paid his own staff,
and certain that the staff must have been a large one.
There is an entry in his petty cash accounts as follows :
' For a booke on Vitruvius for the use of ye office—£3 '.
The name of one famous man employed in his office has
come down to us, that of Nicholas Hawksmoor (1661–
1736), who became his ' scholar and domestic clerk ' at
eighteen, clerk-of-works at Winchester Palace in 1683,
deputy-surveyor at Chelsea Hospital, and clerk-of-works
at Greenwich Hospital in 1698 with a salary of 5s. a day.

In his relations with his numerous clients Wren showed
a great deal of worldly wisdom. Even in 1665, when his
experience of practice was short, he wrote an amusing

letter to his friend the Master of Trinity College, Oxford, about some new buildings projected there, which Wren himself wished to take the form of a long range of chambers, while the subscribers (true to type) clung to the old-fashioned idea of a quadrangle.

' My honoured friend,' he writes, ' I am convinced with Machiavel or some unlucky fellow, 'tis no matter whether I quote true, that the world is generally governed by words. I perceive the name of a Quadrangle will carry with it those whom you say may possibly be your benefactors, though it be much the worst situation for the chambers, and the beauty of the college and of the particular pile of building.' . . . ' Let them have a Quadrangle, though a lame one, somewhat like a three-legged table.'

On another occasion he ventured to play a trick on the civic fathers of Windsor, for whom he was building a new Town Hall.

' The Mayor and Corporation came to make a state inspection when the building was declared finished, and objected that the supports of the floor of the room above the open basement were insufficient. Wren explained the reason of his conviction of its security, but finally consented to add two columns besides those of his plan. These supplementary columns he made of set purpose so short that a space intervened between their capitals and the ceiling. Seen from below, however, all seemed reassuring, and the civic deputation expressed themselves satisfied. The columns stand as they did then, and the space has not lessened between them and the ceiling.' [1]

Wren seems to have been a very painstaking and conscientious architect, and always regarded his work in a businesslike way, avoiding undue extravagance. At times he had his worries, e. g., at one stage in the building of

[1] L. Milman, *Sir Christopher Wren* (London, 1908), p. 192.

St. Stephen's, Walbrook, he is said to have become uneasy about the stability of the structure.[1] There were occasional quarrels with difficult clients, as when he disagreed with Father Smith and the Dean about the organ at St. Paul's ; occasions when royal clients interfered with matters of design, as King William did at Hampton Court ; and disappointments due to the abandonment or curtailment of projected work, as in the cases of the Memorial to Charles I and the Palace at Winchester. But it was not until the early years of the eighteenth century that Wren began to suffer from that series of sordid intrigues, first inspired by a jealous professional rival at Greenwich, later fostered by a handful of narrow-minded and pettifogging clerics on the building committee of St. Paul's, which finally drove him into retirement. Much has been made of this tragic ending to his career ; it is perhaps better to remember that it did not happen until he had reached a very great age, and that up to that time he had shown a surprising skill in dealing with clients of every description, from royalty downwards.

His relations with the numerous contractors and workmen employed on his several buildings appear to have been complicated but highly satisfactory, judging from the quality of the workmanship that he almost invariably obtained. The modern system of dealing with a ' builder ' or general contractor, which makes work so much simpler for the architect, did not then obtain, and at St. Paul's, for example, where the building accounts have been preserved in a long series of thin folio volumes, we find that separate contracts were made with each craft or ' trade ', as is still the case to-day in Scotland and parts of the North of England. Not only was the carpenter distin-

---

[1] L. Milman, *op. cit.*, p. 231.

guished from the joiner, and the bricklayer from the mason, but more than one contractor in one trade was sometimes employed. Thus the first contracts for masonry were made with two separate master-masons, Joshua Marshall and Thomas Strong, the line of demarcation between their contracts being fixed at the centre of a window or door opening. The Strongs were a family of master-masons, who owned quarries in Gloucestershire and built houses in the Cotswolds. When Thomas Strong had once begun to work with Wren, the association continued on many subsequent contracts in his own lifetime and afterwards with his brother and nephew. We have seen that ' young Mr Strong ' partnered young Mr. Wren in a continental tour. The ' master ' in each trade signed the contract and found the necessary labour. Materials for St. Paul's were bought by the Commissioners, either direct from the manufacturer or importer, or from the contractor. Items of material and labour are always differentiated in the accounts. Contract work is described therein as ' Task work ', and was periodically measured up by the Commissioners' measurer to ascertain whether it agreed with the amount allowed in the contract. There was also ' Day work ', in the modern sense. For this ' masters ' were paid 3s. a day (say 10s. to 12s. in pre-war values or 17s. to £1 to-day) and men 2s. 6d. (say 8s. to 10s. pre-war or 14s. to 17s. to-day). The masters were themselves craftsmen (not what the French call *entrepreneurs*, that is, commercial men or contractors who merely employ craftsmen), though doubtless they spent most of their time in supervisory rather than manual work. The work of an architect was therefore very responsible in Wren's time, for he had to ' assemble ' all the different trades and keep them in touch with each other. Nowadays he has something of the same sort in his relation with sub-contractors and specialists, even where a general contractor is employed for the main building work. It is universally admitted that the craftsmanship on Wren's buildings was excellent : and one wonders whether we have lost anything by the introduction of larger combinations under a general contractor, though undoubtedly the modern method makes things easier for the architect, and leads to quicker and better organized progress.

Wren also exercised a very close oversight over all the various decorative craftsmen, including the famous Grinling Gibbons and other carvers, and the equally celebrated Jean Tijou the smith. It is uncertain how far he supplied detail drawings to them himself ; but probably they had to submit detail drawings and models for his approval. There are records of ' boards ' being supplied for Gibbons and Tijou to draw upon, but other evidence makes me think that Wren's own share in detail design was considerable. First of all, the harmony of all his details indicates the working of some master-brain. Then we find in 1695 that a joiner was paid for making models of the exterior of the east end, the altar, the organ-case, and other accessories. Next we have the evidence of Wren's own highly finished drawings and models, in which all decorative details are worked out in advance. Lastly, there is a lengthy report from Wren to the Master of Trinity, Cambridge, accompanied by six sheets of plans, in which he says :

' I suppose you have good masons ; however, I would willingly take further pains to give all the mouldings in great [full size] ; we are scrupulous in small matters ; and you must pardon us ; architects are as great pedants as critics or heralds. Let the mason take his measures and transmit the drawings to me

again, and I shall copy out parts of them at large more proper
for the use of workmen, and give you a careful estimate of the
charges, and return you again the original designs, for in the
hands of the workmen they will soon be defaced.' [1]

Another document,[2] among the Harleian MSS. in the
British Museum, tells us something of the organization
at St. Paul's.

' Sir C. Wren draws all the designs of the building, hath the
universal care thereof, gives all directions to workmen and
other officers, examines all accounts, and agrees for the prices
of workmanship and materials. John Oliver, assistant surveyor,
is constantly attending the work and giving directions to the
workmen. He measures all the masons' work, buys all the
materials that are to be had without travelling into the country,
keeps an account of what stores are delivered to the store-
keeper, and also an account of what stones are brought into
the church. He assists in making contracts and examines all
accounts. His salary is £100 per annum. Lawrence Spencer,
clerk of the works, and paymaster, attends the service of the
work, to take care that carpenters, labourers, &c., who work
by the day, be employed on such business as the surveyor hath
directed to be done ; takes an account, together with the
assistant surveyor, of what stones are brought into the work ;
he receives and pays all the money for workmanship and
materials ; he keeps and makes up all accounts, is chargeable
with all the stores and inspects the delivery thereof to the
workmen ; he is also clerk to the commissioners, and enters all
orders and contracts. His salary is £100 per annum. Thomas
Russel, clerk of the check, he calls over all the labourers,
carpenters and bricklayers who work day work, three times a
day, viz. at six in the morning, one in the afternoon, and at
six at night. He is constantly going from place to place in
the work, to keep those men to their business ; he keeps, like-

---

[1] Quoted in A. Cunningham, *Lives of the Painters, Sculptors, and
Architects* (London, 1831), p. 200.   [2] *Ibid.*, pp. 209–10.

wise, an account of the materials brought into the work, so that both the surveyor and he are checks upon the clerk of works in his accounts. His salary is £50 per annum.'

Throughout the operations Wren was a constant visitor to the fabric, superintending the digging of trial-holes, directing the demolition by gunpowder and battering-ram of the old building from a high platform in the middle of the site, and making alterations to his plans and specifications to meet emergencies as they arose. He strongly objected to bad language in such a place, and put up a notice that ' customary swearing shall be a sufficient crime to dismiss any labourer that comes to the call ' (i. e. casual workers), and that any contractor who failed to ' reform this profanation among his apprentices, servants, and labourers, it shall be construed his fault '. Evelyn's diary [1] contains an interesting account of his discovery of Grinling Gibbons, whom he subsequently introduced to the King and Queen at Whitehall, with a crucifix as a specimen of his carving. The King left the decision to the Queen, the Queen was foolish enough to listen to the opinion of ' a French pedling-woman ', who knew no more of the matter in hand ' than an asse or a monkey ', and the visit was fruitless. However fame came to him shortly afterwards.

As a draughtsman Wren was far more capable than is commonly allowed. There are 270 drawings attributed to him in the All Souls collection at Oxford, in three volumes, and a fourth volume which contains a variety of designs by various hands. A selection of his work has recently been reproduced.[2] He used pencil or ink and wash for studies, ink and wash for more elaborate designs.

[1] For 18 January, 19 February, and 1 March, 1671.
[2] *The Wren Society*, vol. i. (Oxford, 1924), vol. ii. (1925), vol. iii. (1926).

FIG. 39. THE WEST FRONT OF ST. PAUL'S CATHEDRAL

From an original drawing by Sir Christopher Wren

His drawing of the west front of St. Paul's (Fig. 39) is characteristic of his most finished work ; a study (Fig. 40) for the cross on the dome of St. Paul's is typical of his working detail drawings.

Wren used models frequently, e. g. for the new quarters of the Royal Society, for the Sheldonian Theatre, for Emmanuel College, for the Monument, for Greenwich Hospital, and for St. Paul's. The last-named two are preserved in the Royal Naval Museum and in the North Gallery of St. Paul's respectively. The model of St. Paul's represents the ' Rejected ' design, and cost £600 in all (say £1,800 to £2,000 in pre-war values, or £3,000 to £3,500 to-day). Constructed to a scale of about half an inch to a foot, it is of such dimensions that one can stand upright inside it, and form some idea of the internal effect. All the carving, ornamental plasterwork, and gilding was shown ; and it was prepared at the special request of the King. The model is well made of oak, and would still be in excellent condition but for the vandalism of souvenir-hunting visitors, who have done some damage to it in the past. The Greenwich Hospital model is to a much smaller scale (about 28 ft. to 1 inch) and is very carefully made of varnished wood.

A good deal of nonsense has been written about Wren's financial misfortunes and the shabby way in which he was treated. The fact is that he never was a poor man, and in 1713 he bought an estate in Warwickshire for his son at a price of nearly £20,000, representing a very consider-able sum to-day. It is true that he gave his services gratis at Trinity College Library, that he contributed to the building funds at St. Paul's and elsewhere out of his own pocket, as most architects do at the present time. It is also true that he is sometimes recorded to have received small fees for small commissions, e. g. he was paid five guineas in 1672 for designing a temporary ' tabernacle ' at St. Peter's, Cornhill, pending the rebuilding of a permanent church ; but that fee was probably quite adequate. In 1684 he was paid £9 2s. 6d. as comptroller of the works at Windsor Castle, and informs us [1] that ' R. Cottrelel, vermine-killer, received the same '. But Wren's work at Windsor in that year may have involved perhaps one visit, or some correspondence, whereas the vermin-expert's was doubtless a full-time employment. His salary at St. Paul's was meanly withheld for many years because the Commissioners considered him to blame for delays in completion. But, though we admit some hardships, we need not shed tears for Wren's poverty. As regards the City Churches, Sir Lawrence Weaver has pointed out that Wren received exactly 5 per cent. on their cost ; and that, as their total cost was £263,786, he received over £13,000 from this item.[2] For St. Paul's he received £200 a year for 36 years, i. e. £7,200, which is less than 1 per cent. on the estimated outlay of £746,661. But concurrently with all this work he was drawing another salary or retaining fee of £320 a year as Surveyor-General of His Majesty's Works, together with an official residence in Whitehall, consisting of sixteen rooms and a cellar. Besides these various ' retainers ', he seems to have drawn additional fees for each specific service performed, e. g. £1,000 at Chelsea Hospital. If we multiply each of these figures by six, we shall obtain a fair idea of what Wren's remuneration was in present-day purchasing power, and we shall find that he was in receipt of an income of several thousands a year in our currency.

[1] Cunningham, *op. cit.*, p. 228.
[2] Sir L. Weaver, *Sir Christopher Wren*, pp. 123–4.

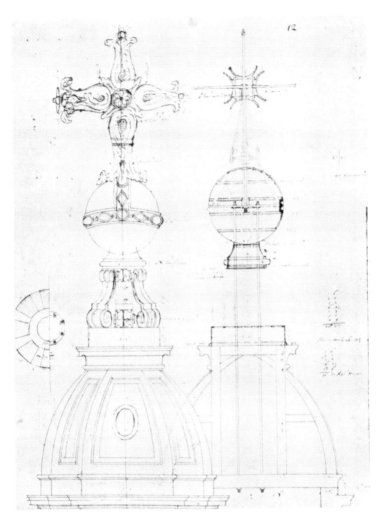

FIG. 40. DETAIL DRAWING OF THE CROSS ON THE
DOME OF ST. PAUL'S CATHEDRAL

By Sir Christopher Wren

His career was incomparably the most brilliant in architectural history, late as he entered the field ; perhaps Sir Gilbert Scott provides its nearest modern counterpart. Wren did not accumulate a vast fortune nor become a marquis, like J. H. Mansart, and his hands were decidedly the cleaner as a result. But he earned the favour of five sovereigns, received the honour of knighthood, represented his country in Parliament, married the daughter of a peer, and was the chosen companion of eminent men like Evelyn and cheery souls like Pepys. The professional interest of his career, as well as the magnitude of his achievement, must be the excuse for the comparatively full treatment accorded to it in these pages.

Of Wren's contemporaries in the seventeenth century little need be said. Talman and Sir Roger Pratt, Bell of Lynn and Grumbold of Cambridge, were all overshadowed by the great master, and Nicholas Stone, though an admirable designer of tombs, was a sculptor rather than an architect.

Sir Balthazar Gerbier (*d.* 1662) was a predecessor of Wren's, but the two little books that he wrote on architecture at the end of his life doubtless found a place on Sir Christopher's well-stocked shelves. The first, published in 1662, is entitled : *A Brief Discourse Concerning the Three chief Principles of Magnificent Building, viz. Solidity, Conveniency, and Ornament.* It is a tiny duodecimo volume, the first part consisting of lengthy dedications to the King and 'The Lords and Commons Assembled in Parliament ', all in very large type, some forty words to a page ; and the remainder, only 44 pages, dealing with ' Orders of Colombs ', &c. Its importance is negligible.

His other little volume is equally minute but much more interesting, and appeared after his death, in 1663. It is entitled : *Counsel and Advise to all Builders ; for the Choice of Their Surveyors, Clarks of their Works, Brick-layers, Masons, Carpenters and other Work-men therein concerned. As also, in respect of their Works, Materials, and Rates thereof. Together with several Epistles to Eminent Persons, who may be Concerned in Building.* This lengthy title is followed by no less than forty separate dedications (the first to the Queen Mother, the last to the Courteous Reader), occupying nearly 100 pages of text. After all this, we come to the text itself, covering only a few pages more than the dedications, but containing a little useful information as to the architect's status.

' Whosoever is disposed to Build, ought in the first place to make choice of a skilful Surveyour, from whose Directions the several Master work-men may receive Instructions by way of Draughts, Models, Frames, &c., For the better managing their intended work. . . . An exact Architect must have the Art of Drawing, and Perspective. . . . The readiest way to try a Surveyour, is to put him to draw a ground Plot in the Builder's presence. . . . A good Surveyour sheweth his Art, both within the Building, as on its Front ; and in the fit mixture of Materials, Morter, Brick and Stone. . . . All Surveyours ought to cause the wooden Molds (on which Masons must work), to be tryed by lifting them as high as the Stone or wooden Figure is to be placed ; to see how it may please the Judicious Eye ; which is the best Jury and compasse. . . .'

The book concludes with a valuable list of contemporary building prices. From this we learn that ' bricks in some parts are delivered at the work for 16s. 8d. the thousand ', that the cost of brickwork per rod of 16½ feet square and 1½ bricks thick, including all materials, was about £5, and that marble and pantiles were imported from Holland.

In 1678 was published an amusing little work on building construction, *Mechanick Exercises*, written by one Joseph Moxon, mathematician, hydrographer, shopkeeper, and Fellow of the Royal Society—a characteristic product of his age and a native of Wakefield, who came up from Yorkshire to London to seek his fortune. This book, first published in serial parts, affords a welcome change from albums of the Orders prefaced by fulsome dedications, and it throws much light on building methods in Wren's time. I have quoted extensively from it elsewhere in connexion with the building crafts of bygone days.[1]

.   .   .   .   .   .

It is impossible here to deal individually with the host of well-known English architects of the eighteenth century. Instead, I propose to adopt the method that I have used in previous chapters, and, by collating the biographies of some thirty famous men, to attempt some generalization as to type, though the individuals are as various in type as could well be imagined. The architects selected for this purpose are : Hawksmoor, Vanbrugh, Archer, James, Campbell, Lord Burlington, Lord Pembroke, Kent, Langley, Gibbs, the two Woods, ' Carr of York ', Ripley, Aldrich, Clarke, Burrough, Essex, Vardy, Ware, the two Dances, Flitcroft, Brettingham, Taylor, Paine, Morris, Robert Adam, Chambers, and Gandon. At the outset one must exclude at least six who were definitely amateurs ; Lord Burlington, Lord Pembroke, Dean Aldrich, ' Doctor ' Clarke, Sir James Burrough, and James Essex. The first two were *virtuosi* of the best sort ; they certainly did much to foster an interest in architecture of the academic sort that was favoured in their day, and they were directly instrumental in furnishing opportunities

[1] M. S. Briggs, *A Short History of the Building Crafts* (1925), *passim*.

of study and advancement to promising young architects. Thus Lord Burlington actually lodged Kent in his own house for many years. The architect of this period dedicated his frequent folios to these ' noble patrons ' in terms of nauseating servility, but he did depend on them very largely for his livelihood. It was part of a gentleman's education to understand ' architecture ' (i. e. the Orders), to make the Grand Tour, and to build himself a colossal mansion with suites of monumental rooms, based on the formal principles of Palladio. Aldrich and Clarke at Oxford, Burrough and Essex at Cambridge, did actual building ; but taken as a whole, their work in the two most beautiful towns in England was for worse rather than for better, and the buildings they have left us are poor compensation for those that they destroyed or mangled.

But whatever we may think of their excursions into architectural practice, and of their relations with architects whom they employed as ' ghosts ', the fact remains that the influence of these aristocratic amateurs on eighteenth-century architecture was enormous and that much of it was in the direction of advancement of the art. While they certainly expended vast sums on houses for themselves, often pompous and grandiose, they encouraged research into the monuments of antiquity and published the results at their own cost. Many of them actively forwarded the work of the Society of Dilettanti : admirable when it was confined to the making of records of ancient buildings, less praiseworthy when it involved the wholesale spoliation of those buildings to enrich the galleries of ' noble patrons ' in this country. Horace Walpole was a mordant and partial critic, but his acumen in matters of architectural taste is undeniable. Pope and Gay as friends of Lord Burlington were always ready to support, with their satirical pens, the architects whom he befriended, and hardly any architect of the eighteenth century escaped the attacks of some bitter satirist attached to a rival faction. At that period it could never be said that architecture was not a matter of general interest.

Yet we find a writer in 1766, at a time when one would have thought that this cultured enthusiasm was at its height, deploring the level of taste prevailing in influential circles. John Gwynn, the author in question, was himself a successful architect, and on occasion he could write with all the sarcasm of his century, as subsequent quotations will show. His *London and Westminster Improved* is primarily a plea for town-planning those cities, and displays a really remarkable foresight which, had it been utilized, might have saved us the squalor of the Euston Road and the Surrey Side, as well as much of the present congestion of our streets. But the book also contains ' A Discourse on Publick Magnificence ; with Observations on the State of Arts and Artists in this Kingdom, wherein the Study of the Polite Arts is recommended as necessary to a liberal Education '. Gwynn regretfully reminds his readers that in the reign of Charles I, a Royal Academy was founded ' . . . where gentlemen were admitted for their education : They were instructed in the living and dead languages, mathematicks, painting, architecture, riding, fortification, antiquities, and the science of medals. Professors in every branch were appointed, . . .' but the scheme collapsed with Charles I's execution, and the idea passed to France.

' In France they enjoy the advantage of every necessary publick establishment that can any way cultivate or improve the polite arts which by custom or habit, are become a necessary as well as beneficial part of education. In England no such establishment exists, instead of meeting with encouragement and cultivation, the arts are left to struggle for themselves (some feeble efforts of the society in the Strand excepted) and instead of their being made a part of education, the youth of this country are only drenched with the dead languages until their stomachs loathe and nauseate every thing that wears the appearance of taste and knowledge, and consequently, instead of encouragers of learning and arts, they in time become only the patrons of buffoons, cheats, and horse-coursers.'

[The defects in general education, already noted, thus account entirely for the prevalent lack of encouragement for artists.]

' If it is indispensably necessary that an artist should, by unwearied application and unremitted study, make himself a master of the art he professes in order to render his works worthy the approbation of the great, is it not equally necessary that his employer, who ought to be supposed his superior in every respect, should be furnished with at least as much knowledge of the art he patronizes as will inable (*sic*) him to form a judgement of the degree of excellence with which it is executed.'

Speaking of the patronage of art by wealthy connoisseurs, Gwynn complains that collectors treat art in too commercial a spirit, and that they prefer antiques and foreign products to the work of living English artists.

' Even the ancient Greeks and modern Romans produced very indifferent as well as very great artists, and in our times the works of the most despicable of these performers are purchased at exorbitant prices, only because they were done by a man who has perhaps lain and mellowed a century or two in his grave.

' The French, whom we copy in their vices and follies, and whose virtues we reject, have . . . a laudable partiality for the works of their own artists.'

After citing the successful direction of the Gobelin factories in France by Le Brun, President of the French Academy, Gwynn continues :

' . . . How much more valuable a manufactory would Birmingham be (as well as many others) to this nation, if it was in the hands of people of taste ! at present, quantity not quality seems principally to be considered, and everything is loaded with much confused and superfluous work, which is falsely called ornament, when less labour, guided by judgement, would be much better, and every article be rendered more valuable by its elegant simplicity in shape and form, and the expence of that unnecessary labour might be added to the quality of the materials, as the making things cheap and good is of infinite advantage to commerce, as cheap and bad are certainly the contrary.'

This is the pure gospel of William Morris, and a truly remarkable passage to find in an eighteenth-century book.

Reverting from John Gwynn's views on public taste to the lives of eighteenth-century architects, we find that, of the twenty-four names remaining on our list after the six ' amateurs ' have been deleted, Campbell, Gibbs, Adam, and Chambers were Scots ; and that Kent, Wood the Elder, Carr, and Ripley were Yorkshiremen, a high proportion of genius for the North, especially as we know nothing of the antecedents of eight of the remainder. Of those whose parentage is recorded, about half came from the upper and professional classes and about half from the artisan class. Three only (Wood the Younger, Dance the Younger, and Robert Adam) were architects' sons, but others were followed by architect-sons who never attained eminence. Vanbrugh, Archer, and Taylor—among others —entered architecture comparatively late in life ; but few of the rest underwent any professional training. Hawks-moor began as Wren's ' scholar and domestic clerk ', and became his clerk-of-works on the Palace at Westminster when he was twenty-two. Kent was apprenticed at four-teen to a coach-painter, but, having been sent to Rome by some ' noble patron ', fell in with Lord Burlington there, after which his career was assured. Batty Langley was at first a landscape-gardener, but later founded a ' school of architecture ' intended chiefly for the education of carpenters ! Gibbs was fortunate, for, after a good educa-tion culminating in a M.A. degree at Aberdeen, he was sent by Lord Mar to Rome to study, and while there he maintained himself by making drawings for aristocratic travellers. John Wood first appears as a surveyor of roads ; Carr as a mason. Ripley, another pushful Yorkshireman, walked all the way to London to seek his fortune, worked as a carpenter there, and at the same time kept a coffee-house. As a young man he married a domestic servant (an imprudence mitigated by the fact that she was employed in Sir Robert Walpole's household) ; but at his second attempt, as a widower, captured an heiress with £40,000. Ware, a chimney-sweep's son, attracted the attention of a ' noble patron ' who sent him to Italy. Dance the Elder is said to have begun as a shipwright, and Flitcroft (a gardener's son) as a joiner.

Travel in Italy was undertaken only by the more fortu-nate, Gibbs, Ripley, and Ware already having been men-tioned ; Chambers travelled extensively. Kent was sent to Rome by Lord Burlington, and Dance the Younger and Robert Adam by their fathers, who evidently attached importance to this mode of study. But apart from those three architects who were trained by their own fathers, we only know of Vardy, Brettingham, Paine, Morris, Gandon and perhaps Hawksmoor who were pupils or assistants in architects' offices. Many of the rest stepped into architecture from the position of a clerk-of-works, a mason, or a carpenter ; while others approached it from painting or sculpture. There is the strange case of Vanbrugh, who was a soldier and a dramatist before he entered the profession. Flitcroft's translation to the higher sphere of building was due to a fortunate tumble off a scaffold in the presence of the all-powerful Lord Burlington. It may therefore be concluded that architectural education in the eighteenth century was almost non-existent ; that though training in an architect's office and travel in Italy were desirable, they were by no means essential ; and that any ambitious craftsman who took the trouble to ' get up ' the Orders found the avenue of success open to him.

The scantiness of the information that we possess of the early days of such prosperous practitioners is accounted for thus by Cunningham : [1]

' Most men of talent, when they rise to distinction, seem reluctant to look back on those early days of toil, hardship, and disappointment, in which they prepared themselves for their fortunes. . . . Nor need we wonder at this. The wealthy or the titled, who patronize the polished scholar or poet, would not perhaps enjoy being frequently reminded that his " clouterly ploughboy carcase " had been exposed to all the winds of heaven ; that their honoured guests had in the days of former years cobbled peasants' shoes, turned a straight furrow, or tasted no better food than porridge and milk for weeks together. Such confessions would be apt to be considered out of place while the feathers of duchesses were fanning his brow, tables laden with plate smoking before him, and obedient lacquies standing in pairs behind him, watching the motions of his knife and fork.'

[1] Cunningham, *Lives of the British Architects*, p. 286.

Of Gandon's early days we know rather more, thanks to the facts that he kept a diary and that his biography has been written by his son,[1] but Gandon's career comes near the end of the century and may not be altogether typical. After spending seven years (1749–56) at a boarding-school, his father's financial embarrassments made it necessary for him to leave at the early age of fourteen. He then worked at home, mainly at classics and mathematics, but in the evenings regularly attended Shipley's Drawing Academy, and also acquired there ' a theoretic knowledge of architecture. This school was at that period the first in London in general estimation '. A few years later Sir (then Mr.) William Chambers settled in London, and soon came to require ' an assistant, a sort of office clerk, or pupil '. Gandon waited on him with a portfolio of drawings, and shortly afterwards was regularly indentured to him ' at a very moderate fee '. He remained with Chambers till 1765, when, at the age of twenty-three, he obtained sufficient work to enable him to begin practice. Thereupon he took lodgings at ' Mr. Babb's, an eminent bookseller in Oxford Street ', then so rural that Gandon said he used to shoot snipe there. Three years later the Royal Academy was founded, and in 1769 offered a gold medal for the best design in architecture, open only to students of the R.A. School. In order to become eligible for this medal, Gandon entered the school as a student. The subject set was a triumphal arch to commemorate the Seven Years War. Before the medal was awarded, the whole architectural class had to undergo a time-test in design (corresponding to what we call to-day in our elegant English phraseology an *esquisse-esquisse*). Subjects for this were drawn from

[1] *The Life of James Gandon*, by his son James Gandon (Dublin, 1846).

a hat. Gandon drew ' an ornamental entrance to a park ', and won the medal. At the mature age of 58, he was awarded the R.A. Travelling Studentship in Architecture, but declined it for reasons of health.

The work done by travelling students in Italy during the eighteenth century varied greatly according to circumstances. The usual route followed was *via* Paris, Lyons, and Avignon, and the length of time spent in Italy depended on a student's resources, which were supplemented in many ways, some of which have already been mentioned. According to Walpole, Kent studied painting in Rome,

' under Cavalier Lutin, and in the academy gained the second prize of the second class, still without suspecting that there was a sister art within his reach more congenial to his talents. Though his first resources were exhausted he still found friends. One of his countrymen, Sir William Wentworth, allowed him £40 a year for seven years.'

Cunningham adds that ' Rome at that period swarmed with wealthy Englishmen, all eager to exchange their gold for the paintings and sculptures of Italy '.[1] Kent made a second pilgrimage to Italy in middle age, for the twofold purpose of improving his acquaintance with Roman architecture, and purchasing pictures for his steady patron, Lord Burlington '.[2]

Gibbs, though he had graduated at Aberdeen and studied architecture in Holland, spent no less than ten years in Rome ' under Garroli, a sculptor and architect of considerable note ',[3] and under Carlo Fontana, deferring the commencement of his practice in London till he was twenty-eight years of age. He financed himself during this long stay in Rome by making drawings for English ' amateurs' residing there. Chambers certainly, and other

[1] *Op. cit.*, p. 302.   [2] *Ibid.*, p. 308.   [3] *Ibid.*, p. 287.

architects probably, studied the work of the early Renaissance masters in Italy, as well as antique monuments and the work of the Palladians. But more striking is the statement that Robert Adam, making his first visit to Italy from 1754 to 1757, actually condescended to notice Romanesque and Gothic buildings, for two centuries regarded by all cultured critics in all countries as barbarian rubbish. It must be stated in his defence that he did not take the Middle Ages seriously, concentrating religiously on 'the antique' all through his long period of travel. But the mere fact that he noted the existence of medieval architecture shows that the heresies afterwards encouraged by Horace Walpole at Strawberry Hill were already taking root. Robert Adam made an intensive study of Roman monumental planning, thus formulating the principles on which the great *thermae* and *fora* had been designed. Then feeling that he ought to study some example of domestic planning on the grand scale, he crossed the Adriatic to Spalato, in company with two draughtsmen whom he had engaged in Rome. He was at first arrested as a spy, but soon got to work, and, after five weeks strenuous labour on the spot, was able to return with the drawings which so greatly enhanced his reputation in after-life, and commenced practice in London in 1764.

At this point we may turn again to John Gwynn,[1] who has some scathing things to say about the travelled architect.

' The powers of inventive genius are, at this time so very little attended to, and the examples of Greece and Rome so firmly established, that nothing more is required to model a youth of moderate parts into a complete architect, than to put him apprentice either to a bricklayer, mason, or carpenter,

[1] Gwynn, *London and Westminster Improved*, &c. (London, 1766), pp. 64–6.

under whose tuition he will acquire the great art of scoring strait lines, and setting off their proportion by scale and compass. His servitude being ended, thus accomplished and furnished with the Rudiments of Architecture, he may be sent to Rome, and after he has spent the usual time allotted for traversing that city, he may cause it to be inserted in the London papers, that Mr. Trowel, the celebrated architect, on account of his vast abilities, has had prodigious honours conferred upon him, and that he shortly intends to re-visit his native country, to which he will no doubt do incredible honour. The trumpet having been thus properly sounded, and the architect furnished in a suitable manner with a collection of the best Italian masters in that science, he may venture to make his appearance in London. His next business is to decorate his house with this borrowed plumage, and then get some friend to beat the drum, and stun the publick with encomiums upon this prodigy of art. This naturally will induce some person of distinction to take a peep at this phenomenon, and if he is possessed of the least spark of *virtú*, he will become almost petrified with amazement, and, in the ardour of astonishment, inquire where this great creature has been hitherto buried ? The answer is obvious, Mr. Trowel is just arrived from Rome ! You see everything is perfectly Italian, his drawings, his air, his cloaths, his servants, all Italian—Bravissimo ! he must undoubtedly be a great genius, Mr. Trowel's name is up, and he may go to bed when he pleases.

' But, to be serious, where is the necessity of this parade of going to Rome, is there a building, or even a fragment of a building in Greece or Italy, of which we have not accurate draughts and measures ? and is it not from these resources that every modern building is compiled without variation, and without the least attempt at novelty or invention ? It is very much to be questioned, if such an attempt was to be made, whether a thoroughbred connoisseur would vouchsafe to bestow a second look upon such a design.

' But this being the case, what becomes of genius and

invention, is the farce of an architect's having been at Rome to supply the want of these, and to exclude every attempt of introducing novelty and elegance, because it is not of foreign extraction? It should seem that people of distinction in England are come to a determination to admire nothing but copies either in painting or architecture, and therefore load the kingdom with the one, and their cabinets with the other. In this view of the state of architecture, it may not be improper to suppose a person of distinction, who, with every other requisite for forming a great character, should also be possessed of a thorough knowledge in building, and that this person should, in conformity to his own ideas of novelty and elegance, require a design for a superb edifice out of the common method of practice ; it is likewise to be supposed that he should be recommended for this purpose to two architects both eminent in their profession, but, with this difference, that one had been in Italy, and the other had not. The question is, from which of these it is to be presumed he would be most likely to obtain what he wanted ; that is a design in which grandeur, elegance and variety should unite to produce a whole which should be new, harmonious, and regular ? It may with the greatest reason be presumed, that he whose ideas had been least confined and shackled with the prejudices of a foreign taste would be the person preferred, for the insurmountable passion for Greek and Roman examples, would prevent the one from striking out any thing which was not strictly conformable to them, and consequently he could produce nothing which had not been seen before ; the other, blinded by no such prejudice, would give his imagination free scope, and by a bold attempt to soar upon his own wings, produce something which if it did not perhaps quite reach the idea of his employer, would at least satisfy him much better, and these trials by being often repeated, must unavoidably produce things new, great, noble, and singular.'

The bitterness of these passages makes one wonder whether Gwynn had some travelled rival in mind. We have no record that he visited Italy himself, but Chambers certainly did, and had appeared upon the scene only a few years before this. In 1755 Gwynn declined the post of Instructor in Architecture to the Prince of Wales (afterwards George III), a post subsequently accepted by Chambers.[1] Robert Adam, as we have seen, commenced practice in 1764 on returning from Italy. ' Almost every one now, who can but make shift to draw neat lines, and is furnished with a few books to borrow from, sets up as an architect....'

In the eighteenth century, as in the twentieth, there was no fixed age at which an architect commenced practice for himself : that depended partly upon his social circumstances, partly upon opportunities that he created for himself by sheer ability. Of the twenty-four typical architects on my list, five at least are men whose date of birth is uncertain, two more (Dance the Younger and Wood the Younger) simply stepped into their fathers' shoes, and there are not more than fourteen about whom we can be even tolerably certain. Of the latter, Hawksmoor and Brettingham worked their way up to independent practice in middle age through subordinate appointments ; Vanbrugh, Archer, Taylor, and Flitcroft entered architecture after attempting other occupations, so hardly afford fair comparisons. For that matter, so did some of the remainder, but they began practice extraordinarily early. Gibbs started practice at twenty-eight years of age, Robert Adam at thirty, and Chambers at thirty-four, all after extensive travel in Italy. George Dance probably began as a shipwright, yet was designing St. Luke's, Old Street, at thirty-two. But ' Wood of Bath ' was launched at twenty-two, ' Carr of York ' (the ex-mason) at twenty-seven and Gandon at twenty-three ; all of them men to whom

[1] *Dict. of Nat. Biog.* s.v. ' Gwynn ' and ' Chambers '.

Italian travel was impossible. The palm must be awarded, however, to that James Paine (1716–89), whose well-known portrait (fig. 41) by Sir Joshua Reynolds hangs in the Ashmolean at Oxford, and who was entrusted with the design and erection of Nostell Priory, a huge mansion in Yorkshire, at the age of nineteen, after which work poured into his office.

It is hardly necessary to remark that in the eighteenth century an architect's career depended in the first instance on his skill or luck in attracting the notice of some wealthy and aristocratic *virtuoso*, and thereafter in retaining a place in Society with a large S. It was not a long journey from the gutter to the palace in such company, but some who made it must surely have found it irksome, especially, one would think, some of those hardy North-countrymen who have always supplied London with new blood and who figure so prominently in the architectural history of the period. Yet Kent, a Yorkshireman, seems to have taken to the social side of his work like a duck to water, though his origin was humble enough. He designed a petticoat for a lady of the Court, with an ingenious pattern of the Five Orders, and his enemies said that his talents consisted solely of a pleasant and engaging manner. Then we find a Scot like Gibbs, from dour Aberdeen, succeeding in fashionable London, and getting a church to build while he remained a stalwart Non-juror. Chambers, another Scot, became a satellite of the Court.

Into this whirlpool of fashion the architect had to cast his net with great skill, and it must be admitted that his catch was nearly as varied as in the days of the Medici in Florence. Military science certainly had passed from his repertoire. The demand for fireworks and public displays seems also to have abated, but Kent designed theatrical scenery, and in 1762 Robert Adam designed a ' trans-

FIG. 41. JAMES PAINE AND HIS SON

From the painting by Reynolds in the Ashmolean Museum, Oxford

parency and illumination ' at St. James's Palace for the
Queen, to greet the King on his return. Kent also designed
in 1732 the great state barge for the Prince of Wales that
is now exhibited in the Victoria and Albert Museum. In
the matter of garden-design there was a change. The
formal parterres and humorous waterworks of the early
seventeenth century, borrowed from Italy, gave way to
landscape gardening, of which Kent was the chief exponent.
The change in ideas which took place on this subject may
be gathered from one of Gwynn's paragraphs : [1]

If a magnificent edifice is to be erected, a common builder,
little if anything superior to a carpenter or bricklayer, in point
of taste or knowledge is consulted, instead of a regular architect ; if an elegant garden or pleasure ground is to be laid out,
a gardener whose utmost knowledge is confined to the nature
of the growth and culture of shrubs, plants and trees, is called
in, instead of consulting the landscape painter, whose studies
relate immediately to the subject, and who is therefore the
person who should be consulted. . . . A good painter will
hardly ever fail, let the situation be ever so bad, to produce
something picturesque, and the best disposed pl sure grounds,
parks, &c., in this country were designed by the late Mr. Kent,
who was a painter, and was the first who ventured to attack
and cut up the Dutch minced-pies of Bridgman, and others of
the same sublime taste and genius.'

Sir William Chambers, whose first steps in architecture
were made in Canton, seems to have lost his generally
steady head when he published his book on Oriental
Gardening in 1772, and laid himself open to the smart
gibes of his critics by paragraphs so absurd and lacking
in humour as the following :

' They keep in these enchanted scenes a surprising variety
of monstrous birds, reptiles and animals, which are tamed by

[1] *Op. cit.*, p. 61.

art, and guarded by enormous dogs of Tibet, and African giants in the habits of magicians. Sometimes in this romantic excursion the passenger finds himself in extensive recesses, surrounded with harbours of jessamine, vines, and roses ; where beauteous Tartarean damsels, in loose transparent robes that flutter in the air, present him with rich wines, and invite him to taste the sweets of retirement on Persian carpets and beds of Camusakin down.'

Gwynn's admirable scheme for town-planning London has already been mentioned in this chapter, but many other instances could be cited. Apart from grandiose projects of lay-out on noblemen's estates, there are Adam's work at the Adelphi and elsewhere in London, his design for a model village at Whitehaven, Carr's work at Harewood in Yorkshire, Hawksmoor's scheme for replanning Cambridge and, most important of all, the fine work of the Woods at Bath.

Towards the end of the century the civil engineer begins to be distinguished from the architect, but the change was very gradual. Most of the chief bridges of the period were designed by architects. Gwynn designed those at Shrewsbury (his native town), Atcham near Shrewsbury, and Worcester ; also Magdalen Bridge at Oxford. Paine designed bridges at Kew, Richmond, Chertsey, and Walton. The bridge at Maidenhead was designed by Sir Robert Taylor ; and old Blackfriars Bridge, after a competition in which many famous architects took part, by Mylne in 1760. But in one case there is mention of a technical assistant who apparently did the engineering work, leaving the general design to the architect. Smeaton (who may be regarded as the father of English civil engineering) was born in 1724, Telford in 1757, and Rennie in 1761. Of these three, only Telford passed into engineering from

the practice of architecture. The separation of the two professions (or rather the introduction of a new one) became
necessary with the rapid developments of canals, and the
increasing complexity of structural work other than building in the ordinary sense. But it was not till the invention
of railways early in the nineteenth century that separation
became complete. The first meeting of the Society of
Civil Engineers was held on 15 April 1793.

But apart from this new factor, the status of the architect
in the eighteenth century is less definite than one would
suppose. In a few instances he is described as the 'master-
carpenter', even when he is known to have previously
designed quite important buildings as an ordinary professional architect under the latter title. So late as 1784,
Gandon found that a Grand Jury in Dublin

' had a very erroneous idea of the profession of an " architect "
as it stood in England. Some of them considered me as a contractor, or, as they termed me, " a projector and undertaker "
not one of those sable personages whose occupation it is to
bury the dead, but to bury stones and mortar.' [1]

But even in England the architect occasionally acted as
contractor and surveyor too. Sir William Chambers did
so on Lord Bessborough's villa at Roehampton in 1769,
and again at Pepperharrow in 1775–6. The architect Jupp
did the same at the East India House in 1799. According to the *Dictionary* of the Architectural Publication
Society,[2] he

' made his design and submitted an estimate upon which he
obtained advances of money, making with the tradesmen his
contracts, which, with the receipts, he produced at the termina-
tion of the works to his client ; and it was customary for the

[1] *Life of James Gandon*, p. 70.   [2] s.v. ' Contractor '.

latter to make a present, beyond the commission, if the works were executed within the estimate ; thus £1,000 is said to have been given in the cases of this building and of the gaol at Nottingham.'

Up to the end of the eighteenth century there seems to be no evidence for the existence of the ' builder ' in the modern sense, i. e. the person who undertakes *all* the various trades required in a building. Where the word ' builder ' occurs (and that is very seldom), it implies either the master-workman of one specific craft, or the building owner or speculator. It is the latter application that Gwynn implies when he writes [1] of ' the fury which seems to possess the fraternity of builders ', and again where he says [2] that,

' In the present state of building, the finest part of the town . . . is left to the mercy of capricious, ignorant persons, and the vast number of buildings, now carrying on, are only so many convincing proofs of the necessity of adopting the following, or some better hints, in order to convince the world that blundering is not the only characteristic of English builders.'

One of Gwynn's brightest passages deals with the status of the architect :

' Nothing can set the present state of architecture in a better light and more explain the estimation in which it is held by people of fashion, than a transaction which actually fell within the observation of the Author, who having some business to transact for a gentleman of fortune, was by him directed to call at a particular part of the town and *consult with his archi-tect*, about an affair of some consequence in a building which the gentleman was at that time erecting. The Author according to the direction given him waited upon the architect, but it is easier to guess than describe his astonishment, when upon

[1] Gwynn, *op. cit.*, p. 16.   [2] *Ibid.*, p. ix.

his approaching the house of this artist, he discovered that he not only built houses for the living, but was also employed in the construction of those in which the dead are usually deposited; in short, he was a coffin-maker. And indeed when it is considered in what a slight wretched manner the greatest part of the new buildings are erected, it may be very justly surmised, that there are not an inconsiderable number of coffin-makers who follow this profession, perhaps with a view to their original business, hoping they may not only bury people in the ruins of their own houses, but also decently inter those whom they have so ingeniously contrived to release from the troubles and difficulties of this transitory life.' [1]

In previous chapters I have endeavoured to describe the attitude of practising architects to the work of their predecessors. Never was this attitude more complex than in the latter part of the eighteenth century, when the Romantic Revival was clumsily floundering into the domain of architecture, barred against everything medieval for two hundred years. It seems to have been at that time a wholly dilettante and artificial movement, not even a reaction against excessive classicism, but merely a new fashion set by Horace Walpole and other smart triflers. All through the previous two centuries there had been continuity in architectural development until the experiments at Strawberry Hill and elsewhere began on a literary basis. Even the Greek Revival that blossomed out at the end of the eighteenth century was an inevitable consequence of the antiquarian enthusiasm of the Society of Dilettanti which had at first interested itself in Roman researches. The quotations from Gwynn (see pp. 306-8) show that even in his day there was at least some protest against the prevailing craze for the antique, but it does not seem likely

[1] *Ibid.*, p. 67.

that either Walpole's sham Gothic or Chambers's absurd *chinoiseries* were signs of revolt, but rather a further flutter in imitative design.

It is curious that the modern and lively outlook voiced by Gwynn finds its expression in the original and graceful designs of eighteenth-century furniture, by Chippendale and others, far more than in architecture. For though, as Mr. Goodhart-Rendel has pointed out,[1] the Gothic spirit had never quite perished in the work of rustic craftsmen who went on building barns and cottages in the old way, it certainly received little sympathy from the professional architects with whose work we are concerned in this book. Batty Langley, least professional of them all, and apparently not a practising architect, certainly invented and published ' the Five Orders of Gothic ', but Walpole, by that time a friend of Gothic as he understood it, said that all that Langley's books achieved ' has been to teach carpenters how to massacre that venerable species, and to give occasion to those who know nothing of the matter, and who mistake his clumsy efforts for real imitations, to censure the productions of our ancestors '. I have come across one or two other isolated references showing that architects of the eighteenth century sometimes treated medieval buildings with respect, but they are few and far between. It is interesting, too, to find Gwynn speculating in 1766 as to the authorship of our ancient cathedrals and churches,[2] another evidence of a fresh and inquiring mind. On the other hand it is unjust to the reputation of the profession as a whole during that period of monumental buildings to assume that architecture had degenerated into

[1] H. S. Goodhart-Rendel, ' English Gothic Architecture of the Nineteenth Century' in *R.I.B.A. Journal*, 5 April 1924.

[2] Gwynn, *op. cit.*, p. 33.

mere copyism of Roman models. In the great mansions
that were the principal output of that aristocratic age, in
Queen Anne's fifty churches, in public buildings like
Somerset House, we find attention being given to an architectural factor that has received too little thought since
that time, the principles of composition. In that respect
especially we must allow to eighteenth-century architects
the credit that is their due. The smaller buildings of the
eighteenth century in England have a homely dignity and
charm that is universally admitted, and in general they
are remarkably free from any pedantry or affectation. It
seems that these admirable qualities are to be attributed
in part to the use by craftsmen, as well as by architects,
of manuals or pattern-books which prevented eccentricity
even if they failed to encourage originality. But it is
equally clear that, before the century was over, individual
design in the crafts had been killed by overdoses of the
same drug.

An advance was made during this period towards the
organization of the profession by the formation in 1791
of the Architects' Club, ' a little convivial association . . .
who met once a month at the Thatched House '[1] in
London and eventually developed into the Royal Institute
of British Architects, as described in the next chapter.
The Royal Academy was founded in 1768, the four
architect-members being Chambers, Sandby, Dance, and
Gwynn. The latter's remarks on the status of the architect, as previously quoted, show that some organization
was becoming necessary to maintain its dignity, but this
need is still more apparent when one looks into the conduct
of architectural competitions. This method of obtaining

---

[1] Cunningham, *op. cit.*, p. 351.

designs is a refreshing alternative to the process of snaring and placating a ' noble patron ', then so much in vogue, but the ' noble patron ' cannot be kept out of the story even by this means. The firm of ' Burlington and Kent ' submitted a design for the Mansion House, and his Lordship was sadly put out when the plans of the City Surveyor were accepted.[1]

The biography of Gandon gives an illuminating example of such a competition, held in 1768 for the Dublin Exchange. The conditions were duly advertised in the press. Gandon being, as we have seen, a young man of push and go, consulted an influential friend in Ireland as to how he should send in his plans to produce the best effect. He was advised not to trust them to the post, but to forward them privately to his patron, who would ' prefer them to the Trustees of the Royal Exchange, and recommend them to their particular attention '. They were duly dispatched in December 1768. Gandon's friend wrote that the designs had arrived and had already been shown to a number of useful people, but that sufficient allowance for ' the declivity of the ground ' had not been made. So he enclosed a site plan with the levels marked thereon. He added that ' Some other plans for our Exchange have come in, one from Mr. Ivory of Northwitch,[2] but none, I think, which should occasion uneasiness.' A later epistle gives a list of the sixty-four competitors and a report of further canvassing done, with a draft of a letter which Gandon's patron thought the architect should send to the Trustees, answering all hostile criticisms which his patron had been at pains to collect. This was done, but the next letter from Ireland mentions one Mr. Cooley as a dark horse, ' a friend of Mr. Mylne's, whose interest with

---

[1] Cunningham, *op. cit.*, p. 325.   [2] Actually, Norwich.

the citizens of London has great weight with some of our merchants here' ; and that 'an unknown author published some remarks the other day upon your plans, as unjust as they were unfair '. The result of the competition was, ' 1 Cooley, 2 Gandon, 3 Sandby ', in spite of Gandon's herculean endeavours.

Another case is the competition advertised in the newspapers during 1776, for ' a Lunatic Hospital ' [the New Bethlehem in Southwark]. A premium of £100 was offered, and ample time was allowed for preparing plans. Gandon with his usual acumen was thus enabled to get into touch with Howard, the great prison reformer, and evidently drew largely upon his wide experience and study. In this instance Gandon was successful, but the comparatively insignificant premium was all that he ever obtained for his work because, in his son's words, the ' carrying out of his own plans . . . was handed over to another person, some man of mere lath and plaster, one wholly incompetent to produce designs or plans of his own '. Yet the preparation of these competition designs, entailing, as it did, many visits to the wards, had caused him sleeplessness, ' horrible dreams of the miserable and afflicting scenes of its wretched inmates ', and finally brain-fever, which very nearly ended his life.

There is not very much more to be said about the methods of work of the eighteenth-century architect which, so far as can be ascertained, were gradually approximating towards modern practice. Innumerable architectural drawings of the period have been preserved, e. g. the Soane Museum contains fifty-three volumes in which are bound between 8,000 and 9,000 drawings and sketches by Robert Adam, bought by Sir John Soane in 1833. There is also a representative collection in the Library of the

Royal Institute of British Architects. The records of the
period seldom refer to models of buildings.

Brief mention must be made of ways by which certain
well-known architects supplemented their incomes, besides
such subsidiary hobbies as purchasing antiques for ' noble
patrons ', designing furniture and costumes for ladies of
fashion, and writing books on the Orders. Vanbrugh
acted as lessee and manager of the Opera House in the
Haymarket, which he bought for £2,000 ; and those
artistic souls the Adams ran a lucrative business in ' real
estate ' in London, abreast of their more legitimate and
professional activities, until an unlucky speculation in
cement brought them to ruin. The Adams seem to have
been fully cognizant of all the accepted methods of architectural advertising—permissible and otherwise.

It was an age of great wealth (for the few), and some
architects made large fortunes. Sir Robert Taylor left
£180,000 to found a school of modern languages at Oxford,
' Carr of York ' left £160,000 to his heirs, and Archer left
£100,000 to a nephew ; Chambers drew £2,000 a year
while employed at Somerset House. These figures are,
however, exceptional, and many of the salaries and fees
recorded are small. Hawksmoor was paid £100 ' to gratify
him for his work ' for the Clarendon Press at Oxford.

Kent's fortune, according to Walpole, ' which, with
pictures and books, amounted to about ten thousand
pounds, he divided between his relations and an actress with
whom he had long lived in particular friendship '. But
the most notable bequest was made by Gibbs, who though
he had done all his professional work at St. Bartholomew's
Hospital without charge, contrived to amass some fifteen
thousand pounds from his other buildings and his writings.
Of this amount, he left a thousand pounds and an income

of £280 a year to the only son of Lord Mar, that ' noble patron ' who had first given him a helping hand but whose Jacobite sympathies had brought to ruin. To the Radcliffe Library, perhaps his greatest building, he left five hundred valuable volumes, many of them on architecture.

This reminds us that on the whole, the most remarkable feature of this somewhat pedantic period was the number of books written by architects. Of the twenty-four taken as typical for my study, at least eighteen published books, some of them many books. The majority of these were either copybooks of the Orders, albums of their own designs for ' Noblemen's Mansions ', or collections of imaginary designs for gigantic mansions that they felt themselves capable of building. Half of them frankly advertise their authors' supposed merits ; nearly all of them contain pages of fulsome flattery of the grandees to whom they are dedicated and by whom they were often financed. Gibbs is said to have made £1,500 by his *Book of Architecture*, in addition to £400 for the plates. But even such few books as were professedly manuals of building-construction and carpentry were mainly occupied with plates of the Orders and of 'Gentlemen's Houses'. Batty Langley's *Builder's Compleat Assistant* (1738) shows this tendency, his *The Builder's Jewel : or, the Youth's instructor and Workman's remembrancer* (1757) even more so, and one cannot fail to notice that none of the simpler processes of building are described or illustrated in any of these books ; they seem to have been taken for granted. When Mr. William Pain, ' Architect and Joiner ', published his *The Practical Builder, or Workman's General Assistant*, in 1774, his object was, according to his own preface, ' Plainly and faithfully to answer the Purpose of the manual Artificer ', yet almost the whole of the book consists of plates of the Orders and of monumental architectural designs, construction being relegated to a few diagrams illustrating the intricacies of geometrical setting-out, and a few more of trussed girders and roofs. His *Practical House Carpenter: or, Youth's Instructor*, is similar in many respects to the last, only 15 plates out of 116 being in the least practical, though there is a valuable appendix containing an exhaustive list of building prices then current.

Of the numerous great folios of the period the most important is the series known as *Vitruvius Britannicus*, of which the first three volumes were produced by Colin Campbell in 1715–25 (under the patronage of Lord Burlington), with the object of illustrating the designs of Inigo Jones and other architects whose work he approved, and incidentally including a few efforts of his own. After his death, supplements to this monumental survey were added in 1767–71 by Wolfe and Gandon.

Very different in character is Sir William Chambers's *Treatise on the Decorative Part of Civil Architecture*. In the third edition of that celebrated book (1791) the author includes an introduction dealing with the qualifications of an architect. After quoting Vitruvius on the same topic, and pointing out how greatly conditions have changed, he proceeds :—

' Such as intend to make it [architecture] their profession should enter the lists with a good store of health, vigor, and agility ; they should neither be lame nor unwieldy ; neither awkward, slow, nor helpless ; neither purblind nor deaf ; nor have any thing ridiculous about them, either natural or acquired. Their understanding should be sound ; the sight and apprehension quick ; the reasoning faculties clear, and unwarped by prejudices ; the temper enterprising, steady, resolute ; and though benevolent, rather spirited than passive, meek, or effeminate. . . .

FIG. 42. SIR WILLIAM CHAMBERS

From an engraving by Bromley, 1792

' And as at the present time few engage in any profession till qualified for the world by a proper school education at least, it must be supposed, that to a competent proficiency in the learned languages, the student adds a thorough knowledge of his own—so as to speak and write it, correctly, at least, if not elegantly ; that he is a good penman, versed in accounts, a ready practitioner in arithmetic, and has received and profited by such other instructions as tend to fix the moral character, to inculcate integrity, to polish the minds, and improve the manners of youth.

' Proficiency in the French and Italian languages is also requisite to him ; not only that he may be enabled to travel with advantage, and converse without difficulty, in countries where the chief part of his knowledge is to be collected ; but also to understand the many, and almost only valuable books treating of his profession, the greater part of which have never been translated.

He must also acquire the technical jargon of his craft, so that his orders may be understood and intelligently executed by the workmen.

' To these qualifications, mental and corporeal, must be united genius or a strong inclination and bias of mind towards the pursuit in question, without which little success can be expected. . . . As many sorts of knowledge, very opposite in their natures, come under the architect's consideration, his genius must be of a complex sort ; endowed with the vivacity and powers of imagination requisite to produce sublime or extraordinary compositions ; and, at the same time, with the industry, patience, and penetration necessary to investigate mathematical truths ; discuss difficult, sometimes irksome subjects ; and enter into details of various sorts, often as tiresome as they are necessary ; a genius equally capable of expanding to the noblest and most elevated conceptions, or of shrinking to the level of the meanest and minutest enquiries : as Dr. Johnson expresses it, a mind that at once comprehends the vast and attends to the minute.

' Of mathematical knowledge, geometry, trigonometry, and conic sections should be understood, as teaching the construction, properties, contents, and divisions of the forms used in building ; likewise of the raising, conveyance, and application of water, as well as for the common uses of life, as to produce many extraordinary effects, very ornamental in gardening, and efficacious in manufactures.'

Commenting on this last paragraph, exactly a century ago, that acute critic Joseph Gwilt observes that ' Mathematics have, perhaps, been too much neglected by some of the Architects of this country. The consequence has been the establishment of a new branch of art whose professors are called civil Engineers.' This statement stands to-day as true as when it was written. Whether one can expect a modern architect, whose repertoire is already extensive enough in all conscience, to recapture the design of bridges and fortifications is very questionable ; but upon his knowledge of mathematics, geometry, and mechanics —with all their recent applications to structural science— depends his ability to retain the increasing amount of building that is essentially scientific in its nature. Certainly the day is long past when Tredgold's empirical formulae can be relied upon to see him through all the problems of his profession.

Returning to Chambers's book, we find the long list of the architect's qualifications set out so fully that much further quotation becomes impossible here. He must be above all things a master of design, he must understand perspective and have ' a perfect acquaintance with all kinds of proportions ', and he ' furthermore must be well versed in the customs, ceremonies, and modes of life of all men his contemporaries ', so that he may provide effectively for their needs. ' Neither must he be ignorant of ancient history . . . as the established stile of decoration collects its forms . . . from these abundant courses, which time, and the concurring approbation of many ages, have rendered venerable.'

Descending to more prosaic matters : 'To the excellence of the designer's art, must yet be added the humbler, though not less useful skill of the mechanic and accountant', including an acquaintance with all building materials and processes, a power ' of regulating the accounts with accuracy ' and of dealing with ' many men of different professions, capacities, and dispositions ; all without violence or clamour, yet with full effect '. He emphasizes the importance of accurate estimating, dismissing with scorn the rough-and-ready method of those who ' Value by the square '. He explains that ' extras ' are due as often to whimsical clients as to careless architects, and urges the value, to all concerned in building, of orders in writing. Finally he shows the importance to the architect of foreign travel, partly, it is true, for the purpose of studying ' the purest models ', but also because ' travelling rouses the imagination ' and broadens the traveller's mind. Nowadays these passages may perhaps be regarded as pompous and verbose, yet there is hardly anything in them that does not apply with equal force to-day ; for though, as in the eighteenth century, architects continually rise from the ranks by sheer force of genius, their talents are developed and their chances of success increased by a liberal and scientific education.

.   .   .   .   .   .

While this book has been passing through the press, there has appeared an interesting study of provincial practice in the eighteenth century : *Georgian Norwich and its Builders*, by Stanley J. Wearing. (Norwich,

Jarrolds, 1927.) Though only a brief sketch, it contains much information as to local building enterprises, competitions, architects' fees and duties, and their use of plans and models. But the book is most valuable in showing how, at that date, carpenters and other building craftsmen turned themselves into ' architects ' by the simple expedient of an advertisement in the newspaper. Thus :

' As the said M^r. [Robert] Brettingham is leaving off his business of Mason, he intends to act in the character of an Architect, in drawing plans and elevations, giving estimates, or putting out work, or measuring up any sort of building, for any Gentleman in the Country.' [1753.]

And Matthew Brettingham's epitaph (1769) in St. Augustine's Church concludes with lines that faithfully portray the eighteenth-century architect :

> ' As a Man his Integrity,
> liberal Spirit and benevolence of Mind ;
> endear'd him to all that knew his Virtues,
> and his Talents as an Architect
> to the Patronage and esteem of the Nobility,
> the most distinguish'd
> for their love of *Palladian* Architecture.'

BIBLIOGRAPHY

(Abbreviations: *A.R.* = 'Architectural Review; *J.* = 'R.I.B.A. Journal'

(a) COLLECTIONS

Chancellor, E. B. *Lives of the British Architects* (1909).
Cunningham, A. *Lives of the British Painters, Sculptors, and Architects* (1829).
(The lives of most of the chief British architects of the Renaissance are given in the *Dict. of Nat. Biog.* and many in the *Encyc. Brit.* ; see also the admirable notices in the *Dict. of the Architectural Publication Society.*)

(b) MONOGRAPHS

Adam, Robert and James. By A. T. Bolton (1922); by J. Swarbrick (1915).
' *Carr of York.*' By S. D. Kitson (*J.* 1910).
Chambers, Sir William. By A. T. Edwards (1924) ; by I. C. Goodison (*A.R.* 1913) ; by T. Hardwick (in Chambers's *Treatise*, &c., 1825).
Dance, George, junior. By R. T. Blomfield (*A.R.* 1901).
Gandon, James. By his son James Gandon (1846).
Grumbold, Robert. By G. Webb, in *Burlington Magazine* (1925–6).
Hawksmoor, Nicholas. By H. S. Goodhart-Rendel (1924).
' *James of Greenwich.*' By M. Judge (*A.R.* 1912).
Jones, Inigo. By P. Cunningham (1848) ; by J. A. Gotch (*J.* 1924) ;
by W. G. Keith (*J.* 1925) ; by W. R. Lethaby (*A.R.* 1912, 1916) ;
by W. J. Loftie (1893) ; by S. C. Ramsey (1924) ; by H. Sirr (*A.R.* 1912) ; by I. Triggs and H. Tanner (1901).
Kent, William. By O. Brackett (*A.R.* 1911).
Smithson Family, The. By M. B. Adams (*J.* 1907) ; by J. A. Gotch (*J.* 1908).
Stone, Nicholas. By A. E. Bullock (1908) ; by W. L. Spiers (Walpole Society, 1919).
Thorpe, John. By H. Sirr (*J.* 1910, 1911).
Vanbrugh, Sir John. By C. Barman (1924) by ; G. H. Lovegrove (1902).
Webb, John. By J. A. Gotch (*J.* 1921) ; by H. Sirr (*A.R.* 1912).
Wren, Sir Christopher. By his son, *Parentalia* (1750) ; by various authors, *R.I.B.A. Bicentenary Volume* (1923) ; by J. Elmes (1823) ; by L. Milman (1908) ; by A. Stratton (1897) ; by L. Weaver (1923). (Also the admirable volumes published in 1924, 1925, and 1926 by the Wren Society.)

VIII

THE NINETEENTH CENTURY
IN ENGLAND

FROM the time of John Shute to that of Sir William Chambers, English architecture drew its chief inspiration, for better or for worse, from Rome. Towards the close of the eighteenth century there was a change, and architects began to look to Greece for ideas. Some critics treat this change as a normal development of the classical tradition, arguing that no abrupt break was involved. But, in the present writer's view, the ' Greek Revival ', as it is commonly called, was as definite a landmark as the Renaissance itself. For nearly 250 years there had been a certain continuity in design (or in borrowing, as hostile writers claim). This continuity was broken at the end of the eighteenth century, and even to-day we are not quite sure of our direction, though the state of architecture is probably healthier than it has been since Wren's time. The nineteenth century has been rightly called ' The Age of Revivals ' in English architecture ; and the effect of revivalism on architects, whether ' Greek·' or ' Gothic ' in their sympathies, can be traced clearly enough in their own careers.

As Mr. Budden has pointed out in his survey [1] of that singular movement, the Greek Revival may be ascribed primarily to the publication of the first volume of Stuart and Revett's *Antiquities of Athens* in 1762. But for 140 years or so prior to that date English travellers had taken some interest in Greek art, though their energies had been

[1] L. B. Budden, ' The Greek Revival in England ' (in *R.I.B.A. Journal*, 1909, p. 177).

FIG. 43. SIR JOHN SOANE

From the painting by Lawrence in the Soane Museum

confined to material loot, and that dangerous architectural weapon—the book of measured drawings—had not yet made its appearance. Stuart and Revett were competent archaeologists, and their admirable work laid the foundation of our present knowledge of Greek monuments. But not all English architects accepted it as their Bible : there were some who took very little notice of the new craze, others who were dabbling in medievalism long before the later Gothic Revival swept them off their feet, and yet others who contrived to make the best of both worlds by designing in the Greek or the Gothic manner with equal readiness according to the dictates of their fancies or their clients.

The following twelve architects may be regarded as typical of those who mainly favoured the Greek Revival : Nash, Sir John Soane, Wilkins, Sir Robert Smirke, Gwilt, Cockerell, Inwood, Basevi, Sir William Tite, Burton, H. L. Elmes, and ' Greek ' Thomson. More than in any previous period we find a measure of similarity in the details of their lives. Most of them were the sons of middle-class parents—indeed, no less than six were architects' sons, while Smirke (son of a famous painter), Decimus Burton (son of a wealthy builder), and Soane (son of a small builder or bricklayer)[1] came from homes where architecture would presumably be understood. Of the remaining three—Nash, Tite, and Thomson—it is possible that the last-named was of humble birth, but to a Scot this has never been an insuperable obstacle.

No longer do we find the architect dropping haphazard into his profession from another walk of life and at any age up to fifty or so. Eleven at least of the twelve men mentioned above studied architecture as pupils in an

[1] Or a stone-mason. Budden, *op. cit.*, p. 179.

architect's office. The only possible exception is Soane, who is said by Mr. Budden[1] to have been ' errand-boy ' to George Dance the Younger, but Mr. Bolton, writing later and more fully,[2] states that he was articled to him. Most of the architects' sons acquired additional experience, after their articles, in the offices of other practitioners. As regards their general education, only Wilkins is known to have attended a university, and that when his father was practising architecture in Cambridge. He entered Caius College as a scholar in 1796, and graduated as sixth wrangler in 1800.

A few examples may be cited showing in further detail how some of the most successful practitioners of this period obtained their professional training. Sir John Soane (1753–1837), most famous of them all, has received especial attention from Mr. A. T. Bolton,[3] the present curator of the Soane Museum, so that we are enabled to reconstruct his early career in some detail. Born only a quarter of a century after Chambers and Adam, and as long before most of the other Greek Revivalists who followed him, Soane is really a link between the eighteenth and nineteenth centuries, but on the whole he belongs to the later phase and may be considered its father.

Mr. Bolton thinks that, as the son of a master bricklayer or mason, Soane's ability may have attracted the notice of one Peacock, chief assistant to the younger George Dance, whose office he entered at fifteen years of age. ' The boy was handsome, quick, enthusiastic, and possessed of considerable charm of manner, as well as of unlimited power of work.' In Dance's office he would see a variety of

[1] Budden, *op. cit.*, p. 179.
[2] A. T. Bolton, ' Life and Work a Century Ago ' (in *R.I.B.A. Journal*, 1922, p. 613).   [3] See Bibliography at end of this chapter.

work, indeed of such varying quality that Mr. Bolton suggests [1] that Soane (long after he left Dance's service) may have played an important part in the design of St. Luke's, Old Street, and of Newgate Prison, works far surpassing in merit anything else that Dance ever produced. At all events Soane in later years not only worked occasionally for his first employer as an emergency draughtsman, but remained on the best of terms of friendship with him. It appears that he soon found Dance a rather eccentric visionary, and in 1770, when he was only seventeen years of age, he moved into the office of Henry Holland, a busy architect of more practical ability who had entered the profession from a family of builders. Here he seems to have remained for some seven years until he went to Italy in 1778. Mr. Bolton assumes that he attained a position of some responsibility in Holland's office, where at the age of twenty-four he was drawing the princely salary of £60 a year. He made a special study of estimating, surveying, and builders' prices, on which he became an expert in later life. From his first coming to London as a poor boy he began to buy books, on mathematics at the commencement, and thus laid the foundation of that magnificent library which he bequeathed on his death to the nation, comprising some eight thousand volumes, of which half deal with architecture and the allied arts. In this large collection are several relics of his purchases in early boyhood. In 1777 he himself prepared and published a small book of designs for garden seats, temples, &c. Some time before 1772 he entered the Royal Academy Schools, for in that year he was awarded the R.A. Measured Drawings Medal for his drawings of Inigo

---

[1] A. T. Bolton, ' St. Luke's Hospital, Old Street ' (in *Architecture*, 1925, p. 210).

Jones's Banqueting Hall.   In 1774 he competed for the
R.A. Gold Medal in Architecture but was disqualified as he
failed to comply with the conditions as to date of delivery.
In 1776 he tried again and was successful. The medal was
awarded to him by Sir Joshua Reynolds, who delivered his
thirteenth 'Discourse' on that occasion, and congratulated
young Soane, as did the influential Sir William Chambers.
After an interview with the King, Soane set out for Italy
in the following spring and commenced practice on his
return to England in 1780.

Cockerell (1788–1863) was born thirty-five years later
than Soane and as an architect's son had a better start in
life. He was educated first at a private school in the City
Road, then at Westminster until he was sixteen, after
which he entered his father's office and remained there
five years. During that period he went on a sketching
tour in the west of England. In 1809 he went as assistant
to Sir (then Mr.) Robert Smirke, and in the following year
commenced his lengthy travels in Greece and Italy, (see
pp. 335-8) returning to commence practice on his own
account at about thirty years of age.

Elmes (1813–47), another architect's son, obtained all
his training in small provincial offices, joined his father
in practice at twenty-two, and never went to Italy. The
remaining architects on my list, so far as can be ascertained,
all commenced practice between the ages of twenty-four
and twenty-nine, except Decimus Burton who was launched
at twenty-one, thanks to his father, a large speculative
builder, who employed him as architect.

The Academy Schools now begin to appear frequently
in the chronicles of architecture. Smirke, Gwilt, and
Burton were among those who studied there, besides
Soane, already mentioned, and Gandon, whose early career

was described in my last chapter (see pp. 304-5). There seems to be some doubt as to whether there was any organized instruction in this School, or whether it was merely an *atelier* where students prepared designs for the annual Gold Medal.

' It may be that Soane was the first professor of architecture to take himself seriously, for we know that his predecessor in office, George Dance the Younger, though he held the post for several years, never gave a lecture. As Dance was one of the original members of the Academy, this fact ranks as a rather remarkable instance of early development in sinecure.' [1]

But it is clear that the main business of training young architects was carried on in the offices where they were articled. Soane himself regarded his responsibilities in this respect seriously, and

gave his pupils plenty of practical work, including surveying, measuring, costing, and superintendence, as well as the making of working drawings. . . . He also established a brilliant academy of fine draughtsmanship. . . . His very beautiful drawings made to illustrate [his Academy] lectures were prepared in his own office, and it is not too much to say that the production of these drawings formed a valuable part of the training provided for his pupils. It is interesting to note that during the 53 years of Soane's practice no less than 357 architectural studies were admitted to the Royal Academy exhibitions from Soane's office staff under their own names. . . . Probably, with about three possible exceptions, no architect since his time has ever provided in his own office—and that a busy office—such a complete or refined education for pupils.' [2]

It was a real disappointment to Soane that his two sons, whom he had sent to Cambridge and given every

[1] Paul Waterhouse, in *Proceedings of Congress on Architectural Education* (1925), p. 31. [2] *Ibid.*

opportunity of a sound start in his own fine practice, had no real inclination for architecture. ' They had vague literary aspirations, and that was all ', says Mr. Bolton. So their distinguished father had to solace himself by helping and befriending his more energetic pupils, of whom Basevi seems to have been his particular pet.

Travel abroad now became more than ever an essential part of an architect's education. Seven of our twelve typical architects travelled in Italy during their student days, and it is significant that five of them extended their tour to Greece. It is noteworthy, too, that all but one of the six architects' sons are found among the travellers (Elmes being the exception), showing that their fathers, not all wealthy men, regarded the study of classical antiquities as important. Travelling in Greece was not only expensive but dangerous, though during the Napoleonic wars Greece was more accessible than Italy. Yet several of the architects under consideration spent many years abroad, Cockerell being absent seven years. Soane and Wilkins at least held travelling studentships, the former from the Royal Academy, the latter as one of ' West's Travelling Bachelors '. Smirke was another successful R.A. student, being awarded the Gold Medal in 1799.

The favourite age for travel in those days seems to have been between twenty-one and twenty-five, that is, after the completion of a pupil's articles and before his venture into independent practice. Soane was therefore rather above the usual age when he set out for Italy in 1778 with a scholarship of £60 a year for three years and a like amount for the expense of the return journey. His companion was Robert Brettingham, an architect's son, three years his senior. They travelled out by way of Paris. Soane was armed with a passport signed by Louis XVI, and the prestige attached to his gold medal found him a circle of influential friends as soon as he arrived in Rome. But he settled down to hard work, measured the Pantheon and other great buildings, and in particular made an elaborate set of drawings of the Temple of Vesta at Tivoli. His friendship with the Bishop of Derry led to his employment as draughtsman by a party of wealthy *cognoscenti* on a tour which embraced Sicily and Malta but never reached Greece. While in Italy, he amused himself with preparing imaginary architectural designs. Among these may be mentioned a ' Design for a British Senate-house ', now preserved in the Soane Museum, which, in his own words, was

' composed at Rome 1779, without regard to expense, or limit as to space, in the gay morning of youthful fancy, amid all the wild imagination of an enthusiastic mind, animated by the contemplation of the majestic ruins of the sublime works of Imperial Rome.' [1]

His tour in Italy was cut short. An invitation to design two houses for the Bishop induced him to abandon his projected visits to Vicenza, and to return home in 1780, but a difficult client, added to his own nervous temperament, made this first commission a fiasco.

Cockerell's travels in Greece read like a sensational story of adventure. His outward voyage in *The Black Joke* to Constantinople was enlivened by incidents with privateers, and his diary contains frequent references to pirates. As he had only a travelling studentship to pay his expenses and was not a rich man's son, he managed to get sent out with dispatches to the fleet and to our Ambassador at Constantinople, but characteristically did not find much

[1] *Description of the House and Museum, &c.* by Sir John Soane (1920 edition), p. 103.

to his taste in that historic city, so moved on to Athens some six months later. We do not know whether accident or design determined his destination : Italy was at that time practically closed to travellers, and for architectural students of a century ago the choice lay between Greece and Italy. It was his work in Greece, of course, that made Cockerell's reputation, and more especially his labours at Aegina, which he visited in April 1811 in company with Foster, a Liverpool architect, and two Germans. Here much excavating and sketching was done, but the chief interest lay in the discovery of sixteen marble statues, known as ' the Aegina marbles '. There was much competition between the British Museum and the Germans for these trophies, which eventually went to the Glyptothek at Munich. In August they proceeded to Olympia, and thence to Bassae or Phigaleia, where measuring and drawing occupied ten days. Some more magnificent marbles were unearthed there at a second visit, and were acquired by the British Government. Between these two visits Foster and Cockerell had travelled in Crete, but the Turks would not allow them to do any drawing there. A short sojourn in the town of Siphanto resulted in Foster's defection :

' Foster found nothing there of interest except numbers of pretty girls, some of whom were so pressing that he found it difficult to get away alone. The fact is, the men of the island being mostly sailors, are away at sea, and the ladies being left in a majority, make the love which in other countries is made to them.' [1]

Cockerell therefore visited Asia Minor and Sicily without Foster. In Sicily he spent several months, devoting part of the time to working up his drawings of Aegina and

[1] Cockerell's diary

FIG. 44. CHARLES ROBERT COCKERELL AS A YOUNG MAN

From a drawing by Ingres

Phigaleia for publication, and learning to cut cameos and to play the guitar. Then followed a further period in Greece, where he had a severe attack of typhoid fever and would probably have died but for the devotion of one of his German friends. The conditions of life for travellers in that country a century ago were always uncomfortable, often almost unbearable, and it is really remarkable that architectural students stayed there so long. When, at the end of 1814, Napoleon's exile opened Italy once more to Englishmen, Cockerell determined to go there. His farewell to Athens was characteristic of the Turkish régime. The Turkish commandant of the fort on the Acropolis told him

' to bring a cart at night to the base of the Acropolis to receive a present, about which he maintained a mysterious reticence. Cockerell obeyed, and as he reached the rendezvous heard a great body crashing down the hill, and rushed to the spot where it came to rest. It was the right-hand slab of the south frieze of the Parthenon. I need not say that such treatment did not improve the sculpture, which still bears the marks of its adventure on its face. Cockerell, however, immediately put it in his cart, and shipped it off from the Piræus. He afterwards presented it to the British Museum, where it is to be found in its due place.' [1]

Leaving Athens early in 1815, he and a German companion travelled slowly to Rome, taking six months on the journey. Arrived there, Cockerell found that the fame of his discoveries in Greece had preceded him, and a galaxy of celebrated artists—including Ingres, Thorwaldsen, and Canova—crowded round him. Even in Rome, Greece had become the fashion. Cockerell soon tired of being

---

[1] R. P. Cockerell, ' The Life of Charles Cockerell ' (in *Architectural Review*, xii. 46).

lionized and fled to Florence to work. But even there he was consulted about the arrangement of some pedimental sculpture in the Uffizi, in which he was very successful. The spell was broken when he was invited to submit designs in competition for a palace for the Duke of Wellington. He complied, but failed ignominiously. This is not remarkable when one remembers that his work abroad had been entirely archaeological : he had not spent part of his time there, as Soane and Adam did, in studying monumental planning, and for six years he had been completely cut off from professional practice. A few months more in Italy, sketching in the northern provinces and restoring the Forum in Rome, completed the term of his long and important travels. Cockerell's researches influenced all his subsequent building, and had a direct bearing on the future of the Greek Revival, which tended to become more and more an exotic movement depending largely on the accurate reproduction of details from his and other books.

What Mr. Ronald Jones has amusingly christened the ' folio period ' of the Georgian Renaissance gave way to another era of architectural book-making in which Cockerell, Wilkins, and Inwood have an honoured place. But their chief books were scholarly volumes on Greek antiquities, thus forming a welcome contrast to the blatant folios of the Georgians. The chair of architecture at the Royal Academy was occupied successively by Soane, Smirke, Wilkins, and Cockerell ; and Soane took three years to prepare a course of six lectures to be delivered from that august position. Many of these men were members of the powerful Society of Dilettanti or of the Society of Antiquaries ; it was essentially a dilettante period, and the Greek Revival a dilettante movement. That fact explains, perhaps, why it gradually expired.

When it became really imitative, as in the work of ' Greek ' Thomson or at Inwood's new church at St. Pancras, it ceased to have any connexion with English habits or modern requirements : it became something culled from a book.

Turning from books and travel to professional practice, we find that nearly all the twelve typical architects of this school had large, some enormous, practices. They must have been busy and rich men. Sir Robert Smirke, who designed the British Museum, the G.P.O., and King's College (London), declined all ' jobs ' of a value less than £10,000 as soon as his feet were on the ladder.

The most striking feature of the early nineteenth century, as compared with the preceding period, is the almost complete disappearance of the ' noble patron ' who figured so prominently in the last chapter. We find architects no longer acting as flunkeys in some aristocratic retinue, but self-respecting professional men. Houses for the wealthy certainly continued to be erected, but not on so gigantic a scale, and other types of building took their place.

Architectural competitions frequently occurred. Soane's first work, on returning from Italy in 1780, was to send in designs for two ' penitentiaries ', a type of institution then recently introduced, but he was unsuccessful. Thereafter he seems to have avoided competitions all through his life, with the single and notable exception of that for the Bank of England in 1788, in which he was placed first, out of fifteen competitors, at thirty-five years of age. Wilkins, who obtained his first commission—Downing College, Cambridge—when he was twenty-six, gained much of his large subsequent practice in competitions, open or limited. Basevi won the competition for the Fitzwilliam Museum at Cambridge in 1835, and Cockerell was successful in two important competitions—Cambridge University Library (1830) and the Taylor and Randolph Building at Oxford (1839)—as well as in the preliminary competition for the Royal Exchange.

But by far the most interesting of these contests was that won by Elmes in 1839, for St. George's Hall at Liverpool. Elmes was only twenty-five at the time, and he had seventy-four competitors against him. But the result had hardly been decided when it was decided to build new Assize Courts ; another competition was held, eighty-six designs were submitted, and again Elmes was placed first. In both instances drawings were submitted under a motto. There seems to be no record of an assessor having been appointed, and Mr. Ronald Jones suggests that Elmes's double success may be due to the City Architect's partiality for Greek architecture, as that official probably had a voice in the award. The original designs for the two buildings in no way resembled the present fine block, for it was decided at a later stage to combine assize-courts and hall in one group, and Elmes succeeded (not without difficulty) in retaining the design of the new building which he had so justly earned by his victories in the earlier stages. The subsequent history of the undertaking has a tragic aspect : Elmes never lived to finish it, and the work was handed over to Cockerell after his death.

The Government Board of Works seems to have provided its ' attached ' architects (who were allowed to continue private practice) with some lucrative and desirable work. The Bank of England is estimated by Mr. Bolton to have cost, during the forty-five years while Soane was in charge, over £850,000 ; £1,000,000 was allowed for the British Museum, designed by Smirke, as was the G.P.O. The National Gallery, the Royal Exchange, the rebuilding of Buckingham Palace, the ' Marble Arch ', and the beautiful screen at Hyde Park Corner were other works of the period. Nash laid out Regent Street, the Quadrant, and the terraces near Regent's Park for the Crown, and all this was work in London alone.

Middle-class revolt against religious restrictions in the older educational foundations led to the building of Mill Hill School (1825) from Sir William Tite's designs, and University College, London (1827), by William Wilkins, while the latter—commonly nicknamed the 'godless college in Gower Street '—was soon followed by King's College, London (1831), by Smirke. A new opportunity for architectural design was provided by the invention of railways. Philip Hardwick was responsible for the Greek propylaea and the lodges at Euston, while Sir William Tite designed a whole series of stations in England and France. The fine example at Newcastle-on-Tyne (1849) is the work of John Dobson. Mention must be made here of the admirable architecture of the tunnels, bridges, and other masonry details of the ' London and Birmingham ' railway, as the line from Euston was then called. This reminds us of the fine series of bridges designed by John Rennie the elder (1761–1821), especially Waterloo, London, and Southwark Bridges. Rennie was trained as a mechanical engineer and I can find no evidence that he pursued any architectural study. Sir Reginald Blomfield quotes, and evidently believes, a legend ' that Rennie got the designs [for Waterloo Bridge] from some broken down architect in prison ', [1] thus accounting for its excellence. His son, Sir John Rennie (1794–1874) completed London Bridge from his father's designs, and himself designed the bridges over the Thames at Staines and over the Serpentine in Hyde

[1] Sir R. Blomfield, *The Touchstone of Architecture* (1925), p. 109.

Park. A recent writer in *The Times* attributes the beauty of Waterloo Bridge to the fact that ' Rennie ' was a F.R.I.B.A., a comfortable but inaccurate statement. The elder Rennie, who designed it, died many years before the R.I.B.A. was thought of, and was not an architect ; his son and namesake was not trained as an architect, and, though his name appears as one of the founders of the R.I.B.A. in 1834, he resigned his membership in the same year. Unless Sir Reginald Blomfield's view can be substantiated, the credit for this great work of art must be conceded to the engineers.

Another branch of architectural practice of the period, and an important one, was connected with speculative building. The early nineteenth century was essentially the age of stucco, and it saw the development of many English spas and seaside towns. This usually decorous, sometimes dull, and now often shabby architecture was often designed by men of considerable ability. Nash— the apostle of stucco—was among those who did such work in London ; Basevi laid out Belgrave Square, Sydney Place, Thurloe Square, and other streets ; and Decimus Burton planned and built most of St. Leonards for his father, and some of the district adjoining Regent's Park. He also designed the gardens of the Zoological Society and the Botanical Society. The meandering walks that characterize his gardens (and others of the period) are in contrast with the severely formal buildings that he erected at their entrances, e. g. the colonnade and lodges in Hyde Park. It may be said in general of the Greek Revival that garden-design made no great progress, that town-planning advanced, and that modern sanitation had hardly come to be considered in the houses of the day. The architects of the early nineteenth century confined themselves for the most part to strictly professional duties, their principal hobby being archaeological research, but we find Nash—a very busy man—coquetting with miniatures and theatrical scenery, and ' Greek ' Thomson—not typical of the school—designing carpets, furniture, and wallpapers.

The accounts of the Bank of England show that a ' builder ' was not employed : Soane dealt direct with contractors in the various trades. But it was in the first years of the nineteenth century that the general contractor, the builder proper, made his appearance. The introduction of quantity-surveyors as a distinct class is attributed to Sir Robert Smirke (1780–1867) ; hitherto any systematic measuring of quantities had been done by specialist clerks in architects' offices. Those offices often contained a considerable staff. Each assistant in Nash's large office had his own compartment and desk. An architect's standard charge for professional services seems to have been established at 5 per cent. on the cost of the work : this appears in the records of the Bank of England, but Soane also made additional charges occasionally for work of a special o_ intricate nature.[1] From records of Nash's speculative ventures in Regent Street and elsewhere it is evident that he remunerated himself from ground-rents in default of fees,[2] and doubtless an examination of Decimus Burton's documents would tell the same tale.

Working-drawings, imaginative designs, and sketches by the chief architects of the Greek Revival are preserved in large numbers at the Soane Museum and in the Library of the R.I.B.A. Draughtsmanship reached a high standard of competency, and perspectives were constantly used.

[1] A. T. Bolton, ' The Bank of England ', in *The Builder*, 17 August 1923.
[2] W. H. Nash, ' John Nash ', in *R.I.B.A. Journal*, 1923.

Generally a fine ink line was adopted, with a free use of
delicate colours.   The Soane Museum also contains a
number of models of buildings designed by its talented
founder.   Mention of office-methods reminds us that
Soane was a tremendous worker.   His office-hours all his
life were from 7 to 7 in summer, from 8 to 8 in winter,
and at one period he walked daily from Ealing to his office
and vice versa.

Finally, the days of the Greek Revival saw the foundation
of the Royal Institute of British Architects in its permanent form.   Originating in that ' little convivial association ', the Architects' Club, that had met regularly since
1791 at the Thatched House tavern in London (see p. 317),
it was established on a firmer basis in 1834 as the ' Institute
of Architects ', and in February 1837 obtained a Royal
Charter.   The names of two of its most famous prizes—
the ' Soane ' and the ' Tite '—commemorate the share
taken in its foundation by two of the protagonists of the
Greek Revival, and Cockerell became its president at a
later period, when the ' Battle of the Styles ' was in full
swing.   But its gradual development from these small
beginnings will be more fittingly described at a later stage
in this study, as it took place after the Greek Revival was
for all practical purposes dead.

That curious movement, sometimes influencing English
architecture for good, sometimes making it merely pedantic,
saw the consolidation of the modern architect's professional status.   There we must leave it, to pass on to the next
phase ; merely remarking that the story of similar movements in Germany and France has been told elsewhere.[1]

.   .   .   .   .   .

[1] See H. H. Statham's article, ' Architecture : Modern ', in the
Encyclopaedia Britannica, eleventh edition.

The Gothic Revival, obscured for the last forty years by a cloud of ridicule, has recently been dragged out into the limelight by an admirer who has tempered his enthusiasm with a lightness of touch that is as rare in such criticism as it is welcome.[1] Fair recognition of this misunderstood movement is certainly long overdue. Few of us to-day are entitled to cast the first stone at its weak points ; for we have seen it replaced successively by revivals of Elizabethan, Jacobean, ' Queen Anne ', Georgian, and even ' Neo-Grec '—all within four decades or so. We may at least admit that the Gothic revivalists were sincere enthusiasts, and even allow a grain of truth in Mr. Goodhart-Rendel's ingenious argument that the spirit of Gothic persisted throughout the seventeenth and eighteenth centuries ; not the full-blown Gothic of our cathedrals but the medieval methods of rustic craftsmen who—undismayed by the thunders of the Palladians—continued to build mullioned windows, steep gables, and bold chimneys. Enough ridicule has surely now been cast on all the ' Eminent Victorians ' by the present generation ; a more sane and generous attitude is suggested by the sound advice in the Book of Ecclesiasticus : ' Let us now praise famous men, and our fathers that begat us.' For the weaknesses of the nineteenth-century architects are at least matched by those of their predecessors ; indeed the Gothic Revival resembled the Palladian Revival most closely when it degenerated into a heresy-hunt. Mr. Goodhart-Rendel thinks that, in this country, ' Vitruvius had never become more than a canonized policeman ',[2] but both his halo and his authority have been evident enough in previous chapters of the present study. At any rate,

[1] H. S. Goodhart-Rendel, ' English Gothic Architecture of the Nineteenth Century ' (*R.I.B.A. Journal*, 1924). [2] *Ibid.*, p. 322.

the readiness with which the early Victorians changed their allegiance is remarkable.

But, though every reader of this book will doubtless have some idea of the date and nature of the Gothic Revival, he may fail to see any reason for dividing the present chapter, as I have done, into three sections corresponding roughly with the Greek Revival, the Gothic Revival, and what may be called the ' Domestic Revival ', initiated by Philip Webb and Norman Shaw. Has this apparently cut-and-dried classification by ' movements ' any definite relation to the story of the architect's development ? The answer is clear : the three movements mentioned are most faithfully reflected in the careers of contemporary architects. But it is quite impossible to draw a sharp line between the several stages, though for convenience they are separated by a space in these pages. For even architectural revivals have their periods of transition, and they overlap.

We are apt to speak of the Gothic Revival as a single movement that swept into England somewhere about 1830 and swept out again some time after 1880. Nothing of that kind took place. It is perhaps too much to say, as Mr. Goodhart-Rendel does, that Gothic never died. He himself admits that the little feeble flame of medieval tradition was only kept alight in village backwaters where craftsmen preferred to copy the models that surrounded them rather than the serio-comic Palladianism of Batty Langley and his kind. But so far as architects were concerned, there was an almost complete break in the Gothic tradition from about 1650 to 1800. The few exceptions, in some of Wren's City churches, ' Tom Tower ', and elsewhere, are mainly due to a desire to harmonize with medieval surroundings. The revival of Gothic came in two waves : the first was due to Horace Walpole, who toyed with it at Strawberry Hill from 1753 to 1776. But there was nothing spontaneous about this work ; it was part of a literary movement, the ' Romantic Revival ', and it lacked everything that makes Gothic architecture great. At the best it was an amusing occupation for a dilettante gentleman's leisure, affording a change from the Chinese and the ' Grecian '.

For forty years at least Gothic made practically no progress. Then came James Wyatt (1746–1813), who lived to become President of the Royal Academy, but whose surgical treatment of our cathedrals earned him the nickname of ' The Destroyer '. In 1796 he commenced a vast house, Fonthill Abbey, for William Beckford. It cost over a quarter of a million, and has now completely disappeared. Wyatt began his career in the way approved in the eighteenth century. At fourteen his talents attracted the attention of a ' noble patron ' who took him to Rome for five or six years. He was then duly articled, and his subsequent doings would have probably followed the stereotyped lines but for his unfortunate infection with the Gothic taste, which led him from the safe classic design that he managed very well to the wild mangling of our great churches that has ruined his reputation for ever. He was a contemporary of most of the Greek Revival architects whom I have mentioned in the early part of this chapter, and it must be remembered that nearly all of them did Gothic of a sort abreast of their Greek designs. It is noteworthy that John Nash, builder of Regent Street and an architect with an immense practice, was building a number of large houses ' in imitation of castellated and monastic structures ' at the very beginning of the nineteenth century.[1] He

[1] B. Ferrey, *Recollections of A. N. W. Pugin* (1861), p. 5.

suggested to the elder Pugin, a French refugee whom he had recently engaged as a draughtsman, that a book of practical details of Gothic architecture would be welcomed by the profession in this emergency. The direct result was Pugin's *Specimens of Gothic Architecture* (1821), dedicated to Nash, but the indirect result was the younger Pugin, the real father of the Gothic Revival in its second stage. Other books contributing to the improvement of taste in the now fashionable movement were John Britton's *Architectural Antiquities of Great Britain* (9 vols. 1805–14), and *Cathedral Antiquities of England* (14 vols. 1814–35) ; and especially Rickman's admirable work, *An Attempt to Discriminate the Styles of Architecture in England from the Conquest to the Reformation* (1817). But though these books supplied valuable information and guidance, the movement lacked life and energy until Welby Pugin arrived on the scene to give it driving power with his vital and passionate personality. We may therefore date the real commencement of the second or mature stage of the Gothic Revival about the year 1837, when Welby Pugin appears in practice ; its full tide was reached with the appearance of Ruskin's *Seven Lamps* in 1849 and the first volume of his *Stones of Venice* two years later ; its decline may be placed in the eighties of last century. To a large extent it was book-architecture, but nevertheless it responded to something in the national temperament that was English and healthy, while eventually it led to an enthusiasm for the building crafts that was altogether praiseworthy. The defects of Ruskin's architectural philosophy have been emphasized so much lately that we are apt to forget its real merits. It is true that he was intensely dogmatic and blindly partisan ; that he exaggerated the purely romantic and ornamental details of architecture while almost ignoring form and proportion ; and that he preferred Italian and French Gothic to our own. He did actual harm, too, in denying that merely utilitarian buildings should be regarded as architecture ; and it was during the height of his influence that industrialism covered our country with hideous factories, cottages, and railway stations. But he created a genuine popular interest in his own pet styles, and on the whole his plea for sound construction and good craftsmanship absolves him for his serious errors in other directions. Moreover, his insistence on the human aspects of architecture as reflecting life, if often fanciful, was a welcome reaction from the lifeless formalism of the aristocratic eighteenth century.

Mr. Halsey Ricardo has recently written an admirable and spirited defence of Ruskin's teaching on architecture,[1] in which he reminds us that we owe to him much that is not obviously Gothic in its nature, such as the care that the best English architects of our day have devoted to good and suitable materials, to local tradition in the crafts, to sound and truthful construction. But his greatest quality, it seems to me, though it was the very quality that most frequently led him astray, was his flaming enthusiasm for good architecture and building. The same trait is found in Welby (the younger) Pugin : indeed it was a consuming fire that burnt him out when he was only forty. In a less degree it appears in Street and Butterfield, as in the minor prophets of the Revival. Occasionally it manifested itself in mere eccentricity and posing, as when Butterfield and Pugin attempted to live a medieval life at home. More often it led to violent pamphleteering and mutual abuse among the various sects of the cult. Ruskin's attack on

[1] See Halsey Ricardo, ' The Architect's Debt to Ruskin ' in *The Builder*, 26 September 1924.

Pugin is a fair sample of the bitterness with which the really great men of the period assailed one another in print. Religious squabbles intensified artistic differences, Pugin being an earnest Catholic and Ruskin a rather aggressive Protestant. In fact religion permeated the Revival, and its disciples were as convinced that Gothic was the only Christian architecture as the Palladians had been that it was barbarous. Questions of ecclesiastical ritual were hotly debated at architectural gatherings. Yet, admitting all these superficial defects, we cannot deny that the leaders of the Gothic Revival in architecture were, for the most part, men of powerful character and great ability, who thoroughly deserved the great reputation and prosperity that they earned. As one reads their lives in detail, one forgets the unctuous phrases of their biographers in the story of remarkable careers made by men who were driven onward and upward by sheer enthusiasm.

Not many architects find a mention in that saga of worldly success, Samuel Smiles' *Self Help*, a typical product of the mild philanthropy of Victorian thought. But one of the most striking features in the story of the Gothic Revival is the way in which its chief practitioners rose to fame at express speed when everything appeared to be against them. For purposes of comparison I will take the following ten men as typical of their time : Sir Charles Barry (1795–1860), Sir Gilbert Scott (1811–78), A. W. N. Pugin the younger (1812–52), W. Butterfield (1814–1900), J. L. Pearson (1817–97), G. E. Street (1824–81), G. F. Bodley (1827–1907), W. Burges (1827–81), A. Waterhouse (1830–1905), and J. D. Sedding (1838–91). Of these men, Barry can hardly be called a convinced medievalist, in fact his own taste led him in the opposite direction, but his position as architect of the Houses of Parliament justifies his inclusion in this group, and thereby simplifies my task. (Norman Shaw, Philip Webb, and Sir Thomas Jackson, though born in the movement and connected with it, are more fittingly mentioned in the third section of this chapter.)

As with their predecessors of the Greek Revival, there is a close similarity in their parentage and upbringing. Every one of the ten men I have selected was of middle-class birth, and most of them were the sons of professional men, though the fathers of Barry and Waterhouse were engaged in commerce and Butterfield was the son of a chemist. Welby Pugin possessed the most picturesque parent of them all, a refugee from France who had fled to England to escape the Revolution, and who entered the service of John Nash in the capacity of a draughtsman. I have already mentioned his famous book on Gothic architecture, which certainly played a prominent part in bringing about the Revival.

Thus we hear very little in this period of the ' noble patron ', and there seem to be no important instances of poor boys of artisan birth springing to fame in the picturesque way that they did in the Italian or English Renaissance. On the other hand, few of these architects' fathers were rich men, so that their success was mainly due to their own genius and perseverance, as will appear later. So far as I can ascertain, none of them had any University education except Burges, and his case is not typical. He was intended to be an engineer, and began to attend lectures at King's College, London, with that object in view. But he changed his mind early, and was articled to an architect at the age of seventeen. Nowadays we have put the clock back in this respect, assuming that seventeen or eighteen is the very earliest age at which a boy

should abandon his general education for technical training. One result of a close study of the biographies of
famous Victorian architects is to raise a doubt as to whether
our modern policy of training is sound. Street, for example, who left school at fifteen, not only became a very
brilliant architect in after-life but wrote at least one book [1]
which is generally regarded as a classic. Barry, Welby
Pugin, and Scott were other men of the period whose
writings and letters bear the stamp of education and
culture, though all entered architecture at a very early age.
But one must not forget that every one of these four men
may fairly be regarded as a genius, and that it would be
absurd to plan our modern training on the assumption that
every student is a budding Pugin or a potential Street.

The Victorian period in architecture was the hey-day of
the pupilage system. No doubt seems to have been cast
upon its efficiency, no alternative method of training
appears to have been suggested. The pupil was bound to
his master for a period varying from two to five years and,
in London at any rate, he often lived in his master's own
house. The early age at which pupilage began, sometimes
at fourteen, explains and justifies this practice. One of
the most amusing passages in the life of Welby Pugin
describes how his father's pupils fared.[2] They had to
submit to an iron system of discipline organized and
administered by Mrs. Pugin. That good lady

' usually retired to rest at nine o'clock and rose in the morning
at four ; she therefore thought it salutary that the pupils
should commence their studies at six o'clock in winter as well
as in summer ; indeed, from the moment the mistress of the
house awoke no one was ever permitted to get any rest. First

[1] *Gothic Architecture in Spain.*
[2] B. Ferrey, *Recollections of A. N. W. Pugin* (1861), pp. 27–8.

Fig. 45. A. N. WELBY PUGIN

From the drawing by Lynch

came the loud ringing of the bell to rouse the maids, then in quick succession the bell to summon the pupils from their beds, and the final peal requiring their presence in the office by six o'clock. A pitiable sight indeed it was to see the shivering youths reluctantly creeping down in the midst of winter to waste their time by a sleepy attempt to work before breakfast. At half-past eight they were summoned to breakfast, and on entering the room Madame was seen already seated at the head of the table : on approaching it each youth made a profound bow, the neglect of which would quickly have been visited with reproof. A short prayer was then said, and breakfast despatched in constrained silence, after which each retired as he entered, making the same obeisance to the head of the table. During dinner the like silent system was enforced, similar obsequious respect paid, and then retiring, the pupils continued to work incessantly at the desk till eight o'clock. The only leisure afforded them was from that hour till ten, when they retired to rest.'

Naturally this Spartan control by ' The Belle of Islington', as she had been known in her girlhood, led to frequent rebellion, so that Pugin *père* was often called in to make peace. Yet, strange to say, his office was always filled with pupils, though he did practically no building and they were mainly employed in working on drawings for his books.

But one need not regard this instance (at the beginning of the nineteenth century) as in the least typical of the average architect's office in Victorian days. Whatever may have been the defects of the pupilage system as it then existed, it is quite certain that in the best offices it worked well, so that architects looked back with gratitude on the memory of the master to whom they had been articled. Butterfield's training was exceptional. At the age of seventeen he was bound to a builder in Horseferry Road, ' to learn the art, trade, or business of a builder,

A a

decorator and furnisher '. According to Professor Lethaby,[1] the term was five years, but the indenture was cancelled when only two had elapsed, and he was then articled to Inwood, architect of the new St. Pancras Church. It is startling to find that the designer of Keble College came from a ' Greek ' pupilage.

Office training was often supplemented by attendance at evening classes of some sort, and usually by sketching and travel. In 1856 Sir Charles Barry wrote an interesting memorandum on the reorganization of the Academy Schools, in which he suggested that students should not be admitted until they had taken a preliminary course of training at University College, King's College, the 'Schools of Design ', or some similar institution. This course was to include a large amount of science and mathematics, knowledge of construction and materials, drawing from the life and from casts, architectural drawing, perspective, and modelling. On admission to the Academy Schools the whole of the curriculum was to be devoted to ' fine art ', i. e. to advanced drawing and design, with special attention to colour and to the principles of composition. He also recommended that students should remain in the Schools for two years, and should be eligible to compete for the Silver Medal in the first year and for the Gold Medal in the second.[2] There is no indication whether the *preliminary* course was to be taken in the daytime or not, but Barry recommended that the Academy Schools should be open on Thursdays all day, and every evening from seven to nine. The system of visits and criticisms by eminent practising architects was inaugurated by Street in 1878.

[1] W. R. Lethaby, ' Philip Webb ', in *The Builder*, 1 May 1925.
[2] Rev. A. Barry, *Memoir of Sir Charles Barry* (1867), pp. 305–11.

It is clear, however, that the chief means by which an articled pupil supplemented his office-training was the sketching and measuring of such old buildings as lay within reach on Saturday afternoons. The successful architects of the period seem to have been tremendous workers from the beginning. They cannot have had time for athletic pursuits, even if they had the inclination, and many of them also devoted their summer holidays to sketching. For a young architect who has any real bent for his work this is no hardship, especially if he is sketching Gothic buildings, which always seem to me to have a freedom of fancy about them that makes sketching a pleasure rather than a task. But, however one regards this way of spending a holiday, it certainly helped to make the careers of more than one of the Gothic Revivalists. Their enthusiasm for medieval architecture was such a consuming passion with them that the discovery of some fresh detail in a village church was far more satisfying than a big score at cricket. Nor was there any pedantry or posing in this attitude : architecture was their hobby as well as their livelihood, and that, I think, was one cause of their success. So we find that Street and his lawyer-brother went year after year in the summer on long walk-ing-tours over England, sometimes trudging thirty miles a day with their knapsacks on their backs, both sketching everything of interest that they passed. The younger Pugin, who had accompanied his father to Paris before he was fifteen, went on a measuring tour to Rochester with Ferrey a few months later, made a complete set of drawings of the Castle, then a restoration, and actually contemplated the preparation and publication of a mono-graph on military architecture. Yet in this very year his mother complains that he has ' had the skin of his nose twice torn off ' in a pillow-fight with his father's articled pupils.

Except the case of Welby Pugin's tours in France with his father, I can find no proof that the other architects with whom I am concerned travelled abroad during their period of pupilage. Burges and Waterhouse both visited Italy, France, and Germany before they commenced practice and before they were twenty-three. But the most interesting record of foreign travel occurs in the life of Sir Charles Barry, who characteristically decided to spend the whole of a small legacy from his father on that object, and set out, at twenty-two years of age, in 1817. Europe was now open to travellers, but further east he encountered some adventures. At first his attention was confined to classical and Renaissance architecture and in Rouen, of all places, he ignored all the medieval buildings. But before his long tour was ended he condescended to notice Gothic too. After nine months in France and Italy, he proceeded to Athens and Constantinople, spending a fortnight in each. In Athens he met one ' Mr. Baillie ', evidently a ' noble patron ' in all but the title, who engaged him as a companion to travel through the Near East for a salary of £200 a year plus all expenses, Mr. Baillie retaining all the sketches done by Barry in the course of their travels ! As Barry had exhibited several drawings at the Royal Academy years before this, and as he handed over some 500 sketches to his generous benefactor at the conclusion of their nine months' trip, Mr. Baillie appears to have driven a highly successful bargain with the young architect. They journeyed up the Nile as far as the Second Cataract, no mean achievement a century ago. Barry was more impressed by the ruins of Egyptian temples and tombs than by anything else that he saw on this tour.

Then they crossed the desert to Gaza, visited Palestine and Syria, and had an exciting escape from Palmyra, where Mr. Baillie's monocle was thought by hostile Arabs to be a treasure-seeker's talisman. In Syria they parted company ; Barry went on to Sicily and thence to Rome, where he found himself quite a lion after his adventures in the mysterious East. His work at Vicenza and elsewhere in Italy followed the stereotyped lines of the eighteenth century. In all, his tour abroad lasted more than three years.

Street's travels can hardly be regarded as part of his student-training, except in the sense that he, like most other ' Eminent Victorians ', never ceased to be a student. His first journey, made in 1850 when he was twenty-six, is characteristic of the man. He did Paris, Chartres, Amiens, Rouen, Caen, and Alençon in ten days, sketching hard the whole time. In the following year he toured the chief centres of Belgium and Germany in three weeks. After that, a foreign holiday became an annual event. He was only twenty-nine when his book on *Brick and Marble Architecture in North Italy* appeared, the fruits of a single summer holiday and of his first visit to Italy. This feat appears still more prodigious when one knows that he cut the blocks for his numerous illustrations with his own hand, and that all this work was done abreast of a busy and increasing practice. His great book on *Gothic Architecture in Spain*, a learned yet interesting work, resulted from three consecutive summer holidays in that country in 1861–3. It is surprising to learn that the elaborate plans of cathedrals that it contains were almost all obtained by ' stepping ' the measurements. His son states that they are reasonably accurate in spite of this.[1] He did most

[1] *Life of G. E. Street*, by A. E. Street (1888), pp. 125, &c.

of his sketches standing, took no notice whatever of cold weather, and never carried an india-rubber. In 1866, when he was preparing his designs for the Law Courts competition, he decided to visit some of the chief buildings of that type abroad. In fourteen days he and his wife rushed round Munich, Vienna, Prague, Dresden, Berlin, and other places, spending seven nights in the train. Mrs. Street was as indefatigable as her husband on these journeys, and saw to it that his daily output of sketches was maintained, if he showed any signs of slackening. But the strain of these ' holidays ' seems to have contributed to her premature death, and, when he married again, his second wife only survived two months, a jaunt to Rome with Street having proved too much for her vitality.

In previous chapters we have seen a procession of architects journeying to Rome, Brunelleschi at their head, to make careful measured drawings from fragments of ' the antique '. Some of them went a stage further, studying not only details of construction but the principles of planning and composition as exemplified in the monumental buildings of the Roman Empire. But after four hundred years there came a change, and the Gothic Revivalists concentrated on picturesque ' bits ' from all parts of Western Europe, sketching rather than measuring. While we must admit that sketching is infinitely more amusing than measuring, especially to an overwrought practising architect on a brief holiday, the thousands of miscellaneous details of carving and ornament that came over to England so freely in the early Victorian period were not an unmixed blessing. Most of the florid and exotic ornament that still survives on the jerry-built villas of the speculative builder, and that not long ago formed the staple of the cast-iron merchant's catalogue, is a sorry caricature from sketches made by Ruskin, Street, and other great draughts-men of the Gothic Revival. Nowadays our taste has become more severe, and rigid economy to some extent limits us in these matters, so that we may still rejoice that the Pugin Studentship of the R.I.B.A. remains to encourage the free sketching of medieval architecture and to per-petuate the name of the great man who broke the Palladian spell.

The architects of the Gothic Revival, though they com-menced practice early, mostly served as assistants in some other office after completing their term of articles. Scott spent some months with a large firm of builders and there-by acquired much useful first-hand knowledge of iron and concrete construction, then in its infancy. In later years he and his partner Moffatt had a huge staff of assistants at their office in Kennington, engaged on the mass-pro-duction of plans for some fifty workhouses. Barry also had a large staff, who formed a ' Barry Club ' as a tribute to their master's reputation. Street must have been a difficult man for an assistant to please, for he worked phenomenally fast himself and disliked to hand over any design, even for details, to subordinates.

Many of the chief architects of the Revival were launched in practice before they were twenty-five, some of them— like Waterhouse—with influential friends to back them, but the majority relying solely on their ambition and ability. A recent writer [1] has made fun of Scott's enter-prising method of obtaining work in his early days, but there was nothing unprofessional in it. In 1834, when his father's death threw him entirely upon his own resources at the age of twenty-three, alterations in the Poor Laws indicated that a large number of workhouses would shortly

[1] H. S. Goodhart-Rendel, *op. cit.*, p. 330.

be required. He thereupon wrote ' a kind of circular ' to every friend of his father's he could think of, ' begging their patronage ', and for weeks together almost lived on horseback, ' canvassing newly formed unions ' for the appointment as architect. Forward manners perhaps, but not more so than we have met ever since the days of Dinocrates, and in this case forced upon the poor parson's son by hard necessity. Sir Gilbert Scott was a great man, thoroughly deserving the success that is sometimes made to look like a crime. Rather later than his workhouse-period, Street came to him as an assistant, and Scott allowed him to commence practice on his own account while still serving in that capacity, until he was firmly established.

The Gothic Revival was contemporaneous with a series of great architectural competitions, of which the first, most important, and most interesting was for the Houses of Parliament, or, more correctly, the Palace of Westminster, in 1835. On the night of October 16 in the previous year, as Barry was returning from Brighton by coach, ' a red glare on the London side of the horizon showed that a great fire had begun '. It was the Houses of Parliament.

' No sooner had the coach reached the office than he hurried to the spot and remained there all night. . . . The thought of this great opportunity, and the conceptions of designs for the future, mingled in Mr. Barry's mind, as in the minds of many other spectators, with those more obviously suggested by the spectacle itself.' [1]

The conditions of competition were announced in the following June. The style was to be ' Gothic or Eliza-bethan ' and designs were to be sent in without any ' formal estimate ' ; a decision was to be made before 20 January

---

[1] Rev. A. Barry, *op. cit.*, pp. 145–6.

FIG. 46. SIR GILBERT SCOTT

From the drawing by Richmond in the National Portrait Gallery

1836 ; four premiums of £500 each were offered ; and the architect placed first was to carry out the work, unless ' some grave cause to the contrary should be discovered ', in which case he was to receive an additional premium of £1,000.

Only five months were available for making this enormous and complicated design, for drawings had to be sent in by 20 November. Barry worked desperately throughout the intervening period, only allowing himself four or five hours for sleep. There were ninety-seven competitors. The award was published on the last day of February, 1836, and Barry proved to be the winner. Thus his fortune was made when he was only just over forty years of age, but from that moment a long line of troubles made their appearance. In their report the Commissioners confessed that in the then imperfect state of knowledge of heating and ventilation they had confined their attention mainly to the appearance of the elevation and to the convenience and dignity of the planning. Nor had cost been considered, the Commission admitting that the building would probably be expensive. Eventually Barry, in conjunction with officials of the Board of Works, estimated the cost at £800,000, excluding the cost of furniture and fittings. (The final cost, including all fees, was about £2,000,000, plus about £500,000 for furniture and fittings.) Meanwhile, three weeks after the announcement of the award, the designs were publicly exhibited. Then came a storm of protest in the Press ; firstly because the design was Gothic ; secondly because the Commissioners were amateurs, and Sir E. Cust, the chief Commissioner, was said to be partial to Barry, who was openly described as ' his tool '. The unsuccessful competitors held a protest meeting, and, though to the honour of their profession there was opposition, succeeded in petitioning Parliament to set aside the award. Barry, much to his credit, remained silent throughout this undignified affair, and had the satisfaction of seeing the whole agitation die down, so that the foundation-stone of the huge building was quietly and informally laid by his wife in 1840. Subsequent incidents connected with this commission will be mentioned later.

The next great public competition in England was for the Government Offices in Whitehall, which took place in 1856 in two stages. From the 219 competitors in the first stage, seventeen were selected for the final stage and premiated. Street, one of the latter, submitted with his designs a pamphlet in defence of Gothic. Sir Gilbert Scott, who was eventually successful, modestly described his own drawings as ' probably the best ever sent in to a competition '. But there was a stormy interlude before his position was secure. When the award was published, Scott was placed third for the Foreign Office block and nowhere for the War Office block. Rumours of intrigue behind the scenes led to a meeting between three of the chief competitors. The aid of the R.I.B.A. was involved, and at last Parliament was induced to appoint a Select Committee, which elicited the interesting fact that the award did not represent the real opinion of the assessors. It appeared that Scott's designs for both blocks had been placed second by the assessors, and as they could not agree that any one else deserved to be first in both cases, he was at last appointed in 1858. Then came a complete change in the requirements for the buildings and a tremendous ' Battle of the Styles ', which seriously shook the Mother of Parliaments. Plans and models were twice exhibited in the tea-room of the House of Commons : angry letters poured into the newspapers. Finally Scott substituted the present Italian Renaissance design for his previous Gothic scheme, and in 1861, five years after the competition took place, his revised plans were approved. The whole sordid tale is related at length in his own *Recollections*.

The third great government competition of the mid-nineteenth century, for the Law Courts in 1866, provides an equally unsatisfactory story. In this case only six architects were originally invited to compete, a premium of £800 being paid to each competitor, but afterwards six more names were added, and, of these twelve, eleven actually submitted designs. The award was made by five laymen and two professional assessors. In July 1867 they published their decision, placing Edmund Barry (son of Sir Charles) first for planning and Street for elevation, a judgement which was not only manifestly absurd but which contained the seeds of bitter strife. There seems to have been some preliminary promise that planning would be regarded as the controlling factor, but in the end Street was employed without Barry and the contract (for some £680,000) was signed in 1874. The facts are singularly obscure, and after reading different accounts of the affair one is quite bewildered as to the rights and wrongs of this very perplexing case. But at all events it is clear enough that such great competitions (one of which may make its winner rich and famous for life) were unsatisfactorily organized in mid-Victorian days. The conditions were too loosely drawn, the assessor's decision was not regarded as final and binding, and there were far too many loopholes for intrigue, wirepulling, and consequent discontent—often quite justifiable—on the part of unsuccessful competitors.

Other important competitions of the period, fortunately not marred by the bitterness that distinguished the three just mentioned, were those for Lille Cathedral, 1855 (won by Clutton and Burges but never built) ; the Crimean Memorial at Constantinople (won by Burges, but handed over to Street) ; St. Nicholas' at Hamburg, the Rathhaus at Hamburg, the Albert Memorial, Edinburgh Cathedral, and St. Pancras Hotel (all won by Sir Gilbert Scott) ; the Reform Club and the Travellers' Club (both won by Sir Charles Barry); and Truro Cathedral (won by Pearson). But plums like these did not drop freely into the mouths of the Victorian giants. Barry, for instance, was unsuccessful in at least eight competitions in his early days, and in one case (the Pitt Press at Cambridge) he submitted four alternative designs.

Architects like Street, Scott, and Waterhouse, in spite of their enthusiasms, were men of the world, capable of dealing successfully with clients of all types ; indeed it was said of Waterhouse that his smile was worth ten thousand a year to him, which must have been an appreciable fraction of his income. But Welby Pugin, who spent his later years ' under restraint ', was always something of a crank, liable at any time to throw up a good commission in a tiff. On one occasion he was asked to design a church, which had to be very large to serve a populous neighbourhood, very handsome to outrival the adjoining sanctuary of another faith, and very cheap in view of scanty funds. He replied at once to the prelate who had commissioned him :

' My dear Lord, Say *thirty shillings* more, and have a tower and spire at once. A. W. P.'

Architectural practice in the mid-Victorian period included a prodigious number of new Gothic churches which, according to the fashion of the moment, had to be ' Early

Pointed ' or ' Middle Pointed ' French or Italian, even ' English ' in the last resort. This movement was accompanied by a zealous crusade, fostered by the Ecclesiological Society, for restoration of medieval buildings all over the country, and ' restoration ' finally became so sweeping and drastic that the very word itself assumed the dignity of inverted commas, and the Society for the Protection of Ancient Buildings came to be founded in 1877 as a protest against the excessive zeal of Sir Gilbert Scott and other famous practitioners. The ' Anti-scrape ', as it is commonly called, is a society that has done work of untold value in preserving not only great buildings but humble cottages, rustic bridges, simple church fittings and so on, from the hands of those who like to make every detail of a building conform to a theory and who would sweep away everything that is not representative of their pet ' period '. There is no doubt that Scott's restorations often went too far in this direction, and that he gloried in making an old cathedral neat and bright and slippery within, eliminating much that was mysterious and picturesque in the process. But all his work was not of this kind : his treatment of the chapter-house at Westminster, for example, was carried out with immense care, and, if Birmingham metalwork and modern tiles are too evident in some of his churches, we must remember that he found many of these buildings in a lamentable state and that he saved them from collapse.

Moreover, the Gothic revivalists, inspired by Barry and Welby Pugin's work at the Houses of Parliament, brought about a real revival of craftsmanship, with Ruskin as their prophet and mentor. From Ruskin and Pugin it is not a far cry to Morris and Webb, founders of the Arts and Crafts Movement and the ' Domestic Revival ' which followed in the seventies. Town-planning and garden-design suffered a distinct set-back during the period. Ruskin was too busy interpreting the carving at St. Mark's to turn the full force of his invective on to the hideous streets that were being run up everywhere by industrial profiteers, and few architects seem to have concerned themselves with civic amenities, the Albert Memorial representing their highest flight in that direction. The one notable exception was Barry, who not only laid out a number of formal gardens in the Italian manner, but also prepared notable schemes for the replanning of Westminster, Whitehall, and the surrounding areas. Naturally, perhaps, architects do not appear to have concerned themselves at that time with the stage, and Welby Pugin is the only one whom we hear of in this connexion. In 1831 he was commissioned to design the medieval setting for the new opera of 'Kenilworth', and this so whetted his appetite for the footlights that he converted the first floor of his father's house in Great Russell Street into a model theatre, with all the mechanical equipment in miniature. Excepting the elder Pugin's designs for confectionery on the royal table at Windsor, his son's model theatre, more than anything else in Gothic Revival days, recalls the versatility of the Renaissance architects in Italy. Barry in boyhood certainly built a ' grotto ' in his bedroom, and Street at first held that an architect should be able to decorate his buildings with painting and sculpture. But prosperity cured him of this Ruskinian attitude, and we find few Admirable Crichtons among these ' Eminent Victorians '.

They were architects pure and simple, for the most part indulging in preaching of one sort and another as a recreation. Welby Pugin certainly practised what he preached, for before he was twenty-three he bought some land near Salisbury, and on it built himself a ' medieval ' house,

' St. Marie's Grange ', at a cost of £2,000. Eight years later he erected a much larger house near Ramsgate, and adjoining it a church on which he is said to have spent £15,000. Here, although he was married, he lived a life approaching as nearly as possible to his monastic ideal, entering his private chapel each morning at precisely six o'clock, saying morning prayers at half-past seven in a cassock and surplice, singing Compline there at ten in the evening, and concluding a very long day of professional work with an hour's reading of historical and theological works before retiring to bed. Burges also preached and practised medievalism ; his bachelor home was furnished to suit his taste, and he had a genuine love for all the crafts. But it is in his drawings that his bent is most clearly manifest. He affected the thirteenth-century style of Villard d'Honnecourt (see pp. 93–5), produced a great parchment ' sketch-book ' on the same lines, and once sent in for the Lille competition a set of drawings so archaic in character that the judges ' wondered at first whether some ancient drawings had not been discovered '.[1] But these two men were extremists. Compared with them, Scott and Street were worldlings, confining their propaganda to pamphlets or lectures, and occasionally indulging in a theological breakfast with Gladstone.

But all of them were tremendous workers. The stories of their energy are appalling. The instances that I have already cited of their hectic Continental tours and their furious efforts in commencing practice are matched by their continued activity after they had become famous and prosperous. They never slowed down. Barry often rose at 4 or 5 a. m., never later than 6, and normally worked till 11 or 12 at night. Pugin wrote most of his letters in the

---

[1] W. R. Lethaby, ' Philip Webb ', in *The Builder*, 1 May 1925.

railway-train, and often continued his drawing during tea, with a board propped up against the table. One day he rushed down to receive instructions for altering a large house near Bournemouth, made his first inspection of the existing building during the afternoon, and submitted sketch designs to his client after dinner the same day. On another occasion he produced two alternative designs for a stained-glass window within a quarter of an hour.[1] He broke down before he was forty, and his medical man said that he had done ' a hundred years work ' in his lifetime. Street habitually dealt with his correspondence before breakfast, beginning at 7.30 a. m., then put in a full working day, and spent 3 or 4 hours every evening at his drawing-board. But the most illuminating sidelight of all upon Victorian success is furnished by the story often related of Sir Gilbert Scott at the height of his immense practice, showing that his ' jobs ' were almost too numerous to remember. He left London by train one morning at six ; when his staff dawdled into the office a few hours later they found a telegram from him at a Midland station asking briefly, ' Why am I here ? ' (This may not be true, but in 1919 I asked a distinguished architect how many War Memorials he then had in hand. He replied that he could not remember, but that there was a list of them pinned up on his office wall.) On another occasion Scott paused to admire a church, and asked for the architect's name. ' Sir Gilbert Scott ', was the laconic reply.[2] It is not surprising to learn that he left a fortune of £120,000.

From such instances of devastating activity one naturally infers that these men produced vast quantities of drawings, often largely assigned to assistants but in other cases done

[1] B. Ferrey, *Recollections of A. W. N. Pugin,* pp. 189, 191.
[2] Lethaby, *op. cit.*

by the master himself. Thus, of 8,000 or 9,000 original drawings prepared for the Palace of Westminster, Barry did ' a large portion ' with his own hand ;[1] and Street disliked handing any design over to a subordinate. Drawings by the chief architects of the period are preserved in the R.I.B.A. Library. For the most part they display careful and skilful draughtsmanship with a rather fine line, wash being sometimes used. Street, though himself a facile draughtsman, distrusted 'draughtsmanship ' as such. He held that every architect should do his own perspectives. He drew his full-size details of mouldings direct in ink, and was able to ' set up ' an elaborate perspective for the Academy in a few hours. The competition designs for the Law Courts by Street and Scott may be cited as typical examples. A visit to the Diploma Gallery of the Royal Academy, however, leaves one with rather mixed feelings about the standard of Victorian design.

Though an architect's remuneration had now been stabilized at the figure of 5 per cent. on the cost of a building, there are several cases where Government offices declined to accept this standard. Nearly fifty pages of Sir Charles Barry's biography are devoted to a sordid dispute about his fees for the Palace of Westminster. The correspondence is long and involved, but it appears that for many years he received no money whatever, and eventually accepted 3 per cent. for his architectural work plus 1 per cent. for quantities.[2] For the Law Courts, Street was paid ' considerably under the recognized fee '. Evidently the Royal Institute of British Architects, in spite of its rapid growth, was not then powerful enough to impose its standard of professional charges upon the Government.

[1] Rev. A. Barry, *op. cit.*, p. 194.
[2] *Ibid.*, pp. 205–27, 369–404.

B b

Barry's disputes about fees at Westminster were complicated by the appearance of 'specialists', in the shape of the civil engineer who supervised the construction of the river-wall, scientists who advised on the selection of stone, a medical man who was introduced to design the whole system of warming and ventilation, the ubiquitous Lord Grimthorpe of St. Alban's fame (then plain Mr. Denison) who undertook to design Big Ben and the clock, and lastly a Fine Arts Commission on which the architect had no place. The medical man's plans subsequently proved quite impracticable and very expensive, so that he was afterwards dismissed ; the Fine Arts Commission later decided to work with the architect ; and in the end the whole vast undertaking adjusted itself. But this is the first instance we have yet encountered of the difficulty caused in modern building operations by their complexity, which involves the employment of many experts besides the architect himself, and thus raises the whole question of his status.

A natural corollary of the Gothic Revival in architecture was a demand for builders and craftsmen who were competent to reproduce medieval forms, even to the extent of producing the effect of medieval workmanship in such details as the texture of stone and the glaze on the surface of encaustic tiles. Such workmen did not exist when Barry and Pugin were making their drawings for the Houses of Parliament ; in fact the previous buildings of the Gothic Revival were chiefly deficient in this quality of craftsmanship. It therefore became necessary for a school to be formed at Westminster, where workers in all the building crafts could be instructed with the aid of casts and specimens of medieval craftsmanship, under the direct supervision of the architects. We hear of similar cases, such as Pugin's new churches, or other men's restoration-work, where an architect gradually trained a builder and craftsmen to work in his way, and then contrived to employ them as far as possible on all his buildings. This personal relation between architect and builder, so difficult of achievement under the modern competitive system, undoubtedly produces good work. But relations were not invariably harmonious in the past. There was a great strike at the Law Courts in 1877 which lasted over seven months. The contractors imported hundreds of workmen from Germany, Italy, Canada, and the United States, but for safety's sake had to house them on the site !

Outside their ordinary professional duties, many of the chief architects of the period—notably Street and Scott —found time to write books, dealing mainly with Gothic architecture and written either as propaganda or from an archaeological standpoint. Some of these books were originally given as Academy lectures. The year 1843 saw the publication of the *The Builder*, the first weekly journal devoted to architecture. Previously the *Gentleman's Magazine* had furnished almost the only forum in which architecture and the other fine arts could be discussed. On p. 344 mention was made of the foundation of the R.I.B.A. in 1834 and of its Royal Charter in 1837. In 1836 its first volume of *Transactions* appeared, in 1837 a register of assistants seeking employment was opened, and the perennial problem of ' Dry Rot ' formed the subject of an evening's discussion ; in 1838 the eternal question of regulating architectural competitions raised its head ; and in 1859 the Institute moved from Grosvenor Street to its present handsome quarters in the heart of West End tailordom. Here it has gradually collected a magnificent library, worthy of being housed in fireproof premises.   In 1862 the first ' Voluntary Architectural Examination ' was held.   The institution of the compulsory examination for Associateship followed in 1882, and a subsequent attempt to close the profession in 1891, which rent the Institute from top to bottom, but especially at the top, is referred to on p. 379.   The R.I.B.A., as I have already noted, was severely shaken by the quarrels between Gothic revivalists and their opponents.   When in 1874 the R.I.B.A. Gold Medal was offered to Ruskin, possibly as a form of soothing syrup, he declined it and utilized the occasion for a brief homily to architects in general.   Meanwhile the Architectural Association was founded, in 1847, and London University had entered the field of architectural education, but not yet with a full-time course.

.   .   .   .   .   .

For the sake of clearness, I have considered the complicated architectural history of the nineteenth century in England under the convenient heads of the 'Greek Revival' and the ' Gothic Revival ', recognizing nevertheless that the two movements ran for a time concurrently, and that such a classification involves the disregarding of many cross-currents.   So, as I reach the last phase of the nineteenth century, which may be shortly styled the ' Domestic Revival ', it is necessary to explain that my brief survey of that period is intended to draw attention to its outstanding characteristics rather than to deal with a host of individual architects.   Moreover, as this book is a *history* of the architect's progress, it seems desirable to exclude from its scope any mention of men still living.

From 1870 to 1900 churches were mainly built in the Gothic style and great public buildings in various forms of revived Renaissance.   But undoubtedly the feature of those years was the awakening of interest in domestic architecture. During the ' revival ' periods architects had progressed very little in that direction ; the ' Battle of the Styles ' had tended to divert public and professional attention from the branch of architecture that concerns the community most intimately—the building of dwelling-houses. Houses were built, of course, throughout that time, but in their design there is little evidence of any attempt to apply artistic treatment to the normal requirements of everyday life.

The architects mainly concerned in this remarkable campaign were George Devey (1820–86), Philip Webb (1830–1915), R. Norman Shaw (1831–1912), W. E. Nesfield (1835–88), and Sir Ernest George (1839–1922). With Philip Webb in the first stages of the movement were associated two men—William Morris (1834–96) and W. A. S. Benson (1854–1924)—both of whom were trained as architects but eventually turned to the crafts.[1] Another great architect contemporary with this group was Sir Thomas Graham Jackson (1835–1924) who, though he carried out comparatively little domestic work, shared many of their enthusiasms and did a great deal by his writings to further their views. Ernest Newton (1856–1922) was a worthy successor of his master Norman Shaw.

The more one reads of Webb and Morris, of the ' Anti-Scrape ' and the ' Arts and Crafts ', the more evident it becomes that this domestic revival in architecture had its birth in the teaching of Ruskin and in the Gothic Revival. It is a far cry from the churches of Street and Butterfield

[1] It is not generally known that Mr. Thomas Hardy was trained as an architect. Born in 1840, he was articled in Dorchester in 1856, came to London as an assistant in 1862, won the R.I.B.A. Essay Medal and the A.A. Design Medal in 1863, and turned to literature finally about 1867.

to the garden cities and country houses that foreign critics for twenty years have regarded as our most successful efforts in modern architecture, yet the steps from one to the other are clearly marked, and it is quite possible to trace a genealogical tree from Pugin to Lutyens.

It was always a defect of the Gothic Revival that so much attention was given to churches and so little to domestic buildings and civic amenities, with the result that the most hideous streets and towns born of industrialism were erected just when Ruskin's influence was at its height. Another defect lay in the artificial spirit behind the whole movement, so that the style of a building came to be dictated by the fashion of the moment—as often as not an exotic fashion—and all its details were carefully copied from the appropriate text-book, perhaps in ' Early French ' or ' Mid-Venetian ' Gothic. Hence, although many of the domestic designs of young revolutionaries like Devey, Webb, and Nesfield included Renaissance elements before 1860, and though the ' Anti-Scrape ' was founded in 1877 as a protest against excessive restoration by Sir Gilbert Scott, it is my belief that ' the Morris group ' were carrying into practical effect the spirit of Ruskin's teaching more consistently than the leaders of the Gothic Revival, who were becoming more and more engrossed in the ' correct ' reproduction of historical styles.

The origin of the ' Domestic Revival ' is commonly assigned to the friendship between Philip Webb and William Morris. Webb, then about twenty-six years of age, was chief or only assistant to Street at the latter's office in Oxford when Morris became an articled pupil there in 1856. Morris had previously drunk deeply of Ruskin's teaching at Oxford, and Webb had already made a sketching-tour in France with Burne-Jones, so that the famous

' group ' that later established the trading firm of ' Morris & Co., Ltd. ' was almost in being. A year of pupilage was enough for Morris, who was the fortunate possessor of a private income of £1,000 a year, together with an exuberant dower of ideas and ideals, and he settled down with Burne-Jones in Red Lion Square to practise designing, painting, and poetry. In 1858 he and Webb travelled in France and on their return Webb ' decided to leave Street, because he saw that modern medievalism was an open contradiction. He resolved to try whether it was not possible to make the buildings of our own day pleasant without pretence of style '.[1]

During their French tour Morris had discussed with Webb a project of building a house to embody their new ideas, and in 1859 Webb started practice on his own account by planning the famous ' Red House ' for Morris near Bexley in Kent. The craftsmanship and decorations of this building show the aims they had already formed, and in 1861 Morris, Webb, Burne-Jones, Rossetti, Madox Brown and two others founded the firm of Morris & Co., ' whose products were to inaugurate a renaissance as well as a revolution in domestic design '.[2]

Norman Shaw entered the office of William Burn at the age of sixteen, and soon afterwards became a student at the Academy Schools. In 1854, at the age of twenty-three, he was awarded the R.A. Gold Medal, and left Burn for a lengthy tour abroad. On his return the Council of the R.A. requested him to publish his drawings, which subsequently appeared as *Architectural Sketches from the Continent* in 1858. He spent a further seven years as assistant, first with Salvin and later with Street, before

---

[1] W. R. Lethaby, ' Philip Webb, in *The Builder* (1925), p. 224.
[2] Holbrook Jackson, *William Morris* (1926), p. 30.

he set up in practice on his own account, sharing rooms but not actually working in partnership with Nesfield, a man four years his junior whom he had met in Burn's office and then again in Salvin's. Nesfield's early career closely resembles Shaw's. He too was articled to Burn at sixteen, and five years later travelled extensively abroad, though apparently not as a prizeman. He too published a book, *Architectural Sketches from France and Italy*, in 1862. But he commenced practice at twenty-four, after only eight years' study, whereas Shaw was not in a position to do so until he was thirty-two. Both had successful careers, but Nesfield's was cut short at a comparatively early age, while Norman Shaw became unquestionably the greatest architect of his day at the end of the century.

' It is largely owing to him that there is now a distinct tendency to approach Architecture as the art of Building rather than as the art of Designing, and the study of old work as one of methods and expressions which are for all time, rather than as a means of learning a language of forms proper only to their period.' [1]

George Devey, born many years earlier than any of the three architects mentioned, was designing houses with Dutch gables and Renaissance details in the fifties, and his work has much in common with that of Webb, Shaw, and Nesfield, but he does not appear to have had any close connexion with the ' Morris group ' and his large country-house practice seems to have been built up on independent lines. Sir Ernest George, a born artist and a really great domestic architect, forms the link between the Gothic Revival and the best modern school of domestic design, for in his office were trained a surprising number of the chief leaders of that school to-day, including Sir Edwin

[1] Anonymous memoir in *Encyclopaedia Britannica*.

Lutyens, Sir Herbert Baker, and Mr. Guy Dawber. He was over sixty years of age and an eminent man when I served for a short time as one of his assistants in 1902, but one could not fail to be struck by his modesty, his energy, and the meticulous care that he took in drawing his beautiful half-inch details in brown ink. W. A. S. Benson was, like Morris, a man of some means who turned to architecture after Oxford, was articled to Basil Champneys, then met Morris and forsook architecture to devote himself to the crafts. When he founded a business in 1880 to manufacture beautiful things for everyday use, he was only repeating an experiment made unsuccessfully by Welby Pugin long before, and carrying out the ideas of Ruskin and Morris. Benson also became chairman of Morris & Co. in 1896, and took a chief part in the foundation of the Arts and Crafts Exhibition Society in 1886. Another characteristic product of this movement was the Art-workers' Guild, founded in 1884. Sir Thomas Jackson, who at one time held the office of Master of that guild, was not a Gothic revivalist nor even a domestic revivalist, but all through his long and brilliant career he fostered the theory, nowadays maintained by Professor Lethaby and his disciples, that architecture at its best is an affair of inspired building rather than of formal design.

The half dozen men who rescued English domestic architecture from mediocrity or worse, and brought it by 1900 or so to a point where it became the cynosure of architects all over the world, were animated by enthusiasms as warm as those which had inspired Brunelleschi or Pugin. Derived direct from Ruskin, their gospel was based upon sound craftsmanship, honest building, and the introduction of good design into every material accessory of modern life. But it had another merit that Ruskin's

teaching generally lacked. Though he was a fervent lover
of Nature, of clouds and mountains, flowers and trees, he
showed less enthusiasm for English architecture, great and
small. His heart had been stolen by Venice and France.
It was left for Morris and Webb to discover the charm of
the English village, with its humble little cottages nestling
in folds of the downs and merging so perfectly into the
landscape that they seem a part of Nature herself. Thus
the work of the ' domestic revivalists ', though a normal
corollary of the Gothic Revival, was ' Gothic in principle
rather than in style '.[1] They concentrated on substance
as well as form, making a study of traditional craftsmanship in the various parts of England where they were
called upon to erect new buildings, and rising to defend
from spoliation even such unconsidered trifles as old barns.
This quality of enthusiasm, while on the one hand it led
' Morris & Co.' to carry on their early business meetings
' like a picnic ',[2] was on the other hand the foundation of
everything that has been admirable in modern English
domestic architecture for the last fifty years, for it was
enthusiasm tempered with common sense. It created the
first ' garden city ' at Bedford Park ; it led to Port Sun-
light, Bournville, Letchworth, and the Hampstead Garden
Suburb. It must have inspired Mr. Raymond Unwin to
formulate the principles of town-planning and Miss Jekyll
to revive the country garden ; and it may conceivably
have set the ' Scapa ' Society on its praiseworthy crusade.
This enthusiasm seldom led to violent conflict, if we except
the heated encounters between Gothic revivalists and
leaders of the ' Anti-scrape ', but it infused into the leaders
of the movement that tremendous energy which we have

[1] C. Marriott, *Modern English Architecture* (1924), p. 162.
[2] Lethaby, *op. cit.*, p. 382.

found again and again in this book among the great masters
of architecture. It was not greed of gold nor even ambition that sent Sir Ernest George out sketching before
breakfast, and inspired Sir Thomas Jackson, when nearly
seventy years of age, to commence the seven volumes in
which he traced the history of architecture from Roman
times ; for both these men had become famous already.
And it was as artists and enthusiasts that Shaw, Jackson,
Webb, and many other distinguished architects, some still
living, raised a public protest in 1891 against an attempt to
make architecture into a close profession like law or
medicine.[1]

The circumstances of their birth and training have
already been briefly noted ; it appears that there was
little variation from conditions prevailing during the Gothic
Revival. The pupilage-system still held the field. In his
preface to his history of Byzantine and Romanesque
Architecture, the first part of the series just mentioned,
Sir Thomas Jackson says that the idea of this work origin-
ated in his informal talks at his own house to his pupils.
Professor Lethaby tells us that Norman Shaw was in the
habit of handing over occasional small commissions to
those of his staff who were about to commence practice.[2]
In fact the relations between master and pupil were admirable in the best offices. But as regards the other side of
the picture, the work done by clever ' ghosts ' for architects of a very different type, the reader should refer to
Professor Prior's bitter and very saddening essay,[3] from
which I am reluctant to quote. Every calling has its

[1] See *Architecture : a Profession or an Art*, edited by R. Norman
Shaw and T. G. Jackson. (London, 1892.)

[2] Lethaby, *op. cit.*, p. 724.

[3] E. S. Prior, *The ' Profession ' and its Ghosts*, in Shaw and Jackson,
op. cit., p. 97.

seamy side, and there is no reason why the most sordid aspect of architecture should be exposed here. Mention of ' ghosts ' suggests architectural competitions, but the chief domestic architects of the late nineteenth century took little part in these. They were mainly but not exclusively engaged in the building of houses large and small. In spite of New Scotland Yard and the Piccadilly Hotel, it is as a domestic architect that Norman Shaw made his reputation. Such notable men as Bentley (a Gothic revivalist at heart), Hare, Belcher, Collcutt, and Stokes are not mentioned in this brief study because their work mainly falls outside the movement with which we are here concerned.

BIBLIOGRAPHY

(Abbreviations : *A.R.* = ' Architectural Review ' ; *S.P.* = ' R.I.B.A. Sessional Paper ' ; *J.* = ' R.I.B.A. Journal.')

(*a*) COLLECTIONS.

Adams, M. B. ' Architects from George IV to George V ' (*J.*1912).
Budden, L. B. ' The Greek Revival in England ' (*J.* 1909).
Eastlake, C. L. *A History of the Gothic Revival* (1872).
Goodhart-Rendel, H. S. ' English Gothic Architecture of the Nineteenth Century ' (*S.P.* 1924).
Gotch, J. A. ' The First Half-century of the R.I.B.A. ' (*S.P.* 1922).
Marriott, C. *Modern English Architecture*. (See Chapter VIII, ' The Gothic Revival ', 1924.)
Statham, H. H., article on ' Modern Architecture ', in *Encyclopaedia Britannica*.
Wood, A. ' The Greek Revival in England ', in *Architectural Association Notes* (1897).
      (The lives of nearly all the chief architects (deceased) of the nineteenth century are given in the *Dictionary of National Biography*, and many of them in the *Encyclopaedia Britannica*, but the fullest biographical notices for the first part of the century are to be found in the *Dictionary of the Architectural Publication Society*.)

(*b*) MONOGRAPHS.

Barry, Sir Charles. By his son, the Rev. A. Barry (1867).

Benson, W. A. S. By the Hon. W. N. Bruce, in Benson's ' Drawing ' (1925).

Bentley, J. F. By W. de l'Hôpital, in ' Westminster Cathedral ', &c. (1920) ; by W. W. Scott Moncrieff (1924) ; by H. Ricardo (*A.R.* 1902).

Bodley, G. F. By E. P. Warren (*A.R.* 1902).

Burton, Decimus. By R. P. Jones (*A.R.* 1905).

Cockerell, C. R. By R. P. Cockerell (*A.R.* 1902) ; by S. P. Cockerell (1903) ; by J. M. Brydon (*S.P.* 1900) ; by E. Prestwich (*J.* 1911).

Devey, George. By W. H. Godfrey (*A.R.* 1907).

Elmes, H. L. By R. P. Jones (*A.R.* 1904).

Jackson, Sir T. G. By H. S. Goodhart-Rendel (*S.P.* 1926).

Morris, William. By J. W. Mackail (1899) ; by W. R. Lethaby (1901); by Holbrook Jackson (1926).

Nash, John. By W. H. Nash (*J.* 1923).

Nesfield, W. E. By J. M. Brydon (*A.R.* 1897).

Newton, Ernest. By his son, W. G. Newton (1925).

Pearson, J. L. By J. E. Newbury (*A.R.* 1897).

Pugin, A. W. N. By B. Ferrey (1861) ; by P. Waterhouse (*A.R.* 1897).

Scott, Sir Gilbert. ' Recollections ' (autobiography) (1879) ; by M. S. Briggs (*A.R.* 1908).

Smirke, Sir Robert. By Sir E. Smirke (*R.I.B.A. Transactions*) (1866).

Soane, Sir John. By A. T. Bolton (*J.* 1922) ; by A. T. Bolton (1924) ; by H. J. Birnstingl (1925).

Stokes, Leonard. By G. Drysdale. (*S.P.* 1926).

Street, G. E. By A. E. Street (1888) ; by W. Millard (*J.* 1918).

' *Greek* ' *Thomson.* By Barclay and Blomfield (*A.R.* 1904) ; by T. Gildard (1888).

Waterhouse, Alfred. By T. Cooper (*J.* 1905).

Webb, Philip. By W. R. Lethaby, in *The Builder* (1925).

EPILOGUE

THE close of the nineteenth century forms a convenient point for ending this book, which otherwise would tend to cross the line between history and contemporary politics. Looking back over the long ages that we have traversed, we have seen the architect gradually consolidating his position as a professional man, then establishing a code of etiquette to govern his professional conduct, founding institutions and societies to further and protect his interests, and at last admitting that the increasing complexity of building operations has put an end to the days when he might with impunity practise any number of the arts as an Admirable Crichton. His hands are now sufficiently full when he sticks to his last. At various periods we have seen him connected with the official hierarchy of a temple or a monastery, as an independent master-craftsman employed by Church and laity alike, as a unit in the great military organization of Imperial Rome, as a satellite of some brilliant court of the Italian Renaissance, and as the protégé of an English nobleman in the eighteenth century. It is therefore impossible to generalize with any confidence about many aspects of his training, status, and work, but two factors seem to remain constant all through this protracted survey.

Firstly, it is clear that a great architect must be *born* something of an artist, with ideals and ambitions beyond mere construction and far beyond the mere earning of a livelihood. He must have real enthusiasm for his work. The inheritance of a practice seems seldom to have brought a man to the top. Secondly, it is evident that such obstacles as humble birth, defective training, and lack of opportunity have proved a positive stimulus to the born architect. If in these pages the ' noble patron ' has sometimes been ridiculed, we must concede that from Lorenzo de' Medici to Lord Burlington he was often instrumental in enabling a poor lad to enter and practise our noble calling. But, nevertheless, the achievements of most of the famous architects in history were due almost entirely to their own ability, ambition, and perseverance. No other profession in the past has offered a more open road to fame, for architecture is at least as much of an art as a profession. In that sense it has always been democratic, and it is my earnest hope that nothing which may happen in the future will close its doors to the youth who has every asset except financial means.

As we turn from retrospect to consider the position of the architect in England to-day, we find that in many ways it has improved during the last half-century. A new system of school training has come into being. In various universities, technical colleges, and schools of art there are full-time day courses in architecture, extending over a period of five years, where students obtain a far more thorough grounding in their work than was possible in the average office under the system of pupilage. The principles of design, formerly acquired mainly by a process of trial and error in public competitions or at the expense of a client, now form the subject of academic study. Entry into these schools depends upon the attainment of a good standard of general education, and the whole of their work is subject to the control of the R.I.B.A. Board of Architectural Education, which grants almost complete exemption from its examinations to those who successfully complete a full course in one of these ' recognized ' schools, including a short period spent in the office of a reputable architect.

But in spite of the recent rapid progress, in numbers and efficiency, of such schools, the majority of those entering the profession still begin as pupils in an architect's office, pick up what they can at evening classes or by attendance one or two days a week at school, and sit for the open R.I.B.A. examinations. Probably most of them are unable to pay the fees for a full-time course, and many certainly live in towns remote from any ' recognized ' school, so that attendance there would entail heavy additional expense for living in lodgings. Others may never have been properly informed about recent changes in architectural training. Only a fraction of this large number can hope to win scholarships for the full-time schools, so the case of the remaining majority must never be overlooked in considering the problem of architectural education as a whole.

Together with this striking development of the school system, there has been an increase in the facilities for architectural study abroad, whether in the British School at Rome, in promiscuous sketching and measuring on the Continent, or in America. Both in number and value, the studentships now available for this purpose far surpass anything that existed fifty years ago. The credit for these various improvements must be ascribed chiefly to the Royal Institute of British Architects, which has grown in less than a century from a small select coterie with a rather dilettante bias to a large and powerful professional organization, capable of making itself heard whenever necessary. Its subscribing members number nearly 6,000, its student and probationary members over 2,000, and its allied societies with over 1,200 members in the provinces and more in the Dominions add to its strength. Since its recent absorption of the Society of Architects, it has included most of the chief practitioners of the profession.

The enormous additions to its membership that have taken place even within my own memory, on one pretext and another, have been made with the expressed view of eventual registration of all reputable architects, thus leading practically if not specifically to the ultimate closing of the profession. This has not yet been achieved, but the status of the architect is improving. For better or for worse, he is becoming first and foremost a professional man.

There are some who regard with genuine regret, even with alarm, this stereotyping of one of the fine arts into professional moulds. Unfortunately it seems to have become inevitable. Combinations for mutual self-defence and self-advertisement, for the maintenance of a minimum wage and a minimum code of honour, surround us on all sides. The architect, like other men, has to live, and it seems to be generally held that he can only live by combining with his brethren. But there are compensating features, and the R.I.B.A. has done much to enhance the reputation and improve the methods of one of the oldest callings in the world. Supporters of registration believe that the Bill now (1927) before Parliament will raise the standard of architecture and architectural practice throughout the country.

The future appears to offer many other problems for solution beyond questions of the architect's training and status. What is to be his precise relation to the engineers who every year play an increasingly important part in the erection and equipment of large buildings ? How can he bring himself more closely into touch with the craftsmen from whom ' big business ' has separated him ? How may the public be made to feel that in these days of gimcrack bungalows, factories, and municipal housing schemes, an architect is able to do something to save rural England from complete uglification, and that he is not a mere luxury ? How is he to convince people that although he admires and studies ancient buildings his chief concern in life is to produce new ones ? Above all, how is he to persuade the man in the street to discard the Ruskinian theory, that modern architecture is not and never can be comparable with the work of our forefathers ?

Many of these questions indicate the need for an improved popular understanding of the real nature and function of modern architecture. Mr. Howard Robertson's recent little book [1] is perhaps the first attempt in this direction that really takes count of the average general reader's needs. Other writers are making use of the public press with some effect, and the Architecture Club is a skilful idea for combining propaganda with geniality.

Up to a few years ago, architectural writers were prone to concentrate their abilities too exclusively on the past. As one who has sinned in this respect, if sin it be, I suggest that it is partly due to a natural reluctance to criticize the work of one's contemporaries, partly to an acute realization of the fickleness of our canons of architectural taste. Architects are often taunted, by engineers and ' hardheaded ' men of business, with being wrapped up in the past and consequently with indifference to the needs of to-day. This book may help to explain why architects are proud of their long ancestry ; but their well-known solicitude to preserve ancient monuments from destruction is all to their credit, for it is by *new* buildings that they live. Much of the misunderstanding on this point may be traced to the over-emphasis assigned to architectural precedents in the revivalist eras of the eighteenth

[1] *Architecture Explained* (1926).

and nineteenth centuries. If our city fathers had listened to the architects who, from Sir Christopher Wren onwards, have published schemes for replanning London, London would be a finer city to-day. The modern science of town-planning is almost entirely due to architects.

When the time comes to write the history of the architect in the twentieth century, it is my confident belief, speaking as one who is now outside the arena of practice, that the historian will regard the best buildings of to-day as modern in spirit, dignified in design, and worthy in every way to be compared with the masterpieces of the past.

INDEX